Focus on GRAMMAR 3

FOURTH EDITION

Marjorie Fuchs
Margaret Bonner
Miriam Westheimer

D0573227

Prezi Presen
Grammar Rules /5
Examples of Cices
own examples /10
Overall Grammar/Spelling /10
Prezi
Presentation Skills /10
Quiz for students /10

Material From: **TEXTBOOKS FOR CHANGE**
www.facebook.com/TextbooksForChange

ALWAYS LEARNING

PEARSON

To the memory of my parents, Edith and Joseph Fuchs—MF
To my parents, Marie and Joseph Maus, and to my son, Luke Frances—MB
To my husband, Joel Einleger, and my children, Ari and Leora—MW

FOCUS ON GRAMMAR 3: An Integrated Skills Approach, Fourth Edition

Copyright © 2012, 2006, 2000, 1994 by Pearson Education, Inc.
All rights reserved.

No part of this publication may be reproduced, stored in a retrieval system,
or transmitted in any form or by any means, electronic, mechanical, photocopying,
recording, or otherwise, without the prior permission of the publisher.

Pearson Education, 10 Bank Street, White Plains, NY 10606

Staff credits: The people who made up the *Focus on Grammar 3, Fourth Edition*
team, representing editorial, production, design, and manufacturing, are Elizabeth Carlson,
Tracey Cataldo, Aerin Csigay, Dave Dickey, Christine Edmonds, Nancy Flaggman, Ann France,
Françoise Leffler, Lise Minovitz, Barbara Perez, Robert Ruvo, and Debbie Sistino.

Cover image: Shutterstock.com
Text composition: ElectraGraphics, Inc.
Text font: New Aster

Library of Congress Cataloging-in-Publication Data

Schoenberg, Irene, 1946–
    Focus on grammar. 1: an integrated skills approach / Irene E. Schoenberg, Jay Maurer. — 3rd ed.
        p. cm.
    Includes index.
    ISBN 0-13-245591-9 — ISBN 0-13-254647-7 — ISBN 0-13-254648-5 — ISBN 0-13-254649-3 —
ISBN 0-13-254650-7 1. English language—Textbooks for foreign speakers. 2. English language—
Grammar—Problems, exercises, etc. I. Maurer, Jay. II. Title.
    PE1128.S3456824 2011
    428.2'4—dc22

                                                                    2011014126

PEARSON LONGMAN ON THE **WEB**

Pearsonlongman.com offers online
resources for teachers and students. Access
our Companion Websites, our online catalog,
and our local offices around the world.

Visit us at **pearsonlongman.com**.

Printed in the United States of America
ISBN 10: 0-13-254648-5
ISBN 13: 978-0-13-254648-5

9 10—V082—16 15

ISBN 10: 0-13-216054-4 (with MyLab)
ISBN 13: 978-0-13-216054-4 (with MyLab)

4 5 6 7 8 9 10—V082—16 15 14

CONTENTS

WELCOME TO *FOCUS ON GRAMMAR*

Now in a new edition, the popular five-level *Focus on Grammar* course continues to provide an integrated-skills approach to help students understand and practice English grammar. Centered on thematic instruction, *Focus on Grammar* combines controlled and communicative practice with critical thinking skills and ongoing assessment. Students gain the confidence they need to speak and write English accurately and fluently.

NEW for the FOURTH EDITION

VOCABULARY

Key vocabulary is highlighted, practiced, and recycled throughout the unit.

PRONUNCIATION

Now, in every unit, pronunciation points and activities help students improve spoken accuracy and fluency.

LISTENING

Expanded listening tasks allow students to develop a range of listening skills.

UPDATED CHARTS and NOTES

Target structures are presented in a clear, easy-to-read format.

NEW READINGS

High-interest readings, updated or completely new, in a variety of genres integrate grammar and vocabulary in natural contexts.

NEW UNIT REVIEWS

Students can check their understanding and monitor their progress after completing each unit.

MyFocusOnGrammarLab

An easy-to-use online learning and assessment program offers online homework and individualized instruction anywhere, anytime.

Teacher's Resource Pack One compact resource includes:

THE TEACHER'S MANUAL: General Teaching Notes, Unit Teaching Notes, the Student Book Audioscript, and the Student Book Answer Key.

TEACHER'S RESOURCE DISC: Bound into the Resource Pack, this CD-ROM contains reproducible Placement, Part, and Unit Tests, as well as customizable Test-Generating Software. It also includes reproducible Internet Activities and PowerPoint® Grammar Presentations.

THE *FOCUS ON GRAMMAR* APPROACH

The new edition follows the same successful four-step approach of previous editions. The books provide an abundance of both controlled and communicative exercises so that students can bridge the gap between identifying grammatical structures and using them. The many communicative activities in each Student Book provide opportunities for critical thinking while enabling students to personalize what they have learned.

- **STEP 1: GRAMMAR IN CONTEXT** highlights the target structures in realistic contexts, such as conversations, magazine articles, and blog posts.
- **STEP 2: GRAMMAR PRESENTATION** presents the structures in clear and accessible grammar charts and notes with multiple examples of form and usage.
- **STEP 3: FOCUSED PRACTICE** provides numerous and varied controlled exercises for both the form and meaning of the new structures.
- **STEP 4: COMMUNICATION PRACTICE** includes listening and pronunciation and allows students to use the new structures freely and creatively in motivating, open-ended speaking and writing activities.

Recycling

Underpinning the scope and sequence of the *Focus on Grammar* series is the belief that students need to use target structures and vocabulary many times, in different contexts. New grammar and vocabulary are recycled throughout the book. Students have maximum exposure and become confident using the language in speech and in writing.

Assessment

Extensive testing informs instruction and allows teachers and students to measure progress.

- **Unit Reviews** at the end of every Student Book unit assess students' understanding of the grammar and allow students to monitor their own progress.
- Easy to administer and score, **Part and Unit Tests** provide teachers with a valid and reliable means to determine how well students know the material they are about to study and to assess students' mastery after they complete the material. These tests can be found on MyFocusOnGrammarLab, where they include immediate feedback and remediation, and as reproducible tests on the Teacher's Resource Disc.
- **Test-Generating Software** on the Teacher's Resource Disc includes a bank of *additional* test items teachers can use to create customized tests.
- A reproducible **Placement Test** on the Teacher's Resource Disc is designed to help teachers place students into one of the five levels of the *Focus on Grammar* course.

COMPONENTS

In addition to the Student Books, Teacher's Resource Packs, and MyLabs, the complete *Focus on Grammar* course includes:

Workbooks Contain additional contextualized exercises appropriate for self-study.

Audio Program Includes all of the listening and pronunciation exercises and opening passages from the Student Book. Some Student Books are packaged with the complete audio program (mp3 files). Alternatively, the audio program is available on a classroom set of CDs and on the MyLab.

THE *FOCUS ON GRAMMAR* UNIT

Focus on Grammar introduces grammar structures in the context of unified themes. All units follow a **four-step approach**, taking learners from grammar in context to communicative practice.

STEP 1 GRAMMAR IN CONTEXT

This section presents the target structure(s) in a natural context. As students read the **high-interest texts**, they encounter the form, meaning, and use of the grammar. **Before You Read** activities create interest and elicit students' knowledge about the topic. **After You Read** activities build students' reading vocabulary and comprehension.

Vocabulary exercises improve students' command of English. Vocabulary is **recycled** throughout the unit.

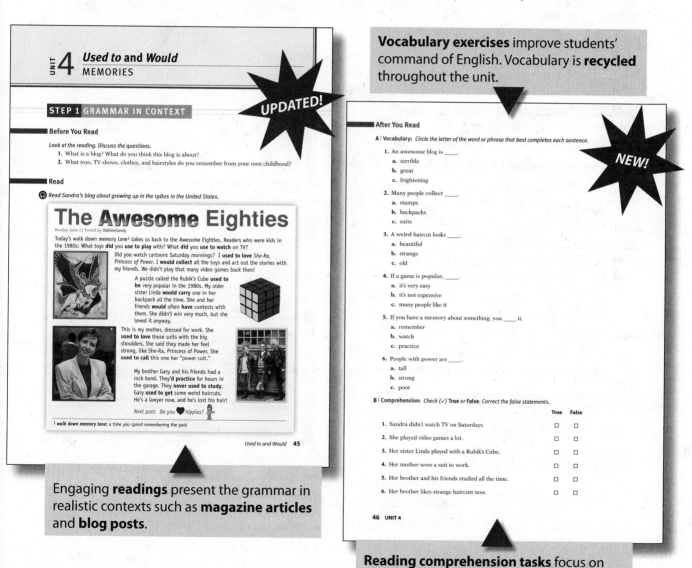

Engaging **readings** present the grammar in realistic contexts such as **magazine articles** and **blog posts**.

Reading comprehension tasks focus on the meaning of the text and draw students' attention to the target structure.

This section gives students a comprehensive and explicit overview of the grammar with detailed **Grammar Charts** and **Grammar Notes** that present the form, meaning, and use of the structure(s).

Grammar Charts present the structure in a clear, easy-to-read format.

Grammar Notes give concise, simple **explanations** and **examples** to ensure students' understanding.

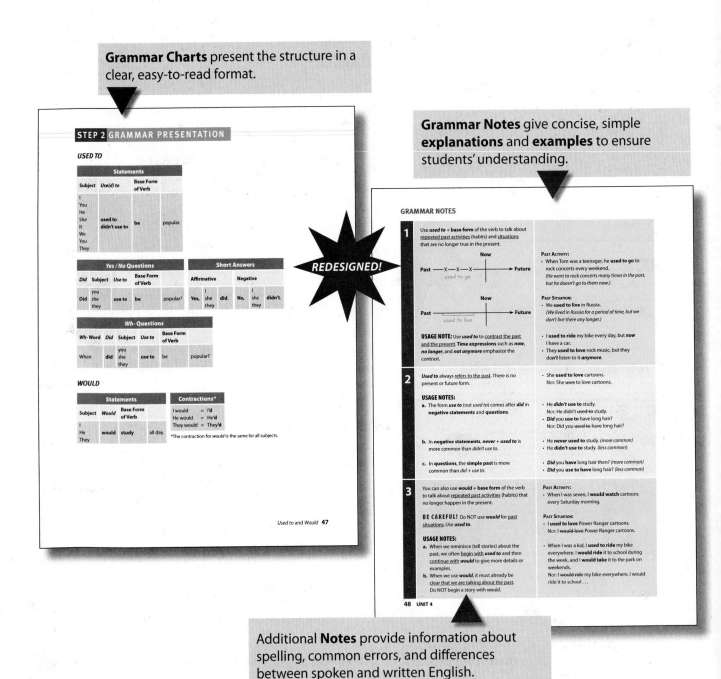

Additional **Notes** provide information about spelling, common errors, and differences between spoken and written English.

STEP 3 FOCUSED PRACTICE

Controlled practice activities in this section lead students to master form, meaning, and use of the target grammar.

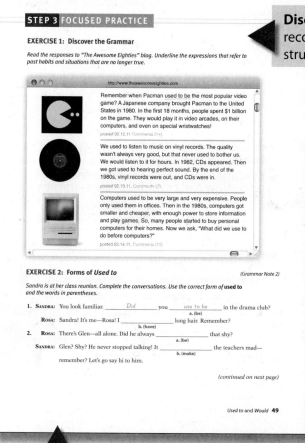

STEP 3 FOCUSED PRACTICE

EXERCISE 1: Discover the Grammar

Read the responses to "The Awesome Eighties" blog. Underline the expressions that refer to past habits and situations that are no longer true.

http://www.theawesomeeighties.com

Remember when Pacman used to be the most popular video game? A Japanese company brought Pacman to the United States in 1980. In the first 18 months, people spent $1 billion on the game. They would play it in video arcades, on their computers, and even on special wristwatches!
posted 02.12.11. Comments (14)

We used to listen to music on vinyl records. The quality wasn't always very good, but that never used to bother us. We would listen to it for hours. In 1982, CDs appeared. Then we got used to hearing perfect sound. By the end of the 1980s, vinyl records were out, and CDs were in.
posted 02.13.11. Comments (7)

Computers used to be very large and very expensive. People only used them in offices. Then in the 1980s, computers got smaller and cheaper, with enough power to store information and play games. So, many people started to buy personal computers for their homes. Now we ask, "What did we use to do before computers?"
posted 02.14.11. Comments (11)

EXERCISE 2: Forms of *Used to*   *(Grammar Note 2)*

*Sandra is at her class reunion. Complete the conversations. Use the correct form of **used to** and the words in parentheses.*

1. **SANDRA:** You look familiar. _____*Did*_____ you ___*use to be*___ in the drama club?
                                                                    a. (be)
    ROSA: Sandra! It's me—Rosa! I _____ long hair. Remember?
                                           b. (have)
2. **ROSA:** There's Glen—all alone. Did he always _____ that shy?
                                                         a. (be)
    SANDRA: Glen? Shy? He never stopped talking! It _____ the teachers mad—
                                                          b. (make)
    remember? Let's go say hi to him.

(continued on next page)

Used to and Would **49**

A **variety of exercise types** engage students and guide them from recognition and understanding to accurate production of the grammar structures.

Discover the Grammar activities develop students' recognition and understanding of the target structure before they are asked to produce it.

An **Editing** exercise ends every Focused Practice section and teaches students to find and correct typical mistakes.

EXERCISE 5: Editing

*Read the journal entry about a high school reunion in Timmins, Ontario, a small town 500 miles north of Toronto. There are nine mistakes in the use of **used to** and **would**. The first mistake is already corrected. Find and correct eight more.*

Shania Twain

> The high school reunion tonight was awesome! I
> talked
> ~~used to talk~~ to Eileen Edwards for a long time. Well,
> she's the famous country pop singer Shania Twain now.
> In high school, she was used to be just one of us, and
> tonight we all called her Eileen. She graduated in 1983,
> the same year as me. Today she uses to live in a
> chateau in Switzerland and has her own perfume
> brand, but her life didn't use to be like that at all! She
> uses to be very poor, and her grandma used to made all her clothes because her
> family couldn't afford to buy them. She was always a good musician, though. In fact, she
> used to earns money for her family that way. On Saturday nights, she would performed
> with a local rock band, and my friends and I would go hear her. She could really sing!
> Her new name, Shania, means "on my way" in Ojibwa (her stepfather's Native American
> language). After she left Timmins, I would think that Timmins wasn't important to her
> anymore—but I was wrong. Now that she's famous, she has a lot of power, and she
> uses it to do good things for our community. And tonight she was just the way she
> used be in high school—simple and friendly!

A school reunion

52 UNIT 4

STEP 4 COMMUNICATION PRACTICE

This section provides practice with the structure in **listening** and **pronunciation** exercises as well as in communicative, open-ended **speaking** and **writing** activities that move students toward fluency.

Listening activities allow students to hear the grammar in natural contexts and to practice a range of listening skills.

STEP 4 COMMUNICATION PRACTICE

EXERCISE 6: Listening

A | *Two friends are talking about their past. Listen to their conversation.*

B | *Read the statements. Then listen again to the conversation and circle the letter of the correct information.*

1. The friends are at a _____.
   a. rock concert   (b.) school reunion

2. Their present lives are very _____ their past lives.
   a. similar to   b. different from

3. They have _____ memories about their past.
   a. good   b. bad

4. They used to play a lot of _____.
   a. video games   b. music CDs

5. The friends are enjoying talking about _____.
   a. a trip   b. the past

C | *Listen again to the conversation. Check (✓) the things the friends used to do in the **past** and the things they do **now**.*

	Past	Now
1. get up very early without an alarm clock	☑	☐
2. use an alarm clock	☐	☐
3. have a big breakfast	☐	☐
4. have a cup of coffee	☐	☐
5. look at the newspaper	☐	☐
6. have endless energy	☐	☐
7. do aerobics	☐	☐
8. take car trips on weekends	☐	☐
9. meet at class reunions	☐	☐

C: *Everybody used to have long hair then.*

EXPANDED!

Pronunciation Notes and **exercises** improve students' spoken fluency and accuracy.

EXERCISE 7: Pronunciation

A | *Read and listen to the Pronunciation Note.*

Pronunciation Note

We often pronounce *used to* like "usta." Notice that the pronunciation of *used to* and *use to* is the same.

EXAMPLES: I **used to** play chess.   →   "I **usta** play chess."
What games did you **use to** play?   →   "What games did you **usta** play?"

Be sure to write *used to* or *use to*, NOT "usta."

We often use the contraction of *would* ('d) in both **speech** and **writing**.

EXAMPLE: We **would** play for hours.   →   "We**'d** play for hours."

NEW!

B | *Listen to the sentences. Notice the pronunciation of **used to** and the contraction of **would**.*

1. I **used to** live in a small town.
2. I didn't **use to** have a lot of friends.
3. I**'d** spend hours alone.
4. On weekends, my sister **used to** play cards with me.
5. She**'d** always win.
6. We**'d** have a lot of fun.

C | *Listen again and repeat the sentences.*

EXERCISE 8: Picture Discussion

Work with a partner. Look at the pairs of pictures and talk about how the people have changed. Then write sentences that describe the changes. Compare your sentences with those of your classmates.

Then	Now

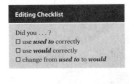 

1. Sharifa _used to be very busy, but now she is more relaxed. She would always be in a hurry._

   _Now she takes things more slowly. She used to wear glasses, but now she doesn't_____

54   UNIT 4

EXERCISE 10: Writing

A | *Write a two-paragraph essay. Contrast your life in the past with your life now. In the first paragraph, describe how your life used to be at some time in the past. In the second paragraph, describe your life today. Remember: We often begin with **used to** and then change to **would**.*

EXAMPLE: I used to live in Russia. I attended St. Petersburg University. I would ride my bike there every day. In those days I used to . . . Today I am living in Florida and attending Miami University . . .

B | *Check your work. Use the Editing Checklist.*

Editing Checklist

Did you . . . ?
☐ use *used to* correctly
☐ use *would* correctly
☐ change from *used to* to *would*

NEW!

Writing activities encourage students to produce meaningful writing that integrates the grammar structure.

An **Editing Checklist** teaches students to correct their mistakes and revise their work.

Speaking activities help students synthesize the grammar through discussions, debates, games, and problem-solving tasks, developing their fluency.

x   The *Focus on Grammar* Unit

Unit Reviews give students the opportunity to check their understanding of the target structure. **Answers** at the back of the book allow students to monitor their own progress.

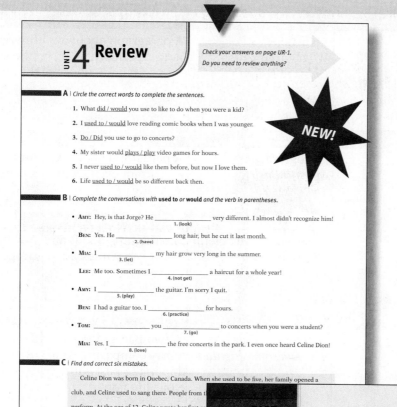

Check your answers on page UR-1.
Do you need to review anything?

UNIT 4 Review

NEW!

A | *Circle the correct words to complete the sentences.*

1. What <u>did / would</u> you use to like to do when you were a kid?

2. I <u>used to / would</u> love reading comic books when I was younger.

3. <u>Do / Did</u> you use to go to concerts?

4. My sister would <u>plays / play</u> video games for hours.

5. I never <u>used to / would</u> like them before, but now I love them.

6. Life <u>used to / would</u> be so different back then.

B | *Complete the conversations with* **used to** *or* **would** *and the verb in parentheses.*

• **Amy:** Hey, is that Jorge? He _____ very different. I almost didn't recognize him!
  1. (look)

  Ben: Yes. He _____ long hair, but he cut it last month.
  2. (have)

• **Mia:** I _____ my hair grow very long in the summer.
  3. (let)

  Lee: Me too. Sometimes I _____ a haircut for a whole year!
  4. (not get)

• **Amy:** I _____ the guitar. I'm sorry I quit.
  5. (play)

  Ben: I had a guitar too. I _____ for hours.
  6. (practice)

• **Tom:** _____ you _____ to concerts when you were a student?
  7. (go)

  Mia: Yes. I _____ the free concerts in the park. I even once heard Celine Dion!
  8. (love)

C | *Find and correct six mistakes.*

Celine Dion was born in Quebec, Canada. When she used to be five, her family opened a club, and Celine used to sang there. People from [...] perform. At the age of 12, Celine wrote her first so[...] it to a manager. At first Celine used to singing only [...] became known in more countries. As a child, Celi[...] to be a singer. Today she is one of the most succes[...]

Extended writing tasks help students integrate the grammar structure as they follow the steps of the **writing process**.

PART I

From Grammar to Writing
COMBINING SENTENCES WITH TIME WORDS

You can often improve your writing by combining two short sentences into one longer sentence that connects the two ideas. The two sentences can be combined by using **time words** such as *while*, *when*, *as soon as*, *before*, *after*, or *until*. The new, longer sentence is made up of a main clause and a time clause.

Example: I was shopping. I saw the perfect dress for her. ➔

TIME CLAUSE   MAIN CLAUSE
While I was shopping, I saw the perfect dress for her.

MAIN CLAUSE   TIME CLAUSE
I saw the perfect dress for her **while** I was shopping.

The time clause can come first or second. When it comes first, a **comma** separates the two clauses.

1 | *Read the paragraph. Underline all the sentences that are combined with a time word. Circle the time words.*

> I always exchange holiday presents with my girlfriend, Shao Fen. Last year, (while) I was shopping for her, I saw an umbrella in her favorite color. As soon as I saw it, I thought of her. I bought the umbrella and a scarf in the same color. When Shao Fen opened the present, she looked really upset. She didn't say anything, and she didn't look at me. I felt hurt and confused by her reaction. Later she explained that in Chinese, the word for "umbrella" sounds like the word for "separation." When she saw the umbrella, she misunderstood. She thought I wanted to end the relationship. After I heard that, I was very upset! When we both felt calmer, we talked about our misunderstanding. At the end, we laughed about it, and I think we're better friends because of it. I discovered something new about Shao Fen's culture. Now I want to learn more about cross-cultural communication.

From Grammar to Writing **69**

SCOPE AND SEQUENCE

UNIT	READING	WRITING	LISTENING
1 page 2 **Grammar:** Present Progressive and Simple Present **Theme:** Different Cultures	An article: *What's Your Cross-Cultural IQ?*	A paragraph about a new experience	Interviews of foreign students studying in the United States
2 page 16 **Grammar:** Simple Past **Theme:** Poets	A biography: *Matsuo Basho, 1644–1694*	A paragraph about important events in your life	An interview with a poet
3 page 31 **Grammar:** Past Progressive and Simple Past **Theme:** Accidents	A newspaper article: *Disaster at Sea*	A paragraph about an event you witnessed	A witness describing a traffic accident
4 page 45 **Grammar:** *Used to* and *Would* **Theme:** Memories	A blog: *The Awesome Eighties*	A two-paragraph essay comparing your life in the past with your life now	Two friends talking about their past
5 page 58 **Grammar:** *Wh-* Questions **Theme:** In Court	An excerpt from a court transcript: *State of Illinois vs. Harry M. Adams*	Interview questions and the interview	A telephone conversation about an accident
PART I **From Grammar to Writing,** page 69 **Combining Sentences with Time Words:** Write a paragraph about a misunderstanding or mistake.			
6 page 74 **Grammar:** Future **Theme:** Space Travel	A radio program transcript: *Space Tourists: Not Just Science Fiction*	A paragraph about your life five years from now	Conversations about future plans and about something happening now
7 page 91 **Grammar:** Future Time Clauses **Theme:** Setting Goals	An article: *Go For It! What are your dreams for the future?*	A goal-planning worksheet	A telephone call to an employment agency
PART II **From Grammar to Writing,** page 103 **Showing the Order of Events:** Write a blog post about your weekend plans.			

SPEAKING	PRONUNCIATION	VOCABULARY	
Find Someone Who . . . *Picture Discussion:* Understanding gestures and facial expressions *Compare and Contrast:* Appropriate cultural questions	Reduction of *What do you* and *What are you* ("Whaddaya")	abroad culture* distance	event misunderstanding native
Compare and Contrast: Two poets *Information Gap:* Celebrity Profile	*Wh-* questions with *did* ("Why'd")	admirer emotion journey	restless topic*
Game: Are You a Good Witness? *Role Play:* Alibi	Pausing after time clauses	alarmed area* calm (adj)	disaster sink (v) survivor*
Picture Discussion: Then and now *Compare and Contrast:* How you used to be and how you are now	Reduction of *used to* ("usta") and contraction of *would* ('d)	awesome collect memory	popular power weird
Role Play: On the Witness Stand *Game:* To Tell the Truth	Intonation of *Wh-* questions asking for information or asking for repetition	defendant frightened in a hurry	indicate* record (n)

SPEAKING	PRONUNCIATION	VOCABULARY	
Making Plans: Finding a time when you and your partner are both free *Reaching Agreement:* Deciding which events to attend	Contraction of *will* ('ll) and reduction of *going to* ("gonna")	edge experience (v) float	incredible sold out takeoff (n)
What About You? Comparing your plans with your classmates' plans *Game:* What's Next?	Intonation in sentences with time clauses	achieve* catalog degree	download goal* interview (n)

* = AWL (Academic Word List) items

SPEAKING	PRONUNCIATION	VOCABULARY	
Role Play: A Job Interview	Intonation in *yes / no* questions and *wh-* questions	consider dramatically* opportunity	positive* residence support (v)
Information Gap: Chores *What About You?* Things you've already done and things you haven't done yet	Contractions of *have* in the present perfect	available* organized professional*	specific* successful
Find Someone Who . . .	Reduction of auxiliary *have* ("books of") and *has* ("hotelz") after a noun	adventure affordable ancient	annual* survey* transportation*
Compare and Contrast: Events last year and this year *Interview:* Asking your partner about a long-distance relationship	Pronunciation of *-ed* in the simple past and past participle of regular verbs	apart arrangement manage	solution temporary* turn down
Find Someone Who . . . *Picture Discussion:* Global warming *Discussion:* Recent changes in your life	Stress in present perfect and present perfect progressive verb phrases	climate design (v)* develop	energy* expert* pollution
Information Gap: Can they do the tango? *Ask and Answer:* Finding someone who can do each task	Distinguishing unstressed *can* /kən/ and stressed *can't* /kænt/	aspiration confused dedication	integrated* perception* talent
Problem Solving: Asking permission *Role Play:* Could I . . . ?	Linking final consonants with *I* or *he:* *can I, could he, may I*	annoyed assume* establish*	guidelines* neat presentation

* = AWL (Academic Word List) items

UNIT	READING	WRITING	LISTENING
15 page 202 **Grammar:** Requests: *Can, Could, Will, Would, Would you mind* **Theme:** Messages	Email and text messages: *Messages 4 u!* Abbreviations for Text Messages	Text messages making requests and answering your partner's requests	Short conversations making and answering requests
16 page 214 **Grammar:** Advice: *Should, Ought to, Had better* **Theme:** Internet Rules	An article: *Netiquette 101* *Cyber Words*	A polite email of complaint to the owner of a school	A radio call-in show about buying a new computer
PART IV From Grammar to Writing, page 227 **Using Appropriate Modals:** Role-play situations, then write and answer emails as the characters in your role plays.			
17 page 232 **Grammar:** Nouns and Quantifiers **Theme:** Time Capsules	An article: *Time in a Bottle*	A note to put in a time capsule	A couple discussing a recipe and making a shopping list
18 page 246 **Grammar:** Articles: Indefinite and Definite **Theme:** Stories	Two fables from Aesop: *The Ant and the Dove* *The Town Mouse and the Country Mouse*	A paragraph about an experience that illustrates the meaning of a moral	Short conversations about books and a video game
PART V From Grammar to Writing, page 262 **Developing a Paragraph with Examples:** Write a paragraph about a special holiday.			
19 page 266 **Grammar:** Adjectives and Adverbs **Theme:** Home	An ad for apartments: *Wakefield House*	An ad that describes your ideal home	A couple discussing online apartment ads
20 page 282 **Grammar:** Adjectives: Comparisons with *As . . . as* and *Than* **Theme:** Food	A restaurant review: *A New Place for Pizza*	A paragraph comparing your country's food with the food of another country	A couple comparing two brands of frozen pizza

SPEAKING	PRONUNCIATION	VOCABULARY	
Making Plans: Requesting help with things on your schedule	Reductions of *you* in requests ("couldja," "wouldja," "willya," and "canya")	appreciate* cheer up deliver	distribute* text (v)
Cross-Cultural Comparison: Advice about customs *Problem Solving:* Discussing everyday situations *Picture Discussion:* Improving a classroom	Reductions of *ought to* ("oughta") and *had better* ("'d better" or "better")	avoid behavior communication*	identity* normal* protect
Quotable Quotes: Time *Problem Solving:* Creating a time capsule	Dropping unstressed vowels ("histry")	civilization create* impressed	intentional interpret* occasion
Game: Quiz Show *Information Gap:* Story Time *Discussion:* What the morals of stories mean; tell a story that illustrates a moral	Two ways to pronounce *the*: /ði/ and /ðə/	enormous* famous immediately	struggle wonderful
What About You? Describing where you live *Compare and Contrast:* Different types of housing *Discussion:* Describing your ideal home *Game:* A Strange Story	Stressing contrasting or new information	charming convenient ideal	located* peaceful satisfied
Compare and Contrast: Pizzas from around the world *Role Play:* Your Restaurant	Reduction of *as* /əz/ and *than* /ðən/	crowded delicious fresh	relaxed* traditional* varied*

* = AWL (Academic Word List) items

UNIT	READING	WRITING	LISTENING
21 page 296 **Grammar:** Adjectives: Superlatives **Theme:** Cities	A travel brochure about Toronto: *A Superlative City*	A fact sheet for your hometown or city	A couple comparing three hotels
22 page 307 **Grammar:** Adverbs: *As . . . as,* Comparatives, Superlatives **Theme:** Sports	A transcript of a TV sports program: *The Halftime Report*	A paragraph comparing two sports figures	Sportscasters describing a horse race
PART VI From Grammar to Writing, page 319 **Using Descriptive Adjectives:** Write a paragraph describing a room.			
23 page 322 **Grammar:** Gerunds: Subject and Object **Theme:** Health Issues	An article: *No Smoking: Around the World from A–Z*	A two-paragraph opinion essay for or against a health or safety issue	A doctor giving advice to a patient
24 page 334 **Grammar:** Infinitives after Certain Verbs **Theme:** Friends and Family	Letters from a newspaper advice column: *Ask Annie*	Emails to two or three friends inviting them to join you for an event	A couple talking to a family counselor
25 page 344 **Grammar:** More Uses of Infinitives **Theme:** Smart Phones	An article: *The World in Your Pocket*	A post for an online bulletin board about using an electronic device	A TV ad for a new phone
26 page 357 **Grammar:** Gerunds and Infinitives **Theme:** Procrastination	An excerpt from an article: *Stop Procrastinating—Now!*	A goals worksheet Three paragraphs about accomplishing each of your goals	An interview with a student about her study habits
PART VII From Grammar to Writing, page 372 **Combining Sentences with *And, But, So, Or*:** Write an email to a friend describing your present life.			

SPEAKING	PRONUNCIATION	VOCABULARY	
What About You? Describing a city you have visited *Discussion:* Some cities in your country	Dropping the final *-t* sound before an initial consonant sound	dynamic* feature* financial*	multicultural public
Compare and Contrast: Famous athletes *Questionnaire:* Work and Play	Linking final consonants to beginning vowels in *as* + adverb + *as*	aggressively consistently* effectively	frequently intensely*
Survey: Opinions about smoking *For or Against:* Smoking in public and private places	Linking final *-ing* with an initial vowel sound	approve of ban (v) illegal*	in favor of permit (v) prohibit*
What About You? Describing childhood relationships *Cross-Cultural Comparison:* How do young people in your culture socialize?	Stress in infinitive phrases	focus (v)* interact* obviously*	similar* solve
Survey: Opinions about cell phones *For or Against:* Pros and cons of new technology *Problem Solving:* Other uses for everyday objects *Discussion:* New uses for a smart phone	Stress in adjective + infinitive phrases	combine device* function (n)*	major* multipurpose old-fashioned
Brainstorming: Ideas for work breaks *Information Gap:* At the Support Group *Quotable Quotes:* Procrastination *Problem Solving:* Ways of stopping clutter	Reduction of *to* /tə/, *for* /fər/, and *on* /ən/	anxious discouraging project (n)*	put off task* universal

* = AWL (Academic Word List) items

UNIT	READING	WRITING	LISTENING
27 page 376 **Grammar:** Reflexive and Reciprocal Pronouns **Theme:** Self-Talk	An article from a psychology magazine: *Self-Talk*	An advice column entitled "Help Yourself with Self-Talk"	Conversations at an office party
28 page 391 **Grammar:** Phrasal Verbs **Theme:** Animal Intelligence	An article about animal behavior expert Cesar Millan: *When He Whispers, They Tune In*	A paragraph about a pet or an animal you've read about or observed	Conversations about a college science class
PART VIII From Grammar to Writing, page 403 **Using pronouns for Coherence:** Write instructions to someone taking care of your home while you are away.			
29 page 408 **Grammar:** Necessity: *Have (got) to, Must, Don't have to, Must not, Can't* **Theme:** Transportation	An article: *Know Before You Go*	A paragraph about an application procedure	Short conversations about driving
30 page 422 **Grammar:** Expectations: *Be supposed to* **Theme:** Wedding Customs	A page from an etiquette book: *Wedding Wisdom*	A short essay about an important life event	Short conversations about a wedding
31 page 434 **Grammar:** Future Possibility: *May, Might, Could* **Theme:** Weather	A transcript of a TV weather report: *Weather Watch*	An email to a friend about your weekend plans	A weather forecast
32 page 446 **Grammar:** Conclusions: *Must, Have (got) to, May, Might, Could, Can't* **Theme:** Mysteries	The beginning of a Sherlock Holmes mystery: *The Red-Headed League*	Possibilities and conclusions based on a story outline	A radio play: the end of *The Red-Headed League*
PART IX From Grammar to Writing, page 461 **Combining Sentences with *Because, Although, Even though*:** Write a letter of complaint.			

SPEAKING	PRONUNCIATION	VOCABULARY	
Questionnaire: Are you an optimist or a pessimist? *Game:* Who Remembers More? *Picture Discussion:* Imagining people's self-talk *Problem Solving:* Feeling better in difficult situations	Stress in reflexive and reciprocal pronouns	fault finally* impact (v)*	maintain* reaction* realize
Making Plans: Organizing a class field trip *For or Against:* Owning a pet	Stress on noun and pronoun objects of phrasal verbs	figure out give up keep on	straighten out take over turn on
Picture Discussion: Traffic signs *Game:* Invent a Sign *What About You?* Describing tasks you have to and don't have to do *Discussion:* Rules and Regulations	Reductions of *have to* ("hafta" and "hasta") and *have got to* ("have gotta" and "gotta")	equipment* hassle (n) inspect*	regulation* strict valid*
Discussion: Important plans that you changed *Cross-Cultural Comparison:* Customs for important life events	Reductions of *supposed to* ("supposta") and *going to* ("gonna")	assistant* ceremony certificate	etiquette role* select*
Conversation: Your weekend plans *Problem Solving:* Predicting what two students might do in the future	Stress in short answers with modals	affect (v)* bundle up exceed*	forecast local trend*
Picture Discussion: Making guesses about a family *Problem Solving:* Giving possible explanations for several situations	Stress on modals that express conclusions	advertisement amazed encyclopedia method*	millionaire position salary

* = AWL (Academic Word List) items

ABOUT THE AUTHORS

Marjorie Fuchs has taught ESL at New York City Technical College and LaGuardia Community College of the City University of New York and EFL at the Sprach Studio Lingua Nova in Munich, Germany. She has a master's degree in Applied English Linguistics and a certificate in TESOL from the University of Wisconsin-Madison. She has authored and co-authored many widely used books and multimedia materials, notably *Crossroads, Top Twenty ESL Word Games: Beginning Vocabulary Development, Families: Ten Card Games for Language Learners, Focus on Grammar 4: An Integrated Skills Approach, Focus on Grammar 3 CD-ROM, Focus on Grammar 4 CD-ROM, Longman English Interactive 3* and *4, Grammar Express Basic, Grammar Express Basic CD-ROM, Grammar Express Intermediate, Future 1: English for Results,* and workbooks for *The Oxford Picture Dictionary High Beginning* and *Low Intermediate, Focus on Grammar 3* and *4,* and *Grammar Express Basic.*

Margaret Bonner has taught ESL at Hunter College and the Borough of Manhattan Community College of the City University of New York, at Taiwan National University in Taipei, and at Virginia Commonwealth University in Richmond. She holds a master's degree in library science from Columbia University, and she has done work toward a PhD in English literature at the Graduate Center of the City University of New York. She has authored and co-authored numerous ESL and EFL print and multimedia materials, including textbooks for the national school system of Oman, *Step into Writing: A Basic Writing Text, Focus on Grammar 4: An Integrated Skills Approach, Focus on Grammar 4 Workbook, Grammar Express Basic, Grammar Express Basic CD-ROM, Grammar Express Basic Workbook, Grammar Express Intermediate, Focus on Grammar 3 CD-ROM, Focus on Grammar 4 CD-ROM, Longman English Interactive 4,* and *The Oxford Picture Dictionary Low-Intermediate Workbook.*

Miriam Westheimer taught EFL at all levels of instruction in Haifa, Israel, for a period of six years. She has also taught ESL at Queens College, at LaGuardia Community College, and in the American Language Program of Columbia University. She holds a master's degree in TESOL and a doctorate in Curriculum and Teaching from Teachers College of Columbia University. She is the co-author of a communicative grammar program developed and widely used in Israel.

ACKNOWLEDGMENTS

Before acknowledging the many people who have contributed to the fourth edition of *Focus on Grammar,* we wish to express our gratitude to those who worked on the first, second, and third editions, and whose influence is still present in the new work. Our continuing thanks to:

- **Joanne Dresner**, who initiated the project and helped conceptualize the general approach of *Focus on Grammar*
- Our editors for the first three editions: **Nancy Perry**, **Penny Laporte**, **Louisa Hellegers**, **Joan Saslow**, **Laura Le Dréan**, and **Françoise Leffler**, for helping to bring the books to fruition
- **Sharon Hilles**, our grammar consultant, for her insight and advice on the first edition

In the fourth edition, *Focus on Grammar* has continued to evolve as we update materials and respond to the valuable feedback from teachers and students who have been using the series. We are grateful to the following editors and colleagues:

- The entire Pearson FOG team, in particular **Debbie Sistino** for overseeing the project and for her down-to-earth approach based on years of experience and knowledge of the field; **Lise Minovitz** for her enthusiasm and alacrity in answering our queries; and **Rosa Chapinal** for her courteous and competent administrative support.
- **Françoise Leffler**, our multi-talented editor, for her continued dedication to the series and for helping improve *Focus on Grammar* with each new edition. With her ear for natural language, eye for detail, analytical mind, and sense of style, she is truly an editor *extraordinaire*.
- **Robert Ruvo**, for piloting the book through its many stages of production
- **Irene Schoenberg** and **Jay Maurer** for their suggestions and support, and Irene for generously sharing her experience in teaching with the first three editions of this book
- **Ellen Shaw** for being a fan and for her insightful and thorough review of the previous edition
- **Sharon Goldstein** for her intelligent, thoughtful, and practical suggestions

Finally, we are grateful, as always, to **Rick Smith** and **Luke Frances**, for their helpful input and for standing by and supporting us as we navigated our way through our fourth *FOG*.

REVIEWERS

We are grateful to the following reviewers for their many helpful comments:

Aida Aganagic, Seneca College, Toronto, Canada; **Aftab Ahmed**, American University of Sharjah, Sharjah, United Arab Emirates; **Todd Allen**, English Language Institute, Gainesville, FL; **Anthony Anderson**, University of Texas, Austin, TX; **Anna K. Andrade**, ASA Institute, New York, NY; **Bayda Asbridge**, Worcester State College, Worcester, MA; **Raquel Ashkenasi**, American Language Institute, La Jolla, CA; **James Bakker**, Mt. San Antonio College, Walnut, CA; **Kate Baldrige-Hale**, Harper College, Palatine, IL; **Leticia S. Banks**, ALCI-SDUSM, San Marcos, CA; **Aegina Barnes**, York College CUNY, Forest Hills, NY; **Sarah Barnhardt**, Community College of Baltimore County, Reisterstown, MD; **Kimberly Becker**, Nashville State Community College, Nashville, TN; **Holly Bell**, California State University, San Marcos, CA; **Anne Bliss**, University of Colorado, Boulder, CO; **Diana Booth**, Elgin Community College, Elgin, IL; **Barbara Boyer**, South Plainfield High School, South Plainfield, NJ; **Janna Brink**, Mt. San Antonio College, Walnut, CA; **AJ Brown**, Portland State University, Portland, OR; **Amanda Burgoyne**, Worcester State College, Worcester, MA; **Brenda Burlingame**, Independence High School, Charlotte, NC; **Sandra Byrd**, Shelby County High School and Kentucky State University, Shelbyville, KY; **Edward Carlstedt**, American University of Sharjah, Sharjah, United Arab Emirates; **Sean Cochran**, American Language Institute, Fullerton, CA; **Yanely Cordero**, Miami Dade College, Miami, FL; **Lin Cui**, William Rainey Harper College, Palatine, IL; **Sheila Detweiler**, College Lake County, Libertyville, IL; **Ann Duncan**, University of Texas, Austin, TX; **Debra Edell**, Merrill Middle School, Denver, CO; **Virginia Edwards**, Chandler-Gilbert Community College, Chandler, AZ; **Kenneth Fackler**, University of Tennessee, Martin, TN; **Jennifer Farnell**, American Language Program, Stamford, CT; **Allen P. Feiste**, Suwon University, Hwaseong, South Korea; **Mina Fowler**, Mt. San Antonio Community College, Rancho Cucamonga, CA; **Rosemary Franklin**, University of Cincinnati, Cincinnati, OH; **Christiane Galvani**, Texas Southern University, Sugar Land, TX; **Chester Gates**, Community College of Baltimore County, Baltimore, MD; **Luka Gavrilovic**, Quest Language Studies, Toronto, Canada; **Sally Gearhart**, Santa Rosa Community College, Santa Rosa, CA; **Shannon Gerrity**, James Lick Middle School, San Francisco, CA; **Jeanette Gerrity Gomez**, Prince George's Community College, Largo, MD; **Carlos Gonzalez**, Miami Dade College, Miami, FL; **Therese Gormley Hirmer**, University of Guelph, Guelph, Canada; **Sudeepa Gulati**, Long Beach City College, Long Beach, CA; **Anthony Halderman**, Cuesta College, San Luis Obispo, CA; **Ann A. Hall**, University of Texas, Austin, TX; **Cora Higgins**, Boston Academy of English, Boston, MA; **Michelle Hilton**, South Lane School District, Cottage Grove, OR; **Nicole Hines**, Troy University, Atlanta, GA; **Rosemary Hiruma**, American Language Institute, Long Beach, CA; **Harriet Hoffman**, University of Texas, Austin, TX; **Leah Holck**, Michigan State University, East Lansing, MI; **Christy Hunt**, English for Internationals, Roswell, GA; **Osmany Hurtado**, Miami Dade College, Miami, FL; **Isabel Innocenti**, Miami Dade College, Miami, FL; **Donna Janian**, Oxford Intensive School of English, Medford, MA; **Scott Jenison**, Antelope Valley College, Lancaster, CA; **Grace Kim**, Mt. San Antonio College, Diamond Bar, CA; **Brian King**, ELS Language Center, Chicago, IL; **Pam Kopitzke**, Modesto Junior College, Modesto, CA; **Elena Lattarulo**, American Language Institute, San Diego, CA; **Karen Lavaty**, Mt. San Antonio College, Glendora, CA; **JJ Lee-Gilbert**, Menlo-Atherton High School, Foster City, CA; **Ruth Luman**, Modesto Junior College, Modesto, CA; **Yvette Lyons**, Tarrant County College, Fort Worth, TX; **Janet Magnoni**, Diablo Valley College, Pleasant Hill, CA; **Meg Maher**, YWCA Princeton, Princeton, NJ; **Carmen Marquez-Rivera**, Curie Metropolitan High School, Chicago, IL; **Meredith Massey**, Prince George's Community College, Hyattsville, MD; **Linda Maynard**, Coastline Community College, Westminster, CA; **Eve Mazereeuw**, University of Guelph, Guelph, Canada; **Susanne McLaughlin**, Roosevelt University, Chicago, IL; **Madeline Medeiros**, Cuesta College, San Luis Obispo, CA; **Gioconda Melendez**, Miami Dade College, Miami, FL; **Marcia Menaker**, Passaic County Community College, Morris Plains, NJ; **Seabrook Mendoza**, Cal State San Marcos University, Wildomar, CA; **Anadalia Mendoza**, Felix Varela Senior High School, Miami, FL; **Charmaine Mergulhao**, Quest Language Studies, Toronto, Canada; **Dana Miho**, Mt. San Antonio College, San Jacinto, CA; **Sonia Nelson**, Centennial Middle School, Portland, OR; **Manuel Niebla**, Miami Dade College, Miami, FL; **Alice Nitta**, Leeward Community College, Pearl City, HI; **Gabriela Oliva**, Quest Language Studies, Toronto, Canada; **Sara Packer**, Portland State University, Portland, OR; **Lesley Painter**, New School, New York, NY; **Carlos Paz-Perez**, Miami Dade College, Miami, FL; **Ileana Perez**, Miami Dade College, Miami, FL; **Barbara Pogue**, Essex County College, Newark, NJ; **Phillips Potash**, University of Texas, Austin, TX; **Jada Pothina**, University of Texas, Austin, TX; **Ewa Pratt**, Des Moines Area Community College, Des Moines, IA; **Pedro Prentt**, Hudson County Community College, Jersey City, NJ; **Maida Purdy**, Miami Dade College, Miami, FL; **Dolores Quiles**, SUNY Ulster, Stone Ridge, NY; **Mark Rau**, American River College, Sacramento, CA; **Lynne Raxlen**, Seneca College, Toronto, Canada; **Lauren Rein**, English for Internationals, Sandy Springs, GA; **Diana Rivers**, NOCCCD, Cypress, CA; **Silvia Rodriguez**, Santa Ana College, Mission Viejo, CA; **Rolando Romero**, Miami Dade College, Miami, FL; **Pedro Rosabal**, Miami Dade College, Miami, FL; **Natalie Rublik**, University of Quebec, Chicoutimi, Quebec, Canada; **Matilde Sanchez**, Oxnard College, Oxnard, CA; **Therese Sarkis-Kruse**, Wilson Commencement, Rochester, NY; **Mike Sfiropoulos**, Palm Beach Community College, Boynton Beach, FL; **Amy Shearon**, Rice University, Houston, TX; **Sara Shore**, Modesto Junior College, Modesto, CA; **Patricia Silva**, Richard Daley College, Chicago, IL; **Stephanie Solomon**, Seattle Central Community College, Vashon, WA; **Roberta Steinberg**, Mount Ida College, Newton, MA; **Teresa Szymula**, Curie Metropolitan High School, Chicago, IL; **Hui-Lien Tang**, Jasper High School, Plano, TX; **Christine Tierney**, Houston Community College, Sugar Land, TX; **Ileana Torres**, Miami Dade College, Miami, FL; **Michelle Van Slyke**, Western Washington University, Bellingham, WA; **Melissa Villamil**, Houston Community College, Sugar Land, TX; **Elizabeth Wagenheim**, Prince George's Community College, Lago, MD; **Mark Wagner**, Worcester State College, Worcester, MA; **Angela Waigand**, American University of Sharjah, Sharjah, United Arab Emirates; **Merari Weber**, Metropolitan Skills Center, Los Angeles, CA; **Sonia Wei**, Seneca College, Toronto, Canada; and **Vicki Woodward**, Indiana University, Bloomington, IN.

1

PRESENT AND PAST

Present Progressive and Simple Present
DIFFERENT CULTURES

STEP 1 GRAMMAR IN CONTEXT

Before You Read

Look at the cartoons. Discuss the questions.

1. What are the people doing?
2. How do they feel?

Read

Read the article about cross-cultural communication.

WHAT'S YOUR CROSS-CULTURAL IQ?[1]

Are you **living** in your native country or in another country? **Do** you ever **travel** abroad? **Do** you **understand** the misunderstandings below?

It's 8:00. Why **is** he **wearing** shorts and a T-shirt? **Is** this the wrong day? I **don't understand**!

PARTY FRIDAY
8:00-MIDNIGHT
63 OAK STREET

What **is** he **doing** here now? It's only 8:00!

What's the matter?[2] Why **is** she **moving** away from me? Maybe she **doesn't like** my perfume!

Why **is** she **standing** so close to me? I **feel** like I **have** no room to breathe!

SITUATION 1

Jason **is standing** at Dan's door. He **thinks** he**'s** on time for the party, but he **doesn't see** any guests, and Dan **is wearing** shorts and a T-shirt! Dan **looks** surprised. In his culture, people never **arrive** at the exact start of a social event. They often **come** at least 30 minutes later.

SITUATION 2

Ina and Marty **are talking**. They **are** both **feeling** very uncomfortable. In Marty's culture, people usually **stand** quite close. This **seems** friendly to them. In Ina's culture, people **prefer** to have more distance between them. This **doesn't mean** they **are** unfriendly.

[1] **What's your cross-cultural IQ?:** How much do you know about other people's cultures?
[2] **What's the matter?:** What's wrong?

After You Read

A | Vocabulary: *Circle the letter of the word or phrase closest in meaning to the word in* **blue.**

1. Are you living in your **native** country?
   a. first
   b. new
   c. favorite

2. Do you ever travel **abroad**?
   a. by boat
   b. to foreign countries
   c. on expensive trips

3. What was the **misunderstanding** about?
   a. fight
   b. argument
   c. confusion

4. They come from different **cultures**.
   a. schools
   b. climates
   c. ways of life

5. They prefer to have more **distance** between them.
   a. streets
   b. space
   c. time

6. There are a lot of parties and other **events** at the Students' Club.
   a. members
   b. languages
   c. activities

B | Comprehension: *Complete each sentence with the correct name.*

1. _____ doesn't have shoes on.

2. _____ isn't expecting people to arrive at 8:00.

3. _____ thinks he's on time.

4. _____ is wearing perfume.

5. _____ wants to stand farther away.

6. _____ probably thinks the other person is a little unfriendly.

PRESENT PROGRESSIVE

Affirmative Statements

Subject	Be	Base Form of Verb + -ing	
I	am		
You	are		
He She It	is	traveling	now.
We You They	are		

Negative Statements

Subject	Be	Not	Base Form of Verb + -ing	
I	am			
He	is	not	traveling	now.
We	are			

Yes / No Questions

Be	Subject	Base Form of Verb + -ing	
Is	he	traveling	now?

Short Answers

Yes,	he	is.
No,		isn't.

Wh- Questions

Wh-Word	Be	Subject	Base Form of Verb + -ing	
Where	are	you	traveling	now?

SIMPLE PRESENT

Affirmative Statements

Subject		Verb
I You		travel.
He She It	often	travels.
We You They		travel.

Negative Statements

Subject	Do	Not	Base Form of Verb	
I	do			
He	does	not	travel	often.
We	do			

Yes / No Questions

Do	Subject	Base Form of Verb	
Does	he	travel	often?

Short Answers

Yes,	he	does.
No,		doesn't.

Wh- Questions

Wh-Word	Do	Subject		Base Form of Verb
Where	do	you	usually	travel?

GRAMMAR NOTES

1 Use the **present progressive** to describe:

a. something that is happening <u>right now</u> (for example, *now, at the moment*)

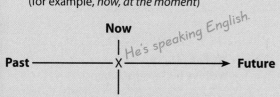

- Diego **is speaking** English *now*.
- He**'s wearing** shorts *at the moment*.

b. something that is happening in a <u>longer present time</u> (for example, *this month, this year, these days, nowadays*), even if it's not happening right now

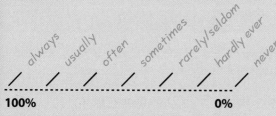

- We**'re studying** U.S. history *this month*. (*But we aren't studying it right now.*)
- Laura**'s studying** in France *this year*.
- **Are** you **studying** hard *these days*?

2 Use the **simple present** to describe what <u>regularly</u> happens (for example, *usually, often, every day, always*).

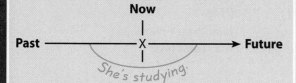

- Diego **speaks** Spanish at home.
- He **wears** jeans *every day*.

3 Use the **simple present** with **adverbs of frequency** to express <u>how often</u> something happens.

always   usually   often   sometimes   rarely/seldom   hardly ever   never

/   /   /   /   /   /   /

100%   **0%**

- In Spain, women *always* **kiss** on both cheeks.
- In France, women *often* **kiss** on both cheeks.
- We *rarely* **stand** very close to each other.
- In China, children *never* **call** adults by their first names.

Adverbs of frequency usually go <u>before</u> the main verb. However, some adverbs, such as *sometimes* and *usually*, can go at the <u>beginning</u> of the sentence too.

- I *sometimes* **wear** shorts at home.
  OR
- *Sometimes* I **wear** shorts at home.

BE CAREFUL! Adverbs of frequency always go <u>after</u> the verb *be*.

- They **are** *never* late.
  NOT: They ~~never are~~ late.

(continued on next page)

4 Use the **simple present** with most **non-action verbs**. Do NOT use the present progressive—even when the verb describes a situation that exists at the moment of speaking.

Non-action verbs usually describe <u>states</u> or <u>situations</u> but not actions. We use them to:

a. express **emotions** (*like, love, hate, want, feel, fear, trust*)

b. describe **mental states** (*know, remember, believe, think [= believe], understand*)

c. show **possession** (*have, own, possess, belong*)

d. describe **senses** and **perceptions** (*hear, see, smell, taste, feel, notice, seem, look [= seem], be, appear, sound*)

- Jane **wants** to go home ***now***.
  Noт: Jane ~~is wanting~~ to go home now.

- We **like** Claude a lot.
- We **love** his sense of humor.

- I **know** a lot of U.S. customs now.
- Ari **remembers** your number.

- Cesar **has** two brothers.
- Some students **own** cars.

- I **hear** the telephone.
- Dina **seems** tired.

5 Some verbs that describe senses and perceptions, such as ***taste***, ***smell***, ***feel***, and ***look***, can have both a **non-action** and an **action** meaning.

Other verbs that have both **non-action** and **action** meaning are ***have*** and ***think***.

USAGE NOTE: We often use ***feel*** in the progressive form to express emotion. The meaning is the same as when we use the simple present form.

Non-Action	Action
The soup **tastes** good. (*It's good.*)	He**'s tasting** the soup. (*He's trying it.*)
His car **looks** great. (*It's beautiful.*)	I**'m looking** at his car. (*I'm examining it.*)
I **have** a new watch. (*I own a new watch.*)	I**'m having** fun. (*I'm experiencing fun.*)
I **think** he's right. (*My opinion: He's right.*)	I**'m thinking** of going. (*I'm considering going.*)

- I **feel** tired. oʀ I**'m feeling** tired.

REFERENCE NOTES

For **spelling rules** on forming the **present progressive**, see Appendix 21 on page A-10.
For **spelling rules** on forming the third person singular of the **simple present**, see Appendix 20 on page A-9.
For **pronunciation rules** for the **simple present**, see Appendix 29 on page A-14.
For **contractions** of *I am, you are*, etc., see Appendix 26 on page A-12.
For a list of **non-action verbs**, see Appendix 2 on page A-2.
For use of the **present progressive** and the **simple present** to talk about the **future**, see Unit 6.

EXERCISE 1: Discover the Grammar

*Read the blog postings by Brian, a Canadian summer exchange student studying in
Argentina. Circle all the verbs that describe what is happening* **now.** *Underline the verbs that
describe what* **regularly** *happens.*

JUNE 28: I'm sitting in a seat 30,000 feet above the Earth en route to Argentina! I usually have
dinner at this time, but right now I have an awful headache from all the excitement. My seatmate
is eating my food. I guess it's good. She looks happy.

JUNE 30: It's 7:30 P.M. My host parents are still working. Carlos, my father, works at home. My
little brother, Ricardo, is cute. He looks (and acts) a lot like Bobby. Right now, he's looking over
my shoulder and trying to read my journal.

JULY 4: The weather is cold here in the summer. I usually spend the first weekend of July at the
beach. Today I'm walking around in a heavy sweater.

AUGUST 6: I usually feel great in the evening, but tonight I feel really tired.

AUGUST 25: I'm feeling very comfortable here now—but it's almost time to go home! My host
parents usually cook a light dinner, but tonight is a special event. They're having a party for me to
say goodbye. I miss them already!

EXERCISE 2: Present Progressive or Simple Present

(Grammar Notes 1–5)

*Some students are talking outside of a classroom. Complete their conversations. Choose
between the present progressive and the simple present forms of the verbs in parentheses.*

A.   **TARO:**   There's Miguel. He _____'s talking_____ to Luisa.
                    1. (talks / 's talking)

    MARISA: Yes. They _____ a class together
                    2. (take / 're taking)

           this semester.

   TARO: They _____ very close to
               3. (stand / 're standing)

           each other. _____ they
                   4. (Do you think / Are you thinking)

           _____?
           5. (date / 're dating)

    MARISA: No. I _____ it _____ anything
               6. (don't think / 'm not thinking)   **7. (means / 's meaning)**

           special. I _____ from Costa Rica, and people usually
               8. (come / 'm coming)

           _____ that close to each other there.
           9. (stand / are standing)

B. LI-WU: Hi, Paulo. What _____?
1. (do you do / are you doing)

PAULO: Oh, I _____ for class to begin.
2. (wait / 'm waiting)

LI-WU: What's the matter? You _____ a
3. (seem / 're seeming)

little down.

PAULO: I'm just tired. I _____ evenings this
4. (work / 'm working)

semester. Hey, is that your teacher over there?

LI-WU: Yes. She _____ to a classmate.
5. (talks / 's talking)

PAULO: What's wrong? He _____ at her. He
6. (doesn't look / 's not looking)

_____ uncomfortable.
7. (seems / 's seeming)

LI-WU: Oh. That _____ anything. In some
8. (doesn't mean / isn't meaning)

countries it's not respectful to look directly at your teacher.

EXERCISE 3: Questions and Statements

(Grammar Notes 1–5)

Other students are talking outside of a classroom. Complete the conversations. Use the present progressive or the simple present form of the verbs in parentheses.

A. RASHA: There's Hans. Why _____ is _____ he

_____ walking _____ so fast? Class _____ at
1. (walk)   2. (start)

9:00. He still _____ 10 minutes!
3. (have)

CLAUDE: He always _____ fast. I think Swiss people
4. (walk)

often _____ to be in a hurry.
5. (appear)

B. IZUMI: Isn't that Sergio and Luis? Why _____

they _____ hands? They already
1. (shake)

_____ each other!
2. (know)

LI-JING: In Brazil, men _____ hands every time they
3. (shake)

_____. It's normal in their culture.
4. (meet)

IZUMI: _____ women _____ hands too?
5. (shake)

EXERCISE 4: Affirmative and Negative Statements

(Grammar Notes 1–2, 5)

Look at Brian's schedule in Argentina. He usually has a regular schedule, but today some things are different. Complete the sentences. Use the present progressive or the simple present. Choose between affirmative and negative.

7:00–8:00	~~run in the park~~	get ready for a field trip
8:30–12:30	~~attend class~~	go on a field trip to the museum
1:00–2:00	eat lunch	
2:00–3:00	~~study with my classmates~~	work on the family Web page
3:00–5:00	work in the cafeteria	
5:00–6:30	~~do homework~~	play tennis
6:30–8:30	~~play tennis~~	watch a video with Eva
8:30–9:30	have dinner	
9:30–10:00	~~write letters~~	take a walk with the family
10:00–10:30	~~take a shower~~	do homework

1. Brian always _runs in the park_ early in the morning, but today he _'s getting ready for a field trip_ .

2. Brian usually _____ between 8:30 and 12:30, but today he _____ .

3. He always _____ between 1:00 and 2:00.

4. It's 1:30. He _____ .

5. He normally _____ after lunch, but today he _____ .

6. Every day from 3:00 to 5:00, he _____ .

7. It's 5:00, but he _____ now.

   He _____ instead.

8. It's 6:45, but he _____ .

   He _____ .

9. It's 8:30. Brian _____ .

10. He always _____ at 8:30.

11. After dinner, Brian usually _____ , but tonight he _____ .

12. It's 10:15, but he _____ .

   He _____ .

EXERCISE 5: Present Progressive or Simple Present

(Grammar Notes 1–5)

Complete the paragraph. Use the correct form of the verbs from the box.

cause	feel	go	live	~~make~~	travel

New food, new customs, new routines—they all _____ make _____ international travel

1.

interesting. But they also _____ culture shock for many travelers going abroad.

2.

_____ you now _____ or _____ in a culture different

3.   **4.**

from your own? If so, why _____ you _____ so good (or so bad)?

5.

Some experts say that we often _____ through four stages of culture shock:

6.

> **Honeymoon Stage:** In the first weeks, everything seems great.
>
> **Rejection Stage:** You have negative feelings about the new culture.
>
> **Adjustment Stage:** Things are getting better these days.
>
> **Adaptation Stage:** You are finally comfortable in the new culture.

EXERCISE 6: Affirmative and Negative Statements

(Grammar Notes 1–5)

A | *Complete the statements in the quiz. Use the correct form of the verbs from the box.*

annoy	improve	~~love~~	think	understand
feel	live	make	treat	want

- [ ] 1. I _____ love _____ it here!
- [ ] 2. People always _____ me very nicely.
- [ ] 3. The customs here often _____ me.
- [ ] 4. I _____ here now, but I _____ I'll stay.
  (negative)
- [ ] 5. Sometimes, I just _____ to go home!
- [ ] 6. My language skills _____ a lot each month.
- [ ] 7. I _____ a lot of new friends these days.
- [ ] 8. I still _____ everything, but I _____ at home here.
  (negative)

B | *Are you living in a culture different from your own? If yes, take the quiz. Check (✓) the statements that are true for you **now**. Then check your quiz results on page 14.*

EXERCISE 7: Editing

Read the student's journal. There are eleven mistakes in the use of the present progressive or simple present. The first mistake is already corrected. Find and correct ten more.

>   *I'm sitting*
> It's 12:30 and ~~I sit~~ in the library right now. My classmates are eating lunch together, but I
> don't feel hungry yet. At home, we eat never this early. Today our journal topic is culture shock.
> It's a good topic for me right now because I'm being pretty homesick. I miss speaking my
> native language with my friends. And I miss my old routine. At home we always are eating a big
> meal at 2:00 in the afternoon. Then we rest. But here in Toronto I'm having a 3:00 conversation
> class. Every day I almost fall asleep in class, and my teacher ask me, "Are you bored?"
> Of course I'm not bored. I just need my afternoon nap! This class always is fun. This semester
> we work on a project with video cameras. My team is filming groups of people from different
> cultures at social events. We are analyze "personal space." That means how close to each other
> these people stand. According to my new watch, it's 12:55, so I leave now for my 1:00 class.
> Teachers here really aren't liking tardiness!

STEP 4 COMMUNICATION PRACTICE

EXERCISE 8: Listening

A | *You are going to listen to short interviews of foreign students studying at a six-week language program in the United States. Before you listen, try to complete the sentences. Then listen and check your answers.*

1. You're living in a new country and experiencing a new _____*culture*_____.

2. In Turkey, I _____ in a very small town, but now I'm living in New York. New York is huge!

3. How do you _____ life in the big city, Eva? Are you experiencing _____ shock?

4. You don't usually _____ a watch? How do you _____ the time?

5. This summer, I _____ grammar and pronunciation.

B | *Listen again to the interviews and check (✓) the things the students* **Usually** *do and the things they are doing* **Now or These Days.**

Students . . .	Usually	Now or These Days
1. a. speak English	☐	☑
b. speak Spanish	☐	☐
2. a. live in a small town	☐	☐
b. live in a big city	☐	☐
3. a. walk slowly	☐	☐
b. move quickly	☐	☐
4. a. wear a watch	☐	☐
b. ask other people for the time	☐	☐
5. a. study grammar and pronunciation	☐	☐
b. study English literature	☐	☐

EXERCISE 9: Pronunciation

A | *Read and listen to the Pronunciation Note.*

> **Pronunciation Note**
>
> In **informal, fast American English**, people often pronounce *What do you . . . ?* and *What are you . . . ?* the same way: "Whaddaya."
>
> **EXAMPLES:** **What do you** read? → "**Whaddaya** read?"
> **What are you** reading? → "**Whaddaya** reading?"

B | *Listen and repeat the questions.*

1. **What are you** studying this semester?
2. **What do you** do after school?
3. **What are you** thinking about?
4. **What do you** usually eat for lunch?
5. **What are you** reading these days?

C | *Work with a partner. Practice asking and answering the questions. Use your own information.*

EXERCISE 10: Find Someone Who...

A | *Walk around your classroom. Ask your classmates questions. Find someone who . . .*

Name

- isn't living in a dormitory

  _____

- likes visiting foreign countries

  _____

- speaks more than two languages

  _____

- is studying something in addition to English

  _____

- doesn't watch sports on TV

  _____

- is planning to travel abroad this year

  _____

- _____

  (add your own)

  _____

> **EXAMPLE:** **A:** Are you living in a dormitory?
> **B:** No, I'm not. I'm living with a family.

B | *Report back to the class.*

> **EXAMPLE:** Tania and José aren't living in a dormitory.

EXERCISE 11: Picture Discussion

Work in pairs. Look at the photographs. Describe them. What's happening? How do the people feel? Discuss possible explanations for each situation. Compare your answers with those of your classmates.

> **EXAMPLE:** **A:** He's pointing. He looks angry.
> **B:** Maybe he's just explaining something.

EXERCISE 12: Compare and Contrast

A | *Work in small groups. Look at the questions. In your culture, which questions are appropriate to ask someone you just met? Which are not appropriate? Compare your choices with those of your classmates.*

- Are you married?
- How much rent do you pay?
- How old are you?
- What are you studying?
- What do you do?
- Where do you live?

B | *What are other examples of inappropriate questions in your culture?*

EXERCISE 13: Writing

A | *Write a paragraph about a new experience you are having. Maybe you are living in a new country, taking a new class, or working at a new job. Describe the situation. How is it different from what you usually do? How do you feel in the situation?*

EXAMPLE: I usually live at home with my parents, but this month I'm living with my aunt and uncle. Everything seems different. My aunt . . .

B | *Check your work. Use the Editing Checklist.*

Editing Checklist

Did you use . . . ?
- ☐ the present progressive to describe something that is happening right now
- ☐ the simple present to describe what regularly happens
- ☐ the simple present with non-action verbs such as **be**, **like**, **want**, and **know**
- ☐ adverbs of frequency in the correct position

QUIZ RESULTS FOR EXERCISE 6

If you checked . . .	*you are in the . . .*
1 and 2	**Honeymoon Stage**
3 and 4 and 5	**Rejection Stage**
6 and 7	**Adjustment Stage**
8	**Adaptation Stage**

A | *Circle the correct words to complete the sentences.*

1. What courses <u>are you taking / do you take</u> this semester?

2. I <u>don't / 'm not</u> understand this phrase. What's *culture shock*?

3. At home, we <u>often speak / speak often</u> Spanish.

4. Look! That's my teacher. He<u>'s talking / talks</u> to Andrea, one of my classmates.

5. <u>Are / Do</u> you feel better today?

B | *Complete the conversation with the present progressive or simple present form of the verbs in parentheses.*

A: What _____ you _____ right now?
         1. (do)

B: Not much. I _____ just _____ a video game. Why?
         2. (play)

A: _____ you _____ to get some lunch?
         3. (want)

B: Sure. I usually _____ this early, but I _____
         4. (not eat)   **5. (feel)**
         pretty hungry right now.

A: Mmm, mushroom soup. It _____ good.
         6. (look)

B: It _____ good, though. I had it yesterday.
         7. (not taste)

A: Hey, there's Costa and Libby. Why _____ they _____ like
                                                                      8. (shout)
         that? _____ they angry?
         9. (be)

B: I don't think so. They always _____ like that. Let's go sit with them.
                                       10. (talk)
         They're fun.

C | *Find and correct five mistakes.*

I live in Qatar, but right now I stay in Wisconsin. I'm studying English here. I have a good

time this summer, but in some ways it's a pretty strange experience. Summer in Wisconsin feel

like winter in Qatar! Every weekend, I go to the beach with some classmates, but I go never

into the water—it's too cold! I'm enjoy my time here though, and my culture shock is going

away fast.

Simple Past
POETS

STEP 1 GRAMMAR IN CONTEXT

Before You Read

Look at the picture and the text above it. Discuss the questions.

1. What did Matsuo Basho do?
2. How long did he live?

Read

Read the short biography of Basho.

Matsuo Basho, 1644–1694

Matsuo Basho **wrote** more than 1,000 *haiku* (three-line poems). He **chose** topics from nature, daily life, and human emotions. He **became** one of Japan's most famous poets, and his work **established** haiku as an important art form.

Basho **was** born Matsuo Munefusa near Kyoto in 1644. ("Basho" is the name he later **used** as a poet.) He **did not want** to become a samurai[1] like his father. Instead, he **moved** to Edo (present-day Tokyo) and **studied** poetry. Then he **became** a teacher, and by 1681 he **had** many students and admirers.

Basho, however, **was** restless. Starting in 1684, he **traveled** on foot and on horseback all over Japan. Sometimes his friends **joined** him, and they **wrote** poetry together. Travel **was** difficult in the 17th century, and Basho often **got** sick. He **died** in 1694 during a journey to Osaka. At that time, he **had** 2,000 students.

As for that flower
By the road —
My horse ate it!
—Matsuo Basho

[1] *samurai:* in past times, a member of the soldier class in Japan

After You Read

A | Vocabulary: *Complete the sentences with the words from the box.*

| admirers | emotions | journey | restless | topic |

1. Basho wrote about everyday things. A frog is the _____ of one of his most famous poems.

2. Basho's students and _____ loved him and called him a great poet.

3. On his first _____, Basho traveled a long way and visited his native village.

4. Basho became _____ and did not want to stay in one place for very long.

5. Basho felt all kinds of strong _____ in his travels, such as fear, loneliness, and happiness.

B | Comprehension: *Check (✓) the boxes to complete the sentences. Check **all** the true information about Basho.*

1. Basho wrote about _____.
   - ☐ flowers
   - ☐ animals
   - ☐ samurai

2. Before Basho, *haiku* _____.
   - ☐ was an important kind of poetry
   - ☐ did not exist
   - ☐ was not an important kind of poetry

3. In Edo, Basho _____.
   - ☐ studied poetry
   - ☐ became a teacher
   - ☐ became a samurai

4. On his journeys, he _____.
   - ☐ traveled in boats
   - ☐ walked
   - ☐ rode horses

5. At the end of his life, Basho _____.
   - ☐ had only a few students
   - ☐ traveled to Osaka
   - ☐ was famous

SIMPLE PAST: *BE*

Affirmative Statements

Subject	*Be*	
I	**was**	
You	**were**	
He She It	**was**	famous.
We You They	**were**	

Negative Statements

Subject	*Be + Not*	
I	**wasn't**	
You	**weren't**	
He She It	**wasn't**	famous.
We You They	**weren't**	

Yes / No Questions

Be	Subject	
Was	I	
Were	you	
Was	he she it	famous?
Were	we you they	

Short Answers

	Affirmative			Negative	
Yes,	you	**were.**	**No,**	you	**weren't.**
	I	**was.**		I	**wasn't.**
	he she it	**was.**		he she it	**wasn't.**
	you we they	**were.**		you we they	**weren't.**

Wh- Questions

Wh- Word	*Be*	Subject	
	was	I	
	were	you	
Where When Why	**was**	he she it	famous?
	were	we you they	

SIMPLE PAST: REGULAR AND IRREGULAR VERBS

Affirmative Statements

Subject	Verb	
I You He She It We You They	**moved** **traveled**	to Japan.
	came **left**	in 1684.

Negative Statements

Subject	*Did not*	Base Form of Verb	
I You He She It We You They	**didn't**	**move** **travel**	to Japan.
		come **leave**	in 1684.

Yes / No Questions

Did	Subject	Base Form of Verb	
Did	I you he she it we you they	**move** **travel**	to Japan?
		come **leave**	in 1684?

Short Answers

Affirmative			Negative		
Yes,	you I he she it you we they	**did.**	**No,**	you I he she it you we they	**didn't**.

Wh- Questions

Wh- Word	*Did*	Subject	Base Form of Verb	
When Why	**did**	I you he she it we you they	**move** **travel**	to Japan?
			come? **leave**?	

GRAMMAR NOTES

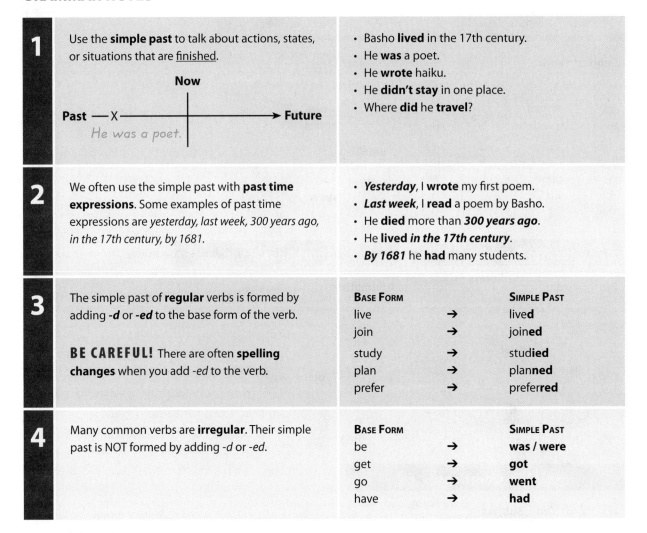

1	Use the **simple past** to talk about actions, states, or situations that are <u>finished</u>. **Now** Past —X————————→ Future *He was a poet.*	• Basho **lived** in the 17th century. • He **was** a poet. • He **wrote** haiku. • He **didn't stay** in one place. • Where **did** he **travel**?
2	We often use the simple past with **past time expressions**. Some examples of past time expressions are *yesterday, last week, 300 years ago, in the 17th century, by 1681.*	• *Yesterday*, I **wrote** my first poem. • *Last week*, I **read** a poem by Basho. • He **died** more than *300 years ago*. • He **lived** *in the 17th century*. • *By 1681* he **had** many students.

3	The simple past of **regular** verbs is formed by adding *-d* or *-ed* to the base form of the verb. **BE CAREFUL!** There are often **spelling changes** when you add *-ed* to the verb.	**BASE FORM** live join study plan prefer	→ → → → →	**SIMPLE PAST** live**d** join**ed** stud**ied** plan**ned** prefer**red**

4	Many common verbs are **irregular**. Their simple past is NOT formed by adding *-d* or *-ed*.	**BASE FORM** be get go have	→ → → →	**SIMPLE PAST** **was / were** **got** **went** **had**

REFERENCE NOTES

For **spelling rules** for the **simple past of regular verbs**, see Appendix 22 on page A-10.

For **pronunciation rules** for the **simple past of regular verbs**, see Appendix 30 on page A-15.

For a list of **irregular verbs**, see Appendix 1 on page A-1.

EXERCISE 1: Discover the Grammar

Read more about Basho. Underline all the verbs in the simple past. Then complete the timeline on the left.

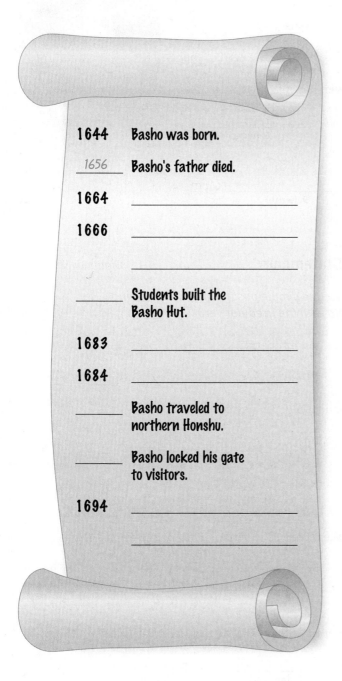

1644	Basho was born.
1656	Basho's father died.
1664	_____
1666	_____
_____	Students built the Basho Hut.
1683	_____
1684	_____
_____	Basho traveled to northern Honshu.
_____	Basho locked his gate to visitors.
1694	_____

As the son of a samurai, Basho grew up in the household of Todo Yoshitada, a young lord. After his father's death in 1656, Basho stayed in the Yoshitada household. He and Todo wrote poetry together, and in 1664, they published some poems. Two years later, Todo died suddenly. Basho left the area.

Basho was a restless young man, and he moved around for several years. In the 1670s, he went to Edo and stayed there. He found friendship and success once again. Basho judged poetry contests, published his own poetry, and taught students. His students built him a home outside the city in 1681. They planted a banana tree (*basho* in Japanese) in front and called his home "Basho Hut." That is how the poet got his name: Basho.

In spite of this success, Basho became unhappy. He often wrote about loneliness. His mother died in 1683, and he began his travels a year later. His trip to the northern part of Honshu in 1689 was difficult, but his travel diary about this journey, *Narrow Road to the Deep North*, became one of Japan's greatest works of literature.

As a famous poet, Basho had many visitors—too many, in fact. In 1693 he locked his gate for a month, stayed alone, and wrote. The following year he took his final journey, to Osaka. He died there among his friends and admirers.

EXERCISE 2: Affirmative Statements

(Grammar Notes 1–4)

Complete the biography of American poet Emily Dickinson. Use the simple past form of the verbs in parentheses. Go to Appendix 1 on page A-1 for help with the irregular verbs.

Emily Dickinson, one of the most famous American poets,

_____*lived*_____ from 1830 to 1886. Her favorite topics
1. (live)

_____ nature, time, and human emotions.
2. (be)

Dickinson _____ an unusual life. During the 1860s, she
3. (lead)

_____ a recluse¹—she almost never _____
4. (become)   **5. (leave)**

her house in Amherst, Massachusetts, and she only _____
6. (wear)

white. Dickinson _____ very few people to visit her, but she
7. (allow)

_____ a lot of friends, and she _____ them
8. (have)   **9. (write)**

many letters.

EXERCISE 3: Affirmative and Negative Statements

(Grammar Notes 1–4)

Complete the list of facts about Emily Dickinson. Use the simple past form of the verbs in parentheses. Go to Appendix 1 on page A-1 for help with the irregular verbs.

1. Dickinson _____*wasn't*_____ only interested in poetry.
   (not be)

2. She also _____ science.
   (like)

3. She _____ topics from science in many of her poems.
   (use)

4. She never _____ far from home, but she _____ many people.
   (go)   **(know)**

5. Dickinson _____ only poetry.
   (not write)

6. She _____ her friends and admirers hundreds of letters.
   (send)

7. Her letters _____ full of jokes, recipes, cartoons, and poems.
   (be)

8. But she _____ the envelopes—other people _____ that for her.
   (not address)   **(do)**

9. Dickinson _____ a typewriter.
   (not own)

10. She _____ the first drafts² of her poems on the back of old grocery lists.
    (write)

11. During her lifetime, 7 of her 1,700 poems _____ in print.
    (appear)

12. She _____ about this, and no one _____ her permission.
    (not know)   **(ask)**

---

¹ **recluse:** someone who stays away from other people

² **first draft:** first copy of a piece of writing, with no corrections

EXERCISE 4: Regular and Irregular Verbs

(Grammar Notes 1–4)

Complete the lines from a poem by Emily Dickinson. Use the simple past form of the verbs from the box. Go to Appendix 1 on page A-1 for help with the irregular verbs.

| bite | ~~come~~ | drink | eat | hop | not know |

A bird _____came_____ down the walk:
       1.
He _____ I saw;
  2.
He _____ an angle-worm in halves
   3.
And _____ the fellow raw.
    4.
And then he _____ a dew
     5.
From a convenient grass,
And then _____ sidewise to the wall
     6.
To let a beetle pass.

EXERCISE 5: Questions and Answers

(Grammar Notes 1–4)

Read the statements about Basho. Then write questions about Emily Dickinson. Write a **yes/no** *question if a verb is underlined or a* **wh-** *question if other words are underlined. Then answer your questions using the information from Exercises 2 and 3.*

1. Basho <u>was</u> a poet.

  Q: *Was Dickinson a poet?*

  A: *Yes, she was.*

2. He was born <u>in 1644</u>.

  Q: *When was Dickinson born?*

  A: *She was born in 1830.*

3. He lived <u>in Japan</u>.

  Q: _____

  A: _____

4. He <u>became</u> famous during his lifetime.

  Q: _____

  A: _____

(continued on next page)

5. Basho's admirers often <u>visited</u> him.

Q: _____

A: _____

6. He <u>traveled</u> a lot.

Q: _____

A: _____

7. Basho wrote <u>more than 1,000 poems</u>.

Q: _____

A: _____

8. He wrote <u>about nature</u>.

Q: _____

A: _____

9. He died <u>in 1694</u>.

Q: _____

A: _____

EXERCISE 6: Affirmative and Negative Statements   *(Grammar Notes 2–4)*

A | *Read the article about a modern writer.*

ANA CASTILLO is a modern poet, novelist, short story writer, and teacher. She was born in Chicago in 1953, and she lived there for 32 years. *Otro Canto*, her first book of poetry, appeared in 1977.

In her work, Castillo uses humor and a lively mixture of Spanish and English (Spanglish). She got her special writer's "voice" by living in a neighborhood with many different ethnic groups. She also thanks her father for her writing style. "He had an outgoing and easy personality, and this . . . sense of humor. I got a lot from him . . ."

Castillo attended high school, college, and graduate school in Chicago. In the 1970s, she taught English and Mexican history. She received a Ph.D. in American Studies from Bremen University in Germany in 1992.

B | *Read the statements. Write **That's right** or **That's wrong**. Correct the incorrect statements.*

1. Ana Castillo was born in Mexico City.

That's wrong. She wasn't born in Mexico City. She was born in Chicago.

2. She lived in Chicago until 1977.

_____

3. Her father was very shy.

_____

4. She grew up among people of different cultures.

_____

5. Castillo got most of her education in Chicago.

_____

6. She taught Spanish in the 1970s.

_____

7. She went to France for her Ph.D.

_____

EXERCISE 7: Editing

Read the student's journal. There are ten mistakes in the use of the simple past. The first mistake is already corrected. Find and correct nine more.

Today in class we read a poem by the American poet Robert Frost.
I really ~~enjoy~~ *enjoyed* it. It was about a person who choosed between two roads
in a forest. Many people believed the person were Frost. He thinked
about his choice for a long time. The two roads didn't looked very
different. Finally, he didn't took the road most people take. He took
the one less traveled on. At that time, he didn't thought it was an
important decision, but his choice change his life.

Sometimes I feel a little like Frost. Two years ago I decide to
move to a new country. It was a long journey and a big change. Did I
made the right decision?

EXERCISE 8: Listening

A | *Read the statements. Then listen to the interview with a poet. Listen again and circle the correct information.*

1. Murat came to the United States <u>before /</u> <u>(after)</u> his parents.

2. He had a wonderful life with his grandparents in <u>Baltimore / Turkey</u>.

3. In Baltimore, he had no friends, so he <u>wrote poems / read books</u>.

4. He wrote his first poem in <u>English / Turkish</u>.

5. In college, Murat studied <u>farming / poetry</u>.

B | *Read the information in the timeline. Then listen again to the interview and write the year for each event.*

| was born | parents left Turkey | moved to the U.S. | began to write poetry | graduated from college | won a poetry award | became a teacher |

1970

EXERCISE 9: Pronunciation

A | *Read and listen to the Pronunciation Note.*

> **Pronunciation Note**
>
> In **wh- questions**, we often pronounce **did** "d" after the *wh-* word.
>
> **EXAMPLES:** Why **did** she write the poem? → "Why**'d** she write the poem?"
> Who **did** they show it to? → "Who**'d** they show it to?"
> How **did** he like it? → "How**'d** he like it?"
>
> Notice that **How'd he** sounds like "Howdy."

B | *Listen to the short conversations. Then listen again and complete the conversations with the words that you hear. Use full forms.*

1. **A:** _____ live?

   B: In Japan.

2. **A:** _____ talk to?

   B: A famous poet.

3. **A:** _____ move?

   B: To be near school.

4. A: _____ feel about their new home?

B: Not great at first.

5. A: _____ study poetry?

B: He loves it.

6. A: _____ go to school?

B: In Mexico.

C | *Listen again to the conversations and repeat the questions. Use short forms. Then practice the conversations with a partner.*

EXERCISE 10: Compare and Contrast

Work in small groups. Reread the information about Matsuo Basho (see pages 16 and 21) and Emily Dickinson (see page 22). In what ways were the two poets similar? How were they different? With your group, write as many ideas as you can. Compare your ideas with those of your classmates.

EXAMPLE: **A:** Both Basho and Dickinson were poets.
B: Basho lived in the 17th century. Dickinson lived in the 19th century.
C: Dickinson stayed at home, but Basho was restless and traveled a lot.

EXERCISE 11: Writing

A | *Write a paragraph about some important events in your life. Do not put your name on your paper. Your teacher will collect all the papers, mix them up, and redistribute them to the class.*

B | *Check your work. Use the Editing Checklist.*

Editing Checklist

Did you . . . ?
☐ use the simple past
☐ spell regular past verbs correctly
☐ use the correct form of irregular past verbs

C | *Read the paragraph your teacher gives you. Then ask your classmates questions to try to find its writer.*

EXAMPLE: Did you come here in 1990? OR When did you come here?

EXERCISE 12: Information Gap: Celebrity Profile

Work in pairs (A and B). **Student A,** *follow the instructions on this page.* **Student B,** *turn to page 30 and follow the instructions there.*

1. Read the profile of an actor who is also a poet, painter, and musician. Ask your partner questions to complete the missing information.

   EXAMPLE: **A:** When was Viggo born?
   B: He was born on October 25, 1958.

2. Answer your partner's questions.

   EXAMPLE: **B:** Where was Viggo born?
   A: He was born in New York.

3. If you don't know how to spell something, ask your partner.

   EXAMPLE: **A:** How do you spell Argentina?
   B: Capital A, R, G, E, N, T, I, N, A.

SCREEN-TIME PROFILE

Date of Birth: October 25, 1958

Place of Birth: New York

Mini Bio:

★ lived in Argentina, Venezuela,

   and _____ as a child

★ attended school in Argentina

★ spoke Spanish, _____, and English

★ returned to the United States in 19_____

★ became a movie actor in 1985

★ first movie was *Witness*

★ played the part of _____ in *Lord of the Rings* (This movie made him famous.)

★ finished his first _____ in 1993 (The title was *Ten Last Night*.)

★ created the paintings for the movie *A Perfect Murder* (He played the part of the artist.)

★ wrote music for *Lord of the Rings*

Viggo Mortensen: actor, poet, painter, musician

When you are finished, compare the profiles. Are they the same?

UNIT 2 Review

Check your answers on page UR-1.
Do you need to review anything?

A | Circle the letter of the correct answer to complete each sentence.

1. Last night I _____ a poem for my English class.
   a. write   **b.** wrote   **c.** written

2. It _____ about my childhood.
   a. be   **b.** were   **c.** was

3. At first, I didn't _____ what to write about.
   a. know   **b.** knowing   **c.** knew

4. My roommate _____ a good suggestion.
   a. makes   **b.** did make   **c.** made

5. Did you _____ a poem for your class?
   a. write   **b.** writing   **c.** wrote

6. I really _____ the experience.
   a. enjoy   **b.** enjoys   **c.** enjoyed

B | Complete the conversation with the simple past form of the verbs in parentheses and a short answer.

A: _____ you _____ out last night? I _____ you, but
                          1. (go)   **2. (call)**

you _____.
       3. (not answer)

B: _____, I _____. I _____ to the movies.
                              4.   **5. (go)**

A: What _____ you _____?
                                  6. (see)

B: I _____ Dead Poets Society. I _____ it very much, though.
          7. (see)   **8. (not like)**

C | Find and correct six mistakes.

The poet Elizabeth Alexander was born in New York City, but she didn't grew up there. Her father taked a job with the government, and her family moved to Washington, D.C. As a child, she have a loving family. Her parents were active in the civil rights movement, and Elizabeth gots interested in African-American history. In her first book, she wrote about important African leaders. She met Barack Obama at the University of Chicago. They both teached there in the 1990s. On January 20, 2009, she reads a poem at President Obama's inauguration.

1. Read the profile of an actor who is also a poet, painter, and musician. Ask your partner questions to complete the missing information.

   EXAMPLE: **A:** When was Viggo born?
   B: He was born on October 25, 1958.

2. Answer your partner's questions.

   EXAMPLE: **B:** Where was Viggo born?
   A: He was born in New York.

3. If you don't know how to spell something, ask your partner.

   EXAMPLE: **B:** How do you spell Argentina?
   A: Capital A, R, G, E, N, T, I, N, A.

SCREEN-TIME PROFILE

Date of Birth: October 25, 1958

Place of Birth: *New York*

Mini Bio:

★ lived in Argentina, Venezuela, and Denmark as a child

★ attended school in _____

★ spoke Spanish, Danish, and English

★ returned to the United States in 1969

★ became a movie actor in 19___

★ first movie was _____

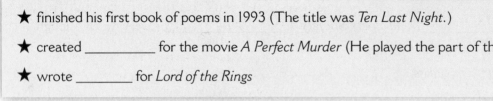

Viggo Mortensen: actor, poet, painter, musician

★ played the part of Aragorn in *Lord of the Rings* (This movie made him famous.)

★ finished his first book of poems in 1993 (The title was *Ten Last Night*.)

★ created _____ for the movie *A Perfect Murder* (He played the part of the artist.)

★ wrote _____ for *Lord of the Rings*

When you are finished, compare the profiles. Are they the same?

Past Progressive and Simple Past
ACCIDENTS

Before You Read

Look at the picture. Discuss the questions.

1. What do you know about the *Titanic?*
2. What happened to the ship?

Read

Read the newspaper article about the sinking of the Titanic.

VOL CCXII, NO 875   MONDAY, APRIL 15, 1912   PRICE ONE CENT

■ DISASTER AT SEA ■

NEW YORK, April 15—It **was** a clear night. The sea **was** calm. The *RMS Titanic*, the largest luxury ship[1] in the world, **was sailing** from Southhampton, England, to New York City. This **was** its first voyage,[2] and it **was carrying** more than 2,200 passengers and crew.[3] At around 11:30 P.M. crew member Frederick Fleet **was looking** at the sea when, suddenly, he **saw** a huge white form in front of the ship. When he **saw** it, Fleet immediately **rang** the ship's bell three times and **shouted**, "Iceberg ahead!" But it **was** too late. The great ship **crashed** into the mountain of ice.

When the *Titanic* **hit** the iceberg, people **were sleeping**, **reading**, and **playing** cards. Some passengers **heard** a loud noise, but they **were** not alarmed. They **believed** the ship **was** unsinkable.[4] But soon it **became** clear that the *Titanic* **was** in danger. There **was** a hole in the side of the ship. Water **was entering** fast, and it **was starting** to sink. There **were** lifeboats, but only 1,178 spaces for 2,224 people. In an attempt to keep everyone calm, the ship's band **played** a lively tune while people **were getting** into the boats.

(*continued on next page*)

---

[1] *luxury ship:* a boat that has many great things (beautiful rooms, swimming pools, restaurants, etc.)
[2] *voyage:* a long trip, usually on a ship
[3] *crew:* the people who work on a ship or airplane
[4] *unsinkable:* cannot go underwater

DISASTER AT SEA

The *Titanic* **was not** the only ship on the sea that night. There **were** several other ships in the area. The *Californian* **was** nearby, but it **did not hear** the *Titanic's* calls for help. And then there **was** the *Carpathia*. While the *Titanic* **was sailing** toward New York, the *Carpathia* **was traveling** from New York to the Mediterranean. When it **heard** the *Titanic's* distress signals,[5] the *Carpathia* **turned** around and **headed** back toward the sinking ship. By the time the *Carpathia* **arrived**, the *Titanic* **was** already at the bottom of the sea, but there **were** 18 lifeboats full of cold and frightened survivors. Thanks to the *Carpathia*, more than 700 people **lived** to tell the story of that terrible night.

[5] **distress signals:** calls for help

After You Read

A | Vocabulary: *Match the words with their definitions.*

_____ **1. disaster**   **a.** one part of a larger place

_____ **2. calm**   **b.** someone who continues to live after an accident

_____ **3. area**   **c.** afraid

_____ **4. survivor**   **d.** to go under water

_____ **5. alarmed**   **e.** a terrible accident

_____ **6. sink**   **f.** quiet

B | Comprehension: *Number the events in order (1–8).*

_____ Water entered the *Titanic*.

_____ Frederick Fleet rang the ship's bell.

_____ The *Titanic* hit an iceberg.

_____ The *Carpathia* arrived and saved the survivors.

_____ The *Titanic* was sailing to New York.

_____ The *Titanic* sank.

_____ Frederick Fleet saw an iceberg.

_____ The *Carpathia* heard the *Titanic's* distress signals.

PAST PROGRESSIVE

Statements

Subject	Was / Were	(Not)	Base Form of Verb + -ing	
I	was			
You	were			
He She	was	(not)	reading eating sleeping	yesterday at 11:30 P.M. when he **called**. while he **was talking**.
We You They	were			

Yes / No Questions

Was / Were	Subject	Base Form of Verb + -ing	
Was	I		
Were	you		
Was	he she	reading eating sleeping	yesterday at 11:30 P.M.? when he **called**? while he **was talking**?
Were	we you they		

Short Answers

Affirmative				Negative		
	you	were.			you	weren't.
	I	was.			I	wasn't.
Yes,	he she	was.		No,	he she	wasn't.
	you we they	were.			you we they	weren't.

Wh- Questions

Wh-Word	Was / Were	Subject	Base Form of Verb + -ing	
	was	I		
	were	you		
Why	was	he she	reading eating sleeping	yesterday at 11:30 P.M? when he **called**? while he **was talking**?
	were	we you they		

GRAMMAR NOTES

1 Use the **past progressive** to focus on the <u>duration</u> of a past action, not its completion.

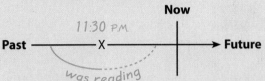

USAGE NOTE: We often use the past progressive with a specific time in the past.

- Paul **was reading** a book last night. *(We don't know if he finished it.)*

- He **was reading** a book *at 11:30 P.M.*

2 Use the **simple past** to focus on the <u>completion</u> of a past action.

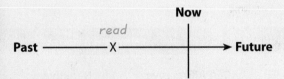

BE CAREFUL! **Non-action verbs** are NOT usually used in the progressive.

- Paul **read** a book last night. *(He finished it.)*

- She **heard** about the disaster. Not: She ~~was hearing~~ about the disaster.

3 Use the **past progressive** with the **simple past** to talk about an action that was <u>interrupted</u> by another action. Use the simple past for the interrupting action.

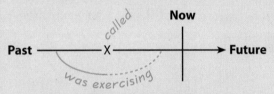

- Use **when** to introduce the **simple past** action.
- Use **while** to introduce the **past progressive** action.

- I **was exercising** when he **called**. *(I was exercising. The phone rang and interrupted my exercising.)*

- He was running **when** he **fell**.
- **While** he **was running**, he fell.

4 Use the **past progressive** with *while* to talk about two actions in progress <u>at the same time</u> in the past. Use the past progressive in both clauses.

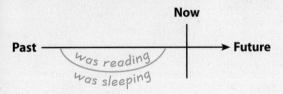

- *While* I **was reading**, Amy **was sleeping**. OR
- Amy **was sleeping** *while* I **was reading**.

5 | **BE CAREFUL!** A sentence with both clauses in the simple past has a very <u>different meaning</u> from a sentence with one clause in the simple past and one clause in the past progressive.

a. Both clauses in the **simple past**:

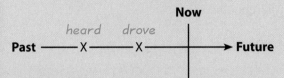

b. One clause in the **simple past**, the other in the **past progressive**:

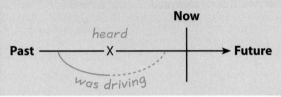

- She **drove** home when she **heard** the news.
(First she heard the news; then she drove home.)

- She **was driving** home when she **heard** the news.
(First she was driving home; then she heard the news.)

6 | Notice that the **time clause** (the part of the sentence with **when** or **while**) can come at the beginning or the end of the sentence.

Use a **comma** after the time clause when it comes at the beginning. Do NOT use a comma when it comes at the end.

- **When you called**, I was eating.
OR
- I was eating **when you called**.

NOT: I was eating, when you called.

REFERENCE NOTES
For **spelling rules** on forming the **past progressive**, see Appendix 21 on page A-10.
For a list of **non-action verbs**, see Appendix 2 on page A-2.

STEP 3 FOCUSED PRACTICE

EXERCISE 1: Discover the Grammar

Read the question. Then circle the letter of the correct sentence.

1. In which sentence did the passengers arrive before the ship left?
   a. When the passengers arrived, the ship was leaving.
   b. When the passengers arrived, the ship left.

2. Which sentence tells us that the ship reached New York?
   a. It was sailing to New York.
   b. It sailed to New York.

(continued on next page)

3. In which sentence do we know that the ship went completely under water?

   a. It was sinking.

   b. It sank.

4. Which sentence talks about two actions that were in progress at the same time?

   a. While the ship was sinking, passengers were getting into lifeboats.

   b. When the ship sank, passengers got into lifeboats.

5. In which sentence was the phone call interrupted?

   a. When he heard the news, he called me.

   b. When he heard the news, he was calling me.

6. In which sentence did the woman leave after the phone call?

   a. When he called her, she left the house.

   b. When he called her, she was leaving the house.

EXERCISE 2: Past Progressive Statements

(Grammar Note 1)

Douglas is sailing to Europe on the SS Atlantic. *Look at his schedule for yesterday. Complete the sentences. Use the past progressive form of the verbs in parentheses. Choose between affirmative and negative.*

S.S. Atlantic

```
10:00  breakfast - Sea Breezes - Donna
11:00  exercise - gym - Michel
12:00  swimming contest - Olympic pool
 1:00  lunch - Oceania - Raul
 2:30  lecture on Italian art - library
 4:00  coffee - Café Rose - Natasha
 5:00  haircut - Jean-Georges Salon - Alain
 7:00  dinner - Thalassa - Kim and Jason
 9:00  card game - Casino Royal - Massimo
```

---

1. At 10:15 Douglas _____ *wasn't sleeping* _____ in his cabin.
                                     a. (sleep)

   He _____ breakfast at Sea Breezes with Donna.
              b. (have)

2. At 11:05 he _____ in the ship's gym with Michel.
                   a. (exercise)

   He _____ in the pool.
              b. (swim)

3. At 1:10 he _____ coffee at Café Rose.
                a. (drink)

   He _____ lunch at Oceania with Raul.
              b. (eat)

4. At 2:40 he _____ for a book in the ship's library.
a. (look)

He _____ to a lecture on Italian art.
b. (listen)

5. At 4:05 he _____ a haircut at the Jean-Georges Salon.
a. (get)

6. At 7:10 he _____ in his room.
a. (rest)

He _____ dinner at Thalassa with Kim and Jason.
b. (enjoy)

7. At 9:15 he _____ cards at the Casino Royal with Massimo
a. (play)

and other friends.

EXERCISE 3: Past Progressive or Simple Past

(Grammar Notes 1–5)

Complete the information about the Titanic *disaster. Use the past progressive or simple past form of the verbs in parentheses. Go to Appendix 1 on page A-1 for help with irregular verbs.*

Eyewitness Accounts[1]

⚓ According to eyewitness Lawrence Beesley, when the ship _____*hit*_____ the iceberg,
1. (hit)

the engines _____. Minutes later, when Professor Beesley _____ on
2. (stop)   3. (go)

deck, he _____ only a few other passengers there. Everyone was calm. A few people
4. (find)

_____ cards in the smoking room. When he _____ out the window,
5. (play)   6. (look)

he _____ an iceberg at the side of the ship.
7. (see)

⚓ Another survivor, Washington Dodge, said that it _____ 11:30 P.M. when the crash
8. (be)

_____. He _____ to go on deck. While the ship _____,
9. (happen)   10. (decide)   11. (sink)

the band _____ a lively tune. At 1:55 A.M. the ship _____ completely
12. (play)   13. (sink)

into the sea.

⚓ While passenger Elizabeth Shutes _____ a chicken sandwich in her cabin, she
14. (eat)

"_____ a shudder travel through the ship." Shortly after, she _____ in
15. (feel)   16. (sit)

a lifeboat in the middle of the ocean with 34 other people. Hours later, someone shouted "a light,

a ship!" When Shutes _____, she _____ a ship with bright lights
17. (look)   18. (see)

coming toward them. It was the *Carpathia*—the only ship in the area that came to help.

⚓ When Harold Bride, one of the ship's two radio operators, _____ some lights in the
19. (notice)

distance, he _____ it was a steamship. It _____ to rescue them. When
20. (know)   21. (come)

the *Carpathia* _____, it _____ all of the survivors—including Mr. Bride.
22. (arrive)   23. (pick up)

---

[1] *eyewitness account:* a report by someone who saw an accident or crime

EXERCISE 4: *Yes/No* and *Wh-* Questions

(Grammar Notes 1–5)

A newspaper is interviewing a Titanic *survivor. Read the survivor's answers. Write the interviewer's questions. Use the words in parentheses and the past progressive or simple past.*

1. **INTERVIEWER:** _What were you doing Sunday night?_
   (what / you / do / Sunday night)
   PASSENGER: I was playing cards with some other passengers.

2. **INTERVIEWER:** _____
   (your wife / play / with you)
   PASSENGER: No, she wasn't. My wife wasn't with me at the time.

3. **INTERVIEWER:** _____
   (what / she / do / while you / play cards)
   SURVIVOR: She was reading in our room.

4. **INTERVIEWER:** _____
   (you / feel / the crash)
   SURVIVOR: Not really. But I heard a very loud noise.

5. **INTERVIEWER:** _____
   (what / you / do / when you / hear the noise)
   SURVIVOR: At first, we all continued to play. We weren't alarmed. Everyone stayed calm.

6. **INTERVIEWER:** _____
   (what / you / do / when the lights / go out)
   SURVIVOR: I tried to find my wife.

7. **INTERVIEWER:** _____
   (what / she / do / while you / look for her)
   SURVIVOR: She was looking for *me*. Thank goodness we found each other!

8. **INTERVIEWER:** _____
   (what / you / do / when you / find her)
   SURVIVOR: We tried to get into a lifeboat.

EXERCISE 5: Statements with *When* and *While*

(Grammar Notes 1–6)

Combine the pairs of sentences. Use the past progressive or the simple past form of the verb. Keep the order of the two sentences. Remember to use commas when necessary.

1. The storm started. Mr. Taylor attended a party.

   When _the storm started, Mr. Taylor was attending a party._ .

2. The electricity went out. The wind began to blow.

   _____ when _____ .

3. He drove home. He listened to his car radio.

   While _____ .

4. He pulled over to the side of the road. He couldn't see anything.

_____ when _____.

5. He listened to the news. He heard about a car crash near his home.

While _____.

6. It stopped raining. Mr. Taylor drove home in a hurry.

When _____.

EXERCISE 6: Editing

Read the journal entry. There are ten mistakes in the use of the past progressive and the simple past. The first mistake is already corrected. Find and correct nine more. Remember to look at punctuation!

April 15

                      went

    This afternoon I ~~was going~~ to a movie at school. It was <u>Titanic</u>. They were showing it because it was the anniversary of the 1912 disaster. What a beautiful and sad film! Jack (Leonardo DiCaprio) was meeting Rose (Kate Winslet) while they both sailed on the huge ship. It was the <u>Titanic's</u> first voyage.

    Rose was from a very rich family; Jack was from a poor family. They fell in love, but Rose's mother wasn't happy about it. When the ship was hitting the iceberg, the two lovers were together, but then they got separated. Rose was finding Jack while the ship was sinking. Seconds before the ship went under, they held hands and were jumping into the water. Rose survived, but Jack didn't. It was so sad. When I left the theater, I still was having tears in my eyes.

    That wasn't my only adventure of the day. When the movie was over I left the school auditorium. While I walked home, I saw an accident between two pedestrians and a car. I was the only one in the area, so while I saw the accident, I immediately called the police. When the police got there, they asked me a lot of questions — there were no other witnesses. I'm glad to say that the accident had a happier ending than the movie!

EXERCISE 7: Listening

A | *You're going to hear a witness describe a traffic accident. Before you listen, look at the pictures. The pictures show three versions of what happened. Work with a partner and describe what happened in each of the three stories.*

1.

2.

3.

B | *Listen to the witness describe the traffic accident. According to the witness, which set of pictures is the most accurate? Circle the number.*

C | *Read the statements. Then listen again to the witness's description and check (✓) **True** or **False**. Correct the false statements.*

	True	False
		saw
1. The woman ~~was in~~ the accident.	☐	☑
2. She was driving down the street.	☐	☐
3. The car was driving very fast.	☐	☐
4. The two men were watching the traffic.	☐	☐
5. The car hit the two men.	☐	☐

EXERCISE 8: Pronunciation

A | *Read and listen to the Pronunciation Note.*

Pronunciation Note

When a **time clause begins a sentence**, we usually **pause** briefly **at the end** of the time clause. In **writing**, we put a **comma** where the pause is.

EXAMPLE: When I saw the movie, I cried.   →   "When I saw the movie [PAUSE] I cried."

B | *Listen to the sentences. Put a comma where you hear the pause.*

1. When the phone rang she answered it.

2. While she was talking I was watching TV.

3. When she saw the storm clouds she drove home.

4. While she was driving home she was listening to the news.

5. When she got home she put the TV on.

C | *Listen again and repeat the sentences.*

EXERCISE 9: Game: Are You a Good Witness?

A | *Look at the picture for 30 seconds. Then close your book and write down what was happening. See how many details you can remember. What were the people doing? What were they wearing? Was anything unusual going on?*

EXAMPLE: A man and a woman were standing by the fireplace. The woman was wearing . . .

B | *When you are finished, compare your list with those of your classmates. Who remembered the most?*

EXERCISE 10: Role Play: Alibi[1]

There was a robbery at the bank yesterday at 2:15 P.M. The thieves stole $100,000. The police are investigating this crime.

A | *Work in groups of three to six. One or two students are police officers; one or two students are witnesses; one or two students are suspects.[2] The police officers are questioning the witnesses and the suspects. Use your imagination to ask and answer questions.*

    EXAMPLE: **OFFICER:** What were you doing when the robbery took place?

                    WITNESS 1: I was standing in line at the bank.

                    WITNESS 2: I was crossing the street in front of the bank. I saw everything.

                    OFFICER: What was happening in the bank? . . .

---

[1] ***alibi:*** the proof that someone was not at the location of a crime at the time of the crime

[2] ***suspect:*** someone who may be guilty of a crime

EXAMPLE: OFFICER: Where were you yesterday at 2:15 P.M.?

SUSPECT 1: At 2:15? I was sitting in class.

SUSPECT 2: I was at home. I was watching TV.

OFFICER: Were there other people with you?

B | *In your group, discuss these questions:*

- What happened at the bank?
- What were the witnesses doing?
- Do the suspects have good alibis?
- What were they doing when the robbery occurred?

C | *Do you believe their alibis? Why or why not?*

EXAMPLE: Suspect 1 said that she was sitting in class yesterday at 2:15. I don't believe her because there was no school yesterday.

EXERCISE 11: Writing

A | *Write a paragraph describing an event that you witnessed: an accident, a crime, a bad storm, a reunion, a wedding, or another event. Use the past progressive and the simple past to describe what was happening and what happened during the event.*

EXAMPLE: While I was going to lunch today, I saw a wedding party. People were waiting for the bride and groom outside a temple. When they saw the couple, they . . .

B | *Check your work. Use the Editing Checklist.*

Editing Checklist

Did you use . . . ?
- [ ] the simple past
- [ ] the past progressive
- [ ] *when* or *while*
- [ ] commas after time clauses at the beginning of a sentence

A | Complete the conversation with the past progressive or simple past form of the verbs in parentheses.

A: _____ you _____ about the big storm last night?
  1. (hear)

B: Yes, I _____ the pictures when I _____ on the news.
  2. (see)   3. (turn)

_____ you _____ home during the storm?
  4. (drive)

A: No. At 6:00, I _____ in my office. So while it _____ really
  5. (work)   6. (rain)

hard, I _____ a report. And just when I _____ work, the rain
  7. (finish)   8. (leave)

_____!
  9. (stop)

B: I'm glad. Those pictures on the news _____ pretty bad.
  10. (look)

B | Combine the sentences. Use the past progressive or simple past form of the verbs.

1. While _____.
   (Danielle watched TV. At the same time, I studied.)

2. _____ when _____.
   (I closed my book. The show Dr. Davis came on.)

3. _____ when _____.
   (Dr. Davis talked to his patient. The electricity went off.)

4. When _____.
   (The electricity went off. We lit some candles.)

5. _____ while _____.
   (We talked about a lot of things. We waited for the lights to come on.)

C | Find and correct five mistakes.

When I turned on the TV for the first episode of *Dr. Davis,* I unpacked boxes in my freshman

dorm room. I stopped and watched for an hour. After that, I wasn't missing a single show while

I was attending school. While I was solving math problems, Dr. Davis was solving medical

mysteries. And *just* while my dumb boyfriend broke up with me, the beautiful Dr. Grace left

Davis for the third time. I even watched the show from the hospital when I was breaking my

leg. The show just ended. I was sad when I see the last episode, but I think it's time for some

real life!

Used to and *Would*
MEMORIES

Before You Read

Look at the reading. Discuss the questions.

1. What is a blog? What do you think this blog is about?
2. What toys, TV shows, clothes, and hairstyles do you remember from your own childhood?

Read

Read Sandra's blog about growing up in the 1980s in the United States.

The Awesome Eighties

Monday June 11 Posted by OldtimeSandy

Today's walk down memory lane[1] takes us back to the Awesome Eighties. Readers who were kids in the 1980s: What toys **did** you **use to play** with? What **did** you **use to watch** on TV?

Did you watch cartoons Saturday mornings? I **used to love** She-Ra, Princess of Power. I **would collect** all the toys and act out the stories with my friends. We didn't play that many video games back then!

A puzzle called the Rubik's Cube **used to be** very popular in the 1980s. My older sister Linda **would carry** one in her backpack all the time. She and her friends **would** often **have** contests with them. She didn't win very much, but she loved it anyway.

This is my mother, dressed for work. She **used to love** those suits with the big shoulders. She said they made her feel strong, like She-Ra, Princess of Power. She **used to call** this one her "power suit."

My brother Gary and his friends had a rock band. They**'d practice** for hours in the garage. They **never used to study**. Gary **used to get** some weird haircuts. He's a lawyer now, and he's lost his hair!

Next post: Do you hippies?

---

[1] **walk down memory lane:** a time you spend remembering the past

After You Read

A | **Vocabulary:** *Circle the letter of the word or phrase that best completes each sentence.*

1. An **awesome** blog is _____.
   a. terrible
   b. great
   c. frightening

2. Many people **collect** _____.
   a. stamps
   b. backpacks
   c. suits

3. A **weird** haircut looks _____.
   a. beautiful
   b. strange
   c. old

4. If a game is **popular**, _____.
   a. it's very easy
   b. it's not expensive
   c. many people like it

5. If you have a **memory** about something, you _____ it.
   a. remember
   b. watch
   c. practice

6. People with **power** are _____.
   a. tall
   b. strong
   c. poor

B | **Comprehension:** *Check (✓)* **True** *or* **False**. *Correct the false statements.*

	True	False
1. Sandra didn't watch TV on Saturdays.	☐	☐
2. She played video games a lot.	☐	☐
3. Her sister Linda played with a Rubik's Cube.	☐	☐
4. Her mother wore a suit to work.	☐	☐
5. Her brother and his friends studied all the time.	☐	☐
6. Her brother likes strange haircuts now.	☐	☐

USED TO

Statements			
Subject	***Use(d) to***	**Base Form of Verb**	
I You He She It We You They	**used to** **didn't use to**	**be**	popular.

Yes / No Questions				
Did	**Subject**	***Use to***	**Base Form of Verb**	
Did	you she they	**use to**	**be**	popular?

Short Answers					
Affirmative			**Negative**		
Yes,	I she they	**did.**	**No,**	I she they	**didn't.**

Wh- Questions					
***Wh-* Word**	***Did***	**Subject**	***Use to***	**Base Form of Verb**	
When	**did**	you she they	**use to**	be	popular?

WOULD

Statements			
Subject	***Would***	**Base Form of Verb**	
I He They	**would**	**study**	all day.

Contractions*	
I would	= I**'d**
He would	= He**'d**
They would	= They**'d**

*The contraction for *would* is the same for all subjects.

GRAMMAR NOTES

1 Use **used to** + **base form** of the verb to talk about repeated past activities (habits) and situations that are no longer true in the present.

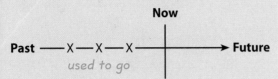

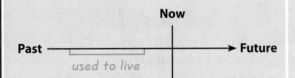

PAST ACTIVITY:
- When Tom was a teenager, he **used to go** to rock concerts every weekend.
  (*He went to rock concerts many times in the past, but he doesn't go to them now.*)

PAST SITUATION:
- We **used to live** in Russia.
  (*We lived in Russia for a period of time, but we don't live there any longer.*)

USAGE NOTE: Use **used to** to contrast the past and the present. **Time expressions** such as **now**, **no longer**, and **not anymore** emphasize the contrast.

- I **used to ride** my bike every day, but **now** I have a car.
- They **used to love** rock music, but they do**n't** listen to it **anymore**.

2 **Used to** always refers to the past. There is no present or future form.

USAGE NOTES:

a. The form **use to** (not *used to*) comes after **did** in **negative statements** and **questions**.

b. In **negative statements**, **never** + **used to** is more common than *didn't use to*.

c. In **questions**, the **simple past** is more common than *did* + *use to*.

- She **used to love** cartoons.
  NOT: She ~~uses~~ to love cartoons.

- He **didn't** use to study.
  NOT: He didn't ~~used to~~ study.
- **Did** you **use to** have long hair?
  NOT: Did you ~~used to~~ have long hair?

- He **never used to** study. (*more common*)
- He **didn't use to** study. (*less common*)

- **Did** you **have** long hair then? (*more common*)
- **Did** you **use to have** long hair? (*less common*)

3 You can also use **would** + **base form** of the verb to talk about repeated past activities (habits) that no longer happen in the present.

BE CAREFUL! Do NOT use **would** for past situations. Use **used to**.

USAGE NOTES:

a. When we reminisce (tell stories) about the past, we often begin with **used to** and then continue with **would** to give more details or examples.

b. When we use **would**, it must already be clear that we are talking about the past. Do NOT begin a story with *would*.

PAST ACTIVITY:
- When I was seven, I **would watch** cartoons every Saturday morning.

PAST SITUATION:
- I **used to love** Power Ranger cartoons.
  NOT: I ~~would love~~ Power Ranger cartoons.

- When I was a kid, I **used to ride** my bike everywhere. I **would ride** it to school during the week, and I **would take** it to the park on weekends.
  NOT: I ~~would ride~~ my bike everywhere. I would ride it to school . . .

EXERCISE 1: Discover the Grammar

Read the responses to "The Awesome Eighties" blog. Underline the expressions that refer to past habits and situations that are no longer true.

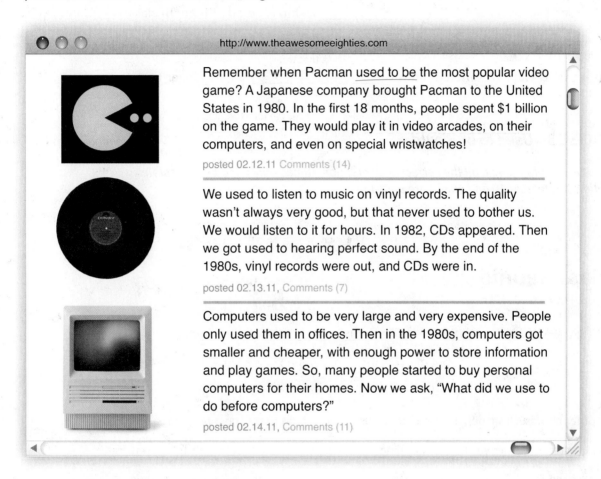

http://www.theawesomeeighties.com

Remember when Pacman <u>used to be</u> the most popular video game? A Japanese company brought Pacman to the United States in 1980. In the first 18 months, people spent $1 billion on the game. They would play it in video arcades, on their computers, and even on special wristwatches!

posted 02.12.11 Comments (14)

We used to listen to music on vinyl records. The quality wasn't always very good, but that never used to bother us. We would listen to it for hours. In 1982, CDs appeared. Then we got used to hearing perfect sound. By the end of the 1980s, vinyl records were out, and CDs were in.

posted 02.13.11, Comments (7)

Computers used to be very large and very expensive. People only used them in offices. Then in the 1980s, computers got smaller and cheaper, with enough power to store information and play games. So, many people started to buy personal computers for their homes. Now we ask, "What did we use to do before computers?"

posted 02.14.11, Comments (11)

EXERCISE 2: Forms of *Used to*

(Grammar Note 2)

*Sandra is at her class reunion. Complete the conversations. Use the correct form of **used to** and the words in parentheses.*

1. **Sandra:** You look familiar. _____*Did*_____ you _____*use to be*_____ in the drama club?

   a. (be)

   Rosa: Sandra! It's me—Rosa! I _____ long hair. Remember?

   b. (have)

2. **Rosa:** There's Glen—all alone. Did he always _____ that shy?

   a. (be)

   Sandra: Glen? Shy? He never stopped talking! It _____ the teachers mad—

   b. (make)

   remember? Let's go say hi to him.

(continued on next page)

3. **ROSA:** _____ you _____ with Gary's band, the Backyard Boys?

                                   a. (play)

    GLEN: Sometimes. We _____ in Gary's garage after school.

                               b. (practice)

4.   **GLEN:** There's Jim and Laura. I think they got married a couple of years ago.

  SANDRA: Really? In high school, they _____ any time together.

                               a. (never / spend)

5.   **LAURA:** I see Sandra! We _____ next to each other in math class.

                               a. (sit)

    JIM: She looks so different now. She _____ glasses.

                               b. (not wear)

  LAURA: We all look different now. We _____ a lot younger back then.

                               c. (be)

EXERCISE 3: *Used to* or *Would*   *(Grammar Notes 1–3)*

Read CityGal's blog. Circle <u>all</u> the correct answers. Sometimes only **used to** is possible. Sometimes both **used to** and **would** are possible.

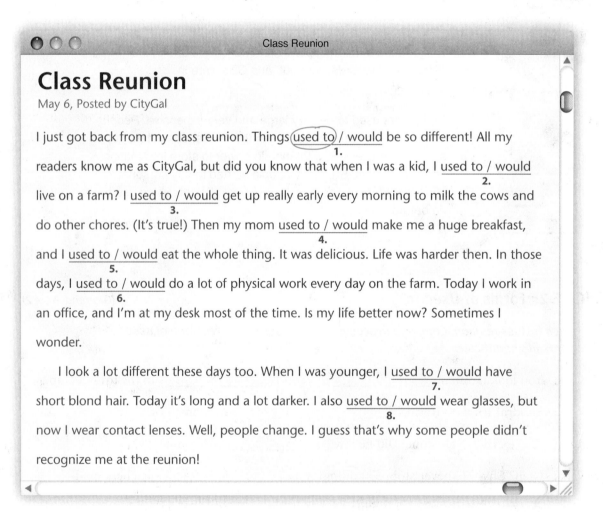

○ ○ ○   Class Reunion

Class Reunion
May 6, Posted by CityGal

I just got back from my class reunion. Things (used to) / would be so different! All my
                                        1.

readers know me as CityGal, but did you know that when I was a kid, I used to / would
                                                      2.

live on a farm? I used to / would get up really early every morning to milk the cows and
               3.

do other chores. (It's true!) Then my mom used to / would make me a huge breakfast,
                                     4.

and I used to / would eat the whole thing. It was delicious. Life was harder then. In those
       5.

days, I used to / would do a lot of physical work every day on the farm. Today I work in
          6.

an office, and I'm at my desk most of the time. Is my life better now? Sometimes I

wonder.

    I look a lot different these days too. When I was younger, I used to / would have
                                                           7.

short blond hair. Today it's long and a lot darker. I also used to / would wear glasses, but
                                                  8.

now I wear contact lenses. Well, people change. I guess that's why some people didn't

recognize me at the reunion!

EXERCISE 4: Contrast: *Used to* or *Would*

(Grammar Notes 1–3)

Sandra is showing her daughter Megan an old photo album. Complete their conversation.
*Use **used to** or **would** and the correct verb from the box. Sometimes both are possible.*

be	drive	~~have~~	love	play	visit	wear

MEGAN: Wow! Look at that! Uncle Gary _____*used to have*_____ a lot of hair! He really looks kind of
                                            1.

    weird in this picture.

SANDRA: Well, right after this photo, he shaved his head.

MEGAN: In this picture, were you going to the gym?

SANDRA: No. We _____ exercise clothes everywhere.
                           2.

MEGAN: You looked cute!

SANDRA: This was your Aunt Linda's new car. After she got it, she _____ her friends to
                                                               3.

    school every day.

MEGAN: That's not Uncle Fred with her.

SANDRA: No, that's Glen. He _____ her boyfriend before she met Fred and fell in love.
                                  4.

MEGAN: Oh! You had a Barbie doll!

SANDRA: Of course. I _____ with it every day.
                        5.

MEGAN: And that's me with Grandma and Grandpa!

SANDRA: Right. You _____ them at the beach every summer. You _____
                              6.   **7.**

    the water.

A 1980s sports car: the Chevrolet Corvette

EXERCISE 5: Editing

*Read the journal entry about a high school reunion in Timmins, Ontario, a small town 500 miles north of Toronto. There are nine mistakes in the use of **used to** and **would**. The first mistake is already corrected. Find and correct eight more.*

Shania Twain

The high school reunion tonight was awesome! I
~~used to talk~~ *talked* to Eileen Edwards for a long time. Well,
she's the famous country pop singer Shania Twain now.
In high school, she was used to be just one of us, and
tonight we all called her Eileen. She graduated in 1983,
the same year as me. Today she uses to live in a
chateau in Switzerland and has her own perfume
brand, but her life didn't use to be like that at all! She
uses to be very poor, and her grandma used to made all her clothes because her
family couldn't afford to buy them. She was always a good musician, though. In fact, she
used to earns money for her family that way. On Saturday nights, she would performed
with a local rock band, and my friends and I would go hear her. She could really sing!
Her new name, Shania, means "on my way" in Ojibwa (her stepfather's Native American
language). After she left Timmins, I would think that Timmins wasn't important to her
anymore — but I was wrong. Now that she's famous, she has a lot of power, and she
uses it to do good things for our community. And tonight she was just the way she
used be in high school — simple and friendly!

A school reunion

EXERCISE 6: Listening

A | *Two friends are talking about their past. Listen to their conversation.*

B | *Read the statements. Then listen again to the conversation and circle the letter of the correct information.*

1. The friends are at a _____.

   a. rock concert   **b.** school reunion

2. Their present lives are very _____ their past lives.

   a. similar to   **b.** different from

3. They have _____ memories about their past.

   a. good   **b.** bad

4. They used to play a lot of _____.

   a. video games   **b.** music CDs

5. The friends are enjoying talking about _____.

   a. a trip   **b.** the past

C | *Listen again to the conversation. Check (✓) the things the friends used to do in the **past** and the things they do **now**.*

	Past	Now
1. get up very early without an alarm clock	✓	☐
2. use an alarm clock	☐	☐
3. have a big breakfast	☐	☐
4. have a cup of coffee	☐	☐
5. look at the newspaper	☐	☐
6. have endless energy	☐	☐
7. do aerobics	☐	☐
8. take car trips on weekends	☐	☐
9. meet at class reunions	☐	☐

EXERCISE 7: Pronunciation

🎧 **A** | *Read and listen to the Pronunciation Note.*

Pronunciation Note

We often pronounce **used to** like "usta." Notice that the pronunciation of **used to** and **use to** is the same.

EXAMPLES: I **used to** play chess.   →   "I **usta** play chess."
            What games did you **use to** play?   →   "What games did you **usta** play?"

Be sure to write **used to** or **use to**, NOT "usta."

We often use the contraction of **would** (**'d**) in both **speech** and **writing**.

EXAMPLE: We **would** play for hours.   →   "We**'d** play for hours."

🎧 **B** | *Listen to the sentences. Notice the pronunciation of* **used to** *and the contraction of* **would**.

1. I **used to** live in a small town.
2. I didn't **use to** have a lot of friends.
3. I**'d** spend hours alone.
4. On weekends, my sister **used to** play cards with me.
5. She**'d** always win.
6. We**'d** have a lot of fun.

🎧 **C** | *Listen again and repeat the sentences.*

EXERCISE 8: Picture Discussion

Work with a partner. Look at the pairs of pictures and talk about how the people have changed. Then write sentences that describe the changes. Compare your sentences with those of your classmates.

Then	Now

1. Sharifa *used to be very busy, but now she is more relaxed. She would always be in a hurry.*

   Now she takes things more slowly. She used to wear glasses, but now she doesn't . . .

Then	**Now**

2. Jean-Marc _____

_____

_____

Then	**Now**

3. Lyric _____

_____

_____

Then	**Now**

4. Mike _____

_____

_____

EXERCISE 9: Compare and Contrast

Work in small groups. Talk about how you used to be and how you are now. Answer the following questions. If you have a picture of yourself from that time, you can bring it in to class and show it to your group.

- How did you use to look?

- What types of things would you do?

- How did you use to dress?

    EXAMPLE: **A:** I used to have very long hair. Now I wear my hair short.
    B: Anton, did you use to have long hair?
    C: *Everybody* used to have long hair then.

EXERCISE 10: Writing

A | *Write a two-paragraph essay. Contrast your life in the past with your life now. In the first paragraph, describe how your life used to be at some time in the past. In the second paragraph, describe your life today. Remember: We often begin with* **used to** *and then change to* **would**.

    EXAMPLE: I used to live in Russia. I attended St. Petersburg University. I would ride my bike there every day. In those days I used to . . . Today I am living in Florida and attending Miami University . . .

B | *Check your work. Use the Editing Checklist.*

Editing Checklist
Did you . . . ?
☐ use ***used to*** correctly
☐ use ***would*** correctly
☐ change from ***used to*** to ***would***

4 Review

Check your answers on page UR-1.
Do you need to review anything?

A | *Circle the correct words to complete the sentences.*

1. What <u>did / would</u> you use to like to do when you were a kid?

2. I <u>used to / would</u> love reading comic books when I was younger.

3. <u>Do / Did</u> you use to go to concerts?

4. My sister would <u>plays / play</u> video games for hours.

5. I never <u>used to / would</u> like them before, but now I love them.

6. Life <u>used to / would</u> be so different back then.

B | *Complete the conversations with* **used to** *or* **would** *and the verb in parentheses.*

- **AMY:** Hey, is that Jorge? He _____ very different. I almost didn't recognize him!
  1. (look)

  BEN: Yes. He _____ long hair, but he cut it last month.
  2. (have)

- **MIA:** I _____ my hair grow very long in the summer.
  3. (let)

  LEE: Me too. Sometimes I _____ a haircut for a whole year!
  4. (not get)

- **AMY:** I _____ the guitar. I'm sorry I quit.
  5. (play)

  BEN: I had a guitar too. I _____ for hours.
  6. (practice)

- **TOM:** _____ you _____ to concerts when you were a student?
  7. (go)

  MIA: Yes. I _____ the free concerts in the park. I even once heard Celine Dion!
  8. (love)

C | *Find and correct six mistakes.*

Celine Dion was born in Quebec, Canada. When she used to be five, her family opened a club, and Celine used to sang there. People from the community would to come to hear her perform. At the age of 12, Celine wrote her first songs. Her family used to record one and sent it to a manager. At first Celine used to singing only in French. After she learned English, she became known in more countries. As a child, Celine Dion would be poor, but she had a dream— to be a singer. Today she is one of the most successful singers in the history of pop music.

UNIT 5

Wh- Questions
IN COURT

STEP 1 GRAMMAR IN CONTEXT

Before You Read

A lawyer is questioning a crime witness. Look at the drawing by a courtroom artist. Discuss the questions.

1. Who is the lawyer? The judge? The witness?
2. What do you think the lawyer is asking?

Read

Read the excerpt from a court transcript.

STATE OF ILLINOIS VS.[1] HARRY M. ADAMS   MARCH 31, 2011

LAWYER: **What happened on the night of May 12?** Please tell the court.[2]
WITNESS: I went to Al's Grill.
LAWYER: **Who did you see there?**
WITNESS: I saw one of the defendants.
LAWYER: **Which one did you see?**
WITNESS: It was that man.
LAWYER: Let the record show that the witness is indicating the defendant, Harry Adams. OK, you saw Mr. Adams. Did he see you?
WITNESS: No, no, he didn't see me.
LAWYER: But somebody saw you. **Who saw you?**
WITNESS: A woman. He was talking to a woman. She saw me.
LAWYER: OK. **What happened next?**
WITNESS: The woman gave him a box.
LAWYER: A box! **What did it look like?**
WITNESS: It was about this long . . .
LAWYER: So, about a foot and a half. **What did Mr. Adams do then?**
WITNESS: He took the box. He looked frightened.
LAWYER: **Why did he look frightened? What was in the box?**
WITNESS: I don't know. He didn't open it. He just took it and left in a hurry.
LAWYER: **Where did he go?**
WITNESS: Toward the parking lot.
LAWYER: **When did the woman leave?**
WITNESS: She was still there when we heard his car speed away.

---

[1] *vs.* (written abbreviation of *versus*): against
[2] *court:* the people (judge, lawyers, jury) who decide if someone is guilty of a crime

After You Read

A | Vocabulary: *Circle the letter of the word or phrase closest in meaning to the word in* **blue.**

1. I saw one of the **defendants**.
   a. people who saw a crime
   b. people who possibly broke a law
   c. people who work in the court

2. It's for the **record**.
   a. music CD
   b. box
   c. written report

3. He looked **frightened**.
   a. dangerous
   b. afraid
   c. unhappy

4. He left **in a hurry**.
   a. quickly
   b. in a storm
   c. by bus

5. The witness is **indicating** Harry Adams.
   a. smiling at
   b. speaking about
   c. pointing to

B | Comprehension: *Check (✓)* **True** *or* **False**. *Correct the false statements.*

	True	False
1. The lawyer is questioning Harry Adams.	☐	☐
2. The witness saw Harry Adams.	☐	☐
3. Harry Adams saw the witness.	☐	☐
4. The witness saw a woman.	☐	☐
5. The woman saw the witness.	☐	☐
6. The witness gave Adams a box.	☐	☐
7. Adams took the box.	☐	☐
8. The woman left before the car sped away.	☐	☐

WH- QUESTIONS: *WHO, WHAT*

Questions About the Subject			Answers		
Wh-Word Subject	**Verb**	**Object**	**Subject**	**Verb**	**Object**
Who	saw	Harry?	**Marta**	saw	him.
		the box?			it.

Questions About the Object				Answers		
Wh-Word Object	**Auxiliary Verb**	**Subject**	**Main Verb**	**Subject**	**Verb**	**Object**
Who(m)	did	Marta	see?	She	saw	Harry.
What						the box.

WH- QUESTIONS: *WHICH, WHOSE, HOW MANY*

Questions About the Subject			Answers		
Wh-Word + Noun	**Verb**	**Object**	**Subject**	**Verb**	**Object**
Which witness			**Mr. Ho**		
Whose lawyer	saw	you?	**Harry's lawyer**	saw	me.
How many people			**Five people**		

Questions About the Object				Answers		
Wh-Word + Noun	**Auxiliary Verb**	**Subject**	**Main Verb**	**Subject**	**Verb**	**Object**
Which witness						the first witness.
Whose lawyer	did	you	see?	I	saw	Harry's lawyer.
How many people						five people.

WH- QUESTIONS: *WHEN, WHERE, WHY*

Questions				Answers		
Wh-Word	**Auxiliary Verb**	**Subject**	**Main Verb**	**Subject**	**Verb**	**Time/Place/Reason**
When						yesterday.
Where	did	Marta	go?	She	went	to the police.
Why						because she was frightened.

GRAMMAR NOTES

1 | Use **wh- questions** (also called *information questions*) to ask for specific information.

Wh- questions begin with **wh- words** such as *who, what, when, where, why, which, whose, how, how many, how much,* and *how long*. | **A:** *Who* did you see at Al's Grill?
B: Harry Adams.

A: *When* did you go there?
B: On May 12.

A: *How many* people saw you?
B: Two.

---

2 | To ask **basic information** about people and things, use **who** and **what**.

a. For questions about the **subject**, use **who** or **what** in place of the subject, and statement word order: **wh- word (= subject) + verb**

b. For questions about the **object**, use **who** or **what** and this word order:
wh- word + auxiliary + subject + verb

REMEMBER: An **auxiliary** verb is a verb such as **do** (*does, did*), **have** (*has, had*), **can**, or **will**. **Be** can be an auxiliary too.

USAGE NOTE: In **very formal** English, we sometimes use **whom** instead of *who* in questions about the **object**.

SUBJECT	SUBJECT
<u>Someone</u> saw you.	<u>Something</u> happened.
↓	↓
Who saw you?	**What** happened?

OBJECT	OBJECT
You saw <u>someone</u>.	He said <u>something</u>.
↘	↘
Who did you see?	**What** did he say?

- **Who will** she defend?
- **What is** he doing?

MORE COMMON	VERY FORMAL
Who did you see?	**Whom** did you see?

---

3 | To ask more **detailed information** about people and things, use:
- **which + noun** (to ask about a choice)
- **whose + noun** (to ask about possessions)
- **how many + noun** (to ask about quantities)

a. For questions about the **subject**, use this word order: **wh- word + noun + verb**

b. For questions about the **object**, use this order:
wh- word + noun + auxiliary + subject + verb

- **Which witness told** the truth?
- **Whose lawyer** do you believe?
- **How many people** saw the trial?

- **Which defendant answered** best?

- **Which defendant did you trust** more?

(continued on next page)

4	To ask about **place**, **reason**, and **time**, use **where**, **why**, and **when**, and this word order: **wh- word** + **auxiliary** + **subject** + **verb**	• **Where will** she go? • **Why does** she want to defend him? • **When did** she arrive?
5	When the main verb is a form of **be** (*am, is, are, was, were*) use: • **wh- word** + **be** OR • **wh- word** + **noun** + **be**	• **Who is** the first witness? • **Where are** the witnesses? • **How many witnesses are** there?

STEP 3 FOCUSED PRACTICE

EXERCISE 1: Discover the Grammar

Match the questions and answers.

   _f_   **1.** Who did you see?

          2. Who saw you?

          3. What hit her?

          4. What did she hit?

          5. Which man did you give the money to?

          6. Which man gave you the money?

a. His wife saw me.

b. She hit a car.

c. I gave the money to Harry.

d. A car hit her.

e. Harry gave me the money.

f. I saw the defendant.

EXERCISE 2: Questions

(Grammar Notes 1–5)

Complete the cross-examination. Write the lawyer's questions. Use the words in parentheses and make any necessary changes.

1. **LAWYER:** *What time did you return home?*
                    (what time / you / return home)
  WITNESS: I returned home just before midnight.

2. **LAWYER:** _____
                    (how / you / get home)
  WITNESS: Someone gave me a ride. I was in a hurry.

3. **LAWYER:** _____
                    (who / give / you / a ride)
  WITNESS: A friend from work.

4. **LAWYER:** _____
                    (what / happen / next)
  WITNESS: I opened my door and saw someone on my living room floor.

5. **LAWYER:** _____
                    (who / you / see)
  WITNESS: Deborah Collins.

6. **LAWYER:** For the record, _____.
   (who / be / Deborah Collins)

   WITNESS: She's my wife's boss. I mean, she *was* my wife's boss. She's dead now.

7. **LAWYER:** _____
   (what / you / do)

   WITNESS: I called the police.

8. **LAWYER:** _____
   (when / the police / arrive)

   WITNESS: In about 10 minutes.

9. **LAWYER:** _____
   (what / they / ask you)

   WITNESS: They asked me to describe the crime scene.

10. **LAWYER:** _____
    (how many police officers / come)

    WITNESS: I don't remember. Why?

    LAWYER: I'm asking the questions here. Please just answer.

EXERCISE 3: Questions

(Grammar Notes 1–5)

Read the answers. Then ask questions about the underlined words or phrases.

1. Court begins <u>at 9:00 A.M.</u>

   When does court begin? _____

2. <u>Something horrible</u> happened.

   _____

3. <u>Five</u> witnesses described the crime.

   _____

4. The witness indicated <u>Harry Adams</u>.

   _____

5. <u>The witness</u> indicated Harry Adams.

   _____

6. The district attorney questioned <u>the restaurant manager</u>.

   _____

7. The manager looked <u>frightened</u>.

   _____

(continued on next page)

8. <u>The judge</u> spoke to the jury.

_____

9. The verdict was "<u>guilty</u>."

_____

10. The jury found Adams guilty <u>because he didn't have an alibi</u>.

_____

11. The trial lasted <u>two weeks</u>.

_____

12. Adams paid his lawyer <u>$2,000</u>.

_____

EXERCISE 4: Editing

Read a reporter's notes. There are nine mistakes in the use of **wh-** questions. The first mistake is already corrected. Find and correct eight more.

<u>Questions</u>

          did Jones go

Where ~~Jones went~~ on January 15?

Who went with him?

What time he return home?

Who he called?

How much money he had with him?

Whom saw him at the station the next day?

How did he look?

Why he was in a hurry?

How many suitcases did he have?

When the witness call the police?

What did happen next?

What his alibi was?

EXERCISE 5: Listening

A | *Someone is on the phone with a friend. There is a bad connection. Listen to the statements. Then listen again and circle the letter of the question the friend needs to ask in order to get the correct information.*

1. **a.** Who did you see at the restaurant?
   b. Who saw you at the restaurant?

2. **a.** Which car did the truck hit?
   b. Which car hit the truck?

3. **a.** When did it happen?
   b. Why did it happen?

4. **a.** Whose mother did you call?
   b. Whose mother called you?

5. **a.** Who did you report it to?
   b. Who reported it?

6. **a.** How many people heard the shouts?
   b. How many shouts did you hear?

7. **a.** Who saw the man?
   b. Who did the man see?

8. **a.** Why do you have to hang up?
   b. When do you have to hang up?

B | *Listen to the short conversations and answer the question in each one.*

1. the teacher
2. _____
3. _____
4. _____
5. _____
6. _____
7. _____
8. _____

EXERCISE 6: Pronunciation

A | *Read and listen to the Pronunciation Note.*

> **Pronunciation Note**
>
> In **wh- questions**, the voice usually **falls at the end**.
>
> **EXAMPLE:** Where do you live?
>
> But sometimes, when we **don't understand someone**, we use *wh-* questions to ask the person to repeat the information. We **stress the *wh-* word** and the voice **rises at the end**.
>
> **EXAMPLE:** **A:** I live in Massachusetts.
>
> **B:** Where do you live?
> **A:** In Massachusetts.

B | *Listen to the questions. Check (✓) if the person is asking for* **information** *or for* **repetition.**

	Information	Repetition
	↗	↗
1. Where did he go?	☐	☑
2. What did he do next?	☐	☐
3. What was in the box?	☐	☐
4. When did the woman leave?	☐	☐
5. How much did it cost?	☐	☐
6. Who called you?	☐	☐
7. Why did you leave?	☐	☐
8. Who saw you?	☐	☐

C | *Listen again and repeat the questions.*

EXERCISE 7: Role Play: On the Witness Stand

Work with a partner. Look at the court transcript on page 58 again. Read it aloud. Then continue the lawyer's questioning of the witness. Ask at least six more questions.

> EXAMPLE: LAWYER: When did the woman leave?
> WITNESS: She was still there when we heard his car speed away.
> LAWYER: What happened next?

EXERCISE 8: Game: To Tell the Truth

A | *Work in groups of three. Each student tells the group an interesting fact about his or her life. The fact can <u>only</u> be true for this student.*

> EXAMPLE: **A:** I play three musical instruments.
> **B:** I speak four languages.
> **C:** I have five pets.

B | *The group chooses a fact and goes to the front of the class. Each student states the same fact, but remember: <u>Only one</u> student is telling the truth.*

EXAMPLE:

C | *The class asks the three students* **wh-** *questions to find out who is telling the truth.*

EXAMPLE: THEA: Ed, which four languages do you speak?
           ED: I speak Russian, French, Spanish, and English.

        LEV: Ed, where did you learn Russian?
        ED: I was born in Russia.

       MEI: Ed, who taught you French?
        ED: My grandmother is French. I learned it from her.

      JOSÉ: Ed, how do you say "witness" in Spanish?
        ED: . . .

EXERCISE 9: Writing

A | *Work with a partner. Think of something exciting or interesting that you once saw. Tell your partner. Then write a list of questions and interview your partner to get more information. Use* **wh-** *questions. Take notes and write up the interview.*

EXAMPLE: **A:** I once saw a bad car accident.
          B: Where did it happen?
          A: On the highway.
          B: How many cars were in the accident?
          A: There was one car and a truck.
          B: What did you do?
          A: I . . .

B | *Check your work. Use the Editing Checklist.*

Editing Checklist

Did you use . . . ?
☐ the correct **wh-** words
☐ the correct word order
☐ auxiliary verbs in questions about the object
☐ auxiliary verbs in questions beginning with **when**, **where**, and **why**

5 Review

Check your answers on page UR-2.
Do you need to review anything?

A | *Match the questions and answers.*

_____ **1.** Where did Feng go Wednesday night?

_____ **2.** When was the movie over?

_____ **3.** How long was it?

_____ **4.** Which movie did he see?

_____ **5.** How many people went?

_____ **6.** Who went with him?

_____ **7.** Whose car did they use?

_____ **8.** Why did they choose that movie?

a. *Date Night.*

b. Because it got great reviews.

c. Xavier's.

d. At 11:00.

e. Laurel and Xavier.

f. Two and a half hours.

g. Three.

h. To the movies.

B | *Circle the correct words to complete the sentences.*

1. Where does Shari <u>work / works</u> now?

2. How <u>did she / she did</u> find that job?

3. Who <u>did tell / told</u> Shari about it?

4. Why <u>she left / did she leave</u> her old job?

5. When did she <u>start / started</u> to work there?

6. Who <u>is her boss / her boss is</u>?

7. What <u>did / does</u> she do at her new job?

C | *Find and correct five mistakes.*

A: What did you did with my math book? I can't find it.

B: Nothing. Where you saw it last?

A: In the living room. I was watching *Lost* on TV. What Zack's phone number?

B: I'm not sure. Why you want to know?

A: He took the class last year. I'll call him. Maybe he still has his book.

B: Good idea. What time does he gets out of work?

From Grammar to Writing

COMBINING SENTENCES WITH TIME WORDS

You can often improve your writing by combining two short sentences into one longer sentence that connects the two ideas. The two sentences can be combined by using **time words** such as *while*, *when*, *as soon as*, *before*, *after*, or *until*. The new, longer sentence is made up of a main clause and a time clause.

EXAMPLE: I was shopping. I saw the perfect dress for her. →

TIME CLAUSE   MAIN CLAUSE
While I was shopping**,** I saw the perfect dress for her.

MAIN CLAUSE   TIME CLAUSE
I saw the perfect dress for her **while** I was shopping.

The time clause can come first or second. When it comes first, a **comma** separates the two clauses.

1 | *Read the paragraph. Underline all the sentences that are combined with a time word. Circle the time words.*

> I always exchange holiday presents with my girlfriend, Shao Fen. Last year, while I was shopping for her, I saw an umbrella in her favorite color. As soon as I saw it, I thought of her. I bought the umbrella and a scarf in the same color. When Shao Fen opened the present, she looked really upset. She didn't say anything, and she didn't look at me. I felt hurt and confused by her reaction. Later she explained that in Chinese, the word for "umbrella" sounds like the word for "separation." When she saw the umbrella, she misunderstood. She thought I wanted to end the relationship. After I heard that, I was very upset! When we both felt calmer, we talked about our misunderstanding. At the end, we laughed about it, and I think we're better friends because of it. I discovered something new about Shao Fen's culture. Now I want to learn more about cross-cultural communication.

2 | *Look at the student's paragraph. Combine the pairs of underlined sentences with time words such as **when**, **while**, **as soon as**, **before**, and **after**. Use your own paper.*

> I usually keep my wallet in my back pocket when I go out. <u>Two weeks ago, I was walking on a crowded street. I felt something.</u> I was in a hurry, so I didn't pay any attention to it at the time. <u>I got home. I noticed that my wallet was missing.</u> I got frightened. It didn't have much money in it, but my credit card and my driver's license were there. <u>I was thinking about the situation. My brother came home.</u> He told me to report it to the police, just for the record, in case someone found the wallet. <u>I called the police. They weren't very encouraging.</u> They said that wallets often get "picked" from back pockets. They didn't think I would get it back. Now I'm a lot more careful. <u>I go out. I put my wallet in my front pocket.</u>

  EXAMPLE: Two weeks ago, **while** I was walking on a crowded street, I felt something.

3 | *Before you write . . .*

1. We often say, "Learn from your mistakes." Think about a misunderstanding or a mistake that you experienced or observed. How did your behavior or thinking change because of your experience?

2. Describe the experience to a partner. Listen to your partner's experience.

3. Ask and answer questions about your experiences, for example: *When did it happen? Why did you . . . ? Where were you when . . . ? How did you feel? What do you do now . . . ?*

4 | *Write a draft of your story. Follow the model below. Remember to use some of the time words and include information that your partner asked about.*

as soon as	before	until	when	while

I (or My friend) always / often / usually / never _____

_____

_____ .

Last week / Yesterday / In 2010, _____

_____

_____

_____ .

Now, _____

_____ .

5 | *Exchange stories with a different partner. Complete the chart.*

1. The writer used time words to connect ideas.　　**Yes** ☐　　　**No** ☐

2. What I liked in the story:

   _____

   _____

   _____

3. Questions I'd like the writer to answer in the story:

   Who _____?

   What _____?

   When _____?

   Where _____?

   How _____?

   (Your own question) _____?

6 | *Work with your partner. Discuss each other's chart from Exercise 5. Then rewrite your own paragraph and make any necessary changes.*

THE FUTURE

UNIT	GRAMMAR FOCUS	THEME
6	Future	Space Travel
7	Future Time Clauses	Setting Goals

STEP 1 GRAMMAR IN CONTEXT

Before You Read

Look at the photo. Discuss the questions.

1. Where do you think the first space tourists will travel?
2. Why do people want to travel into space? Would you like to?

Read

Read the transcript of a radio program about space tourism.

SPACE TOURISTS: NOT JUST SCIENCE FICTION[1]

ROHAN: Good evening, and welcome to *The Future Today*. I'm Enid Rohan, and tonight Dr. Richard Starr, president of YourSpace, Inc., **is going to talk** to us about space tourism. Dr. Starr, **is** this really **going to happen**?

STARR: **Yes**, it **is**, Enid. We're already building the space planes. And we're selling tickets and planning our first trips now. In fact, our training program for passengers **is starting** next January.

ROHAN: Where **will** these tours **go**? **Will** they **travel** to the Moon? Mars?

STARR: **No**, they **won't**. The first space tourists **aren't going to go** that far. They**'re** only **going to travel** about 100 kilometers, or 62 miles above the Earth. That's the edge of space. A trip **will last** about three hours.

ROHAN: But the tickets cost $200,000! Who**'s going to pay** that much for just three hours?

STARR: A lot of people. It**'s going to be** an incredible trip. Come and see! We**'ll save** one of our best seats for you.

ROHAN: What **will** a trip **be** like?

STARR: First of all, you**'ll experience** zero gravity[2]—and let me tell you, it's an amazing feeling. And you**'ll get** a bird's-eye view of the Earth from space. You **won't believe** your eyes! You**'re going to think** about the Earth in a whole new way. Besides, tickets **won't** always **be** so expensive. Costs **are going to fall** a lot.

ROHAN: **Will** I **need** a spacesuit?

STARR: **No**, you **won't**. That **will be** one of the great things about this trip. No spacesuits and no seat belts except for takeoff and landing. The cabins **will be** large, so passengers **will float** freely during the trip.

ROHAN: Sounds great. I think I**'ll ask** my boss to send me on a trip. Maybe I**'ll** even **do** a show from space! So tell me, when **does** the first flight **leave**?

STARR: It **leaves** on January 1, two years from now. But you **won't be** on that one—our first three flights are already sold out!

---

[1] *science fiction:* stories about the future, often about space travel and scientific discoveries

[2] *gravity:* the force that makes things fall to the ground. (In *zero gravity*, things do not stay on the ground.)

After You Read

A | Vocabulary: *Complete the sentences with the words from the box.*

| edge | experience | float | incredible | sold out | takeoff |

1. There are no more tickets for the space tour. It's _____.

2. We live at the _____ of a forest. Sometimes bears come into our yard!

3. Sy took _____ photos on his trip to Antarctica. He saw some strange and wonderful sights.

4. As a space tourist, you'll _____ a lot of feelings—amazement, excitement, fear, and much more.

5. I was only scared at _____—when the space plane left the ground. After that, I felt OK.

6. What did I do on vacation? I lay on the beach and watched the clouds _____ by.

B | Comprehension: *Based on the information in the reading, which of the statements are true right **Now**? Which will be true only in the **Future**? Check (✓) the correct boxes.*

	Now	Future
1. Companies are building space planes.	☐	☐
2. Tourists are buying tickets.	☐	☐
3. A training program for passengers is starting.	☐	☐
4. Space tours travel about 100km (62 miles) above the Earth.	☐	☐
5. Tickets are very expensive.	☐	☐
6. The first flight is ready to leave.	☐	☐

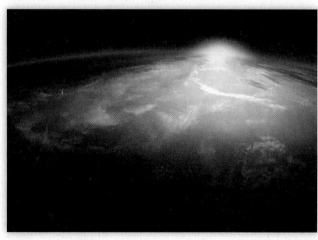

The edge of space

BE GOING TO FOR THE FUTURE

Statements				
Subject	*Be*	*(Not) Going to*	Base Form of Verb	
I	am			
You	are			
He She It	is	(not) going to	leave	soon.
We You They	are			

Yes / No Questions				
Be	Subject	*Going to*	Base Form of Verb	
Am	I			
Are	you			
Is	he she it	going to	leave	soon?
Are	we you they			

Short Answers						
Affirmative			Negative			
	you	are.		you're		
	I	am.		I'm		
Yes,	he she it	is.	No,	he's she's it's	not.	
	you we they	are.		you're we're they're		

Wh- Questions				
Wh- Word	*Be*	Subject	*Going to*	Base Form of Verb
When Why	are	you	going to	leave?

WILL FOR THE FUTURE

Statements			
Subject	***Will (not)***	**Base Form of Verb**	
I You He She It We You They	will (not)	leave	soon.

Yes / No Questions			
Will	**Subject**	**Base Form of Verb**	
Will	I you he she it we you they	leave	soon?

Short Answers					
Affirmative			**Negative**		
Yes,	you I he she it you we they	will.	No,	you I he she it you we they	won't.

Wh- Questions			
***Wh-* Word**	***Will***	**Subject**	**Base Form of Verb**
When	will	you	leave?

PRESENT PROGRESSIVE FOR THE FUTURE

Statements		
Subject + *Be*	**(Not) + Base Form + *-ing***	
We're	(not) leaving	soon.
It's		

SIMPLE PRESENT FOR THE FUTURE

Statements		
Subject		**Verb**
We	leave	Monday at 6:45 A.M.
It	leaves	

GRAMMAR NOTES

1

There are several ways to talk about the **future**. You can use:

- **be going to**
- **will**
- **present progressive**
- **simple present**

        Now
         |
Past ——+———— X ———→ **Future**
         | *meeting*

USAGE NOTE: Sometimes only one form of the future is appropriate, but in many cases more than one form is possible.

- They**'re going to have** a meeting.
- I think I**'ll go**.
- It**'s taking** place next week.
- It **starts** at 9:00 A.M. on Monday.

2

To talk about **facts** or things you are certain will happen in the future, use:

- **be going to**
  OR
- **will**

- The sun **is going to rise** at 6:43 tomorrow.
  OR
- The sun **will rise** at 6:43 tomorrow.

3

To make **predictions** about things you are quite sure will happen in the future, use:

- **be going to**
  OR
- **will**

BE CAREFUL! Use **be going to** (NOT *will*) when something that you <u>see right now</u> makes you almost certain an event is going to happen.

- I think a lot of people **are going to travel** to space.
  OR
- I think a lot of people **will travel** to space.

A: Look at those dark clouds!
B: It**'s going to rain**.
  NOT: It'll rain.

4

To talk about future **plans** or things you have already decided, use:

- **be going to**
  OR
- **present progressive**

USAGE NOTE: We often use the **present progressive** for plans that are <u>already arranged</u>.

- I**'m going to fly** to Chicago next week.
  OR
- I**'m flying** to Chicago next week.
  NOT: I'll fly to Chicago next week.

- I**'m flying** to Chicago next week. I already have a ticket.

5	For **quick decisions** (made as you are speaking), or to make **offers** or **promises**, use **will**.	**QUICK DECISION:** **A:** The Space Show is opening next week. **B:** Sounds interesting. I think I**'ll go**. **OFFER AND PROMISE:** **A:** I'd like to go too, but I don't have a ride. **B:** I**'ll drive** you. But I'd like to leave by 7:00. **A:** No problem. I**'ll be** ready.
6	To talk about **scheduled future events** (timetables, programs, schedules), use the **simple present**. We often use **verbs** such as **start**, **leave**, **end**, and **begin** this way.	• The shuttle **leaves** at 9:00 A.M. • The conference **starts** tomorrow morning.

REFERENCE NOTES

For **contractions** of *I am*, *you are*, *I will*, *you will*, etc., see Appendix 26, page A-12.

For a complete presentation of **present progressive** and **simple present** forms, see Unit 1, page 4.

Will can also be used for **making a request**; see Unit 15 on page 205.

STEP 3 FOCUSED PRACTICE

EXERCISE 1: Discover the Grammar

A | *Read the transcript of an interview with a future space tourist. There are thirteen forms of the future. The first form is already circled. Find and circle twelve more.*

OUT OF THIS WORLD

ROHAN: This is Enid Rohan, reporting from Spaceport America. Lyn Filipov is in the training program here for a flight with YourSpace, Inc. She's going to fly to the edge of space very soon. So. Lyn, which flight are you taking?

FILIPOV: The one that leaves on March 30. The earlier ones were all sold out.

ROHAN: What's the training like?

FILIPOV: Well, at 100 kilometers—that's 62 miles—above the Earth, there won't be any gravity, so we're practicing moving around in zero-g. It's an incredible feeling—like floating in water, or flying. You feel really free.

ROHAN: Aren't you even a little scared?

FILIPOV: Right now, I can't wait to go. I'm pretty sure I'll be terrified on takeoff, but it'll be worth it. Totally.

(*continued on next page*)

ROHAN: How can you afford this? Are you an Internet millionaire?

FILIPOV: No, I'm not. Actually, I won a big lottery. When I saw my winning numbers, my first thought was, "I'll buy a ticket for a space tour."

ROHAN: What an amazing story! But you're very young. How does your family feel about this?

FILIPOV: I'm not *that* young. I'll be 23 next month. But my parents are nervous, of course. My mother is really afraid I'm going to love space travel and I'll want to keep doing it. And my younger brother is jealous.

ROHAN: What do you say to make them feel better?

FILIPOV: I tell my mother, "Listen, Mom, this is a once-in-a-lifetime thing. I won't make a habit of space travel, I promise." My brother? He wants a career in space travel, so he's going to study a lot harder from now on. That's what he says, anyway.

ROHAN: Have a great time, Lyn. And let us know what it was like.

FILIPOV: Thanks. I'll send you photos.

B | *Complete the chart. List the thirteen future verb forms. Then check (✓) the correct column for each form.*

	Facts	Predictions	Plans	Quick Decisions	Offers and Promises	Schedules
1. 's going to fly			✓			
2. are you taking			✓			
3. leaves						✓
4. won't be	✓					
5.						
6.						
7.						
8.						
9.						
10.						
11.						
12.						
13.						

EXERCISE 2: *Will* for Facts and Predictions

(Grammar Notes 2–3)

It is the year 2020, and an international group of space tourists are getting ready for their space flight. Part of the training program includes a Question and Answer (Q & A) session with astronaut William R. Pogue. Complete the questions and answers. Use the verbs in parentheses with **will** *or* **won't**.

It'll Be Great!

Q: _____Will_____ it _____take_____ a long time to get used to zero gravity?
1. (take)

A: No, _____it won'____. Every day you _____will feel_____ more comfortable, and after three
2.   **3. (feel)**

days you _____become_____ used to being in space.
4. (become)

★ ★ ★

Q: _____Will_____ I _____feel_____ sick?
5. (feel)

A: Yes, you might feel sick for a little while. But it _____won't last_____ long.
6. (last)

★ ★ ★

Q: I love to read. How _____will_____ I _____keep_____ my book open to the right page?
7. (keep)

A: Actually, reading a book in space can be quite a problem. You _____won't need_____ strong
8. (need)

clips to hold the book open. It can be a little frustrating at first, but after a while you

_____will get_____ used to it.
9. (get)

★ ★ ★

Q: _____Will_____ I _____look_____ the same?
10. (look)

A: Actually, you _____won't look_____ the same at all. Your face and eyes _____will get_____ puffy.
11. (look)   **12. (get)**

The first time you look in a mirror, you probably _____won't recognize_____ yourself.
13. (recognize)

★ ★ ★

Q: _____Will_____ I _____float_____ in my sleep?
14. (float)

A: Yes, if you are not tied down. And then you should be careful because you _____will bump_____
15. (bump)

into things all night long. Trust me. You can get hurt!

★ ★ ★

Q: I like salt and pepper on my food. Can I still use them in zero gravity?

A: Yes, you _____will_____ still _____have_____ salt and pepper, but not like you do on
16. (have)

Earth. You _____use_____ small, squeezable bottles with salt water and pepper water so
17. (use)

the grains don't float away. You just squeeze it on your food. Don't worry about it.

It _____be_____ great!
18. (be)

EXERCISE 3: *Be going to* for Prediction

(Grammar Note 3)

Look at the pictures. They show events from a day in the life of Professor Starr. Write predictions or guesses. Use the words from the box and a form of **be going to** *or* **not be going to**. *Choose between affirmative and negative.*

answer the phone	get out of bed	give a speech	have dinner	~~take a trip~~
drive	get very wet	go to sleep	rain	~~watch TV~~

1. ___He's going to take a trip.___

2. ___He's going to ride on the train___

3. ___He's going to stay at Hotel___

4. ___He isn't going to stay outside___

5. ___He's going to give a speech___

6. ___He's going to answer the phone___

7. ___He's going to eat - dinner have___

8. ___He's going to read a newspaper___

9. _____   10. _____

EXERCISE 4: Present Progressive for Plans

(Grammar Note 4)

Write about Professor Starr's plans for next week. Use the information from his calendar and the present progressive.

	Monday	Tuesday	Wednesday	Thursday	Friday	Saturday
A.M.	Teach my economics class	Take the train to Tokyo	Do the interview for <u>The Space Show</u>	Work on the Space Future website	Go to an exercise class	Answer emails from the Space Future website
P.M.		Meet friends from England for dinner	Answer questions from the online chat	↓	Fly to New York for the Space Transportation Conference	Write a speech for the next space travel conference

1. On Monday morning _he's teaching his economics class_____.

2. On Tuesday morning _____.

3. On Tuesday evening _____.

4. On Wednesday morning _____.

5. On Wednesday afternoon _____.

6. All day Thursday _____.

7. On Friday morning _____.

8. On Friday evening _____.

9. On Saturday morning _____.

10. On Saturday afternoon _____.

EXERCISE 5: Simple Present for Schedules

(Grammar Note 6)

It is June 2050. You and a friend are planning a trip to the Moon. Your friend just got the schedule, and you are deciding which shuttle to take. Use the words in parentheses to ask questions, and look at the schedule to write the answers. Use the simple present.

2050 SHUTTLE SERVICE TO THE MOON
Fall Schedule

All times given in Earth's Eastern Standard Time

SEPTEMBER		OCTOBER		NOVEMBER	
Leave Earth	Arrive Moon	Leave Earth	Arrive Moon	Leave Earth	Arrive Moon
9/4 7:00 A.M.	9/7 6:00 P.M.	10/15 4:00 A.M.	10/18 3:00 P.M.	11/4 1:00 P.M.	11/8 12:00 A.M.
9/20 10:00 A.M.	9/23 9:00 P.M.	10/27 11:00 A.M.	10/30 10:00 P.M.	11/19 6:00 P.M.	11/23 5:00 A.M.

1. (when / the shuttle / fly to the Moon this fall)

   A: *When does the shuttle fly to the Moon this fall?*

   B: *It flies to the Moon in September, October, and November.*

2. (how many / shuttle flights / leave this fall)

   A: _____

   B: _____

3. (how often / the shuttle / depart for the Moon each month)

   A: _____

   B: _____

4. (when / the earliest morning flight / leave Earth)

   A: _____

   B: _____

5. (what time / the latest shuttle / leave Earth)

   A: _____

   B: _____

EXERCISE 6: Forms of the Future

(Grammar Notes 1–6)

Two people are having a cup of coffee and planning their trip to the Space Conference. Read their conversation and circle the most appropriate future forms.

JASON: I just heard the weather report. It's raining / It's going to rain tomorrow.
1.

ARIEL: Oh no. I hate driving in the rain. And it's a long drive to the conference.

JASON: Wait! I have an idea. We'll take / We're going to take the train instead!

ARIEL: Good idea! Do you have a train schedule?

JASON: Yes. Here's one. There's a train that will leave / leaves at 7:00 A.M.
3.

ARIEL: What about lunch? Oh, I know. I'll make / I'm making some sandwiches for us.

JASON: OK. You know, it's a long trip. What are we doing / are we going to do all those hours?
5.

ARIEL: Don't worry. We'll think / We're thinking of something.
6.

JASON: Maybe I'll bring / I'm bringing my laptop, and we can watch a movie.
7.

ARIEL: Great. Hey, Jason, your cup will fall / 's going to fall! It's right at the edge of the table.
8.

JASON: Got it! You know, we have to get up really early. I think I'm going / I'll go home now.
9.

ARIEL: OK. I'm seeing / I'll see you tomorrow. Good night.
10.

EXERCISE 7: Editing

Read the student's report on space travel. There are eleven mistakes in the use of the future. The first mistake is already corrected. Find and correct ten more.

travel
Both astronauts and space tourists will ~~traveling~~ in space, but tourists going to have a much

different experience. Space tourists ~~is~~ going to travel for fun, not for work. So, they ~~willn't~~ have

to worry about many of the technical problems that astronauts worry about. For example,

space tourists will ~~need not~~ to figure out how to use tools without gravity. And they ~~isn't~~ going to

go outside the spaceship to make repairs. For the most part, space tourists ~~will~~ just going to

see the sights and have a good time.

Still, there will be similarities. Regular activities be the same for astronauts and space

tourists. For example, eating, washing, and sleeping will ~~turned~~ into exciting challenges for

everyone in space. And on long trips, everyone is going to ~~doing~~ exercises to stay fit in zero

gravity. And both astronauts and space tourists ~~will going~~ to have many new adventures!

EXERCISE 8: Listening

A | *Listen to six short conversations. Decide if the people are talking about something happening* **Now** *or in the* **Future**. *Then listen again and check (✓) the correct column.*

	Now	Future
1.	☐	✓
2.	☐	☐
3.	☐	☐
4.	☐	☐
5.	☐	☐
6.	☐	☐

B | *Read the statements. Then listen again to the conversations and check (✓)* **True** *or* **False** *about each conversation. Correct the false statements.*

	True	False
	doesn't have any special plans	
1. The woman ~~plans to go out with friends~~.	☐	✓
2. The woman doesn't think the photos are very good.	☐	☐
3. Professor Starr won't take the call.	☐	☐
4. The lecture is about traveling to Mars.	☐	☐
5. The man isn't going to meet his parents at the airport.	☐	☐
6. The train to Boston left five minutes ago.	☐	☐

EXERCISE 9: Pronunciation

A | *Read and listen to the Pronunciation Note.*

Pronunciation Note

In **conversation**, we often pronounce *will* "ll" after consonants.

EXAMPLE: The trip **will** last three hours. → "The trip**'ll** last three hours."

We also often pronounce *going to* "gonna."

EXAMPLE: I'm **going to** be 23 soon. → "I'm **gonna** be 23 soon."

But do NOT use "gonna" in **writing**. Use *going to*.

    A: I think I'm **going to** go to the park tomorrow.

    B: That **will** be nice. Are you **going to** go in the morning?

    A: Yeah. The park **will** be crowded in the afternoon. Want to come?

    B: Yeah, I do. There's **going to** be an art show there tomorrow.

    A: Maybe Jane **will** have some things in the show. She takes incredible photos.

    B: Oh, wait! I think my parents are **going to** be here tomorrow.

    A: OK. Maybe we**'ll** do something together next weekend.

C | *Listen again to the conversation and repeat each statement or question. Then practice the conversation with a partner.*

EXERCISE 10: Making Plans

A | *Complete your weekend schedule. If you have no plans, write **free**.*

	Saturday	Sunday
12:00 P.M.		
1:00 P.M.		
2:00 P.M.		
3:00 P.M.		
4:00 P.M.		
5:00 P.M.		
6:00 P.M.		
7:00 P.M.		
8:00 P.M.		
9:00 P.M.		

B | *Now work with a partner. Ask questions to decide on a time when you are both free to do something together.*

    EXAMPLE: **A:** What are you doing Saturday afternoon? Do you want to go to the movies?

                B: I'm going to go to the library. How about Saturday night? Are you doing anything?

EXERCISE 11: Reaching Agreement

Work with your partner from Exercise 10. Look at the weekend schedule of events. Then look at your schedules from Exercise 10. Decide which events to attend and when.

Riverside

WEEKEND EVENTS IN RIVERSIDE
June 20 and 21

EVENTS	WHERE AND WHEN
Art in the Park Painting, photography, jewelry, and more! Support our local artists.	River Park, all day Saturday and Sunday
International Food Festival Moussaka, pad thai, spaetzle—you'll find plenty of interesting tastes here. International music and dance too.	Conference Center, Saturday 1:00 P.M.–7:00 P.M.
Walking Event 5 kilometers for Jay Street Clinic. Join us and help the city's only free clinic.	Start at River Park, Sunday 11:00 A.M. End at the clinic, 10 W. Jay St.
Zero G Experience space travel in this new film. On the big, big IMAX screen, it'll feel like you're really there.	Science Museum, starts Sunday Show times: 10:00 A.M. and 3:00 P.M.
Dancing with the Stars Free concert, with plenty of room for dancing. Bring a picnic and your own chairs.	Brown's Beach, Saturday 7:00 P.M.–Midnight

EXAMPLE:　A: What are you doing Sunday? Do you want to go to see the space travel movie, *Zero G*?

B: Hmm. Maybe. What else is happening on Sunday?

EXERCISE 12: Writing

A | *Write a paragraph about your life five years from now. Answer the following questions.*
Include plans, predictions, and facts.

- Where will you live?
- What kind of job will you have?
- What transportation will you use?

EXAMPLE: Most of my family lives in Los Angeles, so I'm probably going to live there too. I'm
graduating from college in two years, and I'm going to look for a job in space travel.
I'll probably drive an electric car because I'm sure gas will get more expensive. I'll be
25 in five years, so I think I'll probably be married. Maybe I'll even have a child.

B | *Check your work. Use the Editing Checklist.*

Editing Checklist

Did you use . . . ?
- ☐ *will* and *be going to* for predictions and facts
- ☐ *be going to* and the present progressive for plans

A | *Circle the correct words to complete the sentences.*

1. We <u>'ll go</u>/ <u>'re going</u> to a concert on Saturday. I already have the tickets.

2. You can give me that envelope. I <u>'ll</u> / <u>'m going to</u> mail it for you on the way to school.

3. Look out! That vase <u>will</u> / <u>is going to</u> fall off the shelf!

4. Take your umbrella. It <u>'ll</u> / <u>'s going to</u> rain.

5. Sara <u>gives</u> / <u>is giving</u> a party tomorrow night.

B | *Complete the sentences about the future with the correct form of the verbs in parentheses.*

1. It's almost June. What _____ we _____ this summer?
   (do)

2. Don't eat so much. You _____ sick tomorrow.
   (feel)

3. The package _____ in a few days.
   (arrive)

4. That driver _____ a speeding ticket. The police are right behind him.
   (get)

5. Bye. I _____ you tomorrow.
   (see)

6. Look at Tommy's face. I think he _____.
   (cry)

7. What time _____ the movie _____?
   (start)

8. _____ Mahmoud _____ back this afternoon?
   (call)

9. Don't worry. He _____ to call you.
   (not forget)

10. Bye. I _____ to you next week.
    (speak)

C | *Find and correct five mistakes.*

1. When will Ed gets home tomorrow?

2. The movie starts at 7:30, so I think I go.

3. Do you want to go with me, or are you study tonight?

4. What you are going to do next weekend?

5. I'm going be home all day.

STEP 1 GRAMMAR IN CONTEXT

Before You Read

Look at the picture. Discuss the questions.

1. What is the girl thinking?
2. What are some typical goals that people have?
3. What will people do to reach those goals?

Read

Read the article about setting goals.

GO FOR IT! What are your dreams for the future?

Will you have your degree **when you're 22**? Will you start your own business **before you turn 40**? We all have dreams, but they'll remain just dreams **until we change them to goals**. Here's how.

PUT YOUR DREAMS ON PAPER. After you write a dream down, it will start to become a goal. Your path will be a lot clearer. For example, Latoya Jones wrote this:

> **Before I turn 30,** I'm going to be a successful businessperson.

Now her dream is starting to become her goal.

LIST YOUR REASONS. When things get difficult, you can read this list to yourself and it will help you to go on. This is what Latoya put at the top of her list:

> My parents will be proud of me **when I'm a successful businessperson.**

WRITE DOWN AN ACTION PLAN. What are you planning to do to achieve your goal? This is Latoya's action plan:

> I'm going to go to business school **as soon as I save enough money to pay for it.**

> **When I graduate,** I'll get a job with a big company.

> **After I get some experience**, I'll find a better job.

TAKE YOUR FIRST STEPS TODAY. Here are the first steps Latoya is going to take:

> **Before I apply to schools,** I'm going to download some online[1] catalogs.

> I'll prepare carefully for interviews **after I apply.**

> I won't decide on a school **until I visit several of them.**

You can do exactly what Latoya did to achieve your own goals. Keep this article in a safe place. **When you decide to start,** you'll know what to do. Remember, the longest journey starts with the first step!

---

1 *online:* on the Internet

After You Read

A | Vocabulary: *Circle the letter of the word or phrase that best completes each sentence.*

1. When you **achieve** something, you get it _____.
   a. as a gift
   b. after hard work
   c. from your family

2. Sam got a college **catalog** because he wanted to _____.
   a. pay his bill
   b. look at a homework assignment
   c. find information about classes

3. Melissa got a **degree** when she _____.
   a. mailed her college applications
   b. graduated from college
   c. listened to the weather report

4. When you **download** something from the Internet, you _____.
   a. put it on your computer
   b. throw it away
   c. email it

5. A **goal** is _____.
   a. not very important to you
   b. something you plan and work for
   c. a person who gives you advice

6. At a college **interview**, you _____.
   a. meet with someone from the school
   b. go on a tour of the college
   c. take a language test

B | Comprehension: *For each pair of sentences (**a** or **b**), check (✓) the action that comes first.*

Latoya's action plan:

1. _____ **a.** She will download school catalogs.   _____ **b.** She will apply to schools.

2. _____ **a.** She will save money.   _____ **b.** She will go to business school.

3. _____ **a.** She will get a job with a big company.   _____ **b.** She will graduate.

FUTURE TIME CLAUSES

Statements					
Main Clause			**Time Clause**		
I **will** I **am going to**					I **graduate**.
She **will** She **is going to**		**get** a job	**when**		she **graduates**.
They **will** They **are going to**					they **graduate**.

Yes / No Questions				
Main Clause			**Time Clause**	
Will you **Are** you **going to**		**get** a job	**when**	you **graduate**?

Short Answers				
Affirmative			**Negative**	
Yes,	I	will. am.	No,	I	won't. 'm not.

Wh- Questions				
Main Clause			**Time Clause**	
Where	**will** you **are** you **going to**	**get** a job	**when**	you **graduate**?

GRAMMAR NOTES

1

Use **future time clauses** to show the time relationship between <u>two future events</u>.

The verb in the **main clause** is in the **future**. The verb in the **time clause** is in the **present**.

BE CAREFUL! Do NOT use *be going to* or *will* in a future time clause.

The **time clause** can come at the <u>beginning</u> or at the <u>end</u> of the sentence. The meaning is the same.

Use a **comma** after the time clause when it comes at the <u>beginning</u>. Do NOT use a comma when it comes at the end.

• She'll find a job *when* she graduates.

MAIN CLAUSE   TIME CLAUSE
• He**'s going to move** *after* he **graduates**.
(First he'll graduate. Then he'll move.)

MAIN CLAUSE   TIME CLAUSE
• We**'ll miss** him *when* he **leaves**.
(First he'll leave. Then we'll miss him.)

NOT: after he ~~is going to graduate~~.
NOT: when he ~~will leave~~.

• *Before* she applies, she'll visit schools.
OR
• She'll visit schools *before* she applies.

NOT: She'll visit school✗before she applies.

(continued on next page)

2 Future time clauses begin with **time expressions** that show the <u>order of events</u>.

a. **When**, **after**, and **as soon as** introduce the <u>first</u> event.

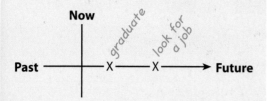

b. **Before** introduces the <u>second</u> event.

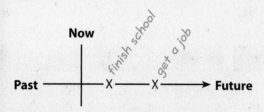

c. **Until** also introduces the <u>second</u> event. It means "only up to the time" of the second event.

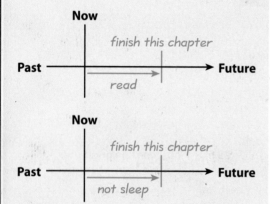

d. **While** introduces an event that will happen <u>at the same time</u> as another event.

You can use either the **simple present** or **present progressive** with an action verb after *while*.

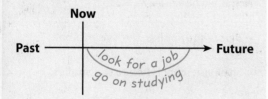

- **When** I graduate, I'll look for a job.
- I'll look for a job **after** I graduate.
  (*First I'll graduate. Then I'll look for a job.*)

- **As soon as** I graduate, I'll look for a job.
  (*First I'll graduate. Immediately after that, I'll look for a job.*)

- **Before** I get a job, I'll finish school.
  (*First I'll finish school. Then I'll get a job.*)

- I'll read **until** I finish this chapter.
  (*I'll keep reading, but only up to the time that I finish this chapter. Then I'll stop.*)

- I won't sleep **until** I finish this chapter.
  (*I'll stay awake, but only up to the time that I finish this chapter. Then I'll go to sleep.*)

- **While** I look for a job, I'll go on studying.
  OR
- **While** I'm looking for a job, I'll go on studying.
  (*I'll look for a job and study at the same time.*)

because of

(non)

EXERCISE 1: Discover the Grammar

Read the numbered sentence. Then circle the letter of the two sentences that have a similar meaning.

1. Amber will open her own business when she finishes school.

   a. Amber will open her own business. Then she'll finish school.

   (b.) Amber will finish school. Then she'll open her own business.

2. Denzell won't quit until he finds another job.

   a. Denzell will find another job. Then he'll quit.

   b. Denzell will quit. Then he'll find another job.

3. Jake will retire as soon as he turns 60.

   a. Jake will retire. Then he'll turn 60.

   b. Jake will turn 60. Then he'll retire.

4. After the Morrisons sell their house, they'll move to Florida.

   a. The Morrisons will sell their house. Then they'll move to Florida.

   b. The Morrisons will move to Florida. Then they'll sell their house.

5. Marisa will call you when she gets home.

   a. Marisa will call you. Then she'll get home.

   b. Marisa will get home. Then she'll call you.

6. Dimitri is going to live with his parents until he gets married.

   a. Dimitri is going to get married. Then he'll live with his parents.

   b. Dimitri will live with his parents. Then he'll get married.

7. While Li-jing is in school, she'll work part-time.

   a. Li-jing will finish school. Then she'll get a part-time job.

   b. Li-jing will go to school. At the same time she'll have a part-time job.

8. Marta will have her degree before she turns 21.

   a. Marta will get her degree. Then she'll turn 21.

   b. Marta will turn 21. Then she'll get her degree.

9. Adel and Farah won't buy a house until their son is two years old.

   a. They'll buy a house. Then their son will turn two.

   b. Their son will turn two. Then they'll buy a house.

10. Ina will live in Paris while she studies French cooking.

    a. First she'll study French cooking. Then she'll move to Paris.

    b. She'll study French cooking. At the same time, she'll live in Paris.

EXERCISE 2: Simple Present or Future

(Grammar Note 1–2)

Complete the student's worksheet. Use the correct form of the verbs in parentheses.

GOAL PLANNING WORKSHEET

A. What is your most important goal?

- I _____'ll get_____ a job after I _____graduate_____.
  - 1. (get)   2. (graduate)

B. List the reasons you want to achieve this goal.

- When I _____ a job, I _____ more money.
  - 3. (get)   4. (have)
- When I _____ enough money, I _____ a used car.
  - 5. (save)   6. (buy)
- I _____ happier when I _____ employed.
  - 7. (feel)   8. (be)
- I _____ new skills while I _____.
  - 9. (learn)   10. (work)

C. What is your action plan?

- Every morning when I _____, I _____ online for
  - 11. (get up)   12. (check)

  employment ads.

- When I _____ to my friends, I _____ them if they know
  - 13. (talk)   14. (ask)

  of any jobs.

- I _____ information about résumé writing before I _____
  - 15. (download)   16. (write)

  a new résumé.

- While I _____ to find a job, I _____ my
  - 17. (try)   18. (improve)

  computer skills.

- Before I _____ on an interview, I _____ how to
  - 19. (go)   20. (know)

  use Excel and PowerPoint.

D. What are the steps you will take right away?

- Before I _____ anything else, I _____ a list of people to
  - 21. (do)   22. (write)

  contact for help.

- As soon as I _____ all the people on my list, I _____ on
  - 23. (contact)   24. (work)

  fixing up my résumé.

EXERCISE 3: Order of Events

(Grammar Notes 1–2)

Combine the pairs of sentences. Use the future and the simple present or present progressive form of the verb. Decide which sentence goes first. Remember to use commas when necessary.

1. Sandy and Jeff will get married. Then Sandy will graduate.

   _____*Sandy and Jeff will get married*_____ before _____*Sandy graduates*_____.

2. Jeff is going to get a raise. Then they are going to move to a larger apartment.

   As soon as _____.

3. They're going to move to a larger apartment. Then they're going to have a baby.

   After _____.

4. They'll have their first child. Then Sandy will get a part-time job.

   _____ after _____.

5. Sandy will work part-time. Then their child will be two years old.

   _____ until _____.

6. Jeff will go to school. At the same time, Sandy will work full-time.

   _____ while _____.

7. Jeff and Sandy will achieve their goals. Then they'll feel very proud.

   When _____.

EXERCISE 4: Editing

Read the journal entry. There are ten mistakes in the use of future time clauses. The first mistake is already corrected. Find and correct nine more. Remember to look at punctuation!

> Graduation is next month! I need to make some plans now because when exams
>   start
> ~~will~~ start, I don't have any free time. What am I going to do when I'll finish school?
>
> My roommate is going to take a vacation before she'll look for a job. I can't do that
>
> because I need to earn some money soon. I think that after I'll graduate I'm going to
>
> take a desktop publishing class. As soon as I learn the software I look for a job with a
>
> business publisher. It's hard to find full-time jobs, though. Part-time jobs are easier to find.
>
> Maybe I'll take a part-time job after I find a good full-time one. Or maybe I'll take a
>
> workshop in making decisions, before I do anything!

EXERCISE 5: Listening

A | *A woman is calling Jobs Are Us Employment Agency. Read the list of steps she will take to get a job. Then listen to her conversation. Listen again and number the steps in order.*

The woman is going to:

_____ **a.** speak to a job counselor

_____ **b.** have an interview at the agency

__1__ **c.** send a résumé

_____ **d.** receive more job training

_____ **e.** go to companies

_____ **f.** take a skills test

B | *Read the statements. Then listen again to the call and circle the correct information.*

1. The agency is going to <u>hire the woman</u> / (<u>help the woman find a job</u>).

2. The woman's goal is to work for <u>her college</u> / <u>a company</u>.

3. The woman has <u>a college degree</u> / <u>a lot of work experience</u>.

4. The man thinks she's going to need more <u>training</u> / <u>experience</u> before she goes on interviews.

5. The man will send the woman <u>his résumé</u> / <u>a brochure</u>.

EXERCISE 6: Pronunciation

A | *Read and listen to the Pronunciation Note.*

Pronunciation Note

When the **time clause comes first**, the voice often **falls at the end of the time clause**. It falls **more** at the end of the **second clause**.

EXAMPLE: *When I finish the homework,* I'm going to have lunch.

B | *Listen to the short conversations and notice the intonation in the answers.*

1. **A:** When are you going to call Dan?

   B: After I do my homework, I'll call him.

2. **A:** Are you going to look for a full-time job?

   B: No. Until I graduate, I'm only going to work part-time.

3. **A:** Are we going to read something new now?

   B: As soon as we take the test, we'll begin a new chapter.

4. **A:** How is Marta doing in her new job?

   B: Great. Before she's 30, she'll open her own business.

5. **A:** Philippe's new house is far from work. How will he get there?

   B: After he moves, he's going to buy a car.

C | *Listen again to the conversations and repeat the answers. Then practice the conversations with a partner.*

EXERCISE 7: What About You?

A | *Complete the sentences with your own information.*

1. I'm going to continue studying English until _____.

2. While I'm in this class, _____.

3. When I finish this class, _____.

4. I'll stay in this country until _____.

5. As soon as _____, I'll _____.

6. I'm not going to _____ until _____.

7. I'm going to feel a lot better after _____.

8. Before _____, _____.

B | *Work in small groups and compare your answers with those of your classmates. How many different answers are there? Remember that all sentences refer to future time.*

EXAMPLE: **A:** I'm going to study English until I pass the TOEFL exam. What about you?
                  B: I'm going to continue studying until I get a job.
                  C: Me too!

EXERCISE 8: Game: What's Next?

Work in a group and form a circle. One person says a sentence with a future time clause. Use your imagination—your sentences don't have to be true! The next person begins a new sentence using information from the main clause. Continue around the circle as long as you can.

EXAMPLE:

EXERCISE 9: Writing

A | *Complete the worksheet for yourself. Use future time clauses.*

GOAL PLANNING WORKSHEET

A. What is your most important goal?

1. _____

B. List three reasons you want to achieve this goal.

1. _____

2. _____

3. _____

C. What are the first three steps of your action plan?

1. _____

2. _____

3. _____

B | *Check your work. Use the Editing Checklist.*

Editing Checklist

Did you use . . . ?
☐ sentences with future time clauses
☐ the present in the time clauses
☐ the future in the main clauses
☐ a comma when the time clause comes first

UNIT 7 Review

Check your answers on page UR-2.
Do you need to review anything?

A | *Circle the correct words to complete the sentences.*

1. What are you going to do after you <u>will graduate</u> / <u>graduate</u>?

2. We won't start a new chapter until we <u>finished</u> / <u>finish</u> this one.

3. <u>When</u> / <u>Until</u> Jorge gets a raise, he's going to buy a new car.

4. <u>Is</u> / <u>Will</u> Andrea find a job by the time she graduates?

5. Where will you live while you're <u>learning</u> / <u>going to learn</u> English?

6. We won't start the test <u>until</u> / <u>when</u> the teacher arrives. She has the tests.

7. <u>Will you</u> / <u>Are you</u> going to take another class after you finish this one?

B | *Complete the sentences with the correct form of the verbs in parentheses.*

1. Yuri is going to take night classes while he _____ full time.
   (work)

2. Until he buys a new computer, he _____ for online courses.
   (not register)

3. When he takes online courses, he _____ more time at home.
   (spend)

4. He'll help his daughter with her homework while he _____ for his
   (study)
   own courses.

5. He _____ for a new job before he graduates.
   (not look)

6. By the time he _____, he's going to have a lot of work experience.
   (graduate)

7. Before he starts his new job, he _____ a vacation.
   (take)

C | *Find and correct six mistakes. Remember to look at punctuation.*

A: Are you going to call Phil when we'll finish dinner?

B: No, I'm too tired. I'm just going to watch TV after I go to sleep.

A: Before I wash the dishes, I'm going answer some emails.

B: I'll help you, as soon as I'll drink my coffee.

A: No rush. I have a lot of emails. I won't be ready to clean up until you'll finish.

PART II

From Grammar to Writing

SHOWING THE ORDER OF EVENTS

When you write about your future plans and goals, use sentences with future time clauses to show the relationship between two future events. Use **time words** (*as soon as*, *after*, *before*, *by the time*, *when*, *while*, and *until*) to introduce the time clause. The time words show the order of the events.

EXAMPLE: First I'll go to the gym. Then I'll call my friend. →

SECOND EVENT   FIRST EVENT
I'll call my friend **after** I go to the gym.

FIRST EVENT   SECOND EVENT
After I go to the gym, I'll call my friend.

The time clause can come first or second. When it comes first, a **comma** separates the two clauses.

1 | *Read the blog post about weekend plans. Underline the future time clauses. Circle the time words in the future time clauses.*

The Weekend: Plan Ahead for a Good One!

It's Sunday night, and once again, I'm wondering, *Where did the weekend go?* So from now on, before the weekend arrives, I'm going to make a plan. My goal: have some fun *and* get the chores done. Here's how I'll achieve that goal next weekend. First, after I finish this blog post, I'm going to buy movie tickets for Saturday night online. Next, no more sleeping late on Saturday! As soon as the alarm clock rings, I'm going to jump out of bed. Then I'll clean the apartment. (And this time, I'll keep working until I finish.) Finally, coffee! While I have my first cup, I'll talk to my friends about the film festival that night. After coffee, it'll be time do the grocery shopping. This will be incredible—I'll actually get to the farmers market before the good stuff is sold out. After that, I'll just relax until it's time to go out. On Sunday, my sister and her family are coming to lunch. No problem! By the time they get here, I'll be ready. In fact, I probably won't even start cooking until I finish my workout at the gym. Is this a plan or an impossible dream? When next Sunday night rolls around,[1] I'll let you know!

---

[1]*roll around:* to arrive

2 | *Look at the pairs of events from Gary's plans. What will happen first? Number the events in each pair: **1** for first event; **2** for second event; write **1** for both events when they happen at the same time.*

a. __2__ the weekend arrives   __1__ I make a plan

b. _____ the alarm clock rings   _____ I jump out of bed

c. _____ I have my first cup of coffee   _____ I talk to my friends

d. _____ get to the farmers market   _____ the good stuff is sold out

e. _____ my sister and her family get here   _____ I'm ready

f. _____ I start to cook   _____ I finish my workout

g. _____ next Sunday rolls around   _____ I let my readers know

3 | *Before you write . . .*

1. Think about the coming weekend. What are some necessary chores? Will you do something for fun? Where will you go? What friends or family members will you see?

2. Talk about your plans with a partner. Listen to your partner's plans. Ask and answer questions about your plans, for example: *What's the most important thing? What will you do after that? Where are you going to . . . ? Who will . . . ?*

3. Complete the timeline with the things you plan to do this weekend.

EXAMPLE:

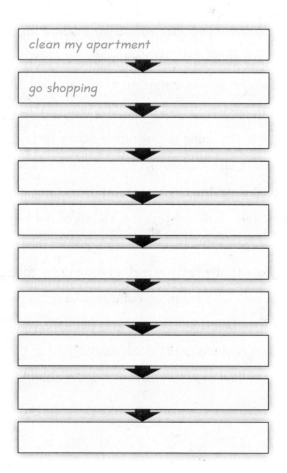

clean my apartment

go shopping

4 | *Write a first draft of a blog post about your weekend plans. Use the blog in Exercise 1 as a model and your timeline to organize your ideas. Include information that your partner asked about. Remember to use the present in future time clauses.*

EXAMPLE: Tomorrow is Saturday, and my friends are coming to dinner. My apartment is a mess, but I have a plan! As soon as I get up Saturday morning, I'm going to clean the apartment. When I finish, I'll . . .

5 | *Exchange drafts with a different partner. Complete the chart.*

---

1. The writer used future time clauses   **Yes** ☐   **No** ☐

2. Check (✓) the time words and phrases the writer used to connect the time clauses:

   ☐ *after*   ☐ *as soon as*   ☐ *before*   ☐ *by the time*   ☐ *when*   ☐ *while*   ☐ *until*

3. What I found most interesting in the paragraph:

   _____

   _____

   _____

4. Questions I'd like the writer to answer in the story:

   Who _____?

   When _____?

   Why _____?

   (Your own questions) _____?

   _____?

   _____?

---

6 | *Work with your partner. Discuss each other's charts from Exercise 5. Then rewrite your own paragraph and make any necessary changes.*

PRESENT PERFECT

Present Perfect: *Since* and *For*
CAREERS

STEP 1 GRAMMAR IN CONTEXT

Before You Read

Look at Bob Burnquist's sports card. Discuss the questions.

1. What are his interests?
2. What are your interests?
3. What is Bob's motto[1]?
4. Do you have a motto? What is it?

Read

Read the article about a champion skateboarder.

by Mariana Andrade

When he was only 11 years old, Bob Burnquist's life changed dramatically. A skate park opened just three blocks from his house in São Paulo, Brazil. Bob got his very first skateboard and started skating. He**'s been** a skater **since then**.

At first he did it just for fun, but soon he turned pro.[3] His first big international contest was in Canada in 1995. Bob won. **Since then** he **has taken** home many more first-place prizes and gold medals. He **has** also **earned** enough money to support himself while doing what he loves most. In 2002 he was voted "King of Skate" in a California contest.

Bob **has lived** in California **since 1995**, but he frequently returns to Brazil. He**'s had** dual citizenship (Brazil and the United States) **for many years**. Does he consider himself American? Bob says, "I'm American, South American. . . . A citizen of the world."

The skateboard isn't the only board he uses. Bob also enjoys snowboarding and surfing. **Since he moved to California**, he **has been** close to snow-topped mountains and the beach. His backyard and, of course, the streets provide opportunity for skating. As he once said, "If you snowboard, surf, and skate, you pretty much cover the whole earth."

Sports Card

Bob Burnquist

Date of Birth: October 10, 1976
Place of Birth: Rio de Janeiro, Brazil
Residence: California, U.S.
Citizenship: Brazil and U.S.
Started Skateboarding: 1987
Turned Professional: 1991
Other Interests: Reading, travel, photography, snowboarding, mountain biking, surfing
Motto: "Be good, be positive, respect individuality[2] and nature."

Sports Card

---

[1] *motto:* a short statement of your life goals or beliefs
[2] *individuality:* the way people are different from each other
[3] *turn pro:* to become a professional (do a sport for money)

After You Read

A | Vocabulary: *Circle the letter of the word or phrase closest in meaning to the words in* **blue.**

1. Bob's life changed **dramatically**.
   a. slowly and a little
   b. dangerously
   c. quickly and a lot

2. He earned enough money to **support himself**.
   a. pay for skating lessons
   b. pay for his own food, clothing, and home
   c. buy an expensive skateboard

3. Does Bob **consider himself** American?
   a. want to be
   b. like being
   c. think he is

4. The streets provide **opportunity** for skating.
   a. some dangers
   b. good chances
   c. a lot of contests

5. Bob's **residence** is in California.
   a. home
   b. office
   c. family

6. Bob always says, "**Be positive.**"
   a. Be 100 percent certain.
   b. Believe good things will happen.
   c. Be strong.

B | Comprehension: *Check (✓)* **True** *or* **False.** *Correct the false statements.*

	True	False
1. Bob Burnquist doesn't skate anymore.	☐	☐
2. He has won only one first-place prize since 1995.	☐	☐
3. Bob moved to California in 1995.	☐	☐
4. Bob is a citizen of many countries.	☐	☐
5. He lives close to the beach.	☐	☐

PRESENT PERFECT WITH *SINCE* AND *FOR*

Statements				
Subject	*Have (not)*	Past Participle		*Since / For*
I You* We They	have (not)	been	here	since 1995. for a long time.
He She It	has (not)	lived		

*You is both singular and plural.

Contractions	
Affirmative	Negative
I have = I've you have = you've we have = we've they have = they've he has = he's she has = she's it has = it's	have not = haven't has not = hasn't

Yes / No Questions				
Have	Subject	Past Participle		*Since / For*
Have	I you we they	been	here	since 1995? for a long time?
Has	he she it	lived		

Short Answers					
Affirmative			Negative		
Yes,	you I / we you they	have.	No,	you I / we you they	haven't.
	he she it	has.		he she it	hasn't.

Wh- Questions				
Wh- Word	*Have*	Subject	Past Participle	
How long	have	I you we they	been	here?
	has	he she it	lived	

Short Answers
Since 1995. For many years.

GRAMMAR NOTES

1	Use the **present perfect** with *since* or *for* to talk about something that <u>began</u> in the past and <u>continues</u> into the present (and may continue into the future). 	• Bob **has been** a skater *since* 1987. *(He became a skater in 1987, and he is still a skater.)* • He **has been** a skater *for* many years. *(He became a skater many years ago, and he is still a skater.)*
2	Use *since* + **point in time** (*since yesterday, since 5:00, since Monday, since 1995, since then*) to show <u>when</u> something started. *Since* can also introduce a **time clause**. Use a **comma** after the clause with *since* when it comes <u>first</u>. Use *for* + **length of time** (*for 10 minutes, for two weeks, for years, for a long time*) to show <u>how long</u> something has lasted. Expressions with *since* or *for* can go at the <u>beginning or end</u> of the sentence.	• He **has won** many contests *since 1995*. • *Since then* he **has become** famous. • He **has loved** sports *since he was a child*. • *Since he turned pro,* he **hasn't taken** a vacation. • Bob **has owned** a restaurant *for years*. • He **hasn't broken** a board *for a long time*. • *Since then* he has become famous. OR • He has become famous *since then*.
3	The present perfect is formed with *have* + **past participle**. a. The **past participle** of **regular verbs** is formed by adding *-d* or *-ed* to the base form of the verb. It is the same as the regular simple past form of the verb. **BE CAREFUL!** There are often **spelling changes** when you add *-ed* to the verb. b. Many common verbs are **irregular**. Their past participle is NOT formed by adding *-d* or *-ed*. Here is a list of many of the **irregular verbs** used in this unit. It shows both the simple past and the past participle of each verb. Notice that most irregular verbs have a past participle form that is different from the simple past form.	• He **has lived** there for years. • They **have been** partners since 1998. | BASE FORM	SIMPLE PAST	PAST PARTICIPLE | |---|---|---| | love | love**d** | love**d** | | want | want**ed** | want**ed** | | | | | | marry | marr**ied** | marr**ied** | | stop | stop**ped** | stop**ped** | | | | | | be | was | **been** | | become | became | **become** | | go | went | **gone** | | have | had | **had** | | meet | met | **met** | | take | took | **taken** | | wear | wore | **worn** | | win | won | **won** | | write | wrote | **written** |

REFERENCE NOTE
For a more complete list of **irregular verbs**, see Appendix 1 on page A-1.

EXERCISE 1: Discover the Grammar

*Read the information about Caterina and Roque. Then circle the letter of the sentence (**a** or **b**) that best describes the situation.*

1. Caterina has been a skater since 2003.

    (a.) She is still a skater.

    b. She is not a skater anymore.

2. She has lived in the same apartment for five years.

    (a.) She lived in a different apartment six years ago.

    b. She moved two years ago.

3. Caterina and Roque have been married for five years.

    a. They are not married now.

    (b.) They got married five years ago.

4. They haven't been on a vacation since 2006.

    a. They are on a vacation now.

    (b.) They were on a vacation in 2006.

5. Caterina hasn't won a contest for two years.

    (a.) She won a championship two years ago.

    b. She didn't win a championship two years ago.

6. She has stayed positive about her career since she won her last contest.

    (a.) She expects to win more contests.

    b. She isn't hopeful anymore.

EXERCISE 2: *Since* or *For*   (Grammar Note 2)

*Complete the sentences about Brazilian sportswriter Mariana Andrade. Use **since** or **for**.*

1. Mariana Andrade has lived in São Paulo _____*since*_____ 1995.

2. She has supported herself as a sportswriter _____*for*_____ four years.

3. _____*Since*_____ June she has written several articles about skateboarding.

4. This sport has been very popular in Brazil _____*for*_____ many years.

5. Mariana has met Burnquist twice _____*since*_____ she started her job.

6. She loves to skate, but she hasn't had much opportunity _____*for*_____ a long time.

7. She has been married to Alvaro, another skater, _____*since*_____ 2003.

EXERCISE 3: Forms of the Present Perfect

(Grammar Note 3)

Complete the article about Roque Guterres. Use the correct form of the verbs in parentheses.

Roque Guterres _____ has loved _____ skating since he was a little boy. He
       1. (love)

began skating when he was 10, and he _____ hasn't stop _____ since that time. Roque
       2. (not stop)

_____ has been _____ a professional skater now for several years. He and Caterina
  3. (be)

_____ have live _____ in Rio since they got married. They _____ have had _____
   4. (live)   **5. (have)**

the same one-bedroom apartment for five years. They _____ haven't taken _____ a vacation for
                             6. (not take)

many years, but they _____ have gone _____ to several skating contests since Roque turned
            7. (go)

pro. Roque _____ has skated _____ in four international contests since last year.
        8. (skate)

He _____ has won _____ two second-place prizes since then. Since he was a child,
     9. (win)

he _____ has wanted _____ to be a pro. "Ever since my dream came true," says Guterres,
     10. (want)

"I _____ have consider _____ myself a lucky man."
    11. (consider)

EXERCISE 4: Forms of the Present Perfect with *Since* or *For*

(Grammar Notes 2–3)

Complete the sentences. Use the present perfect form of the verbs in parentheses and **since**
or **for**.

- Skateboarding _____ has been _____ popular _____ for _____ more than 50
       1. (be)   **2.**

 years. People all over the world love the sport.

- Skateboards _____ have been _____ around _____ for _____ a long
       3. (be)   **4.**

 time. In the 1930s, the first ones were simple wooden boxes on metal wheels. They

 _____ have changed _____ dramatically _____ since _____ then!
     5. (change)   **6.**

- The first skateboarding contest took place in California in 1963. _____ Since _____ then,
                                         7.

 thousands of contests _____ have taken _____ place all over the world.
       8. (take)

- In 1976, the first outdoor skate park opened in Florida. _____ Since _____ then, hundreds of
                                   9.

 parks _____ have opened _____ in countries around the world.
    10. (open)

- Skateboarding can be dangerous. _____ Since _____ the 1960s, hundreds of thousands of
                       11.

 people around the world _____ have gone _____ to hospital emergency rooms because
       12. (go)

 of injuries.

(continued on next page)

When he was seven years old, Jon Comer lost his right foot as a result of a car accident. But that didn't stop him. ___Since___ then he ___has become___ one of the

13. 14. (become)

best-known professional skateboarders in the world, thanks to his great skill and very positive attitude.

Tony Hawk ___hasn't competed___ professionally ___for___ many years,

15. (not compete) 16.

but he is still the most famous and successful skateboarder in the world.

EXERCISE 5: Questions, Statements, and Short Answers   *(Grammar Notes 1–3)*

A | *Amy Lu is applying for a job as a college sports instructor. Look at her online résumé and the interviewer's notes. The year is 2011.*

Amy Lu
525 Ahina St
Honolulu, HI 96816

INTERVIEWED
09/18/11

Education:
2003 Certificate (American College of Sports Medicine)
2000 M.A. Physical Education (University of Texas) moved to Honolulu in 2001

Employment:
2002–present part-time physical education teacher (high school)
2000–present sports trainer (private)
teaches tennis, swimming

Skills:
speak English, Portuguese, and Chinese
martial arts got black belt in tae kwon do 2 mos. ago

Other Interests:
travel, sports photography, skateboarding, surfing

Awards:
2003 Teacher of the Year Award
2000 First Prize in Sunburn Classic Skate Contest

Memberships:
2003–present member of National Education Association (NEA)

B | *John Sakaino is interviewing Amy Lu for a job as a college sports instructor. Complete his questions. Use the words in parentheses.*

1. (how long / live in Honolulu)

   JOHN: *How long have you lived in Honolulu?*

   AMY: *I've lived in Honolulu for 15 years.* OR *I've lived in Honolulu since 1991.*

2. (how long / have your M.A. degree)

   JOHN: Have long have you had M.A. degree?

   AMY: She have had M degree since 2000

3. (have any more training / since / you get your M.A.)

   JOHN: Have you had any training sine?

   AMY: I have had a certificate since 2003

4. (how long / be a physical education teacher)

   JOHN: How long have been a physical education teacher

   AMY: I have been a since 2002

5. (how long / work as a sports trainer)

   JOHN: How long have you work as a sports

   AMY: _____

6. (how long / have a black belt in tae kwon do)

   JOHN: How long have you had

   AMY: _____

7. (win any awards since then)

   JOHN: I see you won a medal in skateboarding. _____

   AMY: _____. I won the Teacher of the Year Award in 2003.

8. (how long / be a member of NEA)

   JOHN: _____

   AMY: _____

C | *Imagine you are Amy Lu. Answer the questions. Use the information in her résumé and use contractions when possible.*

EXERCISE 6: Editing

*Read the posts to an online skateboard message board. There are ten mistakes in the use of the present perfect with **since** and **for**. The first mistake is already corrected. Find and correct nine more.*

The Skateboarding Board
Tell us your skating stories here!

I've had
~~I have~~ my skateboard for two years. For me, it's much more than just a sport. It's a form of transportation. It's much faster than walking!

Jennifer, U.S.

I've been a skater since five years. Since December I won two contests. I'd love to turn pro one day and support myself skating.

Paulo, Brazil

Help! I've broken three boards for January!!! Is this normal? How long you have had your board?

Sang-Ook, South Korea

Broken boards?! That's nothing! Consider yourself lucky! I've break my wrist twice since I started skating!

Marta, Mexico

Last year, my board hit a rock while I was skating in the street. I fell and hit my head and had to go to the emergency room. I always worn a helmet since then!

Megan, Australia

I live in California since 2006. My first love is surfing, but when there aren't any waves, I jump on my skateboard and take to the streets! My motto is "Make the best of what you have!"

Ming, U.S.

Wow! Yesterday, my friend gave me a copy of the video "OP King of Skate." I've watch it three times since then. The Burnquist part is awesome!

Todd, Canada

At last! A skate park opened near my home last week. Since then I gone every day. It's a lot more fun than skating in the streets!

Sylvie, France

EXERCISE 7: Listening

A | *Read the statements. Then listen to the interview. Listen again and circle the correct information.*

1. Eliana is a <u>professional athlete</u> / <u>college student</u> / <u>(sports announcer)</u>.

2. She wants to work for a <u>college</u> / <u>radio station</u> / <u>sports team</u>.

3. She lives in <u>Tampa</u> / <u>L.A.</u> / <u>São Paulo</u>.

4. She works <u>full time</u> / <u>part time</u> / <u>for a TV station</u>.

5. She writes articles about <u>sports</u> / <u>L.A.</u> / <u>job interviews</u>.

6. She considers herself <u>a sports writer</u> / <u>an athlete</u> / <u>a sports announcer</u>.

B | *Listen again to the interview and complete the interviewer's notes. Use **since** and **for**.*

WSPR Radio

Eliana Serrano   Interviewed Sept. 9

Eliana has been an athlete   *for 15 years*   .
                                                            1.

She's been an announcer _____.
                                                            2.

She's lived in L.A. _____.
                                                            3.

She's worked part time at WABC _____.
                                                            4.

She's written sports articles _____.
                                                            5.

She's considered herself an announcer _____.
                                                            6.

EXERCISE 8: Pronunciation

A | *Read and listen to the Pronunciation Note.*

Pronunciation Note
In *yes/no* **questions**, the voice usually **rises** at the end of the question.
In *wh-* **questions**, the voice usually **falls** at the end of the question.
EXAMPLES: **Are** you a student?   **Where** do you go to school?

B | *Listen to the short conversations. Notice how the voice rises or falls at the end of the questions. Draw arrows going up (↗) or down (↘).*

1. **A:** How long have you been a student?
   B: Since 2008.

2. **A:** Have you worked since you moved here?
   B: Yes, I have.

3. **A:** How many jobs have you had since then?
   B: I've had two jobs since I moved here.

4. **A:** Have you been at your job for a long time?
   B: No, I haven't.

5. **A:** How long have you lived here?
   B: For three years.

C | *Listen again and repeat each question. Then practice the conversations with a partner.*

EXERCISE 9: Role Play: A Job Interview

A | *Chin Ho Cho and Clara Reston are applying for a job as a college music teacher. Look at their résumés. Work with a partner and write five or more interview questions. Begin your questions with* **How long, How many,** *and* **Have you . . . since?**

Chin Ho Cho

Education:
2000   M.A. in Music Education
       (Boston University)

Teaching Experience:
2000–present The Juilliard School

Courses Taught:
Voice and Piano
History of Music
Symphonies of Beethoven
20th Century Jazz

Publications:
"Introducing Computers into Music Class"
(*The Journal of Music*, 2002)

Awards:
Teacher of the Year, 2002
Winner of University of Maryland Piano
  Competition, 2009

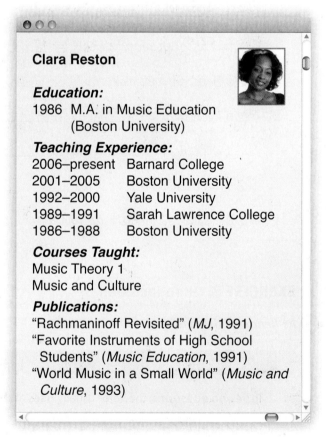

Clara Reston

Education:
1986 M.A. in Music Education
      (Boston University)

Teaching Experience:
2006–present   Barnard College
2001–2005   Boston University
1992–2000   Yale University
1989–1991   Sarah Lawrence College
1986–1988   Boston University

Courses Taught:
Music Theory 1
Music and Culture

Publications:
"Rachmaninoff Revisited" (*MJ*, 1991)
"Favorite Instruments of High School
  Students" (*Music Education*, 1991)
"World Music in a Small World" (*Music and
  Culture*, 1993)

EXAMPLE: How long have you been a music teacher?

B | *Work with your partner. Role-play two interviews (one for Chin Ho Cho and one for Clara Reston). Take turns being the interviewer.*

EXAMPLE: **A:** How long have you been a music teacher, Chin Ho?
B: I've been a music teacher since 2000.

C | *Work in small groups. Decide who to hire for the job and why. Remember to use* **since** *and* **for**.

EXAMPLE: **A:** Chin Ho Cho has had the same job since he got his M.A. degree.
B: Clara Reston has a lot of experience. She's been a teacher since 1986.
C: Chin has taught . . .

EXERCISE 10: Writing

A | *Write a paragraph about someone's accomplishments. It can be someone famous or someone you know. Use the present perfect with* **since** *or* **for**.

EXAMPLE: Amy Lu has been a high school physical education teacher and a private sports trainer for many years. She has received two awards since 2000, one for teaching and the other for skateboarding. She has been a member of the National Education Association since 2003. Amy has many interests. She speaks three languages. She has also been a student of martial arts for a long time, and she has had her black belt in tae kwon do for two months.

B | *Check your work. Use the Editing Checklist.*

Editing Checklist

Did you use . . . ?
☐ *since* and *for*
☐ *have* + the correct past participle

Check your answers on page UR-2.

Do you need to review anything?

A | Complete the sentences with **since** or **for**.

1. Sara has lived in San Francisco _____ 10 years.

2. She has wanted to be a tennis player _____ she was a little girl.

3. She's been a professional player _____ several years.

4. Sara has had the same trainer _____ a long time.

5. _____ 2010 she has won several competitions.

6. _____ the past few weeks, she has had a wrist injury.

7. _____ then she hasn't been able to practice.

B | Complete the sentences with the present perfect form of the verbs in parentheses.

1. I _____ a skateboarder for many years.
   (be)

2. Since 2010 I _____ any skating accidents.
   (not have)

3. My brother _____ the sport since he was a little boy.
   (love)

4. Together we _____ in many competitions.
   (compete)

5. He _____ several competitions since last year.
   (win)

6. We _____ each other for a few months.
   (not see)

C | Find and correct seven mistakes.

1. Marta and Tomás lived here since they got married in 1998.

2. Tomás has been a professional tennis player since he has come to this country.

3. He has won several competitions for then.

4. Since I have known Tomás, he had three different coaches.

5. I haven't see Marta for several weeks.

6. She have been in Brazil since April 1.

7. I've wanted to visit Brazil since years, but I haven't had any vacation time since I got

   this new job.

Present Perfect: *Already, Yet,* and *Still*
PARTY PLANNING

STEP 1 GRAMMAR IN CONTEXT

Before You Read

Look at the title of the article. Discuss the questions.

1. How do you feel about parties?
2. Which do you prefer: giving a party or going to one? Why?

Read

Read the article about how to plan a party.

It's Party Time!

It's almost the end of the year, and you**'ve already been** to several parties, but you **haven't given** one **yet**. You're a little nervous, but you decide it's time to take the plunge.[1]

First things first: **Have** you **chosen** the date **yet**? What about the time?

OK. You**'ve already chosen** the date and the time and **mailed** the invitations. But you **still haven't decided** on the menu, and now your party is just one week away! Don't panic!

We spoke to Patty Cake, a professional party planner. She says, "It *is* very important to be organized, but remember: You don't need a whole new set of skills. Think about your everyday life. You**'ve already done** many of the things you need to do for a party. You know how to shop for food, put it on plates, and introduce friends to one another. Now, all you need to do is just bring your many skills together."

Still need help? Party planners, like Patty Cake, can offer specific advice. She says, "We**'ve already helped** hundreds of people plan successful parties—big and small. If you **haven't used** a party-planning service **yet**, you should give it a try." And you don't have to spend a lot of money. Free advice is available on the Internet. There you will also find handy[2] lists where you can check off things you**'ve already done** (and see the things you **haven't done yet**!). So, take a deep breath, relax, and enjoy the party!

_____

[1] *take the plunge:* to do an activity that seems difficult or frightening
[2] *handy:* useful; easy to use

After You Read

A | Vocabulary: *Complete the sentences with the words from the box.*

available	organized	professional	specific	successful

1. OK. The drinks are on the table over there. Extra chairs are in the bedroom. The cake is in the refrigerator. I'll take it out at 8:00 P.M. That's it! I think I'm quite _____.

2. I can meet you for lunch any day this week to discuss plans for your party. You can also call me anytime—day or night. As you can see, I'm pretty _____.

3. Marta has a Ph.D. in economics, and she's already written three books. Her latest book is on the bestseller list! She's really _____.

4. Please bring two 10-ounce bags of Crispy Chips. The ones in the blue bag—they're low in fat, but not low in salt. You'll find them at Shopwise in aisle 6. I know I'm being very _____, but I want to be sure you get the right ones!

5. Jake offered to paint the apartment, but I prefer to hire _____ painters. They have training, job experience, and insurance if something goes wrong!

B | Comprehension: *Reread the article. Check (✓) the correct answers.*

The party giver . . .

☐ **1.** went to several parties

☐ **2.** gave a party

☐ **3.** chose a date for the party

☐ **4.** chose the time

☐ **5.** sent invitations

☐ **6.** decided on a menu

A party invitation

PRESENT PERFECT: *ALREADY, YET,* AND *STILL*

Affirmative Statements: *Already*					
Subject	*Have*	*Already*	**Past Participle**		*Already*
They	**have**		**mailed**	the invitations.	
She	**has**	*already*	**chosen**	the menu.	
They	**have**		**mailed**	the invitations	
She	**has**		**chosen**	the menu	*already*.

Negative Statements: *Yet*				
Subject	*Have not*	**Past Participle**		*Yet*
They	**haven't**	**mailed**	them	
She	**hasn't**	**chosen**	it	*yet*.

Negative Statements: *Still*				
Subject	*Still*	*Have not*	**Past Participle**	
They		**haven't**	**mailed**	them.
She	*still*	**hasn't**	**chosen**	it.

Yes / No Questions: *Yet*				
Have	**Subject**	**Past Participle**		*Yet*
Have	they	**mailed**	them	
Has	she	**chosen**	it	*yet*?

Short Answers			
Affirmative		**Negative**	
	they **have**.		they **haven't**.
Yes,	she **has**.	**No,**	she **hasn't**.
			not yet.

GRAMMAR NOTES

1 Use the **present perfect** with *already*, *yet*, or *still* to talk about things that happened or did not happen at an <u>indefinite</u> (not exact) time in the past.

a. Use *already* in **affirmative statements** to talk about something that has happened before now.

- I've *already* **mailed** the invitations.
- Jenna **has** *already* **met** Carlos.

b. Use *yet* in **negative statements** to talk about something that has not happened before now (in the near past).

A: Jenna **hasn't called** *yet*.
B: Oh, I'm sure we'll hear from her later.

c. You can also use *still* in **negative statements**. *Still* has a similar meaning to *not yet*, but it shows that the speaker is <u>surprised</u> or <u>unhappy</u> with the situation.

- I *still* **haven't mailed** the invitations!
  (I haven't mailed the invitations yet, and I really need to do it!)

d. Use *yet* in **questions** to ask if something has happened before now. Notice the different possible ways of giving **negative answers**.

A: Have you **bought** the soda *yet*?
B: No, I haven't. OR **No,** *not yet*. OR *Not yet*.

(continued on next page)

2 USAGE NOTES:

a. We sometimes use *already* in **questions** to express <u>surprise</u> that something has happened <u>sooner than expected</u>.

- **Has** Carlos **arrived** *already*? The party doesn't start until 8:00!

b. In American English, we sometimes use the **simple past** with *already* and *yet*.

- Jenna **has** *already* **left**. OR
- Jenna *already* **left**.

BE CAREFUL! When we use *already*, *yet*, or *still* + **present perfect** we do <u>NOT use past time expressions</u>.

- We've *already* met Carlos.
  NOT: We've already met Carlos ~~last month~~.

3

Already usually goes <u>between</u> *have* and the past participle. It can also go at the <u>end</u> of the clause.

- I've *already* **baked** the cake. OR
- I've **baked** the cake *already*.

Yet usually goes at the <u>end</u> of the clause.

- They **haven't arrived** *yet*.

Still goes <u>before</u> *haven't*.

- They *still* **haven't arrived**.

REFERENCE NOTES

For a list of **irregular past participles**, see Appendix 1 on page A-1.
For more about the **indefinite past**, see Unit 10 on page 134.

STEP 3 FOCUSED PRACTICE

EXERCISE 1: Discover the Grammar

Read the first statement. Then decide if the second statement is **True (T)** *or* **False (F)**.

1. I've already given many parties.
   _F_ This will be my first party.

2. I haven't baked the cake yet.
   ____ I plan to bake a cake.

3. Has Bev arrived yet?
   ____ I'm surprised that Bev is here.

4. Tom and Lisa still haven't arrived.
   ____ I expect them to arrive.

5. Has Jenna left already?
   _T_ I'm surprised that Jenna left.

6. Have you had a cup of tea yet?
   ____ I don't know if you had a cup of tea.

7. Carlos has already met my sister.
   ____ I need to introduce Carlos to her.

8. I still haven't called Mehmet.
   ____ I don't plan to call him.

9. Has Tom bought the chips yet?
   ____ I think Tom is going to bring the chips.

10. I still haven't talked to the party planner.
    ____ I should call her.

11. Have you taken any photos yet?
    ____ I saw you take some photos.

12. Is it 9:00 already?
    ____ I thought it was later than 9:00.

EXERCISE 2: Questions, Statements, and Short Answers

(Grammar Notes 1–3)

Complete the conversations. Use the present perfect form of the verbs in parentheses with **already** *or* **yet** *and short answers. Use contractions when possible. Go to Appendix 1 on page A-1 for help with irregular verbs.*

1. **A:** This is a great party. Marta made the cake. She's a professional baker. _____ Have _____

   you _____ tried _____ it _____ yet _____?
   (try)

   B: _____ No _____, I _____ haven't _____. But I'm going to have a piece now.

2. **A:** Jenna, I'd like you to meet my friend Carlos.

   B: We _____ have _____ already _____ met _____. Marta introduced us.
   (meet)

3. **A:** Would you like another cup of coffee?

   B: No, thanks. I _____ haven't _____ already _____ have _____ three cups!
   (have)

4. **A:** _____ Has _____ Jenna _____ already _____ left _____? It's still early!
   (leave)

   B: _____ No _____, she _____ haven't _____. She's in the kitchen.

5. **A:** _____ Have _____ you _____ seen _____ Tarantino's new movie _____ yet _____?
   (see)

   B: _____ Yes _____, I _____ have _____. It's great. What about you?

   A: I _____ haven't _____ seen _____ it _____ yet _____, but I want to.
   (see)

6. **A:** This was a great party. I'm giving my own party next week. I _____ have _____

   _____ already _____ planned _____ the whole thing, but I'm still nervous about it.
   (plan)

   B: Don't worry. If you organize it well, the rest will take care of itself!

EXERCISE 3: Affirmative and Negative Statements

(Grammar Note 3)

*Read Fabrizio's party-planning checklist. Write statements about the things that he **has already done** and the things that he **hasn't done yet** (or the things that he **still hasn't done!**). Use contractions when possible. Go to Appendix 1 on page A-1 for help with irregular verbs.*

Things to Do

- ✓ pick a date
- ☐ choose a time!!
- ✓ find a location
- ✓ write a guest list
- ✓ buy invitations
- ☐ send invitations!!
- ☐ ask friends to help
- ☐ plan the menu!!
- ✓ pick out music
- ☐ shop for food
- ☐ clean the house
- ✓ borrow some chairs

1. *He's already picked a date.*
2. *He hasn't chosen a time yet.* OR *He still hasn't chosen a time.*
3. He's already found a location.
4. He's already written a guest list.
5. He's already bought invitations. He hasn't sent invitations yet.
6. He hasn't asked friends to help yet.
7. He hasn't planned the menu yet.
8. He has already picked out music.
9. He still hasn't shopped for food.
10. He still hasn't cleaned the house.
11. He's already borrowed some chairs.
12. _____

EXERCISE 4: Editing

Read the online bulletin board. There are nine mistakes in the use of the present perfect with **already** *and* **yet***. The first mistake is already corrected. Find and correct eight more.*

Ask the Party Planner!

Doug asked: Help! My party is next week, and I ~~already~~ *still* haven't figured out the food! I'm not at all organized. I've ~~yet~~ *already* wasted three days worrying, and I still don't have any ideas. What should I do?

The Party Planner's Advice: Don't panic! Your guests haven't started arriving ~~already~~ *yet*, so there's still time. Ask everyone to bring something! (You've already invited people, right?) Or order pizza. I haven't met anyone ~~already~~ *yet* who doesn't like pizza.

• •

Rosa asked: I'd like to find a "theme" for my next birthday party. I've already ~~have~~ *had* a pasta party (10 kinds of pasta!), and I've already ~~gave~~ *given* a movie party (everyone dressed up as a movie character). Both were very successful, but I haven't ~~still~~ decided what to do this time. Any ideas?

The Party Planner's Advice: Sure. ~~Has~~ *Have* you tried this one yet? Ask each guest to bring a baby photo of himself or herself. Collect the photos. People try to match the photos with the guests! Your guests will love it!

STEP 4 COMMUNICATION PRACTICE

EXERCISE 5: Listening

A | *Some friends are planning a party. Look at their "To Do" list. Then listen to their conversation. Listen again and check (✓) the things they've already done.*

To Do

✓ 1. choose a date
2. find a place
3. invite people
4. borrow extra chairs
5. figure out food
6. buy soda
7. find someone to help set up
8. select music

Who...?	the man	the woman	Jason	Ella
1. is nervous about the party	✓	☐	☐	☐
2. has already invited everyone	☐	☐	☐	☐
3. has already agreed to have the party at his/her place	☐	☐	☐	☐
4. has already borrowed extra chairs	☐	☐	☐	☐
5. asks about food and drinks	☐	☐	☐	☐
6. hasn't decided on the food yet	☐	☐	☐	☐
7. offers to pick up soda	☐	☐	☐	☐
8. is available to help set up	☐	☐	☐	☐
9. sounds pretty organized	☐	☐	☐	☐
10. has already taken care of the music	☐	☐	☐	☐

EXERCISE 6: Pronunciation

🎧 **A** | *Read and listen to the Pronunciation Note.*

Pronunciation Note

In **conversation**, we almost always use **contractions of *have*** when the verbs are in the present perfect.

EXAMPLES: He **has** already left.   →   "**He's** already left."
She **has not** called yet.   →   "She **hasn't** called yet."
We have already seen him.   →   "**We've** already seen him."
I still **have not** mailed the invitations. →   "I still **haven't** mailed the invitations."

🎧 **B** | *Listen to the short conversations and notice the contractions with* **have.**

1. **A:** Who have you called?
   B: **I've** already called Jason.

2. **A:** Is he coming to the party?
   B: He still **hasn't** decided.

3. **A:** Can you come?
   B: Sorry. **We've** already made plans.

4. **A:** When is it?
   B: They **haven't** chosen a date yet.

5. **A:** Should I buy soda?
   B: **She's** already bought the soda.

6. **A:** Where is it?
   B: **He's** already put it away.

7. **A:** Do you have a question?
   B: **You've** already answered it.

8. **A:** Are they coming?
   B: **They've** already said yes.

🎧 **C** | *Listen again to the conversations and repeat the answers. Then practice the conversations with a partner.*

EXERCISE 7: Information Gap: Chores

Work in pairs (A and B). **Student A,** *follow the instructions on this page.* **Student B,** *turn to page 131 and follow the instructions there.*

1. Look at the picture of the Meiers' dining room and at Gisela's "To Do" list. Cross out the chores that Gisela has already done.

2. Answer your partner's questions about Gisela's chores.

    EXAMPLE: **B:** Has Gisela vacuumed the carpet yet?
    A: No, she hasn't. OR No, not yet.

3. Look at Helmut's "To Do" list. Ask your partner questions to find out which chores Helmut has already done. Cross out those chores.

    EXAMPLE: **A:** Has Helmut bought a memory card yet?
    B: Yes, he has. OR Yes, he's already gotten one.

To Do—Helmut
~~buy memory card for camera~~
bake the cake
put the turkey in the oven
mop the floor
wash the dishes
cut up the vegetables

To Do—Gisela
vacuum the carpet
buy flowers
wash the windows
set the table
hang the balloons
wrap the gift

Now compare lists with your partner. Are they the same?

EXERCISE 8: What About You?

Write a list of things that you planned or wanted to do by this time (for example, find a new job, paint the apartment). Include things that you **have already done** *and things that you* **haven't done yet.** *Exchange lists with a classmate and ask and answer questions about the items on the lists.*

> **EXAMPLE:** **A:** Have you found a new job yet?
> **B:** No, not yet. I'm still looking. OR Yes, I have.
> What about you? Have you . . . ?

EXERCISE 9: Writing

A | *Think about a goal you are working on at the moment.*

> **EXAMPLES:** organizing a party, finding a job, finding a new apartment, finding a college, getting a driver's license

B | *Write a list of things people do to reach this goal.*

> **EXAMPLE:** Finding a new apartment
> - choose a neighborhood
> - find information about the neighborhood
> - read newspaper and online ads
> - look at apartments

C | *Write two paragraphs. Describe things you* **have already done** *and things you* **haven't done yet** *to reach your goal.*

> **EXAMPLE:** I would like to find a new apartment. I've already chosen a neighborhood, but I haven't researched it yet . . .

D | *Check your work. Use the Editing Checklist.*

Editing Checklist

Did you use the . . . ?
- ☐ present perfect with *already*
- ☐ present perfect with *still*
- ☐ present perfect with *yet*
- ☐ correct word order

INFORMATION GAP FOR STUDENT B

1. Look at the picture of the Meiers' kitchen and at Helmut's "To Do" list. Cross out the chores that Helmut has already done.

2. Look at Gisela's "To Do" list. Ask your partner questions to find out which chores Gisela has already done. Cross out those chores.

   EXAMPLE: **B:** Has Gisela vacuumed the carpet yet?
   A: No, she hasn't. OR No, not yet.

3. Answer your partner's questions about Helmut's chores.

   EXAMPLE: **A:** Has Helmut bought a memory card yet?
   B: Yes, he has. OR Yes, he's already gotten one.

To Do—Helmut
~~buy memory card for camera~~
bake the cake ✓
put the turkey in the oven ✗
mop the floor ✓
wash the dishes ✗
cut up the vegetables ✗

To Do—Gisela
vacuum the carpet
buy flowers
wash the windows
set the table
hang the balloons
wrap the gift

Now compare lists with your partner. Are they the same?

Check your answers on page UR-3.

Do you need to review anything?

A | *Circle the correct words to complete the sentences.*

1. I've started planning your graduation party last night / already.

2. We still / yet haven't chosen a restaurant for the party. I'm getting nervous.

3. I met Nita yesterday, but I haven't met her boyfriend already / yet.

4. Did / Has Marla left already? The party just started!

5. Have you told / tell your friends about the party?

6. No, not told / yet.

B | *Complete the conversations with the present perfect form of the verbs in parentheses and **already**, **still**, *or* **yet**.*

- ANN: Ed _____ _____ _____! Amazing!
  1. (graduate / already)

  BEN: I know, but don't relax yet. We _____ _____ _____ the party.
  2. (have / still)

- ANN: _____ they _____ the food _____? Should I begin to worry?
  3. (deliver / yet)

  BEN: It just arrived. But Ed _____ _____ _____ the tables.
  4. (set / still)

  ANN: Well, he _____ _____ _____. I'll help him finish.
  5. (start / already)

- BEN: Some of Ed's friends _____ _____ _____.
  6. (arrive / still)

  ANN: I know . . . I don't think his new girlfriend _____ _____ _____.
  7. (arrive / yet)

  ED: Mom and Dad, _____ you _____ Christy _____?
  8. (meet / yet)

C | *Find and correct six mistakes.*

A: I can't believe it's the 10th already. And we still didn't finished planning.

B: We haven't checked the guest list for a while. Who hasn't replies yet?

A: Sally hasn't called about the invitation already. I wonder if she's coming.

B: Maybe she just forgot. Have you called yet her?

A: I've already call her a couple of times. She hasn't still called back.

Present Perfect: Indefinite Past
ADVENTURE TRAVEL

STEP 1 GRAMMAR IN CONTEXT

Before You Read

Look at the title of the article and at the photos. Discuss the questions.

1. What do you think the article is about?
2. Would you like to do the things in the photos? Why or why not?

Read

Read the article about unusual vacations.

Been There? Done That? Maybe it's time for something new . . . (or maybe not!)

by Rosa García

Today's world is getting smaller. People are traveling the globe[1] in record numbers.[2] They**'ve been** to Rome. They**'ve visited** Greece. They**'ve seen** the ancient pyramids of Egypt. They**'ve gone** skiing in the Swiss Alps. Now, they're looking for new places to see and new things to do. They want adventure. *Travel Today* **has just come out** with its annual survey. As part of the survey, the magazine asks its readers the following question: "What would you like to do that you**'ve never done** before?"

Here are some of their answers:

I**'ve made** several trips to Egypt, but I**'ve never ridden** a camel. I**'ve always wanted** to do that.

Moving along.
Camel ride in the desert

Hot-air ballooning! My boyfriend **has tried** this several times, but I**'ve never done** it.

Up, up, and away!
Hot-air ballooning over Turkey

I**'ve ice skated** and I**'ve climbed** mountains, but I**'ve never been** ice climbing. That's something I'd definitely like to try!

Work or play?
Ice climbing in the U.S.

---

[1] **globe:** the world
[2] **in record numbers:** much more than in the past

(continued on next page)

Riding a camel, hot-air ballooning, ice climbing . . . These are just a few activities that travelers can choose from today. All you need is time, money (a lot of it!), and a sense of adventure.[3] But you don't have to go to a faraway place in an unusual type of transportation to have a great vacation! **Have** you **ever spent** the day walking in the woods, **heard** the sound of the wind, or **watched** the sun set over the ocean? These can be wonderful adventures too! And a lot more affordable!

_____

[3] *sense of adventure:* the ability to enjoy new things

After You Read

A | Vocabulary: *Look at the reading. Find a word or phrase with a similar meaning to . . .*

1. very old   _____

2. exciting, unusual experience   _____

3. every year   _____

4. questionnaire   _____

5. way of traveling someplace   _____

6. cheaper   _____

B | Comprehension: *Which activities have the readers of* Travel Today *tried? Check (✓) them.*

☐ **1.** skiing in the Alps   ☐ **3.** hot-air ballooning   ☐ **5.** mountain climbing

☐ **2.** riding a camel   ☐ **4.** ice-skating   ☐ **6.** ice climbing

STEP 2 GRAMMAR PRESENTATION

PRESENT PERFECT: INDEFINITE PAST

Statements		
Subject	*Have (not)*	**Past Participle**
They	**have (not)**	**visited**	Egypt.
She	**has (not)**	**been**	there.

Statements with Adverbs				
Subject	*Have (not)*	**Adverb**	**Past Participle**	**Adverb**
They	**have**	*never*	**visited**	Egypt.
She	**has**	*just* *recently*	**been**	there.
They	**have (not)**		**visited**	Egypt *twice.*
She	**has (not)**		**been**	there *lately.* *recently.*

Yes / No Questions					Short Answers			
Have	**Subject**	**(Ever)**	**Past Participle**		**Affirmative**		**Negative**	
Have	they	**(ever)**	**visited**	Egypt?	**Yes,**	they **have.**	**No,**	they **haven't.**
Has	she		**been**	there?		she **has.**		she **hasn't.**
								never.

Wh- Questions				
Wh- Word	**Have**	**Subject**	**Past Participle**	
How often	**have**	they	**visited**	Egypt?
	has	she	**been**	there?

GRAMMAR NOTES

1

Use the **present perfect** to talk about things that happened at an **indefinite (not exact) time** in the past.

Use the present perfect when you <u>don't know</u> when something happened or when the specific time is <u>not important</u>.

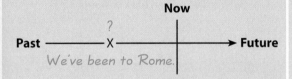

Use the present perfect (not the simple past) to show that the result of the action or state is **important in the present.** The present perfect always has some connection to the present.

USAGE NOTE: For many speakers **been to** and **gone to** have different meanings.

- They**'ve traveled** to Egypt.
  (You don't know the exact time.)

- We**'ve been** to Rome.
  (The exact time isn't important.)

- The hotel **has closed.**
  (So we can't stay there now.)

- He**'s been to** France.
  (At some point in the past, he visited France, but he's not there now.)

- He**'s gone to** France.
  (He's in France now.)

(continued on next page)

2 We can also use the **present perfect** with **adverbs** to talk about the **indefinite past**.

a. Use adverbs like *twice* or *often* to talk about <u>repeated actions</u> at some indefinite time in the <u>past</u>.

- They**'ve seen** the Pyramids *twice*.
- We've *often* **stayed** at that hotel.

b. Use *always* and *never* for actions or states that <u>continue to the present</u>.

- I've *always* **wanted** to go to Rome, but I**'ve** *never* **gone**.

c. Use *ever* to ask questions. It means at <u>any time before now</u>. Use *never* for <u>negative answers</u>.

A: Have you *ever* **been** to Rome?
B: No, I've *never* **been** there. OR **No**, *never*.

d. Use *just*, *lately*, and *recently* to stress that something happened in the <u>very recent</u> (but still indefinite) <u>past</u>.
- *just* = a very short time before now
- *lately* and *recently* = in the near past

- I've *just* **gotten** back from China.
- They **haven't been** there *lately*.
- He**'s** *recently* **flown** a lot.

USAGE NOTE: In American English, we often use *just* and *recently* with the <u>simple past</u>. You can't use *lately* with the simple past.

- I've *just* **returned** OR I *just* **returned**.
  NOT: I returned ~~lately~~.

BE CAREFUL! Do <u>NOT use the present perfect</u> with adverbs that refer to a definite past time.

- I **got** back *yesterday*.
  NOT: ~~I've gotten~~ back yesterday.

3 Notice the **word order** in sentences with the **present perfect** and **adverbs**:

a. Adverbs such as *twice* and expressions such as *many times* usually go at the <u>end of the sentence</u>.

- She**'s been** there *twice*.
- I've **been** there *many times*.

b. Adverbs of frequency such as *always*, *often*, and *never* usually go <u>before the past participle</u>.

- I've *always* **wanted** to stay there.
- We**'ve** *often* **talked** about it.

c. • *Just* goes <u>before</u> the past participle.
- *Lately* goes at the <u>end</u> of the sentence.
- *Recently* can go <u>before</u> the past participle or at the <u>end</u> of the sentence.

- I've *just* **had** dinner.
- I **haven't flown** *lately*.
- He**'s** *recently* **flown** a lot. OR
  He**'s flown** a lot *recently*.

REFERENCE NOTES

For a list of **irregular past participles**, see Appendix 1 on page A-1.
For a complete presentation of all the **present perfect forms**, see Unit 8 on page 110.
For **present perfect** with *already*, *yet*, and *still*, see Unit 9 on page 123.

EXERCISE 1: Discover the Grammar

Read the first statement. Then decide if the second statement is **True (T)** *or* **False (F)**. *If there isn't enough information in the first statement to know the answer, put a question mark* **(?)** *on the line.*

1. Adventure vacations have become very popular.

   _T_   They are popular now.

2. I've been to Italy twice.

   _____   I was there two years ago.

3. I have never been to the Himalayas.

   _____   I went to the Himalayas a long time ago.

4. I've just returned from China.

   _____   I was in China a short time ago.

5. Greg asks you, "Have you ever been to Costa Rica?"

   _____   Greg wants to know when you were in Costa Rica.

6. Marta asks you, "Have you read any good travel books lately?"

   _____   Marta wants to know about a travel book you read last year.

7. We have visited Egypt several times.

   _____   This is not our first visit to Egypt.

8. I've been on an African safari.[1]

   _____   I'm on a safari now.

---

[1] *safari:* a trip through the country areas of Africa in order to watch wild animals

EXERCISE 2: Statements and Questions   *(Grammar Notes 1–2)*

Complete the interview between Travel Today **(TT)** *and travel writer* Rosa García **(RG)**. *Use the present perfect form of the verbs in parentheses. Use contractions when possible.*

TT: As a travel writer, you _____*'ve visited*_____ many places. Any favorites?
                            1. (visit)

RG: Thailand. It's a beautiful, amazing country. I _____ there five times.
                                                   2. (be)

TT: What _____ your most unusual travel experience?
             3. (be)

RG: My *most* unusual? I _____ so many! I _____ near sharks
                          4. (have)   **5. (swim)**

    (in a cage, of course!), I _____ dinner next to a very active volcano,
                                    6. (eat)

    I _____ in an ice hotel in Finland . . .
          7. (sleep)

(continued on next page)

TT: The world _____ a lot smaller. There are fewer and fewer "undiscovered" places.
  8. (become)

_____ you ever _____ a really great place and decided not to tell your
  9. (find)

readers about it?

RG: No, never. I _____ about doing that a few times, but I _____ never
  10. (think)

_____ a place secret. I _____ always _____ about it.
  11. (keep)   12. (write)

TT: Where _____ you _____ recently?
  13. (be)

RG: I _____ just _____ from a hot-air ballooning trip in Australia. It was really
  14. (return)

fantastic. In fact, ballooning is my new favorite form of transportation!

TT: Where are you going next?

RG: On an African safari! I _____ never _____ on one, and I'm really excited.
  15. (be)

I _____ always _____ to do that.
  16. (want)

TT: Good luck! I look forward to your African safari article.

EXERCISE 3: Affirmative and Negative Statements (Grammar Notes 1–3)

*Look at the survey. Then write sentences about things Andy **has done** and things he **hasn't done**. Use contractions when possible.*

Travel Time Survey

Name: _Andy Cheng_

Have you ever done the following activities?
Check (✓) the ones you have done.

1. rent a car ☐
2. rent a motorcycle ☑
3. ride a camel ☐
4. go up in a hot-air balloon ☑
5. have some really unusual food ☑
6. see ancient pyramids ☐
7. sail a boat on the Nile River ☑
8. swim with dolphins in the ocean ☑
9. be on a safari ☐
10. fly around the world ☐

1. *He hasn't rented a car.* OR *He's never rented a car.* _____

2. *He's rented a motorcycle.* _____

3. _____

4. _____

5. _____

6. _____

7. _____

8. _____

9. _____

10. _____

EXERCISE 4: Word Order

(Grammar Note 3)

Complete the conversation. Put the words in parentheses in the correct order. Use the present perfect form of the verbs. Include short answers. Use contractions when possible.

EVAN: Hot-air ballooning! What's it like? _____ *I've never done this* _____ before!

                                                   1. (I / do this / never)

ANDY: You'll love it. _____,

                           2. (I / a few times / go up)

     but _____.

                         3. (not do / it / lately / I)

EVAN: _____?

                4. (you / a lot / travel)

ANDY: Yes, _____. I'm a travel writer, so it's part of my job.

                5.

EVAN: That's great! _____ on a safari?

                6. (you / be / ever)

ANDY: No, _____, but _____.

            7.   **8. (want / to go / always / I)**

EVAN: Me too. _____.

                9. (I / several times / to Africa / be)

     In fact, _____ back from a trip there.

              10. (I / get / just)

     But _____ on a safari.

             11. (never / I / be)

ANDY: Look. _____

              12. (they / finish / just)

     getting the balloon ready. It's time to go up!

EXERCISE 5: Statements

(Grammar Notes 1–2)

Look at some of Rosa's things. Write sentences using the present perfect form of the verbs from the box. Use adverbs when possible.

~~be~~	ride	see	stay	travel	write

1. _She's been to Egypt twice._

2. _____

3. _____

4. _____

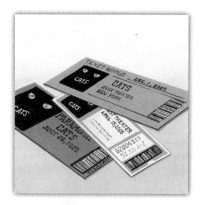

5. _____

6. _____

EXERCISE 6: Editing

Read the comments found on a hot-air ballooning website. There are twelve mistakes in the use of the present perfect and adverbs. The first mistake is already corrected. Find and correct eleven more.

upandaway.com

We *have* ~~has~~ received many comments from our clients. We'd like to share some with you.

Comments 🎈

I have always be afraid of heights. But after I saw the beautiful photos on your website, I knew I had to go hot-air ballooning! This ~~have~~ *has* been one of the best experiences of my life. Thank you!

Britta Kessler, Germany

We've returned ~~just~~ from a fantastic vacation. I've told all my friends about your company.

James Hudson, Canada

I've always wanted to go up in a hot-air balloon. I was not disappointed!

Antonio Vega, Mexico

I just seen some new photos posted on the website! Awesome!

Bill Hampton, USA

I've never ~~went~~ hot-air ballooning, but after visiting your wonderful website, I've decided to sign up!

Amalia Lopes, Brazil

We gave our parents a balloon trip as an anniversary gift. They've just ~~wrote~~ *written* to say it was fantastic. They've *never* ~~ever~~ been very adventurous, but now they want to go rafting!

Pat Calahan, Ireland

You *have* ever seen the face of a kid on a hot-air balloon ride? The cost of the ride: a lot. That look on her face: priceless!

Lydia Hassan, New Zealand

I ~~broken~~ *broke* my leg last month, so I haven't ~~lately~~ been able to do sports—boring! Your mountain balloon trip has just ~~gave~~ *have* me a lift—in more than one way!

May Roa, Philippines

EXERCISE 7: Listening

A | *Read the statements. Then listen to the conversation. Listen again and circle the correct information.*

1. The woman is <u>on vacation</u> / <u>(at a travel agency)</u>.
2. She goes on vacation <u>once</u> / <u>twice</u> a year.
3. She <u>has</u> / <u>hasn't</u> done a lot of adventure traveling.
4. This year she wants to do something she <u>has</u> / <u>hasn't</u> done before.
5. She thinks two of the vacations sound too <u>dangerous</u> / <u>expensive</u>.
6. The last vacation possibility the man mentions <u>is</u> / <u>is not</u> very expensive.

B | *Look at the choices. Then listen again to the conversation and check (✓) the activities Olivia's done before. Circle the number of the best vacation choice for her.*

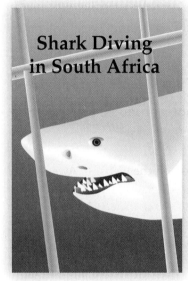

1. ☐

2. ☐

3. ☐

4. ☐

5. ☐

6. ☐

EXERCISE 8: Pronunciation

A | *Read and listen to the Pronunciation Note.*

> ### Pronunciation Note
>
> **After a noun**, we often pronounce:
>
> - *have* like the word *"of"*
>
> - *has* like "s," "z," or "iz."
>
> **EXAMPLES:** The **books have** arrived. → "The **books of** arrived."
> The **book has** arrived. → "The **book's** arrived."
> My **sister has** gone on vacation. → "My **sister'z** gone on vacation."
> The **bus has** been late a lot. → "The **bus'iz** been late a lot."

B | *Listen to the short conversations and notice the pronunciation of* **have** *and* **has.**

1. **A:** My **friends have** just returned from their trip.
   B: Oh, did they have a good time?

2. **A:** The **plane has** just landed.
   B: It was a good flight.

3. **A:** The **book has** arrived.
   B: Great! I can't wait to read it.

4. **A:** The **hotels have** recently closed.
   B: Too bad. We'll have to find new ones.

5. **A:** Our **boss has** left for vacation.
   B: When will she be back?

6. **A:** The **survey has** just come out.
   B: Oh, what does it say?

7. **A:** These **countries have** become very popular.
   B: I know. I'd love to visit them.

8. **A:** The **trip has** become more affordable.
   B: Well, maybe we can go more often now.

9. **A:** I think **class has** started.
   B: Let's go in.

C | *Listen again to the conversations and repeat the first statement in each one. Then practice the conversations with a partner.*

EXERCISE 9: Find Someone Who . . .

A | *Ask your classmates questions. Find out how many people have ever done any of the following things. Add four more activities. When someone answers* **yes,** *ask more questions. Get the stories behind the answers.*

- ride a horse
- take a long car trip
- climb a mountain
- eat something unusual
- be on a boat
- go camping

- see ancient Roman ruins
- hear a mariachi band
- _____
- _____
- _____
- _____

> **EXAMPLE:**   **A:** Have you ever ridden a horse?
> **B:** Yes, I have. A couple of times.
> **A:** Did you enjoy it? Did anything exciting happen?

B | *Share your answers and stories with the class.*

> **EXAMPLES:** Two people have ridden a horse. Miguel has ridden twice. Once when he . . .
> No students have . . .

EXERCISE 10: Writing

A | *Read the quote. Then write a paragraph that answers the questions.*

"My favorite thing is to go where I've never been."
Diane Arbus (1923–1971, photographer, U.S.)

What does Arbus mean? Do you feel the same way? Where have you been? Would you like to go there again? Where have you never been that you would like to go?

> **EXAMPLE:**   I've read the quote by Diane Arbus. I think it means . . .

B | *Check your work. Use the Editing Checklist.*

Editing Checklist

Did you use the . . . ?
- ☐ present perfect without adverbs of time
- ☐ present perfect with adverbs of time such as *twice, always, never, just, recently, lately*
- ☐ correct word order

A | *Circle the correct words to complete the sentences.*

1. Have you twice / ever been to Egypt?

2. I've just / lately returned from Cairo.

3. I've was / been there twice, and I'm returning next summer.

4. Has / Have Jon ever ridden a camel?

5. I haven't read any good travel books lately / never.

6. One of my classmates is / has recommended a good book.

B | *Complete the sentences with the present perfect form of the correct verbs from the box.*

| be | give | read | see | show | take | want |

1. _____ you ever _____ the pyramids?

2. I _____ never _____ to Egypt.

3. Elena _____ just _____ an interesting book about ancient Egypt.

4. She _____ _____ it to me to read.

5. I _____ always _____ to ride a camel.

6. My brother _____ _____ several trips there.

7. He _____ recently _____ me his photos.

C | *Find and correct seven mistakes.*

1. I've lately traveled a lot.

2. We've returned just from an African safari.

3. I've never have so much fun before.

4. Have you been ever on a safari?

5. No, but I've recently went hot-air ballooning.

6. My wife and I has decided to go next summer.

7. I've saw a lot of great photos on a hot-air ballooning website.

Present Perfect and Simple Past
LONG-DISTANCE RELATIONSHIPS

Before You Read

Look at the picture and read the title of the article. Discuss the questions.

1. What do you think a "long-distance marriage" is?
2. Where are the two people living?
3. What are some reasons married people might live apart?

Read

Read the excerpt from an article in Modern Day *magazine.*

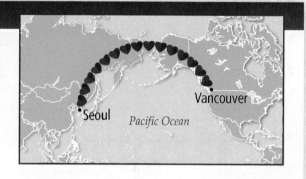

LIFESTYLES

An Ocean Apart

He lives in South Korea. She lives in Canada. But Lee Shinjeng and Park Sunmi **have been** married for four years. So why are they living apart? The couple has a "long-distance marriage." And they are not alone. Many couples around the world **have found** this arrangement to be a temporary solution in difficult economic[1] times.

When they **got** married, both Shinjeng and Sunmi **had** very good jobs. Then, two weeks after the wedding, Sunmi, a professional violinist, **lost** hers. After looking for a job for almost a year, she **got** an offer in Vancouver, Canada. Sunmi **didn't want** to leave Seoul, but she **felt** she **couldn't turn** it **down**. So she **moved**, and her husband, an engineer at a large company in Seoul, **didn't**. How **has** this **worked out**? It **hasn't been** easy. With airfares being so high, the couple **has not been** able to afford many trips to see each other. Last year they **saw** each other just three times (twice when Sunmi was performing abroad), and so far this year, they**'ve** only **seen** each other once.

The marriage, however, remains strong. How do they stay emotionally close when they are geographically so far away? Sunmi says, "Thanks to email, instant messages, text messages, and cell phones, we**'ve managed** to be in touch several times a day—not easy with the 17-hour time difference! At 6:00 A.M. I**'ve** just **prepared** breakfast and am getting ready to start my day, but for Shinjeng it's 11:00 P.M. and he**'s** already **had** dinner and is getting ready for bed." **Has** all this trouble **been** worth it? "Yes!" says the couple in unison[2]. "We both have jobs that we really like," says Shinjeng. "Besides, we really need the money."

"But," adds Sunmi, "we're really looking forward to the day we can be together again."

---

[1] *economic:* about business and money
[2] *in unison:* at the same time

After You Read

A | Vocabulary: *Circle the letter of the word or phrase closest in meaning to the word in* **blue.**

1. How do they like the new **arrangement**?

    a. choice

    b. way of doing something

    c. art show

2. Sometimes they think their problem has no **solution**.

    a. answer

    b. reason

    c. cause

3. They don't like living **apart**.

    a. in different places

    b. together

    c. in an apartment

4. She **managed** to get a new job.

    a. tried

    b. wanted

    c. was able

5. She couldn't **turn down** the offer.

    a. say no to

    b. say yes to

    c. think about

6. It's a **temporary** job.

    a. well-paying

    b. short-time

    c. long-distance

B | Comprehension: *Check (✓)* **True** *or* **False.** *Correct the false statements.*

	True	False
1. Shinjeng and Sunmi plan to get married.	☐	☐
2. They are now living together in South Korea.	☐	☐
3. Their jobs are very important to them.	☐	☐
4. They take a lot of trips together.	☐	☐
5. The couple has a close relationship.	☐	☐

PRESENT PERFECT AND SIMPLE PAST

Present Perfect	Simple Past
She **has been** here since 2008.	She **was** in South Korea in 2007.
They**'ve lived** here for 20 years.	They **lived** there for 10 years.
We**'ve spoken** once today.	We **spoke** twice yesterday.
He **hasn't flown** this month.	She **didn't fly** last month.
Has she **called** him today?	**Did** she **call** him yesterday?

GRAMMAR NOTES

1   现在完了形

Use the **present perfect** to talk about things that started in the past, <u>continue up to the present</u>, and may continue into the future.

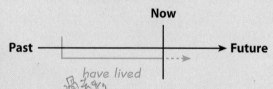

过去〜现在

Use the **simple past** to talk about things that happened in the past and have <u>no connection to the present</u>.

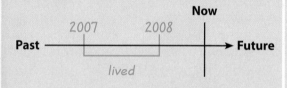

- They **have lived** apart *for the past three years*.
  (They started living apart three years ago and are still living apart.)

- They **lived** together *for one year*.
  (They lived together until 2008. They no longer live together.)

2   Use the **present perfect** to talk about things that happened at an <u>indefinite time</u> in the past.

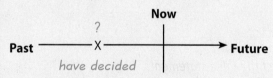

Use the **simple past** to talk about things that happened at a <u>specific time</u> in the past. The exact time is known and sometimes stated.

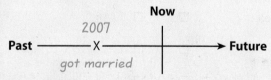

BE CAREFUL! Do <u>NOT use the present perfect</u> with a specific point in time. The only exception is with *since*.

- They **have decided** to live apart.
  (We don't know exactly when the decision was made, or the time of the decision is not important.)

- They **got married** *in 2007*.

- I **lived** in Seoul *in 2007*.
  NOT: ~~I've lived~~ in Seoul in 2007.
- I**'ve lived** in Seoul *since 2007*.

3

Use the **present perfect** to talk about things that have happened in a time period that is <u>not finished</u>, such as *today*, *this morning*, *this month*, *this year*.

Use the **simple past** to talk about things that happened in a time period that is <u>finished</u>, such as *yesterday*, *last month*, *last year*.

BE CAREFUL! Some time expressions such as **this morning**, **this month**, or **this year** can refer to an <u>unfinished or finished</u> time period. Use the present perfect if the time period is unfinished. Use the simple past if the time period is finished.

- He**'s called** three times *today*.
  (*Today isn't finished, and it's possible that he'll call again.*)

- He **called** three times *yesterday*.
  (*Yesterday is finished.*)

- It's 10:00 A.M. She**'s had** three cups of coffee *this morning*.
  (*The morning isn't finished.*)

- It's 1:00 P.M. She **had** three cups of coffee *this morning*.
  (*The morning is finished.*)

REFERENCE NOTES

For the **simple past**, see Unit 2.
For the **present perfect** with *since* and *for*, see Unit 8.
For the **present perfect** for **indefinite past**, see Unit 10.
For a list of **irregular verbs**, see Appendix 1 on page A-1.

STEP 3 FOCUSED PRACTICE

EXERCISE 1: Discover the Grammar

Read the information about Sunmi and Shinjeng. Then circle the letter of the sentence (a or b) that best describes the situation.

1. It's 2011. Sunmi moved to Vancouver in 2008. She still lives there.
   a. She lived in Vancouver for three years.
   b. She's lived in Vancouver for three years.

2. Last year Sunmi and Shinjeng enjoyed their vacation in Paris.
   a. They had a good time.
   b. They've had a good time.

3. Sunmi is telling her friend about her present job. Her friend asks,
   a. "How long were you there?"
   b. "How long have you been there?"

4. Shinjeng is telling Sunmi that the weather in Seoul has been too hot for the past five days.
   a. The weather is uncomfortable now.
   b. The weather is comfortable now.

(continued on next page)

5. Sunmi studied the piano for 10 years, but she doesn't play anymore.

    a. She has played the piano for 10 years.

    b. She played the piano for 10 years.

6. Shinjeng is an engineer. He is interviewing for an engineering job in Vancouver. He says,

    a. "I was an engineer for five years."

    b. "I've been an engineer for five years."

7. This year the couple has met once in Los Angeles. They'll meet in Paris.

    a. They've seen each other only once this year.

    b. They saw each other only once this year.

8. Sunmi's mother visited her once in Vancouver. When she got home, she wrote,

    a. "It was a great visit."

    b. "It has been a great visit."

9. Shinjeng and Sunmi haven't emailed each other this week.

    a. Shinjeng's computer was broken.

    b. Shinjeng's computer has been broken.

EXERCISE 2: Present Perfect or Simple Past

(Grammar Notes 1–3)

Complete the postings to an online board for people in long-distance relationships. Circle the correct verb forms.

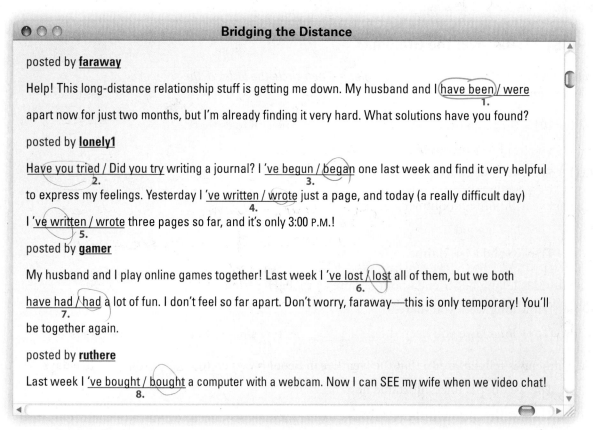

Bridging the Distance

posted by **faraway**

Help! This long-distance relationship stuff is getting me down. My husband and I have been / were
1.
apart now for just two months, but I'm already finding it very hard. What solutions have you found?

posted by **lonely1**

Have you tried / Did you try writing a journal? I 've begun / began one last week and find it very helpful
2.   3.
to express my feelings. Yesterday I 've written / wrote just a page, and today (a really difficult day)
                        4.
I 've written / wrote three pages so far, and it's only 3:00 P.M.!
     5.

posted by **gamer**

My husband and I play online games together! Last week I 've lost / lost all of them, but we both
                                        6.
have had / had a lot of fun. I don't feel so far apart. Don't worry, faraway—this is only temporary! You'll
7.
be together again.

posted by **ruthere**

Last week I 've bought / bought a computer with a webcam. Now I can SEE my wife when we video chat!
     8.

posted by **greenbay**

My wife and I have been / were married for 10 years, but last year I 've had to / had to relocate
9.   10.
because of my job. My wife couldn't come, so we have a phone date every night. It's true: Absence

makes the heart grow fonder.

posted by **singleman**

Forget about it! I 've learned / learned from experience. This long-distance stuff is for the birds!
11.
I 've tried / tried it a few years ago, and it 's been / was awful. It's true what they say: Out of sight,
12.   13.
out of mind.

posted by **lilypad**

Last night I 've called / called my husband while I was having dinner. Luckily, we're in the same time
14.
zone, so he was having dinner too. We 've stayed / stayed on the phone, and it 's felt / felt like we were
15.   16.
eating together! But, to be honest, we 've been / were apart for too long, and I'll be happy when we
17.
can REALLY be together again.

EXERCISE 3: Present Perfect or Simple Past Statements
(Grammar Notes 1–3)

*Complete the entry in Sunmi's journal. Use the present perfect or simple past form of the
verbs in parentheses.*

Thursday, September 28

   This is my first journal entry. Yesterday, I _____found_____ a website for couples
1. (find)
living apart. A few hours ago, someone _____posted_____ a suggestion. They said that
2. (post)
keeping a journal can really help. So, here goes!

   It's 8:00 P.M. It _____been_____ a hard day, and it's not over yet. I still have to
3. (be)
practice that new violin concerto. I _____ working on it a few days ago, but
4. (begin)
I _have learned_ only about half of it so far. And we begin rehearsing tomorrow. Work
5. (learn)
_____has bee_____ difficult lately. I _____worked_____ late every night this week.
6. (be)   7. (work)
I feel exhausted, and I _____ much sleep last night. And of course, I miss
8. (not get)
Shinjeng. Even though I _____ him last month, it seems like a long time ago.
9. (see)
This long-distance relationship is beginning to get me down. We _____ apart
10. (live)
for too long. Oh, there's the phone. I hope it's him!

EXERCISE 4: Present Perfect or Simple Past Contrast (Grammar Notes 1–2)

Shinjeng and Sunmi met in 2005. Since then, Shinjeng has changed. Write sentences describing how he has changed. Use the words in the lists.

In 2005	**Since then**
1. have / long hair	wear / his hair very short
2. wear / a beard and moustache	be / clean shaven
3. be / thin	gain / weight
4. wear / blue glasses	have / contact lenses
5. be / a student	become / an engineer
6. live / with his parents	buy / an apartment
7. be / single	get / married

1. _In 2005 he had long hair._

   Since then, he has worn his hair very short.

2. In 2005 he wore a beard and moustache

   Since then, he has been clean shaven

3. In 2005 he was thin

   Since then he has gained weight

4. In 2005 he wore blue glasses.

   Since then, he has contact lenses

5. In 2005 he was a student

   Since then he has become an engineer.

6. In 2005 he lived with his parents

   Since then, he has bought an apartment.

7. In 2005 he was single

   Since then he got married.

EXERCISE 5: *Wh-* Questions

(Grammar Notes 1–3)

Read the magazine article on page 146 again. Imagine that you wrote the article. You asked Shinjeng questions to get your information. What were they? Write questions. Use the words in parentheses. Choose between the present perfect and simple past.

1. (how long / be married)

   You: *How long have you been married?*

   Shinjeng: Four years.

2. (when / get married)

   You: _____

   Shinjeng: In 2007.

3. (when / your wife / lose her job)

   You: _____

   Shinjeng: Two weeks after our wedding.

4. (when / she / get a new job offer)

   You: _____

   Shinjeng: About a year later.

5. (how long / you / live apart)

   You: _____

   Shinjeng: For three years.

6. (how often / see each other last year)

   You: _____

   Shinjeng: Just three times.

7. (how often / see each other this year)

   You: _____

   Shinjeng: Only once so far.

8. (how / you / manage to stay close)

   You: _____

   Shinjeng: Through email, instant messages, text messages, and the cell phone.

EXERCISE 6: Editing

Read Sunmi's blog post. There are twelve mistakes in the use of the present perfect and the simple past. The first mistake is already corrected. Find and correct eleven more.

○ ○ ○   Long-Distance Relationships

I'm Not Alone!

Wednesday, September 7.20.11

    I've just finished reading an interesting article about Felicia Mabuza-Suttle. Actually, ~~I read~~ *I've read* several

articles about her this year. She's a well-known international businesswoman, and up until 2004 she ~~has been~~ a talk-show host in South Africa. Guess what! We have something in common! Although they now

live together, she and her husband ~~have had~~ a "long-distance marriage" for more than 15 years! She ~~lived~~

in Johannesburg, South Africa; he ~~lived~~ in Atlanta, Georgia. Just like me and my husband, that's a whole

ocean apart! They ~~have met~~ in the 1970s. In the first 10 years of their marriage,

they ~~have~~ lived in more than 10 cities. Then, in the early 1990s, she ~~has~~ returned to

South Africa to help her country. In 2003, she ~~has gone~~ back to the States, and she

and her husband lived there together since then. So, it looks like things have

worked out for them! That's encouraging! She still makes several trips back to

South Africa every year—this year she ~~was~~ there twice so far. Here's a photo of her:

    I love Vancouver and my job, but I really miss my husband. We ~~didn't~~ manage to see each other that

much since I left Seoul. I ~~have been~~ much happier when we ~~have~~ lived together. I know the situation is

temporary, but I hope, like Mabuza-Suttle and her husband, we can find a way to be together again soon.

Posted by Park Sunmi at 10:54 PM   0 Comments

STEP 4 COMMUNICATION PRACTICE

EXERCISE 7: Listening

A | *A student working for the school newspaper is interviewing two college professors. Read the list. Then listen to the interview. Listen again and check (✓) the items that are now true.*

The professors _____.

☑ **1.** are married

☐ **2.** live in different cities

☐ **3.** are at the same university

☐ **4.** live in Boston

☐ **5.** are in Madison

☐ **6.** have a house

B | *Read the statements. Listen again to the interview and circle the correct information.*

1. The couple has been married for two / (ten) years.

2. For a long time, they couldn't find a job / an apartment in the same city.

3. Now they work at the same company / university.

4. They have lived / lived in Boston for six years.

5. They have lived / lived in Madison for almost a year.

6. They have finally been able to buy a car / house.

7. They no longer need to drive / fly to see each other on weekends.

EXERCISE 8: Pronunciation

A | *Read and listen to the Pronunciation Note.*

Pronunciation Note

The **simple past** form and the **past participle** of **regular verbs** are the same. They both end in **-ed**.

EXAMPLE: visit   visit**ed**   have visit**ed**

The **-ed** ending has **three** different pronunciations:

EXAMPLE: /t/   /d/   /ɪd/ (this ending adds a syllable to the word: *visit-ed*)

hop**ed**   liv**ed**   visit**ed**

B | *Listen to the short conversations. Notice the pronunciation of the simple past forms and past participles. Check (✓) the correct pronunciation of the ending.*

	/t/	/d/	/ɪd/
1. A: Have you **visited** Dino this month?	☐	☐	☐
B: Yes, I **visited** him last weekend.	☐	☐	☐
2. A: Have you **tried** out your webcam?	☐	☐	☐
B: Yes, we **tried** it out last night.	☐	☐	☐
3. A: Have you ever **lived** abroad?	☐	☐	☐
B: I **lived** in Turkey for two years.	☐	☐	☐
4. A: Have you ever **wanted** to move?	☐	☐	☐
B: I **wanted** to move to Mexico right after college.	☐	☐	☐
5. A: Have you **finished** your homework?	☐	☐	☐
B: I **finished** hours ago.	☐	☐	☐
6. A: Has Sunmi **practiced** the violin today?	☐	☐	☐
B: She **practiced** for two hours this morning.	☐	☐	☐

C | *Listen again. Practice the conversations with a partner.*

EXERCISE 9: Compare and Contrast

Work in pairs. Look at Sunmi's records from last year and this year. It's now the end of August. Compare what she did last year with what she's done this year. You can use the verbs from the box.

attend	give	go	have	perform	practice	see	study

LAST YEAR					
January	**February**	**March**	**April**	**May**	**June**
• concert in N.Y. • L.A. – violin workshop	• L.A. – violin workshop • 1 seminar	• concert in N.Y.	• attend lecture	• 10 vacation days	• 2 concerts – Ottawa • 1 concert – Toronto
July	**August**	**September**	**October**	**November**	**December**
• Sue's wedding	• music conference – Seoul ♥ Shinjeng	• Mom's visit • attend lecture	• concert in Toronto	• <u>Modern Day</u> interview	• 10 vacation days ♥ Shinjeng

THIS YEAR					
January	**February**	**March**	**April**	**May**	**June**
• concert in San Francisco	• concert in N.Y. • attend lecture	• Nan's wedding	• concert in Toronto	• concert in Paris ♥ Shinjeng	• 5 vacation days • 1 seminar
July	**August**	**September**	**October**	**November**	**December**
• Barry's wedding	• music conference • attend lecture				

EXAMPLE: **A:** Last year she performed in New York twice.

B: So far this year she's only performed there once.

EXERCISE 10: Interview

A | *Many people have long-distance relationships with a friend or family member. Work with a partner. Interview each other about a long-distance relationship that your partner is in. Use the words to ask questions. Remember to use the present perfect and the simple past.*

- Who / have / this relationship with?
- How long / know / this person?
- Who / move away?
- Why / move away?
- When / last see each other?

- How often / be in contact / this year?
- How often / be in contact / last year?
- How / manage / to stay close?
- be / difficult?
- miss each other?

> **EXAMPLE:** **A:** Who have you had a long distance-relationship with?
> **B:** I've been in a long-distance relationship with my best friend for five years. She lives in Mexico.

B | *Continue the interview with questions of your own.*

EXERCISE 11: Writing

A | *Write two paragraphs about a long-distance relationship that you have or someone you know has. Use the present perfect and simple past.*

> **EXAMPLE:** My classmate's family lives more than halfway around the world from him, but he has managed to stay in close contact with them. Last month, he flew home to see them. They had a great time, and . . .

B | *Check your work. Use the Editing Checklist.*

Editing Checklist

Did you use the . . . ?

☐ present perfect for things that started in the past and continue up to the present

☐ simple past for things that happened in the past and have no connection to the present

☐ present perfect for things that happened at an indefinite time in the past

☐ simple past for things that happened at a specific time in the past

☐ present perfect for things that have happened in a time period that is not finished

☐ simple past for things that happened in a time period that is finished

Review

Check your answers on page UR-3.

Do you need to review anything?

A | Imagine you are interviewing Ken. Write questions with the words in parentheses. Use the present perfect or the simple past.

Ken moves to Vancouver		gets engineering degree	starts first professional job	marries Tina	loses job	moves to Singapore to work	Tina joins him in Singapore
2005	2006	2007	2008	2009	2010	2011	July, this year

1. _____
   (when / move to Vancouver)

2. _____
   (how long / be an engineer)

3. _____
   (work / in Vancouver for a long time)

4. _____
   (when / get married)

5. _____
   (how many years / live in Singapore)

6. _____
   (your wife / live in Singapore long)

B | Complete the paragraph with the present perfect or the simple past form of the verbs in parentheses.

I _____ in Singapore for a month, and it still feels special to see Ken every
      1. (be)

day. There's so much to do! We _____ five apartments last week, and so far this
                              2. (see)

evening we _____ three places off our list. Maybe we'll actually decide on one
           3. (cross)

before we fall asleep! I still _____ very much of the city, but this morning we
                              4. (not see)

_____ a boat tour. It _____ great! Ken _____ some
   5. (take)   **6. (be)**   **7. (learn)**

Chinese already, so he _____ lunch for us. I _____ much Chinese in
                       8. (order)   **9. (not learn)**

Vancouver, but I'll learn fast.

C | Find and correct five mistakes.

Tina and Ken lived apart for a while, but then Tina found a job in Singapore. She has moved

there last month. Here are some of their thoughts:

KEN: I'm so glad Tina is finally here. Last year has been the hardest time of my life.

TINA: Before I got here, I didn't understood Ken's experiences. But I was in culture shock since

   I arrive, and I'm learning a new job too! Now I know what a rough time Ken had at first.

UNIT 12

Present Perfect Progressive and Present Perfect

CLIMATE CHANGE

STEP 1 GRAMMAR IN CONTEXT

Before You Read

Look at the picture. Discuss the questions.

1. What is happening to the Earth?
2. Why does the Earth have a thermometer in it?
3. Look at the title. What is a hot topic?

Read

 Read the article about climate change.

Global Warming¹: A Hot Topic

By Dr. Jane Owen

The Earth's climate **has changed** many times. Warm oceans covered the Earth for millions of years. Then those oceans turned to ice for millions more. If the climate **has been changing** for five billion years, why is global warming such a hot topic today? What are people arguing about?

Almost everyone agrees that the Earth **has been getting** hotter. But not everyone agrees about the cause. Most climate experts think that human activities **have added** to global warming. The coal and oil we burn for energy **have been sending** more and more gases into the air around the Earth. The gases keep the heat in the atmosphere² and also cause air pollution. These experts believe humans can slow global warming.

Others say global warming is mostly the result of natural causes, such as changes in the sun. They don't believe that human activities can make things better or worse.

Human or natural, the effects of global warming **have been** powerful. Here are just two examples:

• In the Arctic,³ ice **has been melting** quickly. As a result, polar bears and other animals **have become** endangered species.⁴ Arctic towns and villages are also in danger as sea levels rise.

• In parts of Africa, rainfall **has decreased**. Water and food **have become** very scarce. Both people and animals **have been suffering** badly.

Does it really matter what causes global warming? Yes! If we **have been** part of the cause, then we can be part of the solution. Recently, people **have been developing** ways to use clean solar energy. In addition, they **have been designing** homes and cars that use less energy. Will it help? Maybe. Is it worth a try? You decide—it's your world too!

---

¹ *global warming:* the continuing increase in the Earth's temperatures (including air and oceans) since the 1950s
² *atmosphere:* the air that surrounds the Earth
³ *the Arctic:* the most northern part of the Earth
⁴ *endangered species:* a type of animal or plant that may not continue to exist

Present Perfect Progressive and Present Perfect **159**

After You Read

A | Vocabulary: *Match the words with their definitions.*

_____ **1. expert**   **a.** power that makes machines work

_____ **2. climate**   **b.** to create a drawing that shows how to build something

_____ **3. develop**   **c.** someone with special knowledge of a subject

_____ **4. energy**   **d.** the typical weather in an area

_____ **5. design**   **e.** something unhealthy in the air or water

_____ **6. pollution**   **f.** to work on a new idea or product to make it successful

B | Comprehension: *Circle the letter of the word or phrase that best completes each sentence.*

1. In the past, the Earth's climate was always _____.

     a. cooler

     b. hotter

     c. changing

2. Most experts think the Earth is now _____ than before.

     a. cooler

     b. hotter

     c. no different

3. Some people think that one cause of global warming is _____.

     a. humans

     b. polar bears

     c. ice

4. Other people think that our activities are making _____.

     a. the sun hotter

     b. the Earth cooler

     c. almost no difference

5. One idea for slowing global warming is for us to _____.

     a. protect endangered animals

     b. use clean energy

     c. move to the Arctic

PRESENT PERFECT PROGRESSIVE AND PRESENT PERFECT

Present Perfect Progressive

Statements				
Subject	Have (not)	Been	Base Form of Verb + -ing	(Since / For)
I You* We They	have (not)	been	working	(since 2009). (for years).
He She It	has (not)			

*You is both singular and plural.

Yes / No Questions				
Have	Subject	Been	Base Form of Verb + -ing	(Since / For)
Have	you	been	working	(since 2009)? (for years)?
Has	she			

Short Answers						
Affirmative			Negative			
Yes,	I / we	have.	No,	I / we	haven't.	
	she	has.		she	hasn't.	

Wh- Questions				
Wh- Word	Have	Subject	Been	Base Form of Verb + -ing
How long	have	you	been	working?
	has	she		

Present Perfect Progressive and Present Perfect

Present Perfect Progressive	Present Perfect
They **have been living** here for many years.	They **have lived** here for many years.
I**'ve been reading** this book since Monday.	I**'ve read** two books about solar energy.
Dr. Owen **has been writing** articles since 2000.	Dr. Owen **has written** many articles.
She**'s been working** in Kenya for a year.	She**'s worked** in many countries.

GRAMMAR NOTES

1

We often use the **present perfect progressive** to show that something is <u>unfinished</u>. It started in the past and is still continuing. The focus is on the <u>continuation</u> of the action.

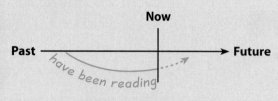

We often use the **present perfect** to show that something is <u>finished</u>. The focus is on the <u>result</u> of the action.

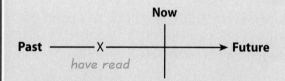

USAGE NOTE: We also use the **present perfect progressive** for <u>finished</u> actions that ended in the <u>very recent past</u>. You can often still see the results of the action.

BE CAREFUL! We usually do NOT use **non-action verbs**, such as *be*, *have*, and *know* in the **progressive**.

- I**'ve been reading** a book about solar energy.
  (I'm still reading it.)

- She**'s been writing** an article.
  (She's still writing it.)

- I**'ve read** a book about solar energy.
  (I finished the book.)

- She**'s written** an article.
  (She finished the article.)

- Look! The streets are wet. It**'s been raining**.
  (It stopped raining very recently.)
  NOT: It's ~~rained~~.

- She**'s had** the same job since 2000.
  NOT: She's ~~been having~~ the same job since 2000.

2

We often use the **present perfect progressive** to talk about *how long* something has been happening.

We often use the **present perfect** to talk about:
- *how much* someone has done
- *how many things* someone has done
- *how many times* someone has done something

- I**'ve been reading** books about wind energy *for two months*.

- I**'ve read** *a lot* about it.
- She**'s written** *three* articles.
- I**'ve read** that book *twice*.

3 Sometimes you can use either the **present perfect progressive** or the **present perfect**. The meaning is basically the same. This is especially true with verbs such as *live*, *study*, *teach*, and *work* with *for* or *since*.

- Jane is a climate expert. She**'s been studying** global warming *for* 10 years.

  OR

- Jane is a climate expert. She**'s studied** global warming *for* 10 years.
  (In both cases, she is still studying it.)

USAGE NOTES:

a. We often use the **present perfect progressive** to show that something is <u>temporary</u>.

- They**'ve been living** here *since* 1995, but they are moving next month.

b. We often use the **present perfect** to show that something is <u>permanent</u>.

- They**'ve lived** here *since* they were children. They've always lived here.

REFERENCE NOTES

For a list of **non-action verbs**, see Appendix 2 on page A-2.
For use of the **present perfect** with *since* and *for*, see Unit 8 on page 110.
For use of the **present perfect** for the **indefinite past**, see Unit 10 on page 134.

STEP 3 FOCUSED PRACTICE

EXERCISE 1: Discover the Grammar

Read the sentences. Then check (✓) the correct box to show if the action is finished or unfinished.

	Finished	Unfinished
1. Professor Owen has been reading a book about global warming.	☐	☑
2. She's read a book about global warming.	☐	☐
3. She's written a magazine article about air pollution.	☐	☐
4. She's been waiting for some supplies.	☐	☐
5. They've lived in Ontario since 2002.	☐	☐
6. They've been living in Ontario since 2002.	☐	☐
7. We've been developing plans with the leaders of many countries.	☐	☐
8. We've developed these plans with many leaders.	☐	☐
9. Look out the window, it's been raining.	☐	☐
10. Look. Someone has watered the plants.	☐	☐

EXERCISE 2: Present Perfect Progressive or Present Perfect (Grammar Notes 1–3)

Complete the statements. Circle the correct form of the verbs. In some cases, both forms are correct.

1. Professor Owen is working on two articles for the next issue of *Green Earth* magazine. She has written / (has been writing) these articles since Monday.

2. *Green Earth* magazine has published / has been publishing its third annual report on the environment. It is an excellent report.

3. Professor Owen has discussed / has been discussing global warming many times.

4. She has spoken / has been speaking at our school many times about climate change.

5. Congress has created / has been creating a new study group to find solutions to climate change. The group has already developed some interesting ideas.

6. The new group has a lot of work to do. Lately, the members have studied / have been studying the use of solar energy for homes. They're learning about pollution from buildings.

7. Professor Owen was late for a meeting with the members of Congress. When she arrived the chairperson said, "At last, you're here. We 've waited / 've been waiting for you."

8. Professor Owen has lived / has been living in Kenya for the last two years, but she will return to the United States in January.

9. She has worked / has been working with environmentalists in Kenya and Tanzania.

10. Kenyans have planted / have been planting 30 million trees since the 1970s.

EXERCISE 3: Present Perfect Progressive (Grammar Note 1–2)

A | *Look at the two pictures of Professor Jane Owen.*

B | Complete the sentences describing what has been happening in the pictures. Use the present perfect progressive form of the verbs in parentheses. Choose between affirmative and negative.

1. She _____'s been working_____ in her office.
   (work)

2. She _____ to climate experts.
   (talk)

3. She _____ a book.
   (write)

4. She _____ the newspaper.
   (read)

5. She _____ coffee.
   (drink)

6. She _____ tea.
   (drink)

7. She _____ her sandwich.
   (eat)

8. She _____ TV.
   (watch)

9. She _____ hard.
   (work)

10. It _____ all day.
    (rain)

EXERCISE 4: Statements

(Grammar Notes 1–3)

Complete Jane Owen's blog about the Solar Decathlon, a competition for the best solar houses (houses that get all their energy from the sun). Use the present perfect progressive or the present perfect form of the verbs in parentheses.

Greenmail

The house designed by the team from Spain.

A beautiful solar village _____has appeared_____ in the
1. (appear)
middle of Washington, D.C. Sorry, the houses aren't for sale. Universities in Canada, Europe, and the United States _____ them here for an
2. (bring)
international competition of solar houses. Universities _____ in this competition since 2004. For all the contests, talented students
3. (participate)
_____ the houses, and they _____ them as well! Over the years,
4. (design)   5. (build)
the homes _____ more energy efficient *and* more beautiful. This year, students
6. (get)
from Canada _____ energy solutions for very cold climates. The team from Spain
7. (find)
_____ a roof that moves to follow the sun. German designers _____
8. (design)   9. (develop)
a home that owners can control over the Internet. (If you forget to turn off the stove, you can do it online!) This year, 20 houses _____ the competition. I _____
10. (enter)   11. (visit)
the houses since I got here, and I _____ also _____ to many of
12. (talk)
the student designers. So far, what I hear most often is, "I could *totally* live in this house!" I agree.

Check next week's blog for the winners.

EXERCISE 5: Questions and Answers

(Grammar Note 2)

Professor Owen is interviewing one of the student designers at the Solar Decathlon. Use the words in parentheses to write Dr. Owen's questions. Use her notes to complete the student's answers. Choose between the present perfect progressive and the present perfect.

> started project two years ago
>
> cost—$250,000
>
> house tours—all afternoon
>
> visitors this week—so far about 30,000
>
> interest in solar energy—started 3 years ago
>
> total energy production today—more than the house needs!
>
> the team's third competition
>
> one prize for lighting design

1. (how long / your team / work / on this project)

    OWEN: *How long has your team been working on this project?*

    STUDENT: *We've been working on this project for two years.*

2. (how much money / the team / spend / on the house)

    OWEN: _____

    STUDENT: _____

3. (how long / you / lead tours / today)

    OWEN: _____

    STUDENT: _____

4. (how many people / visit / this week)

    OWEN: _____

    STUDENT: _____

5. (how long / you / be / interested in solar energy)

    OWEN: _____

    STUDENT: _____

6. (how much energy/ the house / produced today)

OWEN: _____

STUDENT: _____

7. (how many competitions / your team / entered)

OWEN: _____

STUDENT: _____

8. (how many prizes / your team / win)

OWEN: _____

STUDENT: _____

EXERCISE 6: Editing

Read the student's email. There are eight mistakes in the use of the present perfect progressive and the present perfect. The first mistake is already corrected. Find and correct seven more.

Hi guys,

written
Sorry I haven't ~~wrote~~ sooner. I haven't been having any free time since we arrived in Madrid for

the solar house competition. (Our house got here before us!) I'm really excited and also really

tired. Since we arrived, we've been lived on pizza and coffee. I haven't sleeping more than a few

hours since … well, I can't remember when. Our team has been working day and night for the

last two weeks, and today the house looks wonderful. I'm so proud—we've designed a home

that's beautiful AND reduces pollution. We're finally ready for the judges, so I've spent most of

the day looking at other teams' houses. I've been visiting 10 houses today. They are so interesting

and creative! For the last hour, I've just been hanging out in a café with some people from the

other teams. I've already been drinking three cups of coffee—it's delicious, but really strong!

We been practicing our Spanish with the Madrid team. I still don't understand too much, but our

teammate Eloy Ruiz is from Puerto Rico, and he's been helped me out a lot. Wish us luck and

check your email for photos of the house.

Katie

EXERCISE 7: Listening

A | *You're going to listen to five short conversations. Before you listen, look at the pairs of pictures. Each pair shows two different versions of a recent activity. Work with a partner and describe what has happened and what has been happening in each picture.*

1.

a.

b.

EXAMPLE: In this picture, they've planted one tree.   Here they've planted two.

2.

a.

b.

3.

a.

b.

4.

a.

b.

5.

a.

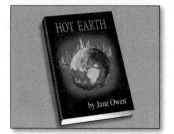
b.

B | *Listen to the conversations. Listen again and circle the letter of the picture that illustrates the activity the people are talking about.*

C | *Look at the pictures again. Complete the sentences with the correct verb form for the pictures you chose in Part B. Then listen again to the conversations and check your work.*

1. They _____*'ve planted*_____ some trees in front of the new library.

2. We _____ this pizza.

3. It _____ a lot since we spoke, but today we _____ on it.

4. We just sent the house, and I _____ all my stuff.

5. Well, for one thing, she _____ a book about global warming.

EXERCISE 8: Pronunciation

A | *Read and listen to the Pronunciation Note.*

> **Pronunciation Note**
>
> In **affirmative sentences**, we usually **stress** the **main verb**, but NOT the auxiliary verb such as *have* or *has*.
>
> **EXAMPLES:** I've been **working** in the library. I've **finished** my report.
>
> In **negative sentences**, we **stress** both the **main verb** and the **auxiliary verb**.
>
> **EXAMPLES:** He **hasn't** been **calling** lately. We **haven't seen** him very often either.

B | *Listen to the short conversations and complete the answers with the verb forms that you hear. Use contractions.*

1. **A:** *Avatar* is playing at the college theater.

   B: Oh, I _____ it.

2. **A:** I didn't see Emma yesterday.

   B: She _____ Mondays.

3. **A:** I just handed in my research paper. What about you?

   B: Well, I _____ it.

4. **A:** There's a new student in our class.

   B: I _____ about her.

5. **A:** Did you decide on a vacation?

   B: We _____ about it.

C | *Listen again and repeat the responses. Then practice the conversations with a partner.*

EXERCISE 9: Find Someone Who . . .

A | *Interview your classmates. Ask questions with the present perfect progressive or present perfect. Find someone who has recently . . .*

- been enjoying this weather
- been working hard
- changed jobs
- seen a good movie
- moved
- been learning a new hobby or skill
- talked to an interesting person
- taken a trip

> **EXAMPLE:** **A:** Hi Eloy. What have you been doing lately? Have you been enjoying this weather?
> **B:** Oh, yeah. I've been spending a lot of time outside.

B | *Then ask more questions. Keep the conversation going!*

> **EXAMPLE:** **A:** Oh, what have you been doing?
> **B:** I've been riding my bike in the park and going for long walks.

EXERCISE 10: Picture Discussion

Work with a partner. Discuss the picture. Think about the questions. Then compare your ideas with those of another pair of students.

- What does the picture show?
- What does it mean?
- Is it a strong message? Why or why not?
- Do you agree with the message?

> **EXAMPLE:** **A:** In this picture, there's a polar bear . . .
> **B:** I think it means . . .

EXERCISE 11: Discussion

Have a discussion in small groups. What changes have you made or experienced recently? Use the present perfect progressive and the present perfect to talk about them.

Have you changed . . . ?

- your opinions about society or the environment
- the way you look or dress
- the people you hang out with
- your hobbies or interests
- your goals
- *(other)* _____

> **EXAMPLE:** **A:** Recently, I've gotten more interested in the environment. I've been recycling paper and other things. I've also been walking or riding my bike more.
> **B:** I've just started a job, so I've been wearing business clothes instead of jeans.
> **C:** You look good, Ben! For myself, I've been . . .

EXERCISE 12: Writing

A | *Write an email to friends or family about what you've been doing lately. You can use ideas from Exercises 9 and 11.*

EXAMPLE: Hi Everyone,

A new semester has started, and I've been pretty busy lately. I've been working really hard on a science project. We're learning how to check the water quality in the lake. I've gotten more interested in the environment because of this project, so I've been riding my bicycle almost everywhere—it's great exercise *and* good for the environment. Oh, and I've just finished a very interesting book about global warming. Life hasn't been all work, though. I've also been hanging out with some interesting new friends . . .

B | *Check your work. Use the Editing Checklist.*

Editing Checklist

Did you use the . . . ?

☐ present perfect progressive for things that are unfinished

☐ present perfect for things that are finished

☐ present perfect progressive to talk about how long something has been happening

☐ present perfect to talk about how much, how many, and how many times something has happened

UNIT 12 Review

Check your answers on page UR-3.

Do you need to review anything?

A | Circle the correct words to complete the sentences.

1. Professor Ortiz <u>has written / has been writing</u> 10 articles on global warming.

2. Today she <u>has been choosing / has chosen</u> the title for a new article: *It's Melting!*

3. I <u>'ve read / 've been reading</u> one of her books. I'll give it to you when I'm finished.

4. My sister <u>has read / has been reading</u> it twice already.

5. I wanted to finish it today, but I <u>'ve had / 've been having</u> a headache all day.

6. I <u>'ve taken / 've been taking</u> two aspirins for it.

B | Complete the conversations with the present perfect progressive or present perfect form of the verbs in parentheses.

- **A:** How long _____ you _____ in Dallas?
  1. (live)

  B: I _____ here for more than 10 years. What about you?
  2. (be)

  A: I moved here last month. I _____ it a lot.
  3. (enjoy)

- **A:** _____ you _____ any books by Peter Robinson?
  4. (read)

  B: Yes. In fact, I'm reading one now.

  A: Really? How many books _____ he _____?
  5. (write)

- **A:** Why are your books all over the place? I _____ to clean up!
  6. (try)

  B: I _____ for my exam.
  7. (study)

- **A:** How long _____ Vilma _____ a student here?
  8. (be)

  B: This is her third semester.

  A: _____ she _____ her major?
  9. (choose)

C | Find and correct five mistakes.

1. Janet hasn't been writing a word since she sat down at her computer.

2. Since I've known Dan, he's been having five different jobs.

3. I've drunk coffee all morning. I think I've been having at least 10 cups!

4. We've been lived here for several years, but we're moving next month.

From Grammar to Writing

THE TOPIC SENTENCE AND PARAGRAPH UNITY

A **paragraph** is a group of sentences about **one main idea**. Writers often state the main idea in one sentence, called the **topic sentence**. The topic sentence is often near the beginning of the paragraph.

1

A | *Read the personal statement for a job application. First cross out any sentences that do not belong in the paragraph. (Later you will choose a topic sentence.)*

Please describe your work experience.

_____
(topic sentence)

While I was in high school, I worked as a server at Darby's during the summer and on weekends. ~~Summers here are very hot and humid.~~ I worked with many different kinds of customers, and I learned to be polite even with difficult people. They serve excellent food at Darby's. Because I was successful as a server, I received a promotion after one year. Since high school, I have been working for Steak Hut as the night manager. I have developed management skills because I supervise six employees. One of them is a good friend of mine. I have also learned to order supplies and to plan menus. Sometimes I am very tired after a night's work.

B | *Now choose one of the sentences as the topic sentence and write it as the first sentence of the paragraph.*

- I feel that a high school education is necessary for anyone looking for a job.

- My restaurant experience has prepared me for a position with your company.

- Eating at both Darby's and Steak Hut in Greenville is very enjoyable.

- I prefer planning menus to any other task in the restaurant business.

2 | *You can use a cluster diagram to develop and organize your ideas. Complete the cluster diagram for the paragraph in Exercise 1.*

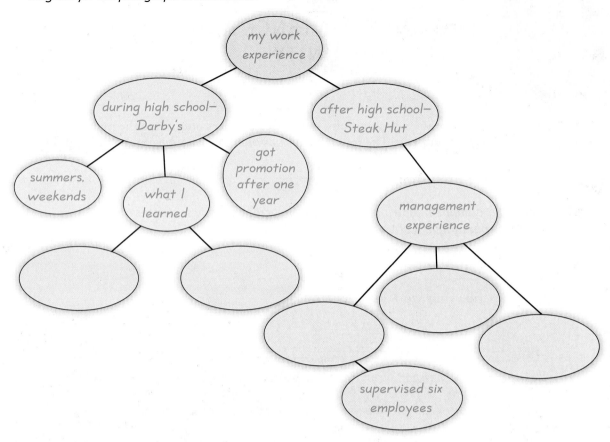

3 | *Before you write . . .*

1. On a separate piece of paper, make a cluster diagram for your accomplishments. Do not include a topic sentence.

2. Work with a small group. Look at each other's diagrams and develop a topic sentence for each one.

3. Ask and answer questions to develop more information about your accomplishments.

4 | *Write a personal statement about your accomplishments. Use your diagram as an outline.*

MODALS AND SIMILAR EXPRESSIONS

"Got your e-mail, thanks."

Ability: *Can, Could, Be able to*

DANCE

STEP 1 GRAMMAR IN CONTEXT

Before You Read

Look at the article. Discuss the questions.

1. What are the people in the photo doing?
2. Look at the title of the article. Guess the main point.

Read

Read the article about a dance company.

Born to Dance

by V. Gupta

"Who made up the rule that you **can** only **dance** on your two feet?" asks Mary Verdi-Fletcher, president and founding director[1] of Dancing Wheels. She is also one of its main dancers. Verdi-Fletcher was born with a medical condition called spina bifida.[2] As a result, by the age of 12, she **wasn't able to stand** or **walk**. But that didn't stop her from dancing. People said, "You **can't walk**; how **can** you **be** a dancer?" Verdi-Fletcher, however, *knew* it was possible to dance in a wheelchair because, as she says, "Dance is an emotion that comes from within."

When she entered her first dance competition, the audience was confused. "She's in a wheelchair. How **can** she **dance**?" But at the end of the performance, they stood and applauded. Not only **could** she **dance**, but she **could hypnotize**[3] an audience with her talent. When the artistic director of the Cleveland Ballet first saw her, he thought, "*That* is a dancer. . . . You **can't take** your eyes off her."

Dancing Wheels was the first integrated dance company in the United States with both "sit-down dancers" and "stand-up dancers." The group presents a new definition of dance. It also changes the perception of what people **can** or **cannot do**. "Through our dance," says Verdi-Fletcher, "we want to show that anything is possible and achievable. . . . People need to see they **can achieve** their dreams and aspirations—but not without a lot of hard work and dedication."

[1] *founding director:* someone who starts a company or business
[2] *spina bifida:* a condition in which the bones of the spine do not develop in a normal way
[3] *hypnotize:* to be so interesting that people cannot think about or look at anything else

A | **Vocabulary:** *Circle the letter of the word or phrase that best completes each sentence.*

1. A **confused** person _____.
   a. isn't able to dance
   b. doesn't understand something
   c. won't applaud

2. A person with **talent** _____.
   a. works hard
   b. talks a lot
   c. has natural ability

3. An **integrated** group is one with _____ members.
   a. a lot of
   b. different kinds of
   c. very interesting

4. Dancing Wheels changed my **perception** of dance. In other words, the group changed my _____ of dance.
   a. enjoyment
   b. ideas
   c. performance

5. If you have a lot of **aspirations**, you have _____.
   a. strong desires to do something
   b. serious health problems
   c. interests that you enjoy

6. Someone with **dedication** _____.
   a. dances very well
   b. often changes his or her mind
   c. continues to work hard

B | **Comprehension:** *Read each statement. Circle the correct information.*

1. Verdi-Fletcher shows that people <u>can</u> / <u>can't</u> dance in a wheelchair.

2. She is a <u>"sit-down"</u> / <u>"stand-up"</u> dancer.

3. She is also the director of <u>The Cleveland Ballet</u> / <u>Dancing Wheels</u>.

4. She believes that the ability to dance comes from <u>inside</u> / <u>outside</u> a person.

5. At the end of her first dance competition, the audience <u>loved</u> / <u>was confused by</u> her performance.

6. Verdi-Fletcher believes it is <u>easy</u> / <u>difficult</u> to reach your life goals.

ABILITY: *CAN* AND *COULD*

Statements			
Subject	***Can / Could (not)***	**Base Form of Verb**	
I You He She We You They	**can (not)**	**dance**	now.
	could (not)		last year.

Contractions		
cannot OR can not	=	**can't**
could not	=	**couldn't**

Yes / No Questions		
Can / Could	**Subject**	**Base Form of Verb**
Can	I you he she we you they	**dance?**
Could		

Short Answers					
Affirmative			**Negative**		
Yes,	you I he she you we they	**can.**	**No,**	you I he she you we they	**can't.**
		could.			**couldn't.**

Wh- Questions			
***Wh-* Word**	***Can / Could***	**Subject**	**Base Form of Verb**
How well	**can**	she	**dance?**
	could	you	

ABILITY: *BE ABLE TO*

Statements			
Subject	***Be***	***(Not) Able to***	**Base Form of Verb**
I	**am**		
You	**are**		
He She	**is**	**(not) able to**	**practice.**
We You They	**are**		

Yes / No Questions			
Be	**Subject**	**Able to**	**Base Form of Verb**
Is	she	able to	practice?
Are	you		

Short Answers			
Affirmative		**Negative**	
Yes,	she **is.**	No,	she **isn't.**
	I **am.**		I'm **not.**

Wh- Questions				
Wh- Word	**Be**	**Subject**	**Able to**	**Base Form of Verb**
When	**is**	she	able to	practice?
How often	**are**	you		

GRAMMAR NOTES

1 Use **can**, **could**, or a form of **be able to** to talk about natural or learned **ability**.

- She **can dance**, but she **can't sing**.
- We **could ride** bikes, but we **couldn't drive**.
- Soon, you**'ll be able to write** to me in English.

2 **Can** and **could** are **modals**. Like all modals:

- They are followed by the <u>base form</u> of a verb:
  modal + base form of verb

  - Mary **can dance**.
  - Not: Mary can ~~to~~ dance.

- They have the <u>same form for all subjects</u>. (They do NOT use -s for the third-person singular.)

  - I **can** dance, and she **can** dance too.
  - Not: She ~~cans~~ dance.

- They form the negative with *not*. (They do NOT use *do*.)

  - She **can't** sing.
  - Not: She ~~doesn't can~~ sing.

- They go before the subject in questions. (They do NOT use *do*.)

  - **Can** Antonio dance too?
  - Not: ~~Does~~ can Antonio dance too?

Be able to is an expression **similar to a modal**, but it isn't a real modal: it has <u>different forms</u> (*am, is, are; was, were; will be*).

  - **Was** she **able to dance** when she was young?
  - **Will** he **be able to learn** the tango by Monday?

(continued on next page)

(continued on next page)

can or sometimes _am/is/are able to_ for **present ability**.

- She **can speak** English, but she **can't speak** French.

a. _Can_ is much <u>more common</u> than _be able to_ in everyday speech about present ability.

MORE COMMON: **Can** you **speak** French?
LESS COMMON: **Are** you **able to speak** French?

b. We use _be able to_ when the ability to do something comes after a lot of <u>hard work</u>.

- French was difficult for me, but now I**'m able to have** a conversation because I spent a year studying in France.

4 Use _can_ or _will be able to_ for **future ability** when you are talking about <u>plans or arrangements</u>.

- I **can buy** the tickets _tomorrow_.
  OR
- I**'ll be able to buy** the tickets _tomorrow_.

BE CAREFUL! Use _will be able to_ (but NOT _can_) to talk about <u>things you learn</u>.

- When I finish this course, I**'ll be able to speak** French well.
  NOT: When I finish this course, I ~~can~~ speak French well.

5 Use _could_ or _was/were able to_ for **past ability**.

- **Could** he **dance** when he was a child?
  OR
- **Was** he **able to dance** when he was a child?

BE CAREFUL! Do NOT use _could_ in affirmative statements for a <u>single event</u> in the past. Use _was/were able to_.

- After a lot of hard work and dedication, they **were able to win** first prize in the _2002 dance competition_.
  NOT: . . . they ~~could~~ win first prize . . .

However, it is possible to use _couldn't_ for single past events.

- They **couldn't win** first prize in the _2003 dance competition_.

REFERENCE NOTES

Can and _could_ are also used for **permission** (see Unit 14) and for **requests** (see Unit 15).
Can't and _could_ are also used for **conclusions** (see Unit 32).
Could is also used for **future possibility** (see Unit 31).
For a list of **modals and their functions**, see Appendix 19 on page A-8.

EXERCISE 1: Discover the Grammar

Mary Verdi-Fletcher

1955	born in Ohio
1975	graduated from high school got job as keypunch operator
1978	learned to drive
1979	entered Dance Fever Competition
1980	began Dancing Wheels enrolled in Lakeland Community College, Ohio took course in public speaking
1980–1988	worked for Independent Living Center
1984	married Robert Fletcher
1989–1990	tour director for Cleveland Ballet
1990–present	founding director and dancer, Dancing Wheels teaches dance to people with and without disabilities
Some Awards	Invacare Award of Excellence in the Arts (1994) Governor's Award for Outreach (1998) Emmy Award for hosting TV series "Shortcuts to Happiness" (2007)
Other Interests	watching football and soccer games

Look at the information about Mary Verdi-Fletcher. Then check (✓) **True** *or* **False** *for each statement. Check* **?** *if there isn't enough information.*

	True	False	?
1. Verdi-Fletcher was able to get a job after high school.	☑	☐	☐
2. She can't drive a car.	☐	☑	☐
3. She couldn't participate in dance competitions.	☐	☑	☐
4. She can speak foreign languages.	☐	☐	☑
5. She was able to start a dance company.	☐	☐	☐
6. She couldn't finish college.	☐	☑	☐
7. She can probably speak well in front of large groups of people.	☑	☐	☐
8. She's able to help people with disabilities learn to dance.	☐	☐	☐
9. She can play the piano.	☑	☐	☐
10. She's so busy she can't have other interests.	☐	☐	☐

EXERCISE 2: Statements with *Can* and *Could*

(Grammar Notes 1–5)

Complete the paragraphs. Use **can, can't, could,** *or* **couldn't.**

1. For a long time, Jim and Marie _____couldn't_____ agree on a family sport. Jim loves tennis,
   a.

   and Marie takes lessons, but she still _____ play. Marie _____can_____
   b.   **c.**

   swim, but Jim hates the water. They recently took up dancing and discovered a new talent.

   Now, they _____can_____ do the swing *and* spend time together.
   d.

2. Stefan has made a lot of progress in English. Last semester he _____ order a
   a.

   meal in a restaurant or talk on the telephone. His friends helped him do everything. Now he

   _____can_____ speak English in a lot of situations.
   b.

3. Bill almost _____ make his class presentation last semester because he was
   a.

   so nervous. He _____ usually communicate well in small groups, but he still
   b.

   doesn't feel comfortable in big ones. He plans to take a course in public speaking. I'm sure

   that with his dedication he _____ improve quickly.
   c.

4. Last year I _____ dance at all, but when I met Stan, I signed up for a class
   a.

   right away. He _____ really dance, and I wanted to dance with him. Now I
   b.

   _____ do the basic steps. I _____ do the waltz yet, but we're
   c.   **d.**

   planning to waltz at our wedding next month.

EXERCISE 3: Statements and Questions with *Be able to*

(Grammar Notes 2–5)

Complete each conversation. Use the correct form of **be able to** *and the verb in parentheses.*
Choose between affirmative and negative.

1. **Austin:** I heard your sister wanted to take lessons. _____Was_____ she _____able to start_____ ?
   a. (start)

   Julia: Yes, she was. She started last month. She can do the fox-trot now, but even with

   lessons and a lot of practice, she still _____ the waltz.
   b. (do)

2. **Evan:** _____ you _____ Mrs. Suraikin at the studio yesterday?
   a. (find)

   Kayla: Yes. She says I _____ in the tango contest next month!
   b. (compete)

   Evan: Great! We all believe you have the talent to win too.

   Kayla: Thanks. Mrs. Suraikin really _____ my perceptions of my
   c. (change)

   abilities. Now I think I can too.

3. **EMMA:** _____ you _____ Russian as a child, Olga?

a. (speak)

   OLGA: Yes, I was. We spoke it at home, so I _____ _____ it fluently when I

b. (speak)

   was very young.

   EMMA: Do your children speak Russian too?

   OLGA: Unfortunately, no. We spoke French at home, so they _____ never

   _____ really fluent.

c. (become)

4. **JENNA:** I _____ _____ the waltz last weekend because I hurt my ankle.

a. (practice)

   COLE: That's too bad. _____ you _____ next week?

b. (practice)

EXERCISE 4: *Can, Could,* or *Be able to*

(Grammar Notes 3–5)

*Two friends are at a dance performance. Complete their conversations. Use **can, could,** or*
***be able to** and the correct verb from the box. You will use some of the verbs more than once.*
*Use **can** or **could** when possible. Choose between affirmative and negative.*

dance	do	get	lend	pay	pronounce	see

1. **NINA:** _____Can_____ you _____see_____ the stage OK?

a.

   LEÓN: Yes, I _am able to see_ it fine. What about you?

b.

   NINA: No. I _can't see_ it very well at all. The man in front of me is too tall.

c.

   LEÓN: Change seats with me. You _____ it better then.

d.

2. **LEÓN:** Wow! This performance is great. This group _____ _____ sure

   _____ beautifully!

a.

   NINA: I know. I'm glad I _could get_ tickets. Last year I _couldn't get_ any.

b.   c.

   They were sold out every time I tried.

   LEÓN: What's their name?

   NINA: I'll spell it for you. It's P-i-l-o-b-o-l-u-s. I'm not sure I _can pronounce_ it correctly!

d.

3. **LEÓN:** It's intermission. Would you like to get something to eat?

   NINA: Oh, I'm afraid I _____ anything. I left my wallet at home by mistake.

a.

   LEÓN: No problem. I _____ you some money.

b.

   NINA: Thanks. I _____ you back tomorrow.

c.

(continued on next page)

4. NINA: This performance makes *me* want to dance. _____ you

_____ the tango?

a.

LEÓN: Not yet! But I'm taking dance lessons, so I _____ it soon!

b.

EXERCISE 5: Editing

Read the review of a dance performance. There are ten mistakes in the use of **can, could,** *and* **be able to.** *The first mistake is already corrected. Find and correct nine more.*

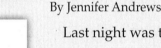

The Dance Desk

How They Can Do That?

They Can They

By Jennifer Andrews

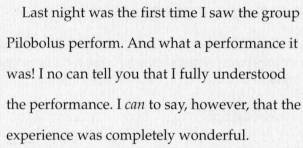

Piliobolus Dance Theatre, photo by John Kane

Last night was the first time I saw the group Pilobolus perform. And what a performance it was! I no can tell you that I fully understood the performance. I *can* to say, however, that the experience was completely wonderful.

Pilobolus is a very unusual group. The performers have no background in dance. When they began, they thought, "Maybe we can't dancing, so why try?" So they just made interesting shapes with their bodies. Well, this group certainly cans dance, and they are able to do much more. The six dancers in the group are athletic, artistic, and very talented. They are able do amazing things with their bodies. In many dances, they move together as a single unit.

My theater companion and I had great seats. We could saw the entire stage (not always true in some theaters). The sound system, though, had a few problems, and we didn't able to hear the music clearly all the time.

Some people in the audience asked: "Is it dance or is it gymnastics?" You can decide for yourself. Many people weren't able to got tickets for the first two performances of this series, but you can still buy tickets for next week. This is the type of dance performance everyone can enjoys.

Highly recommended.

EXERCISE 6: Listening

A | *Karl is interviewing for the job of office manager at Carmen's Dance Studio. What does the interviewer say? Read the statements. Then listen to the conversation. Listen again and circle the correct information.*

1. The office is very (busy)/ quiet.

2. Many of the students are foreign / talented.

3. She asks Karl about his computer / math skills.

4. They're thinking of designing a monthly newsletter / new studio.

5. Many of the students take private language / dance lessons.

6. She may need Karl to drive / dance sometimes.

B | *Listen again to the conversation and check (✓) all the things that Karl can do now.*

☑ **1.** answer the phones   ☐ **5.** design a monthly newsletter

☐ **2.** speak another language   ☐ **6.** schedule appointments

☐ **3.** do spreadsheets   ☐ **7.** drive

☐ **4.** type 50 words per minute   ☐ **8.** dance

EXERCISE 7: Pronunciation

A | *Read and listen to the Pronunciation Note.*

> **Pronunciation Note**
>
> In statements:
>
> • *can* is **NOT stressed**, and it's pronounced /kən/
>
> • *can't* is **stressed**, and it's pronounced /kænt/
>
> EXAMPLES: I **can** dance, but I **can't** sing.
>
> She **can** speak French, but she **can't** speak Spanish.

B | *Listen to the statements. Circle the words you hear.*

1. I can / can't dance.

2. They can / can't speak Chinese.

3. He can / can't fly a plane.

4. We can / can't understand you.

5. She can / can't swim, but she can / can't dive.

6. He can / can't drive.

C | *Listen again and repeat the statements.*

EXERCISE 8: Information Gap: Can they do the tango?

Students at Carmen's Dance Studio are preparing for a dance recital in June. It is now the end of April. Can students do all the dances featured in the recital at this time? Work in pairs (A and B). **Student A,** *follow the instructions on this page.* **Student B,** *turn to page 188 and follow the instructions there.*

1. Ask your partner for the information you need to complete the schedule below.

   EXAMPLE: **A:** Can the students do the Argentine tango?
   B: No, they can't. But they'll be able to do it by the end of May.

2. Your schedule has the information your partner needs to complete his or her schedule. Answer your partner's questions.

   EXAMPLE: **B:** Can they do the cha-cha?
   A: Yes, they can. They could do it in March.

CARMEN'S DANCE STUDIO
Schedule of Dance Classes

Dances	March	April	May
Argentine tango			✔
Cha-cha	✔		
Fox-trot			
Hip-hop		✔	
Hustle			✔
Mambo			
Merengue	✔		
Salsa			✔
Swing			
Tango		✔	
Waltz			

When you are finished, compare schedules. Are they the same?

EXERCISE 9: Ask and Answer

A | *Work in small groups. Imagine you are planning a class presentation. Look at the list of skills and find someone who can do each one. Add to the list.*

- do research online
- create a website
- make charts and graphs
- do a spreadsheet
- photocopy handouts
- take photographs

- videotape the presentation
- interview people
- give a PowerPoint presentation
- _____
- _____
- _____

> **EXAMPLE:**   **A:** Can you do research online?
> **B:** Sure. But I can't create a website yet.
> **C:** I can do that. I just learned how.

B | *Report back to the class.*

> **EXAMPLE:**   **A:** Theo and Alicia can do research online, but . . .

EXERCISE 10: Writing

A | *Write one or two paragraphs about a person who is or was successful in spite of some kind of disability or problem. Choose someone you know or a famous person.*

> **EXAMPLE:**   My aunt had a difficult childhood. She grew up in a poor family. When she was 16, she quit school because she had to stay home and help her mother take care of her younger brothers and sisters. She made all the meals, and by the time she was 18, she could cook and bake very well. She even won a local baking contest. People began ordering cakes from her, and before long she was able to save enough money to start her own small business . . .

B | *Check your work. Use the Editing Checklist.*

Editing Checklist

Did you use . . . ?
- [ ] *can* or *can't* for present ability
- [ ] *be able to* for present ability when this ability comes after hard work
- [ ] *can* or *will be able to* for future ability when you are talking about plans or arrangements
- [ ] *could* or *was/were able to* for past ability
- [ ] the base form of the verb after *can*, *could* or *be able to*

---

1. The schedule below has the information your partner needs to complete his or her schedule. Answer your partner's questions.

   EXAMPLE: **A:** Can the students do the Argentine tango?
   B: No, they can't. But they'll be able to do it by the end of May.

2. Ask your partner for the information you need to complete your schedule.

   EXAMPLE: **B:** Can they do the cha-cha?
   A: Yes, they can. They could do it in March.

CARMEN'S DANCE STUDIO
Schedule of Dance Classes

Dances	March	April	May
Argentine tango			✓
Cha-cha	✓		
Fox-trot		✓	
Hip-hop			
Hustle			
Mambo		✓	
Merengue			
Salsa			
Swing	✓		
Tango			
Waltz	✓		

When you are finished, compare schedules. Are they the same?

A | Circle the letter of the correct answer to complete each sentence.

1. How many languages can you _____?

   a. speak   **b.** speaks   **c.** speaking

2. After a lot of practice, Steve _____ win his first tennis game.

   a. could   **b.** can   **c.** was able to

3. Keep trying and you _____ do the tango in a just few weeks.

   a. 're able to   **b.** 'll be able to   **c.** can

4. Sorry, I _____ pick up the concert tickets tomorrow.

   a. couldn't   **b.** not able to   **c.** can't

5. They worked hard—that's why they _____ win first prize last night.

   a. able to   **b.** were able to   **c.** can

B | Complete the paragraph with **can**, **could**, or **be able to** and the verbs in parentheses. Use **can** or **could** when possible. Choose between affirmative and negative.

As a boy, Carlos Acosta _____ out of trouble, but he sure _____
                          1. (stay)   **2. (kick)**
a soccer ball. Break dancing (a type of street dancing) was his other hobby. His father

_____ Carlos off the streets, so he put him in ballet school. Carlos had problems
     3. (keep)
at first, but by age 16, he _____ first place in an international dance competition.
                              4. (win)
Today, Acosta _____ still _____ beautifully. He _____
                                          5. (dance)   **6. (jump)**
higher than any other dancer, and he _____ in the air longer too. But, now in
                                          7. (stay)
his 30s, he _____ much longer. In a few years, he'll return to Cuba. There he
              8. (perform)
_____ his own dance company, and he and his wife _____ a family.
     9. (start)   **10. (raise)**

C | Find and correct five mistakes.

A: I can't to see the stage. The man in front of me is very tall.

B: Let's change seats. You be able to see from this seat.

A: Thanks. I don't want to miss anything. I no can believe what a great dancer Acosta is.

B: I know. He was so good as a kid that he could win a break dancing contest before he was nine.

A: I didn't know he was a street dancer! Well, I'm glad you were abled to get tickets.

Permission: *Can, Could, May, Do you mind if*
ROOMMATES

STEP 1 GRAMMAR IN CONTEXT

Before You Read

Look at the cartoons. Discuss the questions.

1. Where are these people?
2. What is their relationship?
3. What do two of the people want?
4. How do the others feel about it?

Read

Read the article about getting along with a roommate.

ALWAYS ASK FIRST

Oh, you're awake! **Can I wear** your new jacket today?

Could my friend **stay** here for a few weeks?

Heather immediately liked Tara, her neat, non-smoking college roommate. Their first week together was great. But the second week, the cookies from Heather's mom disappeared. Tara didn't ask Heather, "**Could I have** one?" She just assumed it was all right. Tara's friends always helped themselves to[1] food without asking permission. The third week, Tara looked annoyed whenever Heather's friends stopped by to visit. Heather never asked Tara "Hey, **do you mind if** they **hang out** here for a while?" At home, Heather's friends were always welcome. By October, Heather and Tara weren't speaking to each other. Luckily, their dorm counselor was able to help them fix their relationship with three simple rules.

1. Always ask permission before you touch your roommate's stuff. Say: "My computer isn't working. **Could I use** yours for a few hours?"
2. Establish times when it's OK to have visitors. If it's not "visiting hours," ask your roommate's permission: "**Can** Luis and Ming-Hwa **work** here tonight? We're doing a presentation in class tomorrow."
3. Try to solve problems. Say: "Your music is too loud for me, but you **can borrow** my headphones."

Follow these guidelines, and who knows? You may gain a happier roommate *and* a good friend.

---

[1] **help yourself to something:** to take something you want without permission

After You Read

A | Vocabulary: *Circle the letter of the word or phrase that best completes each sentence.*

1. Ahmed is **annoyed** at his roommate. He is _____ him.
   a. a little angry at
   b. very pleased with
   c. surprised by

2. I have no **guidelines** for this report. Could you give me some _____?
   a. paper
   b. instructions
   c. time

3. Marcia is very **neat**. Her room is always _____.
   a. full of friends
   b. bright
   c. organized

4. I just **assumed** it was OK to eat the cookies because you _____.
   a. told me it was OK
   b. usually don't mind
   c. hid them in your closet

5. We **established** those rules. That means we both _____ to follow them.
   a. agreed
   b. tried
   c. refused

6. For his **presentation**, Raoul _____ about getting along with roommates.
   a. showed a video to his class
   b. talked to his dorm counselor
   c. emailed his best friend

B | Comprehension: *Read each question. Check (✓) all the correct answers.*

Who...?	Heather	Tara	Counselor
1. took the cookies without permission	☐	☐	☐
2. had a lot of visitors without asking first	☐	☐	☐
3. was annoyed	☐	☐	☐
4. helped establish some guidelines	☐	☐	☐

PERMISSION: *CAN, COULD, MAY, DO YOU MIND IF*

Yes /No Questions: *Can / Could / May*

Can / Could / May*	Subject	Base Form of Verb	
Can Could May	I he she we they	stay	here?

Short Answers

Affirmative	Negative
Certainly. Of course. Sure. No problem.	Sorry, but . . .

Can, *could*, and *may* are modals. Modals have only one form. They do not have -*s* in the third-person singular.

Wh- Questions: *Can / Could / May*

Wh-Word	Can / Could / May	Subject	Base Form of Verb
When	can could may	I he she we they	call?

Statements: *Can / May*

Subject	Can / May (not)	Base Form of Verb	
You He She	can (not) may (not)	stay	here.

Contractions*

cannot OR can not	=	can't

*There is no contraction for ***may not***.

Questions: *Do you mind if*

Do you mind if	Subject	Verb	
Do you mind if	I we they	stay	here?
	he she it	stays	

Short Answers

Affirmative	Negative
Not at all. **No**, I **don't**. Go right ahead.	Sorry, but . . .

GRAMMAR NOTES

1 Use the modals *can*, *could*, and *may* to ask **permission**.

- **Can** I **borrow** your book?   LESS FORMAL

a. Notice that when you use *could* for permission, it is <u>not the past</u>.

- **Could** he **come** tomorrow?

b. *May* is much <u>more formal and polite</u> than *can* and *could*. We sometimes use it when we are speaking to a person in authority (for example, a teacher, police officer, doctor, librarian, counselor, etc.).

- **May** we **leave**, Professor Lee?
  (student speaking to teacher)   MORE FORMAL

c. We often say *please* when we ask permission. Notice the word order.

- **Could** I **ask** a question, *please*? OR
- **Could** I *please ask* a question?

2 Use the expression *Do you mind if* to ask **permission** when an action may <u>annoy or inconvenience</u> someone.

A: **Do you mind if I clean up** later?
B: Yes, actually, I do. I hate to see a mess in the kitchen.

BE CAREFUL! Do NOT use *please* with *Do you mind if*.

Nᴏᴛ: Do you mind ~~please~~ if I ask a question?

3 There are several **ways to answer** when someone asks permission.

a. We usually use <u>informal expressions</u> instead of modals in answers.

A: **Could** I close the window?
B: *Sure*. OR *Of course*. OR *Go ahead*.

b. When we use a <u>modal</u> in an answer, we almost always use *can*. We do NOT use *could*, and we rarely use *may* in short answers.

A: **Could** I borrow this pencil?
B: *Yes*, of course you **can**.
     Nᴏᴛ: Yes, of course you ~~could~~.

A: **May** I see your notes?
B: *Sure* you **can**. Rᴀʀᴇ: *Yes*, you **may**.

BE CAREFUL! When the response to a question with *Do you mind if* is *Not at all*, or *No, I don't*, we're really saying: *It's OK*. We're giving permission.

A: **Do you mind if** Ian comes over tonight?
B: *Not at all*. OR *No, I don't*.
     (It's OK for Ian to come over tonight.)

c. When we **refuse permission**, we usually <u>apologize</u> and give an <u>explanation</u>.

A: **Can** I please use your computer?
B: *I'm sorry*, but I need it today.

REFERENCE NOTES

For general information on **modals**, see Unit 13, Grammar Note 2, on page 179.
Can and *could* are also used for **ability** (see Unit 13) and for **requests** (see Unit 15).
Could and *may* are also used for **future possibility** (see Unit 31) and for **conclusions** (see Unit 32).
For a list of **modals and their functions**, see Appendix 19 on page A-8.

EXERCISE 1: Discover the Grammar

Read the quiz. Underline all the modals and expressions for permission. Then if you'd like to, you can take the quiz. The answers are below.

Are You a Good Roommate?

Take this short quiz and find out.

1. You want to use your roommate's computer.
You say:
○ **a.** I may use your computer tonight.
○ **b.** Can I use your computer tonight?
○ **c.** I'm using your computer tonight.

2. You don't have any food in the house.
You say:
○ **a.** Can you make dinner for me?
○ **b.** I don't mind eating some of your food.
○ **c.** Do you mind if I have some of your food?

3. You may not have time to wash the dishes tonight.
You say:
○ **a.** Could you wash the dishes?
○ **b.** I can't wash the dishes.
○ **c.** Can I wash the dishes tomorrow?

4. Your roommate asks you: "Could my best friend stay overnight?"
You answer:
○ **a.** Can she stay in a hotel instead?
○ **b.** Sure she can!
○ **c.** I'm sure she could, but I don't want her to!

5. You can find nothing to wear to the party next Friday.
You say:
○ **a.** Could I borrow your new sweater?
○ **b.** I may borrow your new sweater.
○ **c.** You could lend me your new sweater.

6. You want to hang your favorite poster in your dorm room.
You say:
○ **a.** Could I hang my poster here?
○ **b.** Maybe you could hang my poster here.
○ **c.** I assume I can hang my poster here.

ANSWERS: 1. b, 2. c, 3. c, 4. b, 5. a, 6. a

EXERCISE 2: Questions and Answers

(Grammar Notes 1–3)

Look at the signs. Complete each conversation. Use the words in parentheses and the correct pronouns. Write appropriate short answers. There can be more than one correct short answer.

1. **PIERRE:** _Do you mind if_ I _____eat_____ my lunch
   a. (do you mind if / eat)

   here while I get on the Internet? I'll be neat.

   ASSISTANT: _____Sorry_____. Please look at the sign.
   b.

   > No Food or Drink
   > **Computer Lab**

2. **SÉBASTIEN:** Those guys next door are making a lot of noise!

   _____Can_____ they _____do_____ that?
   a. (can / do)

   NATHANIEL: _Yes, they can_. According to the guidelines, it's
   b.

   OK to play music now. It's 8:00 A.M.

   SÉBASTIEN: Well, _____Can_____ I _____borrow_____ your
   c. (can / borrow)

   earplugs? I have to prepare for my English presentation.

   > **Quiet Hours**
   > 11:00 p.m. - 7:00 a.m.
   > Sunday - Saturday

3. **CARMEN:** _____May_____ we _____ride_____ our bikes
   a. (may / ride)

   on this path?

   GUARD: _Yes, you can_.
   b.

4. **DONOVAN:** _____Could_____ I _____bring_____ my dog next
   a. (could / bring)

   semester? My roommate doesn't mind.

   COUNSELOR: _No, you can't_. But some of the other dorms
   b.

   allow pets. _I'm sorry_.

   > No Dogs
   > **Kent Hall**

5. **GABRIELLE:** _____May_____ I _____use_____ my cell
   a. (may / use)

   phone in here?

   LIBRARIAN: _____. People get really annoyed by cell
   b.

   phone conversations.

   > No Cell Phones

EXERCISE 3: Questions and Answers

(Grammar Notes 1–3)

Heather and her roommate Tara are planning a party in Kent Hall. Use the words in parentheses to ask for permission. Answer the questions.

1. Tara's friend Troy is in town. She wants him to come to the party.

   TARA: _Do you mind if Troy comes to the party?_
   _____
   (do you mind if)

   HEATHER: _Not at all._ _____ I'd love to meet him.

2. Heather wants to borrow her roommate's black sweater.

   HEATHER: I have nothing to wear. _Can I borrow your sweater?_
   _____
   (can)

   TARA: _I'm sorry, you can't._ _____ I'm planning to wear it myself!

3. Tara's sister is coming from out of town. Tara wants her to stay in their room.

   TARA: _Do you mind if my sister stays in this room?_
   _____
   (do you mind if)

   HEATHER: _Sure, you can, no, I_ _____ She can sleep on the couch.

4. Heather and Tara would like to have the party in the dormitory lounge. Heather asks her dormitory counselor for permission.

   HEATHER: _May we have the party in the dormitory lounge?_
   _____
   (may)

   COUNSELOR: _I'm sorry, you can't._ _____ It's available next Friday. We just have to establish some guidelines.

5. Heather and Tara would like to hang decorations from the ceiling of the lounge.

   HEATHER: _Could we hang decorations from the ceiling of the lounge?_
   _____
   (could)

   COUNSELOR: _____ Fire regulations won't allow it.

6. Heather and Tara want the party to go until midnight.

   HEATHER: _____
   (could)

   COUNSELOR: _____ Quiet hours start at 11:00 on Friday.

7. Tara wants to play some of her friend Erica's CDs at the party.

   TARA: _____
   (could)

   ERICA: _____ Which ones should I bring?

8. It's Friday night. A student wants to study in the lounge.

   STUDENT: _____
   (can)

   HEATHER: _____ We're having a party. Want to join us?

EXERCISE 4: Editing

Read Emil's English test. There are seven mistakes in the use of **can, could, may,** *and* **do you mind if**. *The first mistake is already corrected. Find and correct six more.*

Class: English 102   **Name:** Emil Kuhn

Directions: These conversations take place on a train. Find and correct the mistakes.

1. **A:** May we board the train now?
                           can't
   B: Sorry, you ~~couldn't~~ board until 12:30.

2. **A:** Can he ~~comes~~ on the train with me?

   B: Sorry. Only passengers can board.

3. **A:** Do you mind if ~~I'm sitting~~ here?

   B: ~~No,~~ I don't. My friend is sitting here.

4. **A:** Could I ~~looked~~ at your newspaper?

   B: Yes, of course you ~~could.~~

5. **A:** Do you mind if my son ~~play~~ his computer game?

   B: No, not at all. It won't disturb me.

   A: Thanks.

STEP 4 COMMUNICATION PRACTICE

EXERCISE 5: Listening

A | *Read the list. Then listen to the short conversations. Who's speaking? Listen again and write the letter of the people next to the number of each conversation.*

Conversation	People
_d_ 1.	**a.** roommate and roommate
____ 2.	**b.** child and parent
____ 3.	**c.** travel agent and customer
____ 4.	**d.** driver and police officer
____ 5.	**e.** boyfriend and girlfriend's mother
____ 6.	**f.** employee and employer
____ 7.	**g.** student and teacher

B | *Listen again to the conversations and decide if permission was given or refused. Check (✓) the correct column.*

Conversation	Permission Given	Permission Refused
1.	✓	☐
2.	☐	☐
3.	☐	☐
4.	☐	☐
5.	☐	☐
6.	☐	☐
7.	☐	☐

EXERCISE 6: Pronunciation

A | *Read and listen to the Pronunciation Note.*

Pronunciation Note

In **informal conversation**, we often **link** the modals **can**, **could**, and **may** with the pronouns *I* and *he* in questions:

can I	→	"cani"	**can he**	→	"can'e" (drop the *h* in *he*)
could I	→	"couldi"	**could he**	→	"could'e" (drop the *h* in *he*)
may I	→	"mayi"			

EXAMPLES: **Can I** open the window? → "**Cani** open the window?"
    Could he have a cookie? → "**Could'e** have a cookie?"

We do **NOT link** these modals with *you, she, we,* or *they.*

B | *Listen to the questions. Circle the word you hear.*

1. Can <u>he / she</u> come with us?

2. <u>Could / Can</u> I ask a question?

3. Can <u>he / she</u> sit over there?

4. May <u>she / we</u> call you tonight?

5. Could <u>he / she</u> get a ride with you?

C | *Listen again and repeat the questions.*

EXERCISE 7: Problem Solving

Work in small groups. Read the situations and decide what to say. Think of as many things to say as possible.

1. You have a small apartment. Two of your friends are coming to visit your town for a week, and they want to stay with you. What can you say to your roommate?

   EXAMPLES: Do you mind if Anton and Eva stay here for a week?
   Could Anton practice his guitar in the evening?
   Can Eva keep her bike in the hall?

2. You're visiting some good friends. The weather is very cold, but they don't seem to mind. Their windows are open and the heat is off. You're freezing.

3. You're at a concert with some friends. You like the performer very much. You have your camcorder and your camera with you. Sometimes this performer talks to fans and signs programs after the concert.

4. You have formed a study group with some classmates. You want to use a classroom on Thursday evenings to study. You would like to use one of your school's video cams to practice a presentation. Some of your classmates come directly from work. They would like to eat their dinner in the classroom. What can you say to your teacher?

EXERCISE 8: Role Play: *Could I . . . ?*

Work with a partner. Read the situations. Take turns being Student A and Student B.

Student A

1. You were absent from class yesterday. Student B, your classmate, always takes good notes.

   EXAMPLE: **A:** Can I copy your notes from class yesterday?
   B: Sure. Here they are.
   A: Could I call you tonight if I have questions?
   B: Of course.

2. You're at work. You have a terrible headache. Student B is your boss.

3. You're a teenager. You and your friend want to travel to another city to see a concert. You want to borrow your mother's (Student B's) car. Your friend has a license and wants to drive.

4. Student B has invited you to a small party. At the last minute, your two cousins show up. They have nothing to do the night of the party.

Student B

1. Student A is in your class. You're always willing to help your classmates.

2. Student A is your employee. You have a lot of work for Student A to do today.

3. Student A is your son / daughter. You like this friend, and you have no objection to lending him or her the car. However, you want the friend to be careful.

4. Your party is a small party for a few of your close friends. It's also at a restaurant, and you have already arranged for a certain number of people to attend.

EXERCISE 9: Writing

A | *Write two short notes asking permission. Choose situations from Exercise 8 or use situations of your own. Then exchange notes with two classmates. Write responses to your classmates' notes.*

EXAMPLES:

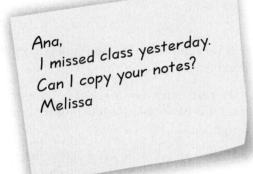

Ana,
I missed class yesterday.
Can I copy your notes?
Melissa

Sorry, Melissa, but
I missed class too!
Ana

B | *Check your work. Use the Editing Checklist.*

Editing Checklist

Did you . . . ?
☐ use the base form of the verb after **can**, **could**, and **may**
☐ use **can** and **may** (not *could*) in your answers
☐ apologize and give an explanation if you refused permission

Check your answers on page UR-4.

Do you need to review anything?

A | *Circle the correct words to complete the questions.*

1. Can my brother <u>come</u> / comes to class with me?

2. <u>Could</u> / Do you mind if I call you at home?

3. Could I <u>borrow</u> / borrowed a pen?

4. Do you mind <u>if</u> / when I ask a question?

5. May I shut please / <u>please shut</u> the door?

B | *Read the situations in parentheses. Then complete the questions to ask permission.*

1. Could _____?
   (You want to borrow a pen.)

2. Can _____?
   (Your sister wants to leave.)

3. Do you mind _____?
   (You want to open a window.)

4. Could _____?
   (You and a friend want to come early.)

5. May _____?
   (You want to ask a question.)

C | *Find and correct ten mistakes.*

1. **A:** Do you mind if I changed the date of our next meeting?

   B: Yes, I do. When would you like to meet?

2. **A:** Could I calling you tonight?

   B: Sorry, but you couldn't. I won't be home.

3. **A:** Mom, I may have some more ice cream?

   B: No you mayn't. You've already had a lot. You'll get sick.

4. **A:** Do you mind if my son turn on the TV?

   B: Not at all. I can't study with the TV on.

5. **A:** Can my sister borrows your bike?

   B: Could I letting you know tomorrow?

   A: Sure. No problem.

Requests: *Can, Could, Will, Would, Would you mind*

MESSAGES

STEP 1 GRAMMAR IN CONTEXT

Before You Read

Look at the title. Discuss the questions.

1. What do you think it means? Check the list of abbreviations on the next page.
2. Why do people use abbreviations in text messages?
3. Do you use text abbreviations in another language?
4. Do you prefer text messages or email? Why?

Read

Read the email and text messages.

Messages 4 u!

From: RheaJones@island.net
To: MarciaJones@dataline.com
Subject: Requests

Marcia, dear—
Can you **drive** me to the Burtons after work today? They've invited me for dinner. Oh, and **will** you **pick up** something special at the bakery before you come? I told them I'd bring dessert.

Thanks, honey.—Mom

P.S. Here's a little cartoon to cheer you up.   :)

"Would you mind talking to me for a while? I forgot my cell phone."

Mom,
I'm sorry, but I can't tonight. I'm working late. Do you want me to ask your favorite son-in-law if he can drive you?
M.
P.S. Thanks for the cartoon. Very funny!

Jsanchez Hi, Marcia. I'll be out of town until Thursday. **Would** you please **copy** and **distribute** the monthly sales report? Thank you. I really appreciate your help! —John

Mjones Hi John. I'd be glad to. I'll text you after I distribute them. Have a good trip. —Marcia

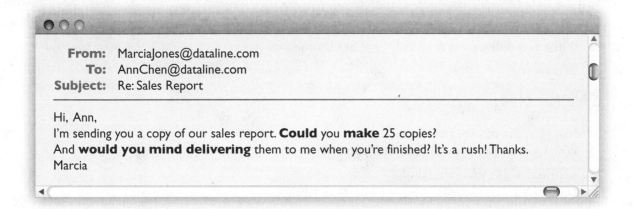

From: MarciaJones@dataline.com
To: AnnChen@dataline.com
Subject: Re: Sales Report

Hi, Ann,
I'm sending you a copy of our sales report. **Could** you **make** 25 copies?
And **would you mind delivering** them to me when you're finished? It's a rush! Thanks.
Marcia

Ejones Mom – I need a ride home from soccer practice 2day. Plz CMB.

Mjones Hi Ethan! I cn pick u up but I'll be late.

Ejones That's OK. CUL8R and TY.

Mjones Jody—**Will** u **cook** dinner 2nite? I'll be home @ 7.

Jjones OK, Mom. I'll get some lasagna out of the freezer.

Mjones TY Jody. ILU.

Jjones ILU2.

Some Abbreviations for Text Messages*

Abbreviation	Meaning	Abbreviation	Meaning
@	at	CUL8R	See you later
2	to, too	LU	Love you
4	for	Plz	Please
CMB	call me back	TY	Thank you
cn	can	u	you

* We use these abbreviations in informal messages to friends and family.

After You Read

A | Vocabulary: *Circle the letter of the word or phrase that best completes each sentence.*

1. When you **text** someone, you _____ to the person's cell phone.
   a. send photos
   b. write a message
   c. record a message

2. When you **deliver** a report, you _____ it to someone.
   a. promise
   b. describe
   c. bring

3. When you **cheer** someone **up**, that person becomes _____.
   a. upset
   b. happy
   c. smart

4. When you **distribute** something, you _____.
   a. give something to each person in a group
   b. organize it by date
   c. keep a copy on your computer

5. When you **appreciate** what someone does for you, you feel _____.
   a. worried
   b. sorry
   c. thankful

B | Comprehension: *Check (✓) True or False. Correct the false statements.*

	True	False
1. Marcia's mother sent Marcia a text message.	☐	☐
2. John needs copies of the sales report.	☐	☐
3. Ann is going to distribute the copies.	☐	☐
4. Marcia is going to make the copies.	☐	☐
5. Ethan needs a ride home from soccer practice.	☐	☐
6. Jody is going to cook dinner tonight.	☐	☐

REQUESTS: *CAN, COULD, WILL, WOULD, WOULD YOU MIND*

Questions: *Can / Could / Will / Would*				Short Answers		
Can / Could / Will / Would*	*You*	**Base Form of Verb**		**Affirmative**	**Negative**	
Can **Could** **Will** **Would**	you	**distribute**	this report for me?	Sure. Certainly. No problem. Of course. I'd be glad to.	I'm sorry, but	I **can't**.
		drive	me to the doctor?			
		pick up	some groceries?		I'm afraid	

*Can, could, will, and *would* are modals. Modals do not have *-s* in the third-person singular.

Questions: *Would you mind*			Short Answers		
Would you mind	Gerund		**Affirmative**	**Negative**	
Would you mind	**distributing**	this report for me?	Not at all. I'd be glad to. No problem. Of course not.	I'm sorry, but	I **can't**.
	driving	me to the doctor?			
	picking up	some groceries?		I'm afraid	

GRAMMAR NOTES

1
Use the modals *can, could, will,* and *would* to make a **request** (ask someone to do something).

a. *Could* and *would* are more polite than *can* and *will*. We use *could* and *would* to soften requests.

b. You can also use *please* to make the request more polite. Notice the word order.

- **Can** you **turn on** the TV?
- **Will** you **bring** dessert?

- **Could** you **text** me?
- **Would** you **close** the door?

- **Would** you **close** the door, *please*? OR
- **Would** you *please* **close** the door?

2
In **affirmative answers** to requests, we usually use expressions such as *sure, certainly, of course,* and *no problem*.

In **negative answers**, we usually apologize and give an explanation.

BE CAREFUL! Do NOT use *would* or *could* in response to polite requests.

A: **Would** you **shut** the window, please?
B: *Sure*. OR *I'd be glad to*. OR *Of course*.

A: **Could** you **deliver** this to Ron, please?
B: *I'm sorry, I can't*. I'm expecting a call.

Nᴏᴛ: Sure I ~~would~~.
Nᴏᴛ: I'm sorry, I ~~couldn't~~.

(continued on next page)

3 We also use **Would you mind** + **gerund** (verb + -ing) to make polite requests. It is even more polite than *could* or *would*.

A: Would you mind waiting? Mr. Caras is in a meeting.

BE CAREFUL! When we answer this type of request with **Not at all** or **Of course not**, it means that we will do what the person requests.

B: Not at all. OR **Of course not.** (OK. I'll do it.)

In **negative answers**, we usually apologize and give an explanation.

B: I'm sorry, I can't. I have another appointment in half an hour.

REFERENCE NOTES

For general information on **modals**, see Unit 13, Grammar Note 2, on page 179.
Can and **could** are also used for **ability** (see Unit 13) and for **permission** (see Unit 14).
Can't and **could** are also used for **conclusions** (see Unit 32).
Could is also used for **future possibility** (see Unit 31).
Will is also used for the **future** (see Units 6 and 7).
For a list of **modals and their functions**, see Appendix 19 on page A-8.

STEP 3 FOCUSED PRACTICE

EXERCISE 1: Discover the Grammar

Mike's roommate, Jeff, is having problems today. Underline Jeff's requests. Then circle the letter of the appropriate response to each request.

1. Mike, would you please drive me to Cal's Computer Shop? I have to bring my computer in.

   a. Yes, I would.   **b.** I'd be glad to.

2. Would you mind lending me five dollars? I'm getting paid tomorrow.

   a. Not at all.   **b.** Yes.

3. Mike, can you lend me your laptop for a minute? I have to email my teacher.

   a. Sorry. I'm working on something.   **b.** No, I can't.

4. Could you lock the door on your way out? My hands are full.

   a. Yes, I could.   **b.** Sure.

5. Jody, can you tell Ethan to come to the phone? It's important.

   a. No problem.   **b.** Not at all.

6. Will you pick up some milk on the way home this afternoon?

   a. No, I won't.   **b.** I'm sorry, I can't. I'll be at work until 8:00.

7. Would you explain this text message from Jody? She uses weird abbreviations.

   a. I'd be glad to.   **b.** No, I wouldn't.

EXERCISE 2: Requests

(Grammar Notes 1, 3)

A | *Look at the pictures. What is each person thinking? Write the letter of the correct thought from the box.*

a. Repair the copier.	d. ~~File these reports.~~	g. Buy some cereal.
b. Call back later.	e. Shut the door.	h. Wait for a few minutes.
c. Get that book.	f. Close the window.	i. Wash your cups and dishes.

1. ___*d*___

2. ___*e*___

3. ___*g*___

4. ___*f*___

5. ___*h*___

6. _____

7. ___*b*___

8. ___*c*___

9. ___*a*___

B | *What are the people in the pictures going to say? Complete their requests. Use the words in parentheses and the information from the pictures.*

1. _____Could you file these reports, please?_____ I've finished reading them.
   (could)
2. _____ I can't think with all that noise in the hall.
   (would)
3. _____ on the way home? We don't have any left.
   (will)
4. _____ It's freezing in here.
   (can)
5. _____ Mr. Rivera is still in a meeting.
   (would you mind)
6. _____ It's getting messy in here.
   (would you mind)
7. _____ I have to leave for a meeting now.
   (could)
8. _____ I can't reach it.
   (can)
9. _____ I need to make copies right away.
   (could)

EXERCISE 3: Requests and Answers

(Grammar Notes 1–3)

Write polite requests. Use **can, could, will, would,** *or* **would you mind** *and the correct form of the words in parentheses. Write appropriate answers.*

1.   **MAN:** ____Would you mind lending me your cell phone____? The battery in mine is dead.
                     a. (lend me your cell phone)

      WOMAN: _____No problem_____. But I'm in a hurry.
                        b.

      _____
           c. (please / keep your conversation short)

      MAN: _____. I just need to text my friend.
                      d.

2.   **STUDENT:** Excuse me, Professor Ruiz. _____?
                       a. (explain reflexive pronouns)

      I don't understand them.

     PROFESSOR: _____ right now. I'm expecting a
                    b.

      call. _____
            c. (come back in 20 minutes)

3.   **WOMAN:** _____? It's blocking my driveway.
                 a. (move your car)

      MAN: _____. I'll do it right away. I'm
                    b.

      really sorry. I didn't notice.

4.   **MANAGER:** _____? Our sales people need it for
              a. (please / distribute this report)

      their meeting this afternoon.

     ASSISTANT: _____. I can't leave my desk right
                    b.

      now. But I can ask Marcia to do it.

EXERCISE 4: Editing

*Read Marcia Jones's response to an email message from her boss. (Her answers are in **red**.) There are eight mistakes in making and responding to requests. The first mistake is already corrected. Find and correct seven more.*

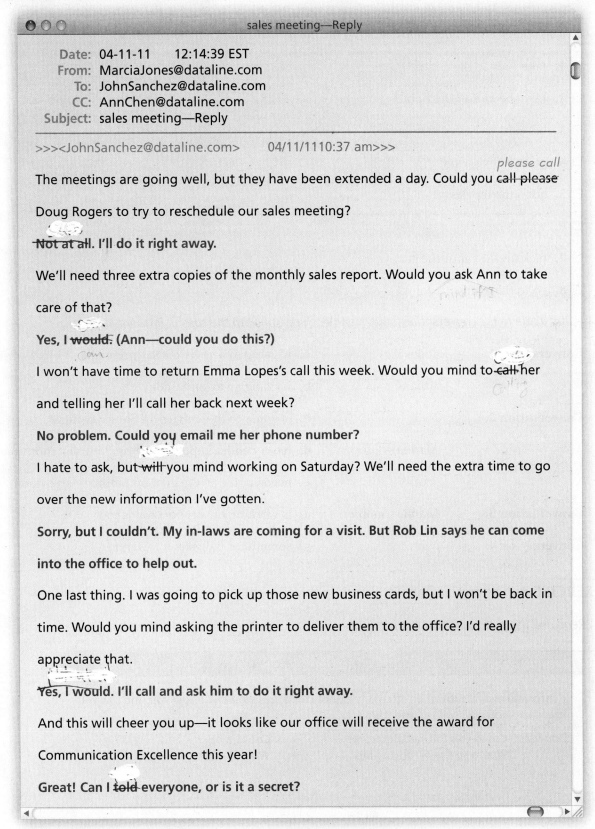

sales meeting—Reply

Date: 04-11-11   12:14:39 EST
From: MarciaJones@dataline.com
To: JohnSanchez@dataline.com
CC: AnnChen@dataline.com
Subject: sales meeting—Reply

>>><JohnSanchez@dataline.com>   04/11/1110:37 am>>>

please call

The meetings are going well, but they have been extended a day. Could you ~~call please~~ Doug Rogers to try to reschedule our sales meeting?

~~Not at all.~~ **I'll do it right away.**

We'll need three extra copies of the monthly sales report. Would you ask Ann to take care of that?

Yes, I ~~would.~~ (Ann—could you do this?)

can

I won't have time to return Emma Lopes's call this week. Would you mind to ~~call her~~ and telling her I'll call her back next week?

No problem. Could you email me her phone number?

I hate to ask, but ~~will~~ you mind working on Saturday? We'll need the extra time to go over the new information I've gotten.

Sorry, but I couldn't. My in-laws are coming for a visit. But Rob Lin says he can come into the office to help out.

One last thing. I was going to pick up those new business cards, but I won't be back in time. Would you mind asking the printer to deliver them to the office? I'd really appreciate that.

~~Yes, I would.~~ I'll call and ask him to do it right away.

And this will cheer you up—it looks like our office will receive the award for Communication Excellence this year!

Great! Can I ~~told~~ everyone, or is it a secret?

EXERCISE 5: Listening

A | *Marcia Jones has planned a busy weekend. Read the list. Then listen to the conversations. Listen again and check (✓) the things that belong on her schedule.*

☑ **1.** take Jody to the dentist

☐ **2.** take the kids to the library

☐ **3.** babysit for Kelly's daughter

☐ **4.** go to Kelly's party

☐ **5.** go to the movies

☐ **6.** walk Mom's dog

☐ **7.** pick up the car at the garage

☐ **8.** go to the gym with John

B | *Listen again to the conversations and match each person with the correct information.*

Conversation 1. __d__ Jody   **a.** is going to a party on Saturday night

_____ Ethan   **b.** is going away on Sunday

Conversation 2. _____ Kelly   **c.** is going to the movies on Saturday night

_____ Marcia   **d.** has a dentist appointment on Saturday morning

_____ Ann   **e.** needs a ride to the gym on Saturday afternoon

Conversation 3. _____ Marcia's mother   **f.** is working on a report for school

Conversation 4. _____ John   **g.** sometimes babysits for Marcia

EXERCISE 6: Pronunciation

A | *Read and listen to the Pronunciation Note.*

Pronunciation Note

In **informal conversation**, we often pronounce *could you*, *would you*, *will you*, and *can you* "couldja," "wouldja," "willya," and "canya."

EXAMPLES: **Could you** call me after work?   →   "**Couldja** call me after work?"

Would you mind driving me home?   →   "**Wouldja** mind driving me home?"

B | *Listen to the short conversations. Notice the pronunciation of* **could you, would you, will you,** *and* **can you.**

1. **A: Would you** mind texting me when you get home?
   B: Not at all. I know you worry.

2. **A: Can you** lend me a pencil? I lost mine.
   B: Sorry, I can't. I only have one.

3. **A: Could you** explain this cartoon? I don't get it.
   B: No problem! It's a joke about cell phones.

4. **A: Will you** turn the TV down, please? I'm studying.
   B: Sure.

5. **A: Would you** email me a photo of the game?
   B: Sorry, I can't. I didn't have time to take one.

6. **A: Could you** help me with this math problem? I don't understand it.
   B: I'd be glad to.

C | *Listen again to the conversations and repeat the requests. Then practice the conversations with a partner. Take turns making the requests and answering them.*

EXERCISE 7: Making Plans

A | *Fill out your schedule for the weekend.*

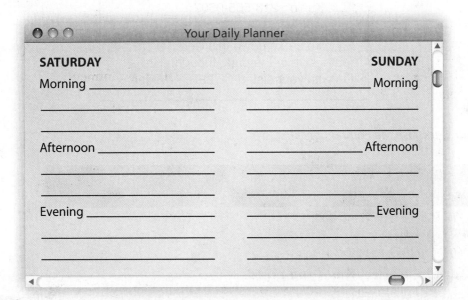

B | *Now work in small groups. Ask group members to help you with some of the things on your schedule.*

EXAMPLE: A: Ali, can you drive me to the mall Saturday morning?
B: Sorry, I can't. I'm working Saturday morning. OR Sure, I'd be glad to.
C: Ria, would you mind . . .

EXERCISE 8: Writing

A | *Read the situations. For each one, write a text message making one or more requests.*

1. Your roommate is going away for the weekend. Your sister from out of town will be visiting you. Write a text message to your roommate.

   EXAMPLE:

   > TO: Viktor M 213-555-4321
   >
   > Hi Viktor. My sister is visiting this weekend. W%d u mind lending her your bike? I'd like 2 take her 4 a ride in the park. Thanks. —Kunio

2. You work at a restaurant on Mondays, Wednesdays, and Fridays. You have to go to the dentist, but the dentist can only see you on Wednesday. Write a text message to a co-worker.

3. You're in school. You have to leave class early in order to help your parents. Write a text message to a classmate.

4. You're going to have a party at your home. You've invited 20 people. Write a text message to your neighbor.

B | *Exchange text messages with a partner. Write responses to your partner's requests.*

   EXAMPLE:

   > TO: Kunio   213-555-0507
   >
   > Hi Kunio. I'm really sorry, but I can't. My bike broke down this week. U cn rent a bike in the park, though. Have fun with your sister! CUL8R. —Viktor

C | *Check your work. Use the Editing Checklist.*

Editing Checklist
Did you . . . ? ☐ use modals correctly ☐ use a gerund after **Would you mind** . . . ☐ use **please** correctly ☐ apologize and give an explanation when you said **No** to a request

A | *Circle the correct words to complete the conversations.*

- **A:** Would you mind <u>to turn / turning</u> off the TV? I'm trying to read.
        1.
  B: <u>Yes, I would. / I'm sorry, I can't.</u> I need to watch the news for a homework assignment.
        2.
- **A:** Will you <u>please text / text please</u> me when you get home?
        3.
  B: <u>Not at all / No problem.</u> I'll probably be home by nine.
        4.
- **A:** Could you <u>picked /pick</u> up some dessert on the way home?
        5.
  B: <u>I'd be glad to / Yes, I could.</u> How about ice cream?
        6.

B | *Read the statements in parentheses. Then complete the questions to make requests.*

1. Would you mind _____?
   (Please lend me five dollars.)

2. Could _____?
   (I'd like you to drive me to school.)

3. Will _____?
   (Please explain this sentence to me.)

4. Can _____?
   (I'd like you to carry this suitcase for me.)

5. Would _____?
   (Please distribute the report.)

6. Would you mind _____?
   (I'd like you to walk the dog tonight.)

C | *Find and correct eight mistakes.*

- **JASON:** Hi Tessa. It's Jason. Could you taking some photos of the game today?

  TESSA: Sorry, Jason, but I couldn't. My camera is broken. Maybe Jeri can help.

- **JASON:** Hi Jeri. Would you came to the game today? I need someone to take photos.

  JERI: Jason, can you mind calling me back in a few minutes? I'm busy right now.

  JASON: Sorry, Jeri, I can't, but I'll email you. Would you give me please your email address?

  JERI: Not at all. It's Rainbows@local.net.

- **JERI:** Hi Jason, it's Jeri. I'm sending you those photos. You could call me when you get them?

  JASON: Thanks, Jeri. The photos are great. Now will teach me how to put them on Facebook?

UNIT 16

Advice: *Should, Ought to, Had better*
INTERNET RULES

STEP 1 GRAMMAR IN CONTEXT

Before You Read

Do you communicate with people on the Internet? Discuss the questions.

1. Is it important to be polite on the Internet? Why or why not?
2. Do you behave differently online than face-to-face with people?
3. What are some rules you follow?

Read

Read the article about being polite on the Internet. If you don't understand a cyber[1] word, look up its meaning on the next page.

Netiquette 101
by Emilia Poster

Email, bulletin boards, and chat rooms open up a new world of communication—and sometimes misunderstanding. To avoid problems, you **should know** these simple rules of netiquette:

- When **should** you **post** to a bulletin board or chat room? Newbies shouldn't jump in right away—they **ought to lurk** a little first. Look through old messages for answers to common questions. Many websites also have FAQs for basic information. After that, post when you have something new to say. You **should keep** your post short and simple.

- **Should** you **use** capital letters to make a strong statement? NO! A MESSAGE ALL IN CAPITAL LETTERS SEEMS LIKE SHOUTING. You **should follow** the normal rules for capital (big) and lowercase (small) letters.

- Did someone make you angry? Wait a minute! You**'d better not reply** right away. Count to 10 first. Don't flame another board or chat room member. You **should** never **forget** that people on the Internet are real people with real feelings.

- Emoticons can help avoid misunderstandings. You **should learn** how to use them to show your feelings.

- Internet safety is part of netiquette. When you post to a bulletin board or a chat room, you **should** always **protect** your identity by using a screen name. Never give your real name or other personal information.

Practice these five rules of netiquette, and most of your emoticons will be smileys! ☺

---
[1] *cyber:* about computers or the Internet

Cyber Words

bulletin board an Internet site where members can post ideas about a special interest

chat room a site for online conversations in "real" time

emoticon a picture of a feeling, for example:

FAQ Frequently Asked Question

flame to send insulting messages to someone

lurk to read messages on a bulletin board but not post any messages

netiquette Internet etiquette (rules for polite behavior)

newbie (or newb) someone new to an Internet site

post to send messages to a bulletin board or chat room

"Got your e-mail, thanks."

After You Read

A | Vocabulary: *Complete the sentences with the words from the box.*

avoid	behavior	communication	identity	normal	protect

1. Never give your real _____ in a chat room. Always use a screen name.

2. It's _____ for newbies to lurk on a site before they post. Many people do that.

3. Don't go to websites where members often flame other members. _____ those groups. Find groups that practice good netiquette.

4. Do you want to improve your online _____? Emoticons will help others understand what you mean.

5. People's _____ in chat rooms is sometimes different from the way they act in real life.

6. _____ yourself on the Internet. Never tell anyone your passwords. People could steal your identity.

B | Comprehension: *Read the sentences. Check (✓)* **OK** *or* **Not OK.**

	OK	Not OK
1. Read some messages before you post.	☐	☐
2. Reply immediately when you're angry.	☐	☐
3. Use all capital letters in your posts.	☐	☐
4. Use emoticons to show feelings.	☐	☐
5. Use your real name in chat rooms.	☐	☐
6. Learn the rules of netiquette.	☐	☐
7. Flame people when you don't like their messages.	☐	☐
8. Write long, complicated messages.	☐	☐
9. Think about people's feelings when you post a message.	☐	☐

STEP 2 GRAMMAR PRESENTATION

ADVICE: *SHOULD, OUGHT TO, HAD BETTER*

Statements		
Subject	***Should / Ought to / Had better*** *	**Base Form of Verb**
I You He She We You They	**should (not)** **ought to** **had better (not)**	**reply.**

Contractions		
should not	=	**shouldn't**
had better	=	**'d better**

*Should and *ought to* are modals. *Had better* is similar to a modal.
These forms do not have -s in the third-person singular.

Yes / No Questions		
Should	**Subject**	**Base Form of Verb**
Should	I he she we they	**reply?**

Short Answers					
Affirmative			**Negative**		
Yes,	you he she you they	**should.**	**No,**	you he she you they	**shouldn't.**

Wh- Questions				
Wh- Word	**Should**	**Subject**	**Base Form of Verb**	
How When Where	**should**	I he she we they	**send**	it?

GRAMMAR NOTES

1 Use the modals **should** and **ought to** to say that something is **advisable** (a good idea).

USAGE NOTES:

a. **Should** is much **more common** than *ought to*.

b. We do NOT usually use the <u>negative</u> of *ought to* in American English. We use **shouldn't** instead.

c. We often <u>soften advice</u> with **maybe**, **perhaps**, or **I think**.

- Derek **should answer** that email.
- You **ought to read** the FAQ.

- You **should read** the FAQ.

- We **shouldn't post** long messages.
  NOT COMMON: We ought not to post long messages.

- Ryan, **maybe** you **shouldn't spend** so much time on the Internet.

2 Use **had better** (an expression similar to a modal) for **strong advice**—when you believe that something bad will happen if the person does not follow your advice.

USAGE NOTE: The full form *had better* is very formal. We usually use the **contraction**.

The <u>negative</u> of *had better* is **had better not**. Notice the word order.

BE CAREFUL! *Had better* always refers to the **present** or the **future**, never to the past (even though it uses the word *had*).

- Kids, you**'d better get** offline now or you won't have time for your homework.

- You**'d better choose** a screen name.
  NOT COMMON: You had better choose a screen name.

- You**'d better not use** your real name.
  NOT: You ~~had not better~~ use your real name.

- You**'d better not call** them **now**. They're probably sleeping.
- You**'d better post** that **tomorrow** or it'll be late.

3 Use **should** for **questions**. We do not usually use *ought to* or *had better* for questions.

You can use **should** in **short answers**, but we often use other <u>expressions</u>.

- When **should** I **sign on**?

- **A:** **Should** I **join** this chat room?
- **B:** Yes, you **should**. It's fun.
  OR
  Why not? Good idea!

(continued on next page)

4 In **very informal** notes, emails, text messages, and Internet posts, we often use "**oughta**" instead of *ought to* and we use ***better*** instead of *had better*.

BE CAREFUL! Do NOT use these forms in more **formal** writing. Use ***ought to*** and ***had better*** or ***'d better***.

- Newbie, don't post so soon. You **oughta** read the netiquette rules first. You **better not** just jump in.
  (informal Internet post)

    Q: When should I start to post?
Not: **A:** You ~~oughta~~ read the netiquette rules first. You ~~better not~~ just jump in.
    (formal FAQ for the site)

REFERENCE NOTES

For general information on **modals**, see Unit 13, Grammar Note 2, on page 179.

Sometimes we use ***must*** or ***have to*** for **very strong advice**. This kind of advice is similar to talking about **necessity** or **obligation** (see Unit 29).

For a list of **modals and their functions**, see Appendix 19 on page A-8.

STEP 3 FOCUSED PRACTICE

EXERCISE 1: Discover the Grammar

Read the posts to an online bulletin board for high school students. Underline the words that give or ask for advice.

Subject: HELP!
From: Hothead

MY BRAIN IS EXPLODING!!! SAVE ME!! What should I do? I'm taking all honors courses this year, and I'm on the debate team, in the school congress, and on the soccer team. OH! And, I'd better not forget piano lessons! I'm so busy I shouldn't even be online now. ☹

From: Tweety

First of all, you should stop shouting. You'll feel better. Then you really ought to ask yourself, "Why am I doing all this?" Is it for you, or are you trying to please somebody else?

From: Loki

Tweety's right, Hothead. Do you really want to do all that stuff? No? You'd better not do it then. You'll burn out before you graduate. 🌀

From: gud4me

You're such a loser. You should get a life. I mean a NORMAL life. Do you have any friends? Do you ever just sit around and do nothing?

From: Tweety

Hey, gud4me, no flaming allowed! That's bad cyber behavior. We really shouldn't fight—it never helps communication. Try to help or keep quiet. ☺

EXERCISE 2: Statements with *Should, Ought to,* and *Had better*   (Grammar Notes 1–2)

Read the posts to a chat room about learning English. Complete the posts. Use the correct form (affirmative or negative) of the words in parentheses. Use contractions when possible.

curly: I think I _____*should watch*_____ more movies to improve my English. Any ideas?
1. (should / watch)

usedit: I loved *The Uninvited*. But you _____had better rent_____ it if you don't like
2. (had better / rent)

scary films.

agurl: That's right. And you _____'d better keep_____ the remote in your hand. That
3. (had better / keep)

way you can fast-forward through the scary parts.

592XY: I think you _____ought to see_____ *Groundhog Day*. The same thing
4. (ought to / see)

happens again and again. It's an old movie, but it's great listening practice—and it's funny!

pati: You _____should turn on_____ the English subtitles. They really help.
5. (should / turn on)

usedit: But you _____should use_____ the subtitles right away. First you
6. (should / use)

_____should listen_____ a few times. That's what rewind buttons are for!
7. (should / listen)

592XY: Good advice. And you really _____ought to read_____ a plot summary before
8. (ought to / read)

you watch. You can find one online. It's so much easier when you know the story.

agurl: Curly, you're a math major, right? Then you really _____ought to watch_____
9. (ought to / watch)

The Da Vinci Code. It's about solving a mystery with math clues.

curly: Thanks, guys. Those are great ideas. But you _____'d better give_____ me any
10. (had better / give)

more advice, or I'll never work on my other courses!

EXERCISE 3: Statements with *Should*, *Ought to*, and *Had better* (Grammar Notes 1–2)

Rewrite the Internet safety tips. Use **should**, **ought to**, or **had better**. Choose between affirmative and negative.

> The Internet is a wonderful place to visit and hang out. Here are some tips to make your trip there a safe one!

1. **I often use my real name online. Is that a problem?**

   Yes! *You should always use a screen name.*
   (Always use a screen name.)
   Protect your identity!

2. **Someone in my chat group just asked for my address.**

   _____
   (Don't give out any personal information.)
   People can use it to steal your identity and your money.

3. **My brother wants my password to check out a group before joining.**

   _____
   (Don't give it to anyone.)
   Not even your brother! He might share it, and then people can steal your information.

4. **I sent a file to someone, and she told me it had a virus.**

   _____
   (Get virus protection and use it.)
   A virus can hurt your computer and destroy important files (and other people's too).

5. **I update my virus protection every month. Is that really necessary?**

   Yes! _____
   (Keep your virus protection up-to-date.)
   Remember: *Old* virus protection is *no* virus protection!

6. **I got an email about a home-based business. I could make $15,000 a month.**

   _____
   (Don't believe any "get rich quick" offers.)
   They sound good, but people almost always lose money.

7. **I got an interesting email. I don't know who sent it, but it's got a file attached.**

   _____
   (Don't open any email attachments from strangers.)
   They could contain dangerous viruses.

8. **The Internet sounds too dangerous for me!**

   Not really. _____,
   (Be careful!)
   but enjoy yourself—it's an exciting world out there!

EXERCISE 4: Questions and Short Answers with *Should*

(Grammar Note 3)

Complete the posts to an online bulletin board. Use the words from the box to complete the questions. Give short answers.

buy one online	forward the email	~~try to repair it~~
check the spelling	say to make them stop	use my birthday
flame him	start posting	use emoticons

1. **Q:** My computer is seven years old and has problems. _____*Should I try to repair it*_____?

   A: _____*No, you shouldn't*_____. That's very old for a computer! Buy a new one!

2. **Q:** I just joined an online discussion group. When _____?

   Right away?

   A: You should really just read for a while. It's always a good idea to "lurk" before you post.

3. **Q:** I just received a warning about a computer virus. The email says to tell everyone I know

   about it. _____?

   A: _____. These warnings are almost always false.

4. **Q:** I hate to go shopping, but I really need a jacket. _____?

   A: _____. It's safe. Just buy from a company you know.

5. **Q:** I type fast and make spelling mistakes. Is that bad? _____?

   A: _____. Use a spell checker! Mistakes are bad netiquette!

6. **Q:** My friends email me a lot of jokes. I don't want to hurt their feelings, but I *really* don't

   want to keep getting these jokes. What _____?

   A: You should be honest and say you are too busy to read them. These jokes can waste an

   awful lot of time!

7. **Q:** I always forget my password. _____ so I don't forget?

   A: _____. It's too easy to guess. Protect your identity.

8. **Q:** A newb on our board is asking dumb questions. _____?

   A: _____! Your behavior should be as polite online as offline.

9. **Q:** _____ in emails? Those smileys are awfully cute.

   A: Sure, go ahead. They're fun. But don't use them in business emails. 😊

EXERCISE 5: Editing

*Read the posts to a bulletin board for international students in the United States. There are twelve mistakes in the use of **should, ought to,** and **had better**. The first mistake is already corrected. Find and correct eleven more.*

Justme: My friend asked me to dinner, and she told me I should ~~to~~ bring some food! What kind of an invitation is that? What I should bring to this strange dinner party?

Sasha: LOL![1] The invitation is totally normal. Your friend is having a potluck—a dinner party where everybody brings something. It's really a lot of fun. You ought bring a dish from your country. People will enjoy that.

Toby: HELP! My first day of class, and I lost my wallet! What ~~ought I~~ do first? My student ID, credit card, and cash are all gone.

R2D2: First of all, you'd ~~not better~~ panic because you need to be calm so you can speak clearly. You should ~~to~~ call your credit card company right away. Did you lose your wallet at school? Then you ought to ~~going~~ to the Lost and Found Department at your school.

Smiley: What should an international student ~~does~~ to make friends? At my college people always smile and say, "Hi, how are you?" but they don't wait for an answer!

4gud: New students should ~~joining~~ some clubs and international student organizations. They also ought to find a student in each class to study with and ask about homework assignments.

Newguy: Hi. I'm new to this board. I'm from Vietnam, and I'm going to school in Canada next year. How should I ~~will~~ get ready?

Smiley: Welcome Newguy! I'm at school in Montreal, and you won't believe how cold it gets here. You're better bring a lot of warm clothes.

Sasha: You ought check the school's website. They might have a Vietnam Students Association. If they do, you should email the association with your questions. Good luck!

---

[1] **LOL:** abbreviation for *Laughing out Loud*

EXERCISE 6: Listening

A | *A radio show host is giving advice to callers about buying a new computer. Read the questions. Then listen to the show. Listen again and check (✓) all the correct answers.*

Who . . . ?	Amy	Jason	Marta	Tim
1. is the host of the show	☐	☐	☐	☑
2. is calling for the first time	☐	☐	☐	☐
3. asks about repairing an old computer	☐	☐	☐	☐
4. gives information about the normal life of a computer	☐	☐	☐	☐
5. is going to buy a new computer	☐	☐	☐	☐
6. says "always protect your identity"	☐	☐	☐	☐

B | *Read the advice in the list. Listen again to the show and check (✓) the sentences that agree with the host's advice.*

☐ **1.** Repair a seven-year-old computer.
☑ **2.** Read online computer reviews.
☐ **3.** Throw away your old computer.
☐ **4.** Always buy the cheapest computer.
☐ **5.** Order a computer from a big online company.
☐ **6.** Shop at a local computer store.
☐ **7.** Consider a service contract.
☐ **8.** Get the most memory you can afford.

EXERCISE 7: Pronunciation

A | *Read and listen to the Pronunciation Note.*

Pronunciation Note

In **informal conversation**:

- We often pronounce **ought to** "oughta".

- For **had better**, we usually pronounce **had** "d", and sometimes we leave out **had** and just say "better."

EXAMPLES: You **ought to** get a new computer. → "You **oughta** get a new computer."
You **had better** get a flash drive too. → "You**'d better** get a flash drive too." OR
"You **better** get a flash drive too."

🔊 **B** | *Listen to the conversation. Notice the pronunciation of* **ought to** *and* **had better.**

A: Do you think I **ought to** buy a new computer?

B: I think you**'d better**. Yours is pretty old.

A: What kind should I get?

B: Maybe you **ought to** get a laptop.

A: Good idea. I think I'll look for a used one.

B: You**'d better** not. A lot of used laptops have problems.

A: OK. I guess I **ought to** read some reviews.

B: Yeah, that's what you really **ought to** do.

🔊 **C** | *Listen again to the conversation and repeat each question or statement. Then practice the conversation with a partner.*

EXERCISE 8: Cross-Cultural Comparison

Work with a partner. Imagine that your partner has been offered a job as a computer expert in a country that you know very well. Give some advice about customs there. Then switch roles. Use these topics:

- calling your boss by his or her first name
- shaking hands when you first meet someone
- calling a co-worker by a nickname
- asking for a second helping when you are a guest

- crossing the street before the light turns green

(Add your own topics.)

- _____
- _____

EXAMPLES: You'd better not call your boss by her first name.
You should shake hands when you first meet someone.

EXERCISE 9: Problem Solving

Work in small groups. Each group member chooses a problem to ask the group about. Group members discuss the problem and give advice.

1. I was studying for exams, and I forgot my girlfriend's birthday. She's really angry at me. What should I do?

   EXAMPLE: **A:** You'd better take her to a nice restaurant.
   B: I think you should apologize and tell her you were really busy.
   C: You'd better not just send her an email. Pick up the phone and call!

2. My best friend from high school is getting married, but I don't have money to travel to her wedding. Should I borrow money for a plane ticket?

3. My boss emails me jokes that aren't really funny. Should I email back and say they're funny?

4. My roommate eats my groceries, and he doesn't clean his room. He's a good friend, and I don't want him to leave. What should I say to him?

5. I work during the day and go to school at night. I don't have much time to go out. How do I make new friends? Should I join online interest groups?

EXERCISE 10: Picture Discussion

Work in pairs. Look at a classroom at the EFL Computer Training Institute. Give advice for ways to improve the institute. Then compare your ideas with the ideas of another pair.

EXAMPLE: A: They should empty the trash.
B: Yes, and they ought to . . .

EXERCISE 11: Writing

A | *Look at the picture in Exercise 10. Imagine you are a student at that institute. Write an email to Mr. Thompson, the owner of the school, to complain about the institute. Don't flame him; follow the rules of netiquette. Give him advice on improvements the institute should make.*

EXAMPLE: Dear Mr. Thompson:
I am a student at the EFL Computer Training Institute. My classes are very good, but the Institute really should make some improvements. First, I think you ought to . . .

B | *Check your work. Use the Editing Checklist.*

Editing Checklist

Did you use . . . ?
☐ **should** and **ought to** for advice
☐ **had better** for strong advice
☐ the correct written forms of **ought to** and **had better**

UNIT 16 Review

Check your answers on page UR-4.

Do you need to review anything?

A | *Circle the letter of the correct answer to complete each sentence.*

1. Doug should _____ that Internet group. I think he'd like it.

   a. join   **b.** joins   **c.** to join

2. He ought _____ some postings before he posts his own.

   a. read   **b.** reads   **c.** to read

3. He should _____ a long message.

   a. n't post   **b.** no post   **c.** post no

4. He'd _____ give too much personal information. It could be dangerous.

   a. better   **b.** better not   **c.** not better

5. He'd better _____ careful.

   a. be   **b.** not be   **c.** not being

B | *Complete the conversations with the words in parentheses and with short answers.*

- **A:** _____ I _____ Suzanne tomorrow?

1. (should / call)

  B: You _____ it tonight. She's been expecting to hear from you.

2. (had better / do)

- **A:** How _____ I _____ Professor Lions? Email?

3. (should / contact)

  B: No. You _____ her. She prefers the phone.

4. (ought to / call)

- **A:** _____ I _____ her for help?

5. (should / ask)

  B: _____, you _____. That's part of her job.

6.

- **A:** _____ I _____ it right now?

7. (should / do)

  B: _____, you _____. It's much too late.

8.

  A: You're right. I _____ until tomorrow morning.

9. (had better / wait)

C | *Find and correct six mistakes.*

1. Vanessa should gets a new computer. She should no keep her old one.

2. She'd better not buying the first one she sees.

3. She ought read reviews before she decides on one.

4. Ought she get one online or should she goes to a store?

From Grammar to Writing

USING APPROPRIATE MODALS

When you write a note, you do more than give information. You perform social functions such as **asking for permission** and **making requests**. Modals help you perform these functions politely.

EXAMPLE: I want you to call me in the morning. ➔
Could you **please** call me in the morning?

1 | *Read the first draft of Ed's email to his co-worker, Chen. Work with a partner and decide which sentences should have modals. Underline the sentences.*

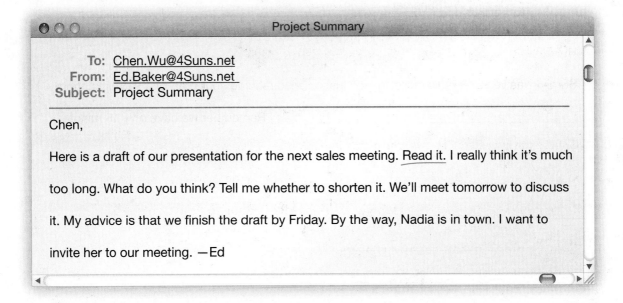

Project Summary

To: Chen.Wu@4Suns.net
From: Ed.Baker@4Suns.net
Subject: Project Summary

Chen,

Here is a draft of our presentation for the next sales meeting. Read it. I really think it's much too long. What do you think? Tell me whether to shorten it. We'll meet tomorrow to discuss it. My advice is that we finish the draft by Friday. By the way, Nadia is in town. I want to invite her to our meeting. —Ed

2 | *Complete Ed's second draft of the email. Use modals to express the functions in parentheses.*

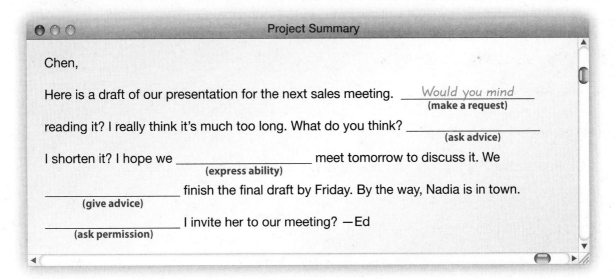

Project Summary

Chen,

Here is a draft of our presentation for the next sales meeting. __Would you mind__
(make a request)

reading it? I really think it's much too long. What do you think? _____
(ask advice)

I shorten it? I hope we _____ meet tomorrow to discuss it. We
(express ability)

_____ finish the final draft by Friday. By the way, Nadia is in town.
(give advice)

_____ I invite her to our meeting? —Ed
(ask permission)

3 | *Complete Chen's reply to Ed. Use modals to express these ideas:*

- Shorten the presentation. *(advice)*

- I'm not going to meet with you today because of another meeting. *(ability)*

- I'd like to meet tomorrow instead. *(request)*

- Please reserve the conference room for the meeting. *(request)*

- Of course Nadia will come to the meeting. *(permission)*

- I hope we'll all have lunch after the meeting. *(ability)*

Re: Project Summary

To: Ed.Baker@4Suns.net
From: Chen.Wu@4Suns.net
Subject: Re: Project Summary

Hi Ed,

Sorry, I was very busy this morning, so I just finished reading your draft of the presentation.

_____ *I think you should shorten it.* _____ Remember we have only 15 minutes.

_____

_____

_____

_____

_____

See you tomorrow morning.

Chen

1. Work with a partner. Choose one of the situations below. Role-play the situation.
   Use modals to express the ideas.

   Situation 1: A salesperson and his or her boss

   You work in a sales office. Recently a customer complained to your boss because he had to wait for service. You want to meet with your boss to explain what happened. You'd like to bring a co-worker who saw the incident. You think the company needs another receptionist for busy times.

   Situation 2: A student and his or her English teacher

   You would like your English teacher to write a letter of recommendation for you. You want him or her to mention that you have good computer skills and are an A student in the class. You're not sure how many hours to work a week, so you ask your teacher. You want to miss class so that you can go to your job interview.

2. Work with another pair. Watch their role play. Make a list of functions they expressed (for example, advice, ability, request) and the modals they used to express those functions. Discuss your list with them. Did they express what they wanted to?

3. Perform your role play and discuss it with the other pair.

EXAMPLES: Dear Barbara,
                Thank you for letting me know about the angry customer. Could you . . . ?

                Pete,
                Thanks for your email. I'll be able to . . .

NOUNS, QUANTIFIERS, AND ARTICLES

Nouns and Quantifiers
TIME CAPSULES

Before You Read

Look at the illustration of a time capsule. Discuss the questions.

1. What things can you name in the capsule?
2. What is a time capsule?
3. Why is the article called "Time in a Bottle"?

Read

Read the article on time capsules.

TIME IN A BOTTLE

An **alarm clock**, **lipstick**, a **toy car**, *some* **fabrics** made out of **cotton** and **wool**. A **picture** of a **baseball**, **money** (a **dollar bill** and *a few* **coins**). **Seeds** (such as **rice** and **corn**). The **Bible**, a written **message** from **Albert Einstein**, and hundreds of **books** and **newspapers** on **microfilm**.[1]

What do these **items** have in common? They all went into a **capsule** 50 **feet** underground in **Flushing Meadows Park**, in **New York City**. The **year** was 1939; the **occasion**, the **New York World's Fair**; and the **instructions** were not to open the **capsule** for 5,000 **years**!

The **Westinghouse Time Capsule** is just one of *many* **capsules** all over the **world**. They hold hundreds of everyday **objects**, but they have just one **purpose**: to tell **people** of the **future** about **life** in the **past**. To help make this happen, **Westinghouse** published a **book**, printed on special **paper** with **ink** that will not fade over **time**. The **book** tells how to find and open the **capsule**. It even explains how to interpret the **capsule's English**, which will be very different from **languages** 5,000 **years** from now!

The **Westinghouse Time Capsule** is an **example** of an intentional **time capsule**, but **history** has given

us unintentional **time capsules** too. The most famous is the ancient Roman **city** of **Pompeii**, in **Italy**. In the **year** 79, **Vesuvius**, a nearby **volcano**, erupted.[2] It buried the **city** under 60 **feet** of **ash** and created an instant **time capsule**. **Archeologists**[3] are still studying it today.

Intentional or unintentional, **time capsules** give us the **chance** to "communicate" with **people** from other **times**. What will **people** think of us when they open the **Westinghouse Time Capsule** in 5,000 **years**? Will they be as impressed with our **civilization** as we are with ancient **Pompeii**? Only **time** will tell—although we certainly won't be there to find out!

---

[1] *microfilm:* a special type of film used for making very small photos of important papers
[2] *erupt:* to explode and send out smoke, fire, and rocks into the sky
[3] *archeologist:* someone who studies ancient cultures by examining their buildings and objects

After You Read

A | Vocabulary: *Circle the letter of the word or phrase closest in meaning to the word in* **blue**.

1. I hear that Emily is having a big party tomorrow night. What's the **occasion**?

    a. starting time

    b. location

    c. reason for the event

2. Some of her friends **created** a birthday "time capsule" for her.

    a. bought

    b. found

    c. made

3. Emily was really **impressed**.

    a. unhappy

    b. full of respect

    c. important

4. James arrived late, but it wasn't **intentional**.

    a. on purpose

    b. very important

    c. too annoying

5. I couldn't **interpret** her email. Was she sad or angry?

    a. exactly describe

    b. completely remember

    c. decide on the meaning of

6. This semester, we're studying the **civilization** of ancient Rome.

    a. government

    b. society

    c. manners

B | Comprehension: *Check (✓)* **True** *or* **False**. *Correct the false statements.*

	True	False
1. Time capsules contain unusual items.	☐	☐
2. There are time capsules all over the world.	☐	☑
3. The Westinghouse Time Capsule is in Italy.	☑	☐
4. The ancient city of Pompeii is an unintentional time capsule.	☐	☑
5. Time capsules teach us about different civilizations.	☑	☐
6. People will soon be able to see the contents of the Westinghouse Time Capsule.	☐	☐

NOUNS AND QUANTIFIERS

Count Nouns			
	Noun	**Verb**	
One	**capsule**	is	in New York.
Two	**capsules**	are	

Non-Count Nouns		
Noun	**Verb**	
Money	is	inside.

Quantifiers and Count Nouns		
	Quantifier	**Noun**
It holds	*some* *enough* *a lot of* *a few* *several* *many*	**fabrics.** **seeds.** **coins.**
It doesn't hold	*any* *enough* *a lot of* *many*	
Does it hold	*any* *enough* *a lot of* *many*	**coins?**

Quantifiers and Non-Count Nouns		
	Quantifier	**Noun**
It holds	*some* *enough* *a lot of* *a little* *a great deal of*	**wool.** **rice.** **money.**
It doesn't hold	*any* *enough* *a lot of* *much*	
Does it hold	*any* *enough* *a lot of* *much*	**money?**

GRAMMAR NOTES

1   There are two categories of nouns:
proper nouns and **common nouns**.

a. Proper nouns are the <u>names</u> of particular
people, places, or things. They are usually
unique (there is only one).

People	Albert Einstein, Emily Lee
Places	New York, Italy
Things	Coca Cola, *Time* magazine
Months	September, October
Nationalities	American, Italian

<u>Capitalize</u> the first letter of proper nouns.

• Have you ever visited **Pompeii**?

b. Common nouns refer to people, places, and
things, but <u>not by their names</u>. For example,
scientist is a common noun, but *Einstein* is a
proper noun.

People	scientist, teacher, archeologist
Places	city, country, continent
Things	soda, newspapers, wool

<u>Do NOT capitalize</u> the first letter of a common
noun unless the noun is the first word in a
sentence.

• Einstein was a **scientist**.
  Not: Einstein was a ~~Scientist~~.

2   **Common nouns** can be **count** or **non-count**.

a. Count nouns are people, places, or things
that you can <u>count separately</u>: *one book,
two books, three books . . .*

• Count nouns can be <u>singular or plural</u>.
• They take <u>singular or plural verbs</u>.
• You can use *a, an* or ***the*** before them.

• He read one **book**. She read two **books**.
• The **book *is*** new, but the **newspapers *are*** old.
• There's **a toy** in **the box**.

b. Non-count nouns are things that you <u>cannot
count separately</u>. For example, you can say
rice, but you cannot say ~~one rice~~ or ~~two rices~~.
To the right are some categories of non-
count nouns.

Abstract words	education, love, time
Activities	exploring, farming, sailing
Courses of study	archeology, history, math
Foods	corn, milk, rice
Fabrics	cotton, silk, wool

Some common non-count nouns do not fit
into categories.

equipment	homework	news
furniture	information	work

• Non-count nouns have <u>NO plural</u> forms.
• They take <u>singular verbs and pronouns</u>.

• She bought a lot of **wool**. Not: ~~wools~~
• **Archeology *is*** an interesting subject. **It *was***
  his favorite subject.
  Not: ~~An archeology~~ is an interesting subject.

• We usually do NOT use *a* or *an* with them.

(continued on next page)

3 Use **quantifiers** with nouns to talk about *how many* or *how much*. Some quantifiers go only with count or with non-count nouns. Other quantifiers can go with both.

a. In **affirmative statements**, use:

- *many*, *a lot of*, *a great many*, and *a great deal of* for a <u>large quantity</u>

- *some* and *several* for a <u>smaller quantity</u>

- *enough* for *the* <u>necessary quantity</u>

- *few / a few* and *little / a little* for a <u>small quantity</u>

BE CAREFUL! The meaning of *few* and *little* is different from *a few* and *a little*. *Few* and *little* usually mean *not enough*.

b. In **negative statements** and in **questions** use:

- *many*, *a lot of*, *any*, and *enough* with <u>count</u> nouns

- *much*, *a lot of*, *any*, and *enough* with <u>non-count</u> nouns

USAGE NOTE: Sometimes, people use *much* instead of *a lot of* in affirmative sentences. This is <u>very formal</u> and <u>not common</u>.

- *Many* **people** worked on the capsule.
- They did *a great deal of* **work**.
- It took *a few* **years** to finish.
- That wasn't *much* **time**.

COUNT NOUNS	NON-COUNT NOUNS
many / a lot of coins	*a lot of* money
a great many jobs	*a great deal of* work
some toys	*some* wool
several books	*some* paper
enough apples	*enough* rice
a few years	*a little* time

- We had *a little* **time** to complete the project. *(We had some time, but not a lot.)*
- We had *little* **time** to complete the project. *(We almost didn't have enough time.)*

- There weren't *many* **students** in class.
- Did you put *any* **seeds** in the capsule?
- There weren't *enough* **books**.

- We didn't have *much* **rice**.
- Does he have *any* **homework**?
- There was never *enough* **time**.

VERY COMMON: They spent *a lot of* money.
NOT COMMON: They spent *much* money.

REFERENCE NOTES

For a list of **irregular plural nouns**, see Appendix 6 on page A-4.
For a list of **non-count nouns**, see Appendix 7 on page A-4.
For **categories of proper nouns**, see Appendix 8 on page A-5.
For **spelling rules** for **regular plural nouns**, see Appendix 25 on page A-11.
For **capitalization rules**, see Appendix 27 on page A-13.

EXERCISE 1: Discover the Grammar

A | *Read the article about Pompeii. Underline the nouns.*

Pompeii: A Window to Ancient History

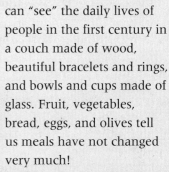

Pompeii was a rich and lively city on the bay of Naples, south of Rome. Wealthy Romans came to spend the summer there in large and beautiful villas.[1] Then, on August 24 in the year 79, Vesuvius erupted. The volcano buried the city under 60 feet of ash and killed thousands of people. It also destroyed a great many of the buildings. But not all of them. The ash preserved many houses, roads, theaters, statues, and a lot of beautiful art.

Pompeii's ruins stayed buried for almost 2,000 years. Then one day in 1748, a Spanish engineer discovered them. Since that time, archeologists have dug up many everyday objects from this ancient civilization.

Furniture, jewelry, money, and even a little food remain from that terrible day. Today we can "see" the daily lives of people in the first century in a couch made of wood, beautiful bracelets and rings, and bowls and cups made of glass. Fruit, vegetables, bread, eggs, and olives tell us meals have not changed very much!

Today Pompeii is "alive" again. Millions of tourists walk its roads each year. This amazing unintentional time capsule shows them what everyday life in ancient Rome was like. It is their window to ancient history.

---

[1] *villa:* an ancient Roman house or farm with land surrounding it

B | *Put nouns from the article into the correct columns. Choose only 16 count nouns.*

Proper Nouns	Common Nouns				
	Count Nouns			**Non-Count Nouns**	
1. Pompeii	1. window	9. bays	1. history	8. time	
2. Wealthy Romans	2. city	10.	2. Money	9.	
3. Naples	3. villas	11. summers	3. glass	10.	
4. August	4. building	12. Furniture	4. fruit	11.	
5. Spanish	5. house	13.	5. bread	12.	
6. Vesuvius	6. road	14. money	6. art	13.	
	7. theater	15.	7. ash		
	8. statue	16.			

EXERCISE 2: Noun and Verb Agreement

(Grammar Note 2)

Emily and James are planning a trip to Pompeii. They are checking a travel website for some tips on packing. Complete the tips. Use the correct form of the words in parentheses. Go to Appendix 7 on page A-4 for help with non-count nouns.

(brackets)

Pompeii Packing Posts

On the Road

Your ___*feet need*___ your help! Good ___*shoes is*___ a must! You'll be walking
1. (foot / need)   **2. (shoe / be)**

for ___*hours*___ among the ___*ruins*___ of this ancient civilization. And, remember, those
3. (hour)   **4. (ruin)**

___*streets are*___ very, very old—almost 2,000 ___*years*___!
5. (street / be)   **6. (year)**

Hey, it's hot out there!

___*Water is*___ essential. You can't buy it once you're inside, so don't forget to take
7. (water / be)

several ___*bottles*___ with you. The ___*sun is*___ VERY hot, so ___*sunblock is*___ very
8. (bottle)   **9. (sun / be)**   **10. (sunblock / be)**

important too. And don't forget your ___*hat*___! Both these ___*things help*___ protect
11. (hat)   **12. (thing / help)**

you from the sun.

Pompeii—It's picture perfect!

Pompeii is amazing, and you'll want to take a lot of ___*pictures*___. So bring a camera and
13. (picture)

an extra memory card. Extra ___*batteries*___ important too!
14. (battery / be)

What to wear

The right ___*clothing*___ a big difference. Pompeii often ___*gets*___ cool at night, so
15. (clothing / make)   **16. (get)**

bring a sweater.

Tempus fugit

That's Latin for ___*time flies*___. Most ___*people spend*___ a whole day at Pompeii.
17. (time / fly)   **18. (people / spend)**

The ___*ruins are*___ huge. Take a map, and take your time!
19. (ruin / be)

EXERCISE 3: Quantifiers

(Grammar Note 3)

Circle the correct words to complete the conversations.

1. **EMILY:** There were so (many) / much people at the ruins today. Was it some kind of special
   occasion or something?
   a.

   JAMES: I don't think so. I heard the guide say it's the most popular tourist attraction in Italy.

   EMILY: And I can understand why. I've never seen so much / many fascinating things.
   b.

2. **EMILY:** My feet hurt! We did a lot of / much walking today!
   a.

   JAMES: Tell me about it! But it sure was amazing.

   EMILY: How many / much pictures did you take?
   b.

   JAMES: I took a few / a lot of pictures—over 200!
   c.

3. **JAMES:** It sure was hot. I'm glad we took some / any water with us. I really drank a lot / much.
   a.   **b.**

   EMILY: Me too. And I used several / a great deal of sunblock. The sun was *really* strong.
   c.

   JAMES: Do we have some / any water left? I'm still thirsty.
   d.

4. **EMILY:** Are you hungry? I saw a little / a few nice-looking restaurants nearby.
   a.

   JAMES: OK. But we need to stop at an ATM first. We only have a little / a few money left.
   b.

   EMILY: That's not a problem. Very little / few restaurants don't accept credit cards these days.
   c.

5. **JAMES:** You know, we should spend some / any time in Naples. Our guidebook says they have
   a.
   a lot of / much art from Pompeii at the Archeological Museum.
   b.

   EMILY: Do we have little / enough time to do that? Tomorrow is our last day.
   c.

   JAMES: True. But I think we can spend few / a few hours there. We don't need enough / much
   d.   **e.**
   time to pack, do we?

   EMILY: I haven't bought some / any souvenirs yet, and I feel like we're running out of time.
   f.

   JAMES: Don't worry. We can do some / a few shopping before dinner. How much / many gifts
   g.   **h.**
   do you need to buy?

   EMILY: Not much / many, I guess. Just some / any things for the family.
   i.   **j.**

(continued on next page)

6. **Emily:** I'm impressed with our guidebook. It does a great job of interpreting the art.

   James: Yes. It has <u>a lot of / many</u> useful information. Maybe it can recommend a restaurant.
   a.

   Emily: What do you feel like eating?

   James: I'd love <u>some / any</u> pasta. What about you?
   b.

   Emily: Sounds good. And <u>a little / a few</u> dessert would be nice too. Maybe they have that
   c.

   Roman apple cake.

EXERCISE 4: Editing

Read Emily's email to her family. There are fifteen mistakes in the use of nouns and in the use of verb and pronoun agreement. The first mistake is already corrected. Find and correct fourteen more.

Hi Everyone!

James and I got back from Pompeii *a* few days ago. We bought a little souvenirs, which I'll mail to you all very soon. We're still unpacking and looking over the many, many photographs (hundreds!) we took of this amazing place. Our Guidebook calls the Pompeii a "time capsule," and I truly felt that we were somehow communicating with this rich and vibrant cultures. There are never enough times for everything on vacation, but that's especially true of Pompeii. Really, there are few places in the world this amazing. You should all try to go. I was so impressed!

I plan to do several blog posts and put up a lot photos to show you what I mean. Speaking of time capsules, I was just in the attic putting away any suitcases, and I discovered a trunk with much old stuff. The old clothing were still in great shape—I might wear some of the skirts and blouses. Oh, and I found a great deal of letters that Grandpa wrote to grandma when he was working in Italy on an archeological dig. A few of them made me cry, and one of them had a recipe for Roman apple cake! I think we'll try to make it, and we'll let you know how it turns out.

Love,

Emily

EXERCISE 5: Listening

🎧 **A** | *Emily and James are discussing a recipe. Look at the list of ingredients. Then listen to the conversation. Listen again and complete the list of ingredients. (You'll complete the shopping list later.)*

Roman Apple Cake

✓ 1 ½ cups _____sugar_____
½ cup vegetable _____
2 _____
2 _____ flour
1 teaspoon baking powder
1 _____ baking soda
¼ teaspoon _____
½ teaspoon cinnamon
1 cup _____
½ cup _____
½ cup _____
3 _____

Shopping List

_____eggs_____

🎧 **B** | *Listen to the rest of the conversation between Emily and James and check (✓) the items on the list of ingredients that they have enough of.*

🎧 **C** | *Listen again to Emily and James's conversation. Complete the shopping list of ingredients they need to buy.*

EXERCISE 6: Pronunciation

🎧 **A** | *Read and listen to the Pronunciation Note.*

Pronunciation Note

In **conversation** we sometimes **do not pronounce unstressed vowels**. For example, in the word *history*, we drop the vowel in the second syllable, *histØry*, and say "histry."

EXAMPLES:	history	→	"histry"
	family	→	"famly"
	camera	→	"camra"

B | *Read the sentences. Which vowels do you think are dropped? Draw a slash (/) through them. Then listen to the sentences and check your answers.*

1. Pompeii is very interesting.

2. We saw several wall paintings.

3. Don't forget your camera!

4. It makes a big difference.

5. I'm studying history.

6. We ate at my favorite restaurant.

7. The vegetables are delicious.

8. I bought some jewelry for my family.

C | *Listen again and repeat the sentences.*

EXERCISE 7: Quotable Quotes

Read the quotes about time. Discuss them with a partner. What do they mean? Do you agree with them?

1. It takes time to build castles. Rome wasn't built in a day.
   —*Irish proverb*

   EXAMPLE: **A:** I think this proverb means that you can't do something important quickly.
   B: I agree. Success isn't instant.

2. Time gives good advice.
   —*Maltese proverb*

3. Be happy while you're living for you're a long time dead.
   —*Scottish proverb*

4. There's no time like the present.
   —*English proverb*

5. Tomorrow is nothing; today is too late; the good lived yesterday.
   —*Marcus Aurelius (121–180, Roman emperor, historian, philosopher)*

6. Time stays long enough for anyone who will use it.
   —*Leonardo da Vinci (1452–1519, Italian painter, sculptor, architect, engineer)*

7. Time is money.
   —*Benjamin Franklin (1706–1790, U.S. statesman, scientist, writer)*

8. Time you enjoyed wasting is not wasted time.
   —*T. S. Eliot (1888–1965, U.S.-British poet)*

9. When you sit with a nice girl for two hours, you think it's only a minute. But when you sit on a hot stove for a minute, you think it's two hours. That's relativity.
   —*Albert Einstein (1879–1955, German-U.S. physicist)*

EXERCISE 8: Problem Solving

A | *Work with a group. Imagine that you are going to create a time capsule to tell people in the future about your present life. You have room in your capsule for only 10 things. Try to use both count and non-count nouns.*

Some categories to consider:

- books
- clothing
- food
- games
- money
- music
- technology
- tools

Answer the questions:

1. Which 10 items will you put in your time capsule? (Give the reasons for your choices.)

   EXAMPLE: **A:** Let's put in some fast food.
   B: A hamburger will go bad in less than a day!
   A: We could put *pictures* of popular kinds of fast food.

2. When do you want people to open it?

   EXAMPLE: **A:** I think people should open it 50 years from now. Then we can see their reactions.
   B: Good. It's enough time for a lot of things to change.

3. Where will you put your time capsule?

   EXAMPLE: **A:** Let's put it in the school basement.
   B: I don't know about that. Maybe the school won't still be here 50 years from now. How about . . . ?

4. What will you call your time capsule? Give it a name.

   EXAMPLE: **A:** Let's just name it after the year.
   B: Good idea. We'll call it Capsule 2011.

B | *Compare your choices with other groups' choices. Have other groups made any of the same choices as your group?*

EXERCISE 9: Writing

A | *Write a note to put in a time capsule. Use information from Exercise 8 or choose at least five items to put in the capsule. Your note is to the people who will open the capsule. Answer the questions:*

1. When did you create the capsule?
2. Where did you put it?
3. What is inside and why did you choose those items? How many or how much did you include?

   EXAMPLE: On October 4, 2010, my classmates and I created a time capsule. We buried it under the oldest tree in Lincoln Park. The capsule contains 10 items. Each item tells something about the lives we live today. For example, we put a few sales receipts inside to show . . .

B | *Check your work. Use the Editing Checklist.*

Editing Checklist

Did you . . . ?
☐ capitalize proper nouns
☐ use non-count nouns with singular verbs and pronouns
☐ use the correct verb (singular or plural) after count nouns
☐ use correct quantifiers

UNIT 17 Review

Check your answers on page UR-5.
Do you need to review anything?

A | *Circle the letter of the correct answer to complete each sentence.*

few …少ししかない
a few …少しだけある
little …少ししかない (不可算)
a little …少しだけある

1. Where would you like to go today? We only have a _____ time.
   a. little **b.** few **c.** great deal of
2. Do we have _____ time for the photography museum?
   a. several **b.** enough **c.** few
3. Sure! They have _____ old photographs of the city, and I'd love to see them.
   a. any **b.** much **c.** a lot of
4. The museum is _____ miles from here. Let's take our bikes.
   a. few **b.** a great deal of **c.** several
5. OK. And we should remember to bring _____ water. It's hot today.
   a. some **b.** a few **c.** little

B | *Complete the suggestions for items to put in a time capsule. Use the correct form of the words in parentheses.*

1. ______________________ essential. Include different kinds.
   (music / be)
2. Family ______________________ relationships, personalities, and a lot more.
   (photograph / show)
3. ______________________ a great item. Include bills and coins.
   (money / make)
4. ______________________ the popular styles and the fabrics of the time.
   (clothing / show)
5. ______________________ bad fast, so put in pictures of food instead.
   (food / go)

C | *Find and correct ten mistakes.*

One night in june, 1,400 Years ago, a volcano erupted in today's El Salvador and buried a village of the great Mayan civilization. Archeologists have already found many large building from this time, but only a little homes of farmers and workers. The village of El Ceren contains perfect examples of a great deal of everyday objects. The archeologists have found some knives (with foods still on them), much pots made of clays, a lot garden tools, a little fabric, and a book. On the wall of one room, they found a few word in an unknown language. There is still a lot to learn from this time capsule, called "the Pompeii of Latin America."

STEP 1 GRAMMAR IN CONTEXT

Before You Read

Look at the pictures on this page and the next. Read the title of each story. Discuss the questions.

1. What kind of a story is a fable?
2. Are fables only for children?
3. Do you know a fable in your first language?

Read

Read the two fables.

Two Fables

Aesop was **a famous storyteller** in Greece more than 2,000 years ago. **The fables** he told are still famous all over **the world**. Here are two of Aesop's fables.

The Ant and the Dove

An ant lived next to **a river.** One day, **the ant** went to **the river** to drink, and he fell into **the water. A dove** was sitting in **a tree** next to **the river. The dove** saw **the ant** struggling in **the water.** She picked **a leaf** from **the tree** and dropped it into **the river. The ant** climbed onto **the leaf** and floated safely to **the shore.**

An hour later, **a hunter** came to **the river** to catch **birds.** He was **the best hunter** in that part of **the country**, and all **the animals** feared him. When **the ant** saw **the hunter**, he wanted to save his friend, but he thought, "How can **a tiny ant** stop **a big man**?" Then he had **an idea**. He climbed on **the hunter's foot** and bit him hard. **The hunter** shouted in pain, and **the noise** made **the dove** fly away.

Importance of help eachother

Help!

return by someone

money doesn't mean happiness

The Town Mouse and the Country Mouse

A town mouse went to visit his cousin in **the country**. **The country cousin** was poor, but he gladly served his town cousin **the only food** he had—**some beans** and **some bread**. **The town mouse** ate **the bread** and laughed. He said, "What **simple food** you **country mice** eat! Come home with me. I'll show you how to live." **The moon** was shining brightly that night, so **the mice** left immediately.

As soon as they arrived at **the town mouse's house**, they went into **the dining room**. There they found **the leftovers** of **a wonderful dinner**. **The mice** were soon eating **jelly** and **cake** and many nice things. Suddenly, **the door** flew open, and **an enormous dog** ran in. **The mice** ran away quickly. "Good-bye, Cousin," said **the country mouse**. "Are you leaving so soon?" asked **the town mouse**. "Yes," his honest cousin replied. "This has been **a great adventure**, but I'd rather eat **bread** in peace than **cake** in fear."

After You Read

A | Vocabulary: *Complete the sentences from another fable with the words from the box.*

enormous	famous	immediately	struggled	wonderful

1. A long time ago, a smart cat lived with a very poor master. The cat _____struggled_____
   to help his master, but it wasn't easy.

2. One day, he had an adventure with a(n) ____enormous____ giant. The giant was 10 feet tall.

3. To show his magic powers, the giant became a tiny mouse, and the clever cat ate him. He and
   his master didn't wait. They ____immediately____ moved into the giant's castle.

4. The cat and his master became ____famous____. Everyone knew about the man and his
   clever cat. People even wrote stories about them.

5. The cat's master married a princess, and they lived a(n) ____wonderful____ life in the castle.
   The cat became rich and powerful and wore beautiful clothes. He only chased mice for fun.

B | Comprehension: *Number the sentences in each group in the correct order (1–5).*

"The Ant and the Dove"

_____ An hour later, a hunter came to the river to catch birds.

_____ She picked a leaf from the tree and dropped it into the river.

__2__ The dove saw the ant struggling in the water.

__1__ A dove was sitting in a tree next to the river.

_____ The ant climbed onto the leaf and floated safely to the shore.

"The Town Mouse and the Country Mouse"

_____ The town mouse ate the bread and laughed.

_____ The mice ran away quickly.

_____ The country cousin was poor, but he gladly served his town cousin the only food he had.

_____ This has been a great adventure.

_____ A town mouse went to visit his cousin in the country.

STEP 2 GRAMMAR PRESENTATION

ARTICLES: INDEFINITE AND DEFINITE

Indefinite

Singular Count Nouns		
	A / An	**(Adjective) Noun**
Let's read	**a**	**story.**
This is	**an**	**old story.**

Plural Count Nouns / Non-Count Nouns		
	(Some)	**(Adjective) Noun**
Let's listen to	**(some)**	**stories** on this CD.
This CD has		**nice music** too.

Definite

Singular Count Nouns		
	The	**(Adjective) Noun**
Let's read	**the**	**story** by Aesop.
It's		**oldest story.**

Plural Count Nouns / Non-Count Nouns		
	The	**(Adjective) Noun**
Let's listen to	**the**	**stories** by Aesop.
I like		**old music** on this CD.

GRAMMAR NOTES

はっきりない

1

We can use **nouns** in two ways:

a. A noun is **indefinite** when you and your listener <u>do not have a specific person, place, or thing in mind.</u>

はっきりしている ✓

b. A noun is **definite** when you and your listener both <u>know which person, place, or thing</u> you are talking about.

A: Let's buy **a book**.
B: Good idea. Which one should we buy?
(A and B are not talking about a specific book.)

A: I bought **the book** yesterday.
B: Good. You've wanted it for a while.
(A and B are talking about a specific book.)

2

To show that a noun is **indefinite**, use the **indefinite article** *a* / *an*, or **no article**, or *some*.

a. Use the **indefinite article** *a* / *an* with <u>singular count nouns</u> that are **indefinite**.

- Use *a* before <u>consonant sounds</u>.
- Use *an* before <u>vowel sounds</u>.

BE CAREFUL! It is the <u>sound</u>, not the letter, that determines whether you use *a* or *an*.

b. Use **no article** or *some* with <u>plural count nouns</u> and with <u>non-count nouns</u> that are **indefinite**. *Some* means an indefinite number.

A: I'm reading *a fable*.
B: Oh really? Which one?

- *a* **r**iver, *a* **t**iny ant
- *an* **i**dea, *an* **e**xciting story

- *a* **E**uropean writer (a "Yuropean")
- *an* **h**onest relative (an "ahnest")

PLURAL COUNT
- I had **(some) leftovers** for dinner.

NON-COUNT
- I should buy **(some) food**.

3

Notice these uses of *a* / *an*, **no article**, and *some*:

a. To **identify** (say what someone or something is), use:

- *a* / *an* with <u>singular count nouns</u>

- **no article** with <u>plural count nouns</u> and <u>non-count nouns</u>

b. To make **general statements**, use **no article** with <u>plural count nouns</u> and <u>non-count nouns</u>.

c. *Some* in general statements means "several, but not all."

A: What do you do?
SINGULAR COUNT
B: I'm *a* **chef**. Not: I'm chef.

A: What's in the pot?
PLURAL COUNT   NON-COUNT
B: They're **beans**. I'm making **soup**.

PLURAL COUNT   NON-COUNT
- Ava loves **stories** and **music**.
  (stories and music in general)
  Not: Ava loves the stories and the music.

- I like *some* **stories**, but a lot of them are boring.

(continued on next page)

4 Use the **definite article *the*** with most common nouns (count and non-count, singular and plural) that are **definite**.

A ← nonspecific

Use ***the*** when:

a. a person, place, or thing is unique—there is only one

- Aesop is famous all over ***the* world**.
- ***The* moon** was shining brightly.

b. the context makes it clear which person, place, or thing you mean

A: Who is she?
B: She's ***the* teacher**.
(*A and B are students in a classroom. A is a new student.*)

c. the noun is mentioned for the second time (it is often indefinite the first time it is mentioned)

- ***An* ant** lived next to ***a* river**. One day, ***the* ant** went to ***the* river** to drink.
- They ate **cake**. ***The* cake** was delicious.

d. a phrase or adjective such as ***first***, ***best***, ***right***, ***wrong***, or ***only*** identifies the noun

- He was ***the best* hunter** in the country.
- He served ***the only* food** he had.

Use the **definite article** with some proper nouns, for example, the names of:
- certain books and documents
- countries and geographical features

- ***the*** Koran, ***the*** U.S. Constitution
- ***the*** United Arab Emirates, ***the*** Alps

5 **Adjectives** often go directly before a noun. When you use an article or *some*, the adjective goes between the article or *some* and the noun.

- ***Old* fables** are great.
- We read ***the first* story** in the book.
- He has **some *wonderful old*** books.

REFERENCE NOTES

For a list of **non-count nouns**, see Appendix 7 on page A-4.
For more information about the use of ***the*** with **proper nouns**, see Appendix 8 on page A-5.
For more information about the **word order of adjectives**, see Appendix 12 on page A-6.

STEP 3 FOCUSED PRACTICE

EXERCISE 1: Discover the Grammar

Read the conversations. Circle the letter of the statement that best describes each conversation.

1. **CORA:** Dad, could you read me a story?

   DAD: Sure, I'd love to.

   a. Dad knows which story Cora wants him to read.

   b. Cora isn't talking about a particular story.

2. FRED: Mom, where's the new book?

    MOM: Sorry, I haven't seen it.

        a. Mom knows that Fred bought a new book.

        b. Mom doesn't know that Fred bought a new book.

3. DAD: I'll bet it's in the hall. You always drop your things there.

    FRED: I'll go look.

        a. There are several halls in the house.

        b. There is only one hall in the house.

4. DAD: Was I right?

    FRED: You weren't even close. It was on a chair in the kitchen.

        a. There is only one chair in the kitchen.

        b. There are several chairs in the kitchen.

5. DAD: Wow! Look at that! The pictures are great.

    FRED: So are the stories.

        a. All books have great pictures and stories.

        b. The book Fred bought has great pictures and stories.

6. FRED: Oh, I forgot . . . I also got a video game. Do you want to play?

    DAD: Sure. I love video games.

        a. Dad is talking about video games in general.

        b. Dad is talking about a particular video game.

EXERCISE 2: Definite Article or No Article
(Grammar Notes 1, 3–5)

*Ben went to a bookstore to buy books for his niece. Complete the sentences. Use **the** where necessary. Leave a blank if you don't need an article.*

BEN: I'm looking for _____the_____ books for my 14-year-old niece. Do you have any
                1.

    recommendations?

CLERK: Let's go to _____the_____ young adult section. Does she like _____/_____
             2.   **3.**

    mysteries? Doris Duncan wrote some good ones for teenagers.

BEN: She's read all _____the_____ mysteries by Duncan. She's _____the_____ fastest
                4.   **5.**

    reader in the family!

CLERK: It's hard to keep up with _____the_____ fast readers. Here's a good one by Gillian
                             6.

    Cross—*Born of* _____ *Sun*. It's about finding a lost Inca city.
                 7.

(continued on next page)

BEN: She'll like that one. She loves _____the_____ books about _____
8.   9.

history—and science too.

CLERK: Then how about *A Short History of* ___the___ *Universe*? It's in
10.

_____the_____ science section.
11.

BEN: This is great! She likes _____the_____ books with beautiful pictures.
12.

CLERK: Well, _____The_____ pictures in this one are wonderful. *Nature Magazine* called this
13.

book _____the_____ best introduction to this subject.
14.

BEN: OK, I'll take _____the_____ mystery by Cross and _____the_____ science book.
15.   16.

Anything else?

CLERK: Well, _____the_____ kids have fun with _____ trivia games. Here's a
17.   18.

good one.

BEN: Great. I'll get _____the_____ trivia game too. Thanks. You've been very helpful.
19.

EXERCISE 3: Indefinite or Definite Article

(*Grammar Notes 1–5*)

Complete the information and the story about Nasreddin. Use **a, an,** *or* **the.**

Nasreddin lived _____a_____ long time ago in Turkey. He
1.

is one of _____the_____ most famous characters in literature.
2.

People often thought he was _____a_____ fool, but he was
3.

_____the_____ very wise man. Here is _____the_____
4.   5.

funny story about him:

Nasreddin Solves _____a_____ Difficult Problem
6.

Nasreddin had _____a_____ little donkey. There was
7.

_____the_____ market in _____the_____ nearby
8.   9.

town, and Nasreddin and his grandson often went there with

_____the_____ donkey. One day, they were traveling to
10.

_____the_____ market when _____a_____ group of people passed by. Someone
11.   12.

shouted, "Look! _____the_____ old man is walking while _____the_____ boy rides!" So
13.   14.

_____the_____ boy got down, and Nasreddin rode. Then they passed _____a_____
15.   16.

storyteller sitting under _____a_____ tree. _____the_____ storyteller called out,
17.   18.

"Why is that poor child walking in _____ _____ hot sun?" So they both rode. Next,

they met _____ old woman. "_____ little donkey is tired!" she
         20.   **21.**

shouted. So Nasreddin said, "_____ best thing is for both of us to walk." Soon
                              22.

they met _____ merchant. _____ merchant's donkey was carrying
         23.   **24.**

_____ enormous bag. "Why are you two walking?" _____ merchant
     25.   **26.**

laughed. "That's _____ strong little donkey!" Nasreddin immediately picked up
                 27.

_____ donkey and carried it on his shoulders. "These people will never leave us
     28.

alone," he told his grandson. "So this is _____ only way to solve _____
                                          29.   **30**

problem."

EXERCISE 4: Indefinite, Definite, or No Article *(Grammar Notes 1–5)*

Circle the correct article to complete the paragraph. Circle Ø if you don't need an article.

People all over the / Ø world know a / the fables of Aesop, but
              1.   **2.**

there is very little information about the / Ø life of this famous
                                       3.

Greek storyteller. Scholars agree that Aesop was born around

620 B.C.E.[1] In his early years, he was a / the slave, and he lived on
                                        4.

Samos, an / a island in an / the Aegean Sea. Even as a / the slave,
         5.   **6.**   **7.**

Aesop had the / Ø wisdom and knowledge. His master respected
              8.

him so much that he freed him. When Aesop became a / Ø free
                                                    9.

man, he traveled to many countries in order to learn and to teach.

In Lydia, the / Ø king invited him to stay in that country and gave Aesop some difficult jobs in
          10.

a / the government. In his work, Aesop often struggled to convince people of his ideas. Sometimes
11.

he used a / Ø fables to help people understand what he meant. One time, a / the king sent Aesop to
         12.   **13.**

Delphi with a / Ø gold for a / the people of that city. Aesop became disgusted with the / Ø people's
           14.   **15.**   **16.**

greed, so he sent the / Ø gold back to a / the king. A / The people of Delphi were very angry at Aesop
              17.   **18.**   **19.**

for this, and they killed him. After his death, a / the famous sculptor made a / the statue of Aesop you
                                              20.   **21.**

see in a / the photo above.
       22.

---

[1] **B.C.E.:** the abbreviation for *Before Common Era*, a year-numbering system used in many parts of the world

EXERCISE 5: Indefinite, Definite, or No Article

(Grammar Notes 1–5)

This is a trivia game. Complete the clues for each item. Then, using the clues and the appropriate picture, write the answer. Use **a, an,** *or* **the** *where necessary. Leave a blank if you don't need an article. The answers to the trivia game are on page 260.*

1. **CLUES:** He's _____*a*_____ person in _____ adventure story. In _____ story, he lives in
   a.   **b.**   **c.**
   _____ tree with his wife, Jane, and his son, Boy.
   d.

   ANSWER: He's _____*Tarzan*_____.

2. **CLUES:** It's _____ longest structure in _____ world. _____ emperor started
   a.   **b.**   **c.**
   building it more than 2,000 years ago. _____ bicycle race ended there during the
   d.
   2008 Olympics.

   ANSWER: It's _____.

3. **CLUES:** It's _____ smallest continent. There are _____ kangaroos and other
   a.   **b.**
   interesting animals there. Europeans found _____ gold there in 1851.
   c.

   ANSWER: It's _____.

4. **CLUES:** They are _____ very short stories. _____ stories are about _____
   a.   **b.**   **c.**
   animals, but they teach _____ lessons about how people behave. Aesop wrote
   d.
   _____ most famous ones.
   e.

   ANSWER: They're _____.

5. **CLUES:** She was _____ intelligent and beautiful woman. She was _____ most
   a. b.

   famous queen of Egypt. She ruled _____ country with her brother.
   c.

   ANSWER: She was _____.

6. **CLUES:** They are _____ biggest living animals on Earth. They have _____ fins, but
   a. b.

   they aren't _____ fish.
   c.

   ANSWER: They're _____.

EXERCISE 6: Editing

*Read the article about video games. There are thirteen mistakes in the use of **a**, **an**, and **the**.
The first mistake is already corrected. Find and correct twelve more.*

THE PLUMBER AND THE APE

Once there was a plumber named Mario.
The plumber
~~Plumber~~ had beautiful girlfriend. One

day, a ape fell in love with the girlfriend

and kidnapped her. The plumber chased

ape to rescue his girlfriend. This simple

tale became *Donkey Kong*, a first video

game with a story. It was invented by Shigeru Miyamoto, an artist with Nintendo,

Inc. Miyamoto loved the video games, but he wanted to make them more

interesting. He liked fairy tales, so he invented story similar to a famous fairy tale.

Story was an immediate success, and Nintendo followed it with *The Mario*

Brothers and then with *Super Mario*. The third game became popular all over a

world, and it is still most famous game in video history. Nintendo has continued

to add the new adventures and new ways to play game. Now players can follow

Mario to outer space and play the game on their Wii.[1] But success and space travel

do not change Mario. He is still brave little plumber in a red hat.

___

[1] **Wii** (pronounced "we"): a game system in which players hold a wireless controller and
control the game by their movements and by pressing buttons

EXERCISE 7: Listening

🎧 **A** | *Read the sentences. Then listen to the short conversations. Listen again and circle the words that you hear.*

1. I just finished a / (the) story by Nasreddin.

2. It's a / the new video game. Do you want to try it?

3. She's a / the princess with magic powers.

4. What about Aesop? Have you read a / the fable?

5. You know, I'd like to buy a / the book of fables for Ava.

6. Let's go to a / the bookstore this weekend.

7. Why don't you have a / the sandwich?

8. I think I put it on a / the shelf above the sink.

🎧 **B** | *Read the statements about the conversations. Then listen again to each conversation and circle the letter of the correct statement.*

1. **a.** Ben already knows about the story.

   b. Ben and Amy haven't spoken about the story before.

2. **a.** Ben and Amy have already spoken about this video game.

   b. Ben has never mentioned this video game before.

3. **a.** The story has several princesses. One of them has magic powers.

   b. The story has just one princess.

4. **a.** Ben and Amy have already spoken about this fable.

   b. Amy has never mentioned this fable before.

5. **a.** Amy has a specific book of fables in mind.

   b. Amy isn't thinking of a particular book of fables.

6. **a.** Amy has a specific bookstore in mind.

   b. Amy isn't thinking of a particular bookstore.

7. **a.** There is only one sandwich.

   b. There are several sandwiches.

8. **a.** There is only one shelf above the sink.

   b. There is more than one shelf above the sink.

EXERCISE 8: Pronunciation

A | *Read and listen to the Pronunciation Note.*

> ### Pronunciation Note
>
> *The* can be pronounced in two ways:
> 1. Before a **vowel sound**, say "thee" /ði/
>   **EXAMPLE:** the ant
> 2. Before a **consonant sound**, say "the" /ðə/
>   **EXAMPLE:** the dove

B | *Listen to the sentences. Which pronunciation of **the** do you hear? Check (✓) the box.*

	/ði/	/ðə/
1. We watched **the** new quiz show last night.	☐	☐
2. My sister answered all **the** questions.	☐	☐
3. I only answered **the** easy ones.	☐	☐
4. One question was about *The Mario Brothers*.	☐	☐
5. It's **the** oldest video game with a story.	☐	☐
6. I have one of **the** earliest games.	☐	☐
7. It's **the** only one I still play.	☐	☐
8. My friends like **the** newer games.	☐	☐

C | *Listen again and repeat the sentences.*

EXERCISE 9: Game: Quiz Show

Work with a small group. Choose five interesting or famous things. Write three clues for each thing. Then join another group. Give your clues and ask the other group to guess what each thing is. Look at Exercise 5 on page 254 for ideas. You can use the Internet or a library to find information.

EXAMPLE: **A:** It's a planet. It's the closest one to the Sun. There might be water there.
B: Does it have rings?
C: No, it doesn't.

EXERCISE 10: Information Gap: Story Time

Work in pairs (A and B). **Student A,** *follow the instructions on this page.* **Student B,** *turn to page 260 and follow the instructions there.*

1. Look at the picture below. Ask your partner for the information you need to finish labeling the picture.

   EXAMPLE: **A:** Who's the man in the black cape?
   B: He's the magician.

2. Answer your partner's questions.

   EXAMPLE: **B:** What's the magician holding?
   A: A magic wand.

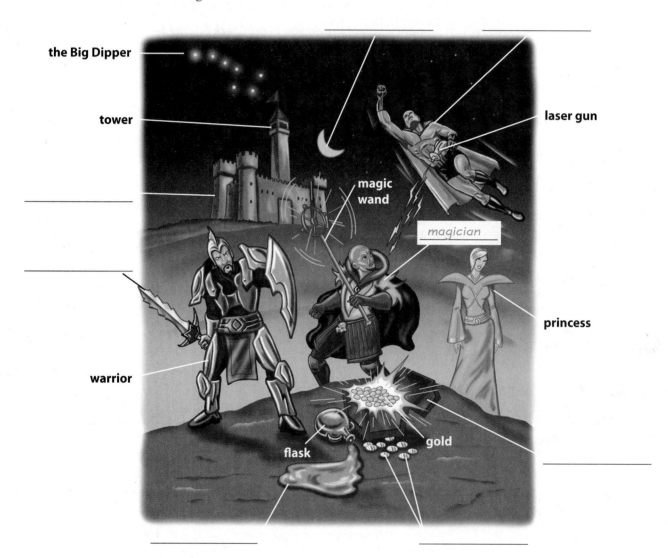

When you are finished, compare pictures. Are the labels the same?

EXERCISE 11: Discussion

A | *Fables often have a moral—a sentence at the end that explains the lesson of the story. Work with a small group. Read the list of morals. Answer the questions.*

- You can't please everyone.
- Sometimes a little friend is a great friend.
- Look before you leap.

- It's better to eat bread in peace than cake in fear.
- Slow and steady wins the race.
- Self-help is the best help.

1. Which ones belong to the two fables on pages 246–247?
2. Which one goes with the Nasreddin story on page 252?
3. What do you think they mean?

EXAMPLE: **A:** "It's better to eat bread in peace than cake in fear" goes with the second fable.
  B: I think this means it's better to have a good life situation with poorer things than a bad life situation with better things.
  C: I agree. You can't enjoy the better things if you're living in fear.

B | *Tell a story that illustrates one of the other morals. The story can be an experience you have had yourself or something you know about. The group will guess the moral.*

EXAMPLE: "When I went to college, my sister wanted to sew some curtains for my dorm room. She wanted the curtains to be really special, so she asked a friend to help her choose the material. The friend promised to help, but she didn't really have time to do it. My sister didn't start the curtains because she kept waiting for her friend . . ."

EXERCISE 12: Writing

A | *Choose one of the morals from Exercise 11. Write a paragraph about an experience that illustrates the meaning of the moral.*

EXAMPLE: "Slow and steady wins the race."
  When I was in high school, I was a good student, but I always waited until the night before a test to study. I learned very fast, so I never had trouble. Then I took a class from Mr. Fox, the toughest teacher in the school . . .

B | *Check your work. Use the Editing Checklist.*

Editing Checklist

Did you use . . . ?

☐ *a*, *an*, *some*, or **no article** with indefinite nouns
☐ *the* with definite nouns
☐ *a*, *an*, *some*, or **no article** to identify and make general statements
☐ *the* when a noun is unique, or it is clear which person, place, or thing it is

INFORMATION GAP FOR STUDENT B

1. Look at the picture below. Answer your partner's questions.

    EXAMPLE: **A:** Who's the man in the black cape?
                B: He's the magician.

2. Ask your partner for the information you need to finish labeling the picture.

    EXAMPLE: **B:** What's the magician holding?
                A: A magic wand.

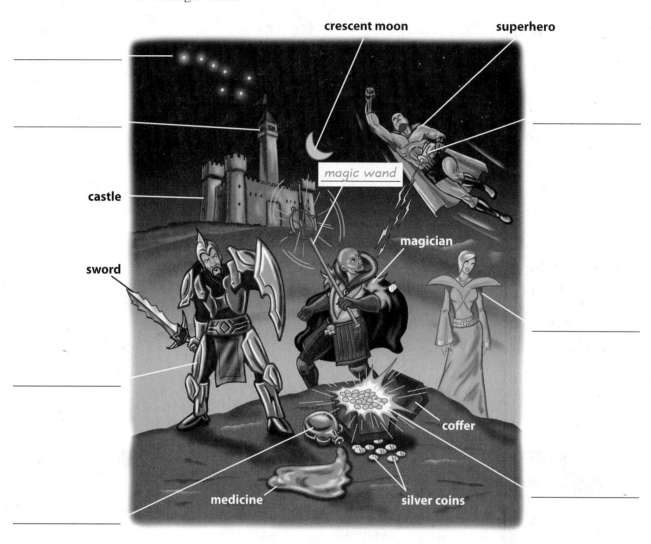

When you are finished, compare pictures. Are the labels the same?

ANSWERS FOR EXERCISE 5:   **2.** the Great Wall of China   **3.** Australia   **4.** fables   **5.** Cleopatra   **6.** whales

UNIT 18 Review

Check your answers on page UR-5.

Do you need to review anything?

A | *Circle the correct articles to complete the sentences. Circle Ø if you don't need an article.*

1. Is there a / the good bookstore around here?

2. I want to buy a / the book for my niece.

3. She really enjoys the / Ø fables.

4. I just read a / an excellent collection of fables.

5. Some / Ø fables have mice in them.

6. My niece is afraid of Ø / the mice.

7. This is a / the best story I've ever read.

8. It's famous all over a / the world.

B | *Complete the conversations with* **a, an,** *or* **the.**

- **A:** Did anyone feed _____ cat today?
   1.

   B: I did. Why?

   A: He's still hungry.

   B: Well, there's more food in _____the_____ kitchen.
   2.

- **A:** Look at this picture of Boots.

   B: It's really cute. What kind of cat is it?

   A: It's not _____a_____ cat. It's _____ dog.
   3.   4.

   B: You're kidding! What _____ unusual animal!
   5.

C | *Find and correct seven mistakes.*

Yesterday I downloaded the movies. We watched comedy and a Argentinian thriller. A comedy was very funny. I really enjoyed it. The thriller wasn't that good. There wasn't enough action in it. Tonight I think I'd rather read the book than watch a movie. I recently bought the book of fables and a mystery. I think I'll read a mystery before I go to bed.

From Grammar to Writing
DEVELOPING A PARAGRAPH WITH EXAMPLES

One way to develop a paragraph is to add **examples**. Examples give more information about the people, places, and things you are describing. They make your writing clearer and more interesting.

EXAMPLE: We celebrate with **food**. →
We celebrate with **food**. **For example, we bake loaves of bread we call "souls."**

1 | *Read the paragraph about a holiday. Write the examples from the box in the correct place in the paragraph.*

My family always hires a mariachi band	**For my sister, we offer toys.**
~~we bake loaves of bread we call "souls."~~	**We also create an altar[1] and put candy skulls[2] on it.**

A Happy Holiday

In Mexico we celebrate *Los Días de los Muertos* ("The Days of the Dead") on November 1 and 2.

On these days, we remember our relatives who have died. We celebrate with wonderful food, special

gifts for the dead, and music. For example, _____we bake loaves of bread we call "souls."_____
1.

They are shaped like people. _____ In addition,
2.

we remember special things our relatives liked, and we buy them gifts. For example, for my

grandfather, we always put out a new hat. _____
3.

On the second day, everyone in my family meets at the cemetery.[3] This sounds like a sad occasion,

but it is really a big party. _____ , and we all sing.
4.

Some people think that *Los Días de los Muertos* is like Halloween, but they are wrong. At

Halloween, people pretend to be afraid of evil spirits, but during *Los Días de los Muertos*, we invite

the friendly spirits of our family to visit us. It's our way of communicating with them.

---

[1] ***altar:*** a special table for religious ceremonies
[2] ***skull:*** the bones of a person's head
[3] ***cemetery:*** a special area where dead people are buried

2 | Complete the outline of the paragraph in Exercise 1.

1. The name of the holiday and when it is celebrated: _____

2. The purpose of the holiday: _____

3. How people celebrate the holiday:

    a. _____ *food* _____

        EXAMPLES: ____ *loaves of bread called "souls"* ____ and _____

    b. _____

        EXAMPLES: ____ *a new hat for my grandfather* ____ and _____

    c. _____

        EXAMPLES: _____ and _____

3 | Before you write . . .

1. Think about a holiday that is special to you. Develop an outline like the one in Exercise 2 for a paragraph about the holiday.

2. Work with a partner. Exchange outlines. Ask questions about your partner's holiday. Answer your partner's questions.

4 | Write a paragraph about a special holiday. Include the information your partner asked you about.

5 | Exchange paragraphs with a different partner. Complete the chart.

	Yes	No
1. Does the paragraph include examples?	☐	☐
2. Do the examples give more information about people, places, and things?	☐	☐
3. Are there more examples that you would like to see?	☐	☐
4. If yes, what would you like an example of? _____		
5. What else would you like to know about this holiday? _____		

_____

6 | Work with your partner. Discuss each other's editing questions from Exercise 5. Then rewrite your own paragraph and make any necessary corrections.

PART VI

ADJECTIVES AND ADVERBS

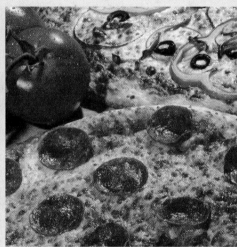

Adjectives and Adverbs

HOME

STEP 1 GRAMMAR IN CONTEXT

Before You Read

Look at the house. Discuss the questions.

1. Is this a good place to live? Why or why not?
2. What is important when looking for a home?

Read

Read the ad for two apartments in the house.

statisfy...満足
させる

WAKEFIELD HOUSE

Are you looking for a **nice** neighborhood with **safe**, **quiet** streets?
Do you love the **big sunny** rooms and **high** ceilings in **interesting old**
buildings—but want **modern** appliances[1] and **high-speed** Internet too?
Apartments in Wakefield House offer that and more. Here's your place to relax **completely** after
a **long hard** day at school or work. We are located in a **peaceful residential** area near **famous**
Lake Forest Park. And you'll still be just a **convenient** drive or bus ride from downtown and the
university. **Exciting** nightlife, shopping, and museums are only minutes away.

It sounds **very expensive**, right? But it's not! A **comfortable one-bedroom** apartment is
surprisingly affordable. We have two **beautifully furnished** apartments **available** right now.
But don't wait! Our apartments rent **very quickly**.

Call 555-1234 now for an appointment.

★ ★

Here's what some of our **satisfied** tenants[2] are saying about life at Wakefield House:

"The neighborhood is like a
small village, with **really friendly**
people and **charming** houses."
—Maggie Chang

"This place is
absolutely perfect.
It's my **ideal** home."
—Luis Rivera

"Weekends here are **so peaceful**—no **annoying**
traffic noise. I love walking through the
nearby park or just sitting on the **front** porch."
—Alice Thompson

---

[1] *appliance:* a piece of equipment, such as a washing machine or stove, that people use in their homes
[2] *tenant:* someone who lives in a house, apartment, or room and pays rent to the owner

After You Read

A | Vocabulary: *Circle the letter of the word or phrase closest in meaning to the word in* blue.

1. We found an **ideal** house today.
   a. perfect
   b. expensive
   c. nearby

2. The bus to town is very **convenient**.
   a. safe
   b. easy to use
   c. comfortable

3. There's a **charming** garden behind the house.
   a. large
   b. quiet
   c. lovely

4. The house is **located in** a residential area.
   a. close to
   b. far from
   c. part of

5. It's on a **peaceful** street.
   a. dangerous
   b. quiet
   c. crowded

6 We were very **satisfied** with the neighborhood.
   a. happy
   b. unhappy
   c. relaxed

B | Comprehension: *Check (✓)* **True** *or* **False**. *Correct the false statements.*

	True	False
1. Wakefield House is in a dangerous neighborhood.	☐	☑
2. The apartments have a lot of light.	☑	☐
3. It's in an exciting area of the city.	☑	☑
4. You'll be surprised that the rent is so low.	☐	☑
5. There are three apartments for rent now.	☑	☐
6. One tenant likes to spend weekends at home.	☑	☐

ADJECTIVES AND ADVERBS

Adjectives	Adverbs of Manner	Degree Adverbs
They are **quiet** tenants.	They talk **quietly**.	They're **very** quiet. They talk **very** quietly.
The house is **beautiful**.	They decorated it **beautifully**.	It's **so** beautiful. They decorated it **so** beautifully.
It looks **good**.	She described it **well**.	This looks **really** good. She described it **really** well.
It's a **fast** elevator.	It moves **fast**.	It's **awfully** fast! It moves **awfully** fast!

Participial Adjectives

-ing Adjective	*-ed* Adjective
The apartment is **interesting**.	One couple is **interested** in the apartment.
It's an **interesting** one-bedroom apartment.	The **interested** couple called again.
My neighbor is **annoying**.	I'm **annoyed** by his loud music.
He's an **annoying** neighbor.	Another **annoyed** tenant complained.

Word Order: Adjectives before Nouns

	Opinion	Size	Age	Shape	Color	Origin	Material	Purpose	Noun (as Adj)	NOUN
a	peaceful	little						residential		area
some	interesting		young							tenants
your				round	blue	Chinese				vase
the		large	old				wooden		kitchen	table

I live in

S

I   young Jap

GRAMMAR NOTES

1 | **Adjectives** and **adverbs** describe or give more information about other words:

a. Use **adjectives** to describe <u>nouns</u> (people, places, or things).

ADJECTIVE   NOUN
- They are *safe* **streets**.

NOUN   ADJECTIVE
- The **streets** are *safe*.
(Safe *tells you more about the streets.*)

b. Use **adverbs** to describe:

- verbs

VERB   ADVERB
- The manager **talks** *quietly*.

- adjectives

ADVERB   ADJECTIVE
- He's *extremely* **quiet**.

- other adverbs

ADVERB   ADVERB
- He works *very* **quietly**.

2 | Notice the **word order** of **adjectives** and **adverbs** and the words they describe:

a. An **adjective** usually goes right <u>before the noun</u> it describes.

ADJECTIVE   NOUN
- This is a *small* **house**.

It can also go <u>after a non-action verb</u> such as *be, look, seem, appear, smell,* or *taste.*

VERB   ADJECTIVE
- This house **looks** *small*.

b. An **adverb** usually goes <u>after the verb</u> it describes.

VERB   ADVERB
- The apartment **rented** *quickly*.

BE CAREFUL! Do NOT put an adverb between the verb and the object.

VERB   OBJECT   ADVERB
- She **decorated** the house *beautifully*.
NOT: She decorated ~~beautifully the house~~.

c. An **adverb** usually goes right <u>before the adjective or adverb</u> it describes.

ADVERB   ADJECTIVE
- It's an *extremely* **nice** house.

ADVERB   ADVERB
- They found it *very* **quickly**.

(continued on next page)

3 Use **adverbs of manner** to describe or give more information about <u>action verbs</u>.

    ACTION VERB   ADVERB
- They **decorated** the apartment ***beautifully***!
- They **rented** it ***quickly***.

a. Form most adverbs of manner by **adding -ly** to the adjective:

adjective + -ly = adverb

    ADJECTIVE
- We need a **quick** decision.

    ADVERB
- You should decide ***quickly***.

Some adverbs of manner also have a **form without -ly** (the same as the adjective). The form without -ly is more <u>informal</u>.

MORE FORMAL		MORE INFORMAL
slowly	OR	**slow**
quickly	OR	**quick**
loudly	OR	**loud**
clearly	OR	**clear**

- Don't speak so **loudly**. OR Don't speak so **loud**.

    ADJECTIVE
- It's a **lovely** apartment.

BE CAREFUL! Some **adjectives** also end in -ly —for example, *friendly*, *lonely*, *lovely*, and *silly*.

b. Some **common adverbs of manner** are NOT formed by adding -ly to adjectives:

The adverb form of ***good*** is ***well***.

    ADJECTIVE   ADVERB
- He's a **good** driver. He drives **well**.

Early*, *fast*, *hard*, *late*,** and ***wrong have the <u>same adjective and adverb forms</u>.

    ADJECTIVE   ADVERB
- She is a **hard** worker. She works **hard**.

BE CAREFUL! *Hardly* is not the adverb form of *hard*. *Hardly* means "almost not."
Lately is not the adverb form of *late*. *Lately* means "recently."

- There's **hardly** enough room for a bed.
  (There's almost not enough room for a bed.)
- We haven't seen any nice houses **lately**. We're getting discouraged.

4 Use **degree adverbs** to make adjectives and other adverbs <u>stronger</u> or <u>weaker</u>.

absolutely   awfully   really   pretty   fairly   not at all
completely   terribly   so   quite
           very

100%   0%

A: How fast can you get to work from here?
B: ***Very* fast**. The traffic is**n't** bad *at all*.

A: This apartment is ***absolutely* perfect**!
B: Really? It looks ***very* small** to me.
A: But it's in a ***really* good** neighborhood.
B: True. And you can get to work ***quite* easily**.

Awfully and *terribly* can describe something **good** or something **bad**.

- The landlord was ***awfully* rude**.
- The apartment was ***awfully* nice**.

Not at all means "totally not."

- I did**n't** like the apartment **at all**.
  (I totally didn't like it.)

Notice the word order for ***not at all***:
- After a verb or verb + object
- After or before an adjective or another adverb

- They did**n't** decorate (the place) **at all**.
- It was**n't** nice **at all**. OR It was**n't** **at all** nice.

5 Participial adjectives are adjectives that end with *-ing* or *-ed*. They come from <u>verbs</u>.

VERB
- This story **amazes** me.

ADJECTIVE ADJECTIVE
- It's an **amazing** story. I'm **amazed**.

Participial adjectives often describe **feelings**.

- Use the *-ing* form for someone or something that <u>causes</u> a feeling.

- The fly is **disgusting**.
  (The fly causes the feeling.)

- Use the *-ed* form for the person who <u>has</u> the feeling.

- I'm **disgusted**.
  (I have the feeling.)

6 Sometimes we use **two or three adjectives before a noun**. If these adjectives belong to different categories, we usually follow this **order**:

opinion + size + age + shape + color + origin + material + purpose + noun (used as adjective) + NOUN

(OPINION) (AGE) (PURPOSE)
- It's in a **charming old residential** neighborhood.

(OPINION) (COLOR) (MATERIAL)
- I bought a **nice black leather** couch.

(SIZE) (OPINION) (NOUN AS ADJ)
- It's a **small affordable one-room** apartment. OR

EXCEPTION: Size adjectives (such as *big* and *small*) often go first in a series of adjectives.

(OPINION) (SIZE) (NOUN AS ADJ)
- It's an **affordable small one-room** apartment.

(SIZE) (SHAPE) (ORIGIN)
- I got a **large round Mexican** mirror.
  NOT: I got a large, round, Mexican mirror.

We do **NOT use commas** between adjectives that belong to <u>different categories</u>.

For adjectives that belong to the <u>same category</u>, the **order is not important**. Use **commas** to separate these adjectives.

- She's a **friendly, helpful, nice** woman. OR
- She's a **helpful, friendly, nice** woman. OR
- She's a **nice, helpful, friendly** woman.
  (All the adjectives are opinion adjectives, so the order can change.)

REFERENCE NOTES

For a list of **non-action verbs**, see Appendix 2 on page A-2.
For a discussion of **adverbs of frequency**, see Unit 1, Grammar Note 3, on page 5.
For a list of **participial adjectives**, see Appendix 11 on page A-6.
For the **order of adjectives before a noun**, see Appendix 12 on page A-6.
For **spelling rules** for forming *-ly* adverbs, see Appendix 24 on page A-11.

EXERCISE 1: Discover the Grammar

Read the notice from a university bulletin board. Underline the adjectives and circle the adverbs. Then draw an arrow from the adjective or adverb to the word it is describing.

APT. FOR RENT
140 Grant Street, Apartment 4B

Are you looking for a place to live? This charming apartment is in a new building and has two large comfortable bedrooms and a small sunny kitchen. The building is very quiet—absolutely perfect for two serious students. It's near the campus on a peaceful street. There's convenient transportation. The bus stop is an easy, pleasant walk, and the express bus goes directly into town. You can run or ride your bike safely in nearby parks. The rent is very affordable. Small pets are welcome. The apartment is available on June 1. Interested students should call Megan at 555-5050. We're sure you'll be satisfied. Don't wait! This apartment will rent fast. Nonsmokers, please.

EXERCISE 2: Adjective or Adverb

(Grammar Notes 1–5)

Circle the correct words to complete Maggie's email to her brother.

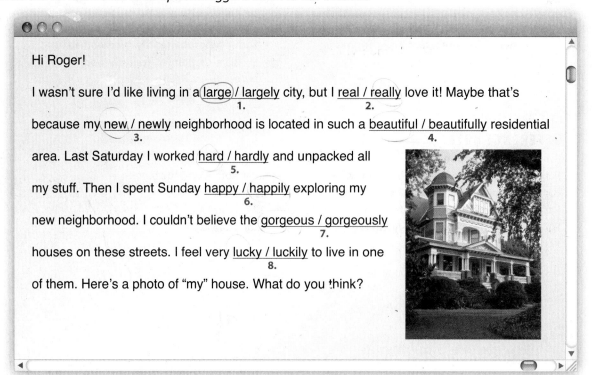

Hi Roger!

I wasn't sure I'd like living in a (large) / largely city, but I real / really love it! Maybe that's
                                          1.   **2.**

because my new / newly neighborhood is located in such a beautiful / beautifully residential
                3.   **4.**

area. Last Saturday I worked hard / hardly and unpacked all
                                   5.

my stuff. Then I spent Sunday happy / happily exploring my
                                        6.

new neighborhood. I couldn't believe the gorgeous / gorgeously
                                                7.

houses on these streets. I feel very lucky / luckily to live in one
                                        8.

of them. Here's a photo of "my" house. What do you think?

My apartment is on the second floor. It's really <u>great / greatly</u>. I'm <u>total / totally</u> satisfied

9.   10.

with it. The other tenants are very <u>nice / nicely</u>. My next-door neighbor, Alice, seemed pretty

11.

<u>shy / shyly</u> at first, but I think we're going to become <u>good / well</u> friends very <u>quick / quickly</u>.

12.   13.   14.

She's an art student, and she likes to visit museums. We're going to the Modern Art Museum

together next Saturday. Life in the city is <u>exciting / excitingly</u>, but I get <u>terrible / terribly</u>

15.   16.

homesick. So I hope you visit me soon!

Love,
Maggie

EXERCISE 3: Adverbs Before Adjectives and Other Adverbs   *(Grammar Notes 2, 4)*

Many different people went to see the apartment described in Exercise 1. Complete their comments about the apartment. Use the correct form of the words in parentheses. Go to Appendix 24 on page A-11 for help with spelling adverbs ending in -ly.

1. I am very interested. I think the apartment is _____ *extremely nice* _____.
                                                    (extreme / nice)

2. I was expecting much bigger rooms. I was _____.
                                  (terrible / disappointed)

3. I thought it would be hard to get to, but the bus was _____.
                                  (surprising / convenient)

4. I think it's a great place. I'm sure it will rent _____.
                                  (incredible / fast)

5. The ad said it was quiet, but I heard the neighbors _____.
                                  (very / clear)

6. I heard them too. I thought their voices were _____.
                                  (awful / loud)

7. The ad described the apartment _____ _____.
                                  (pretty / accurate)

8. To be honest, this place is _____ for me!
                                  (absolute / perfect)

9. I'm going to feel _____ if I don't get it.
                                  (real / upset)

A living room in Wakefield House

EXERCISE 4: Word Order

(Grammar Notes 2–4)

Put the words in the correct order to complete the entry from Sylvie's journal.

I'm a ___*fairly cheerful person*___ most of the time, but yesterday some

1. (cheerful / person / fairly)

_____ happened. The bus _____,

2. (things / upsetting / pretty)   **3. (late / arrived / really)**

so I missed an _____ at work. However, my boss

4. (important / meeting / awfully)

_____. She _____. Later, I

5. (well / quite / reacted)   **6. (at all / angry / didn't / seem)**

looked at a(n) _____. I thought it was exactly what I wanted, but

7. (apartment / charming / absolutely)

I needed to _____. When I called this morning, I found out it was

8. (it / think about / carefully / very)

already rented! Wow—_____! Next time I see a great place, I'll

9. (so / it / happened / quickly)

_____.

10. (it / immediately / take)

EXERCISE 5: Participial Adjectives

(Grammar Note 5)

Luis is talking to his friend Sylvie. Read their conversation. Complete it with the correct participial adjective form (-ing or -ed) of the verbs in parentheses.

Sylvie: These apartment ads are really ___*annoying*___. Just look at this one.

1. (annoy)

Luis: Hmmm. It says, "cozy and _____ apartment." Why are you

2. (charm)

_____ at that?

3. (annoy)

Sylvie: I saw the place—it's tiny, not cozy! And I wasn't _____ at all. In fact, I was

4. (charm)

pretty _____.

5. (disgust)

Luis: Take it easy. It sounds like you had an _____ day. Let's relax and watch a

6. (exhaust)

movie tonight.

Sylvie: You're right. I'm completely _____. I could use a _____

7. (exhaust)   **8. (relax)**

evening. What do you want to watch?

Luis: There's a movie called *Lake House* on TV tonight. I hear it's _____.

9. (fascinate)

Sylvie: *Lake House?* Great title! I'm _____ already. What's it about?

10. (fascinate)

Luis: Well, the story's a little _____, but it happens in a beautiful glass house on a

11. (confuse)

peaceful lake.

Sylvie: That sounds like a pretty _____ house. I wonder if *they're* looking for tenants.

12. (amaze)

EXERCISE 6: Word Order: Adjectives + Noun

(Grammar Note 6)

Sylvie has found a great place, and she's already moved in. Put the words in the correct order to complete the new entry in her journal. Remember to use commas when necessary.

I found a ___*nice, comfortable apartment*___ in this _____!
     1. (apartment / nice / comfortable)   **2. (old / house / charming)**

It's in a _____, and I can see a(n) _____
     3. (residential / neighborhood / peaceful)   **4. (tree / enormous / old)**

outside my _____. There's even a very lovely garden with a
     5. (bedroom / wide / window)

_____. The apartment is nicely furnished too. The kitchen has
     6. (stone / bench / Japanese)

a(n) _____. I do my homework there. And the people here are
     7. (beautiful / table / antique / large)

great. The manager is a _____. I've already met most of my
     8. (man / friendly / helpful)

neighbors. Across the hall from me is a _____. She took me to a(n)
     9. (Polish / young / woman)

_____ for dinner. I know I'll be happy here.
   10. (nice / neighborhood / restaurant / Italian)

EXERCISE 7: Editing

Read reviews of school dormitories. There are fourteen mistakes in the use of adjectives and adverbs. The first mistake is already corrected. Find and correct thirteen more.

RATE YOUR DORM

☆☆☆☆☆ **Jeff W.** The Northwood dorms are pretty ~~awesomely~~ awesome. They're clean and

modern, and they're a convenient walk to class and the dining hall. The halls get ~~noisy~~ terribly

sometimes, though. When I'm studying ~~hardly~~ for exams, I have to go to the library.

☆☆☆☆☆ **Sheryl** Miller Hall is the ideal dorm for freshmen. It's quite small, so I was able

to make friends ~~fastly~~ there. Also, the floor counselors are great. ~~Ours explained clearly the rules.~~

She was a young French ~~nice~~ woman, and she was always available when you needed to talk.

I was ~~extreme~~ satisfied. I would absolutely recommend this ~~dorm amazing~~ to anyone.

☆☆☆☆☆ **Tania** Warning! Keep away! Wyeth Hall is totally ~~disgusted~~. The lounges are

~~incredible~~ dirty. The toilets don't work ~~good~~, and the halls smell ~~badly~~. I had a small brown

depressing room on the ground floor. My parents were ~~shocking~~ when they saw the place.

EXERCISE 8: Listening

A | *A couple is discussing online apartment ads. Read the ads and guess the missing adjectives and adverbs.*

Janslist>bay area> housing > apts/housing for rent

$700 a month _____small_____ , charming 2 bedroom in Smithfield
1.

This is an _____ building very _____ all public transportation.
2.   3.

Keep your car in the garage and relax on the train!

Date: 12-10-2011 posted 10:00 PM PST
Call 555-3296 for an appointment today

FOSTER $750 Light and bright 2 BR on beautiful tree-lined street

This lovely apartment has been newly painted and is in _____ condition.
4.

_____ near shopping and schools.
5.

Date: 12-09-2011 posted 1:00 PM PST
Apply Online   Email for Appointment   See Photos

$650 Cute and Cozy 2 BR in Cumberland!

Our last 2-bedroom apartment has all _____ appliances.
6.

Enjoy the _____ residential area of Cumberland.
7.

Date: 12-14-2011 posted 8:53AM PST
Call 555-2343 ext. 27 OR email blanders@goodproperties.com Sorry, no pets. CLICK for photos.

LINCOLN Beautiful 2 bedroom only $850

Completely renovated building with _____
8.

kitchen and bath. All _____ appliances.
9.

Well-behaved pets welcome. Available _____.
10.

Date: 12-09-2011 posted 7:00 AM PST
Call 555-4478 email: edgar.hodgins@Lincolntownhouse.com

B | *Listen to the couple's conversation. Did you guess the same adjectives that they used to describe the apartments? If not, write the adjectives used in the conversation.*

C | *Read the information in the chart. Then listen again to the conversation and check (✓) the couple's opinion of each apartment.*

Opinion	Apt 1	Apt 2	Apt 3	Apt 4
Sunny				
Sounds terrific!				
Not enough information	✓			
Awfully small				
Can't bring Loki				
Not near stores				

EXERCISE 9: Pronunciation

A | *Read and listen to the Pronunciation Note.*

Pronunciation Note

In phrases that include **adjective + noun**, the adjective and the noun are **both stressed**. When the **noun is new information**, the noun is often **stressed more strongly** than the adjective.

EXAMPLES: A: Are you happy with your **new apartment**?

B: Well, I've got a **noisy neighbor**.

When we contrast information or add new information, we **stress** the **contrasting** or **new information more strongly**.

EXAMPLES: A: This apartment is in a very **safe neighborhood**.

B: No, it's not. It's in a very **dangerous area**.

B | *Listen to the short conversations. Put a small dot (•) or a large dot (●) over the nouns and adjectives to show stress.*

1. **A:** This is a **nice apartment**.

   B: And it's such a **sunny place** too!

2. **A:** Alice seems like a **friendly neighbor**.

   B: Yes, and she's a **helpful neighbor**, too.

3. **A:** It's got a **small kitchen**.

   B: No, it doesn't! It's the **perfect kitchen** for me.

(continued on next page)

4. A: Did the landlord give you **new appliances**?

   B: No. But these aren't **bad appliances**.

5. A: Do you have a **helpful landlord**?

   B: Yes, but he's a **nosy landlord**, too!

6. A: Well, I hope you like your **new home**.

   B: Thanks. I'm going to like it more than my **old home**.

C | *Listen again. Then practice the conversations with a partner.*

EXERCISE 10: What About You?

Work in small groups. Describe where you live. Answer the questions.

1. How did you find the place?
2. How did you first feel about it (pleased, disappointed, etc.)?
3. What does it look like?
4. How did you decorate it?
5. What is special about your place?

EXAMPLE: **A:** I found my apartment last summer. I was taking a walk in a beautiful neighborhood, and I saw . . .
B: At first I was pretty happy about my dorm room, but then . . .
C: My place is cozy, and it's got an old fireplace . . .

EXERCISE 11: Compare and Contrast

Work with a partner. There are many different types of housing. Describe the different types in the list. How are they similar? How are they different? Use your dictionaries to help you. Do these types of housing exist in other places you have lived?

- apartment

- boarding house

- dorm (dormitory)

- mansion

- mobile home

- private home

- rented room in someone's house

- studio apartment

EXAMPLE: **A:** A mobile home can be very convenient. You can move it from place to place.
B: And it's easy to get away from noisy—or nosey—neighbors!

EXERCISE 12: Discussion

What is your ideal home? What does it look like? What kind of roommates, neighbors, and landlord does it have? Work in small groups. Take turns describing this perfect place. Talk about the people and their activities. Here are some words you can use.

Adjectives

affordable	convenient	honest	messy	peaceful
boring	cozy	interesting	modern	relaxed
cheerful	friendly	large	neat	reliable
considerate	helpful	loud	nosy	sunny

Adverbs of Manner

carefully	honestly	quickly
early	late	politely
easily	loudly	seriously
happily	noisily	well

Degree Adverbs

awfully	really
not . . . at all	so
pretty	totally
quite	very

EXAMPLE: **A:** My ideal home is small and modern. It's located . . .
B: My ideal neighbors are really interesting. They . . .
C: The perfect roommates always . . .

EXERCISE 13: Game: A Strange Story

Work in small groups. Student A keeps his or her book open. All the other students close their books. Student A asks each member of the group, in turn, for a type of adjective. Student A fills in the blanks with the words the group members give. At the end, Student A will read the story to the group. Expect a very strange story!

EXAMPLE: **A:** Enrique, I need a size adjective.
B: How about *enormous*?
A: OK. Lee, now I need an opinion adjective . . .

I was walking down the street one day when I saw a(n) _____ _____

                               1. (size adj)   **2. (opinion adj)**

_____ house. It was _____ _____. I took out my camera
3. (color adj)   **4. (degree adv)**   **5. (participial -*ing* adj)**

phone and _____ called my friend. He wasn't at home, so I took a picture.
        6. (-*ly* adv of manner)

The house was _____ _____. It had three _____
             7. (degree adv)   **8. (opinion adj)**   **9. (size adj)**

_____ windows and a _____ _____ door. There
10. (shape adj)   **11. (size adj)**   **12. (material adj)**

were two _____ _____ trees and a lot of _____
      13. (size adj)   **14. (age adj)**   **15. (opinion adj)**

_____ flowers. Under the tree was a(n) _____ _____
16. (color adj)   **17. (age adj)**   **18. (material adj)**

_____ bench. I was _____. I'd never seen anything like it before!
19. (origin adj)   **20. (participial -*ed* adj)**

Source: This game is based on the popular game *Mad Libs* invented in 1953 by Leonard Stern and Roger Price. *Mad Libs* books are published by Price Stern Sloan, an imprint of Penguin Group.

EXERCISE 14: Writing

A | *Write an ad like the one for Wakefield House on page 266. Describe your ideal home.*
Use adjectives and adverbs.

> **EXAMPLE:** Do you want to live in an exciting neighborhood with great stores that stay open late?
> Do you want a large modern apartment with a terrific view of all the action in the
> streets below? The apartments in the Atrium are . . .

B | *Check your work. Use the Editing Checklist.*

Editing Checklist

Did you use . . . ?
☐ adjectives to describe people, places, and things
☐ participial adjectives to describe feelings
☐ adverbs of manner to describe action verbs
☐ degree adverbs to describe adjectives and other adverbs

A | *Circle the correct words to complete the sentences.*

1. My neighbor is so <u>annoyed / annoying</u>. He plays loud music all night long.

2. The bus came <u>late / lately</u>, and I missed my class.

3. This apartment seems <u>perfect / perfectly</u> for you. Are you going to take it?

4. Ken worked very <u>hardly / hard</u> last semester. He deserved those A's.

5. My roommate is <u>surprising / surprisingly</u> shy. She doesn't even like to answer the phone.

B | *Unscramble the words to complete the sentences.*

1. Today I looked at a(n) _____.
   (old / house / interesting)

2. I loved the _____.
   (yellow / big / kitchen / cheerful)

3. The house is on a _____.
   (residential / peaceful / street)

4. Two _____ live next door.
   (international / nice / students / young)

5. But the landlord _____.
   (seem / friendly / didn't / at all)

6. There's a _____ on the corner.
   (little / restaurant / cute / Greek)

7. It has a _____ in the back.
   (garden / beautiful / really)

8. We sat at a(n) _____.
   (round / table / wonderful / wooden / old)

9. I think I have to _____ about this house.
   (quickly / pretty / decide)

10. I have a feeling that it's going to _____.
    (fast / awfully / rent)

C | *Find and correct five mistakes.*

The conditions in Parker Dorm are pretty shocked. The rooms are terrible small, and the furniture is incredibly ugly. The locks on the doors don't work good, so your stuff is never safely. The dorm counselors are great—they're all really nice, friendly people—but they can't make up for the badly conditions.

STEP 1 GRAMMAR IN CONTEXT

Before You Read

Look at the photo. Discuss the questions.

1. Would you like to order the pizza in the photo? Why or why not?
2. How often do you eat out?
3. What types of restaurant food do you enjoy?

Read

Read the newspaper restaurant review.

A New Place for Pizza
by Pete Tsa

AS FRESH AS IT GETS!

PIZZA PLACE, the chain of popular restaurants, has just opened a new one on Main Street, two blocks from the university. The last time that I ate there, the service was **not as good as** at the other Pizza Place restaurants in town. The young staff (mostly students) probably needs time to become **more professional**. But the pizza was incredible! It seemed **bigger** and **better than** at the other six locations in town. As with all food, **the fresher** the ingredients,[1] **the better** the pizza. The ingredients at the new Pizza Place are **as fresh as** you can get (absolutely no mushrooms from a can here!), and the choices are much **more varied than** at their other locations. We ordered two different types. The one with mashed potatoes and garlic was a lot **more interesting than** the traditional pizza with cheese and tomato sauce, but both were delicious.

Each Pizza Place is different. The one on Main Street is a little **larger** (and **louder**) **than** the others. It's also a lot **more crowded** because students love it. At lunchtime the lines outside this new eatery are getting **longer and longer**. Go early for a **quieter**, **more relaxed** meal.

---

[1] *ingredients:* things that go into a recipe (example: tomatoes, cheese, mushrooms, salt . . .)

A | Vocabulary: *Circle the letter of the word or phrase that best completes each sentence.*

1. **Delicious** food _____.
   a. is healthy
   b. tastes very good
   c. costs a lot

2. **Fresh** food _____.
   a. comes in a can
   b. is not old
   c. is always hot

3. If a meal is **relaxed**, you don't feel _____.
   a. in a hurry
   b. too full
   c. comfortable

4. A **varied** menu has _____.
   a. pizza and hamburgers
   b. very good food
   c. a lot of different types of food

5. In a **crowded** restaurant people or things are _____.
   a. close together
   b. not interesting
   c. far apart

6. _____ is NOT a **traditional** pizza ingredient.
   a. Cheese
   b. Tomato sauce
   c. Fruit

B | Comprehension: *Check (✓)* **all** *the words that describe each item.*

1. **the restaurant**	☐ crowded	☐ new	☐ quiet	☐ popular
2. **the staff**	☐ professional	☐ young	☐ relaxed	☐ loud
3. **the food**	☐ delicious	☐ fresh	☐ expensive	☐ good

ADJECTIVES: COMPARISONS WITH *AS . . . AS* AND *THAN*

Comparisons with *As . . . as*				
	(Not) As	**Adjective**	**As**	
The new restaurant is	**(not) as**	large busy good interesting expensive	**as**	the other ones.

Comparisons with *Than*			
	Comparative Adjective Form	***Than***	
The new restaurant is	larger busier better more interesting less expensive	**than**	the other ones.

GRAMMAR NOTES

1 Use *as* + **adjective** + *as* to show how people, places, or things are <u>the same or equal</u>.

- The new menu is **as good as** the old.

Use *just* to make the comparison stronger.

- The new menu is *just* **as good as** the old.
  (*The new menu and the old menu are equally good.*)

Use *not as* + **adjective** + *as* to show how they are <u>NOT the same or equal</u>.

- The new menu is**n't as varied as** the old.
  (*The old menu was more varied.*)

REMEMBER: It is not necessary to mention both parts of the comparison when the meaning is clear.

A: I liked the old menu. It had more choices.
B: Too bad the new one is**n't as varied**.
   (*It isn't as varied as the old menu.*)

2

Use **comparative adjectives** + *than* to show how people, places, or things are <u>different</u>.

- The new room is **bigger than** the old room.
- The new waiters are **more professional than** the old waiters.

Use *even* to make the comparison stronger.

- The old waiters were very professional, but the new waiters are *even* **more professional than** the old waiters.

USAGE NOTE: We usually do NOT use *less...than* with <u>one syllable adjectives</u>. Instead we use:
- *not as...as*

  OR
- another adjective with the <u>opposite meaning</u>.

NOT: Our server is ~~less fast than~~ theirs.

- Our server is**n't as fast as** theirs.

  OR
- Our server is **slower than** theirs.

REMEMBER: It is not necessary to mention both parts of the comparison when the meaning is clear.

- The new tables are **smaller**.
  (*They are smaller than the old tables.*)

3

There are several ways of **forming comparative adjectives**.

a. For **short adjectives** (one syllable and two syllables ending in -*y*), use **adjective** + -*er*.

ADJECTIVE	COMPARATIVE
loud	loud**er**
friendly	friendl**ier**

There are often **spelling changes** when you add -*er*.

late	lat**er**
big	big**ger**
early	earl**ier**

Some short adjectives have **irregular** comparative forms.

good	**better**
bad	**worse**
far	**farther**

b. For **long adjectives** (two or more syllables), use *more / less* + **adjective**.

expensive	**more** expensive
	less expensive

EXCEPTION: The **short adjective** *fun* forms the comparative in the same way as a long adjective.

fun	**more** fun NOT: ~~funner~~
	less fun

c. For **some adjectives**, such as *lively*, *lovely*, *friendly*, and *quiet*, you can use: -*er* or *more*

- The Inn is **livelier** than Joe's.

  OR
- The Inn is **more lively** than Joe's.

(continued on next page)

4	**Repeat the comparative adjective** to show <u>increase or decrease</u>:
	
	comparative adjective + *and* + comparative adjective
	
	With long adjectives, repeat only *more* or *less*.
		• The lines are getting **longer and longer**.
		  (Their length is increasing.)
		
		• It's getting **more and more popular**.
		  (Its popularity is increasing.)
		  Noт: It's getting more ~~popular~~ and more popular.

5	Use **two comparative adjectives** to show <u>cause and effect</u>:
	
	the + comparative adjective *the* + comparative adjective
	
	When both comparative adjectives describe the same person, place, or thing, we often <u>leave out the noun</u>.
		• **The more crowded** the restaurant, **the slower** the service.
		  (The service is slower because the restaurant is more crowded.)
		
		A: The service is really fast here.
		B: **The faster, the better.**
		  (The faster the service, the better the service.)

REFERENCE NOTES

For a list of **adjectives** that use **both forms of the comparative**, see Appendix 9 on page A-5.
For a list of **irregular comparative adjectives**, see Appendix 10 on page A-6.
For **spelling rules** for the **comparative form of adjectives**, see Appendix 23 on page A-11.

STEP 3 FOCUSED PRACTICE

EXERCISE 1: Discover the Grammar

Read the information about two brands of frozen pizza on the next page. Then decide if each statement is **True (T)** *or* **False (F).**

	Maria's Pizza	John's Pizza
Size	12 inches	12 inches
Weight	27 ounces	24 ounces
Price	$5.99	$6.99
Calories*	364	292
Salt content*	731 milligrams	600 milligrams
Fat content*	11 grams	11 grams
Baking time	20 minutes	16 minutes
Taste	★ ★ ★	★ ★ ★ ★

* for a five-ounce serving

1. Maria's pizza is bigger than John's.
2. John's pizza is just as big as Maria's.
3. John's isn't as heavy as Maria's.
4. Maria's is just as expensive as John's.
5. John's is more expensive than Maria's.
6. Maria's is higher in calories than John's.
7. Maria's is saltier than John's.
8. John's pizza is just as high in fat as Maria's pizza.
9. The baking time for Maria's isn't as long as the baking time for John's.
10. John's tastes better than Maria's.

EXERCISE 2: Comparisons with As . . . as

(Grammar Note 1)

*Look at the consumer magazine chart comparing three brands of pizza cheese. Complete the sentences. Use **as . . . as** or **not as . . . as** and the correct form of the words in parentheses.*

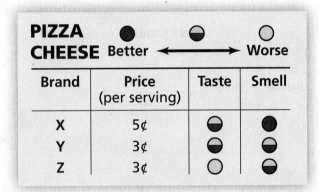

PIZZA CHEESE	Better ⬤ ◗ ◯ Worse		
Brand	Price (per serving)	Taste	Smell
X	5¢	◗	⬤
Y	3¢	◗	◗
Z	3¢	◯	◗

1. Brand Z _____ is as expensive as _____ brand Y.
   (be / expensive)
2. Brand Y _____ isn't as expensive as _____ brand X.
   (be / expensive)
3. Brand X _____ is as ... taste ... as ... as _____ brand Y.
   (taste / good)
4. Brand Z _____ doesn't taste as good as _____ brand Y.
   (taste / good)
5. Brand Y _____ doesn't smell as delicious as _____ brand X.
   (smell / delicious)
6. Brand Y _____ smells as delicious as _____ brand Z.
   (smell / delicious)

EXERCISE 3: Comparisons with *Than*

(Grammar Note 2–3)

*Look at the menu. Then complete the sentences comparing items on the menu. Use the appropriate comparative form of the adjectives in parentheses and **than**.*

1. The sweet-and-sour shrimp is _____ *more expensive than* _____ the steamed scallops.
   (expensive)

2. The beef with red pepper is _____ hotter than or _____ the beef with broccoli.
   (hot)

3. The pork with scallions is _____ less expensive than _____ the sweet-and-sour shrimp.
   (expensive)

4. The chicken with orange sauce is _____ spicier then _____ the steamed scallops.
   (spicy)

5. The steamed vegetables are _____ not so as salty as _____ the pork with scallions.
   (salty)

6. The steamed vegetables are _____ healthier than _____ the beef with red pepper.
   (healthy)

7. The broccoli with garlic is _____ *cheaper than* _____ the chicken with broccoli.
   (cheap)

8. The shrimp dish is _____ *sweeter than* _____ the scallop dish.
   (sweet)

9. The restaurant's hours on Sunday are _____ *shorter than* _____ on Saturday.
   (short)

10. The children's menu is _____ *not as varied as* _____ the adult's menu.
    (varied)

11. The children's menu is _____ *not as expensive as* _____ too.
    (expensive)

12. The chicken wings are _____ *as sweet as* _____ the macaroni and cheese slices.
    (sweet)

EXERCISE 4: Increase or Decrease; Cause and Effect (Grammar Notes 4–5)

Complete the conversations. Use the comparative form of the adjectives in parentheses to show an increase or decrease or a cause and effect.

1. **A:** Wow! The lines here are getting _____ longer and longer _____.
   (long)

   B: I know. And _____ the longer _____ the wait, _____ the hungrier _____ I get.
   (long)   (hungry)

2. **A:** It's worth the wait. The food here is getting _____ better and better _____.
   (good)

   B: But _____ the better _____ the food, _____ the higher _____ the bill!
   (good)   (high)

3. **A:** The lunch crowd is leaving. It's getting _____ less and less crowded _____.
   (crowded)

   B: Great. These books were starting to feel _____ heavier _____.
   (heavy)

4. **A:** The menu is getting _____ more and more interesting _____.
   (interesting)

   B: I know, but that means it's also _____ more difficult _____ to choose something.
   (difficult)

5. **A:** There's Professor Lee. You know, his course is getting _____ more popular _____.
   (popular)

   B: It's amazing. _____ The harder _____ it is, _____ the more popular _____ it gets.
   (hard)   (popular)

   He's a great teacher.

6. **A:** Is it the hot sauce, or has your cough been getting _____ worse _____?
   (bad)

   B: It's the hot sauce, but I love it. For my taste, _____ the spicier _____,
   (spicy)

   _____ the better _____.
   (good)

7. **A:** The service used to be slow here, but it's getting _____ faster and faster _____.
   (fast)

   B: Right. _____ The faster _____ the service, _____ the shorter _____ the lines!
   (fast)   (short)

EXERCISE 5: Editing

Read the student's essay. There are ten mistakes in the use of **as . . . as** *and comparatives* *with* **than.** *The first mistake is already corrected. Find and correct nine more.*

When I was a teenager in the Philippines, I was an expert on snacks and fast foods. I was

growing fast, so the more I ate, the ~~hungry~~ hungrier I felt. The street vendors in our town had ~~the~~

better snacks than anyone else. In the morning, I used to buy rice muffins on the way to

school. They are ~~more~~ sweeter ~~that~~ American muffins. After school, I ate fish balls on a stick

or *adidas* (chicken feet). Snacks on a stick are ~~small~~ than traditional American hot dogs and

burgers, but they are much varied, and the food is much fresher. My friend thought

banana-cue (banana on a stick) was really great. However, they weren't as sweet from

kamote-cue (fried sweet potatoes and brown sugar), my favorite snack.

When I came to the United States, I didn't like American fast food at first. To me, it was

interesting than my native food and less tastier too. Now I'm getting used to it, and it seems

deliciouser and deliciouser. Does anyone want to go out for a pizza?

STEP 4 COMMUNICATION PRACTICE

EXERCISE 6: Listening

A | *Read the statements. Then listen to the conversation. Listen again and circle the correct information.*

1. The couple is in a restaurant / at a supermarket.

2. They are going to have fresh / frozen pizza for dinner.

3. They are comparing two / three brands of pizza.

4. They first discuss the size / price of the pizza.

5. The woman / man reads the nutrition information.

6. The expiration date tells them the latest date they should eat / buy the pizza.

7. In the end, the couple decides to buy Angela's / Di Roma's pizza.

B | *Listen again to the conversation and check (✓) the pizza that is better in each category.*

	Di Roma's	Angela's
1. cheap	✓	☐
2. big	☐	☐
3. healthy	☐	☐
4. tasty	☐	☐
5. fresh	☐	☐

EXERCISE 7: Pronunciation

A | *Read and listen to the Pronunciation Note.*

> **Pronunciation Note**
>
> In **conversation** we often pronounce *as* /əz/ and *than* /ðən/.
>
> **EXAMPLES:** It's **as** good **as** John's pizza.
>   It's better **than** Maria's.

B | *Listen to the short conversations. Notice the pronunciation of* **as** *and* **than***.*

1. **A:** The new restaurant is just **as** crowded **as** the old one.

   B: It's even more crowded **than** the Pizza Place.

2. **A:** The menu was more varied **than** at Joe's.

   B: And the prices were just **as** good.

3. **A:** The fish was just **as** expensive **as** the scallops.

   B: It was even more expensive **than** the shrimp.

4. **A:** The restaurant didn't feel **as** relaxed **as** it used to.

   B: But the service was better **than** it was.

5. **A:** It's just **as** noisy **as** Joe's at lunchtime.

   B: It's even noisier **than** Joe's at dinnertime.

C | *Listen again. Then practice the conversations with a partner.*

EXERCISE 8: Compare and Contrast

Look at some of these favorite international pizza toppings. Discuss them with a partner.
Make comparisons using some of the adjectives from the box.

delicious filling healthy interesting spicy tasty traditional unusual

1. Australia

2. Mexico

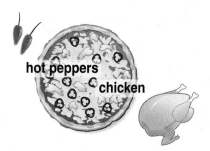

3. Hong Kong

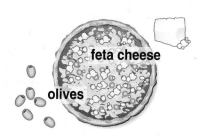

4. Greece

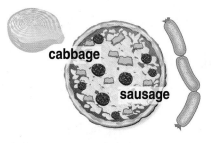

5. Poland

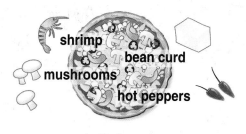

6. Indonesia

EXAMPLE: **A:** The pizza from Hong Kong looks less filling than the one from Mexico.
             B: Yes, but it looks just as spicy.

EXERCISE 9: Role Play: Your Restaurant

A | *Work in small groups. Imagine that you have a small restaurant. Give your restaurant a name and decide what to put on the menu. Discuss dishes and prices for each category. Use comparisons in your discussion.*

> EXAMPLE: **A:** We need a soup. How about chicken noodle?
> **B:** Too boring! Gazpacho is more interesting.

_____

Soups and Appetizers

_____ . . . . $ _____

_____ . . . . $ _____

Entrées

_____ . . . . $ _____

_____ . . . . $ _____

Salads and Side Dishes

_____ . . . . $ _____

_____ . . . . $ _____

Desserts

_____ . . . . $ _____

_____ . . . . $ _____

Beverages

_____ . . . . $ _____

_____ . . . . $ _____

B | *With your group, role-play ordering from your menu. One person is the server; the others are customers.*

> EXAMPLE: **A:** Is the gazpacho as spicy as the hot-and-sour soup?
> **B:** No, the hot-and-sour soup is much spicier.
> **C:** Great! I love spicy food. The spicier the better!

EXERCISE 10: Writing

A | *Write a paragraph comparing your country's food with the food of another country.*

    EXAMPLE: Food in Taiwan is fresher than food in the United States. Taiwan is a small island, and there are a lot of farms . . .

B | *Check your work. Use the Editing Checklist.*

Editing Checklist

Did you . . . ?

☐ use comparisons with *as . . . as* to show how food is or is not similar

☐ use comparisons with *than* to show how food is different

☐ form comparative adjectives (long and short) correctly

☐ use *just* or *even* to make the comparisons stronger

A | Circle the correct words to complete the sentences.

1. Rosa's spaghetti is just as good as / than Maria's.

2. My mother's tomato sauce is good / better than Rizzo's bottled sauce.

3. These chairs are more / as comfortable than the old ones.

4. I don't like the new menu. It's more / less interesting than the old one.

5. The lines in my supermarket are getting long / longer and longer.

6. The longer the line, the more impatient / more impatient I get.

B | Complete the sentences with the comparative form of the words in parentheses.
Use **than** where necessary.

1. Tony's pizza is ___more expensive than___ Sal's, so I can't buy it often.
   (expensive)

2. It's also ___bigger___, so it's worth the price.
   (big)

3. Tony's restaurant is ___larger than___ Sal's. They have more tables.
   (large)

4. But Sal's hours are ___more convenient___. They're open until midnight.
   (convenient)

5. Tony's is ___farther___ from school. It's 10 blocks away.
   (far)

C | Find and correct nine mistakes.

Last night, I had dinner at the new Pasta Place on the corner of Main Street and Grove. This
new Pasta Place is just as good than the others, and it has just as many sauces to choose from.
No one makes a more good traditional tomato sauce them. But there are much interestinger
choices. Their mushroom cream sauce, for example, is as better as I've ever had. Try the
mushroom and tomato sauce for a healthier than meal. It's just as delicious. The new branch is
already popular. The later it is, longer the lines. My recommendation: Go early for a more short
wait. And go soon. This place will only get more popular and more popular!

Adjectives: Superlatives
CITIES

Before You Read

Look at the photo. Discuss the questions.

1. Do you recognize this city? Where do you think it is?
2. What are some important features for a city to have?

Read

Read the travel brochure.

A Superlative[1] City

TORONTO. It's the capital of the province of Ontario. It's also . . .

* 🍁 **the largest** city in Canada

* 🍁 **the most important** economic and financial center of the country

* 🍁 one of **the most multicultural** places on earth (Over 100 languages are spoken in the city!)

* 🍁 one of **the easiest** places to get around (It has **the second largest** public transportation system in North America.)

* 🍁 **the safest** city on the continent, and one of **the most peaceful** of all large, international cities on earth

All of these features, and many more, make Toronto one of **the most dynamic** cities in the world. Come visit and find out for yourself!

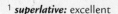

[1] **superlative:** excellent

After You Read

A | Vocabulary: *Circle the letter of the word or phrase that best completes each sentence.*

1. A **financial** center has a lot of _____.
   a. banks
   b. parks
   c. hospitals

2. A **multicultural** city has people from many different _____.
   a. schools
   b. theaters
   c. countries

3. An important **feature** of Toronto is its _____.
   a. city
   b. name
   c. safety

4. The transportation system is **public**. _____ can use it.
   a. Only important people
   b. Everyone
   c. Nobody

5. A **dynamic** city is NOT _____.
   a. interesting
   b. exciting
   c. boring

B | Comprehension: *Check (✓)* **True** *or* **False**. *Correct the false statements.*

	True	False
1. Some Canadian cities are larger than Toronto.	☐	☐
2. Some Canadian cities are more important financially than Toronto.	☐	☐
3. Many cities in the world aren't as multicultural as Toronto.	☐	☐
4. It's easy to get around Toronto.	☐	☐
5. Some cities in North America are safer than Toronto.	☐	☐

ADJECTIVES: SUPERLATIVES

	Superlatives		
	Superlative Adjective Form		
This is	**the largest** **the busiest** **the best**	city	***in** the world. **of** all. I've **ever** visited.*
	the most interesting **the least expensive**		

GRAMMAR NOTES

1	Use **superlative adjectives** to compare <u>one</u> person, place, or thing with other people, places, or things in a <u>group</u>.	• Toronto is **the largest** city in Canada. • It's **the most multicultural** city in the country.

2	There are several ways of **forming superlative adjectives**.	
		ADJECTIVE **SUPERLATIVE**
	a. For **short adjectives** (one syllable and two syllables ending in -*y*), use: ***the** + adjective + **-est***	loud **the** loud**est** pretty **the** prett**iest**
	There are often **spelling changes** when you add **-est**.	late **the** lat**est** big **the** big**gest** early **the** earl**iest**
	Some adjectives have **irregular** superlative forms.	good **the best** bad **the worst** far **the farthest**
	b. For **long adjectives** (two or more syllables), use ***the most / the least** + **adjective**.	expensive **the most** expensive **the least** expensive
	EXCEPTION: The **short adjective** *fun* forms the superlative the same way as a long adjective.	fun **the most** fun NOT: the ~~funnest~~ **the least** fun
	c. For **some adjectives**, such as *lively*, *lovely*, *friendly*, and *quiet*, you can use: ***the . . . -est*** OR ***the most / the least***	• Rio is **the liveliest** city in the world. OR • Rio is **the most lively** city in the world.

3 We often use the superlative with other **words and expressions**:

a. phrases with *in* and *of*

- This is **the least expensive** hotel *in town*.
- It's **the greatest** city *in the world*.
- This was **the best** day *of our visit*.

b. *one of* or *some of*
  Use a plural count noun with *one of*.

- Toronto is *one of* the most dynamic *cities* in the world.
  Not: Toronto is one of the most dynamic ~~city~~ in the world.

  With *some of* you can use:
  - a plural count noun
  - a non-count noun

- *Some of* the best *cities* have large parks.
- Toronto has *some of* the best *food* in Canada.

c. *second (third, fourth . . .)*

- It has **the *second* largest** transportation system.

d. *ever* + **present perfect**

- This is **the biggest** building I*'ve ever seen*.

REFERENCE NOTES

For a list of **adjectives** that use **both forms of the superlative**, see Appendix 9 on page A-5.
For a list of **irregular superlative adjectives**, see Appendix 10 on page A-6.
For **spelling rules** for the **superlative form of adjectives**, see Appendix 23 on page A-11.

STEP 3 FOCUSED PRACTICE

EXERCISE 1: Discover the Grammar

Read more information about Toronto. Underline all the superlative adjectives.

What to Do and See in Toronto

🍁 **Go to the CN Tower**. It's one of <u>the tallest</u> buildings in the world. From there you can get the best view of the city and countryside.

🍁 **Drive along Yonge Street**. At 1,200 miles (1,800 km), it's the longest street in the world. For one weekend in July it's one of the liveliest too. Come and join 1 million others for the exciting Yonge Street Festival.

🍁 **Visit PATH**, the world's largest underground shopping complex.

🍁 **Explore the Old Town of York**. It has the most historic buildings in the whole city.

🍁 **Take the Yuk Yuk's Comedy Tour** of the Entertainment District—you'll have a good time on the funniest bus ride in town.

🍁 **Visit the Toronto Zoo**. There's always something new and fascinating going on. Local people call it the best family outing in Toronto.

EXERCISE 2: Superlative Adjectives

(Grammar Notes 1–2)

Look at the chart. Complete the sentences. Use the superlative form of the correct adjectives in parentheses.

CITY STATISTICS

		BEIJING	SEOUL	MEXICO CITY	TORONTO
👥	**Population**	8,614,000	17,500,000	17,400,000	4,367,000
	Area	748 sq km 289 sq mi	1,049 sq km 405 sq mi	2,072 sq km 800 sq mi	1,655 sq km 639 sq mi
🌡	**Average January Temperature**	–4°C 28°F	–2.7°C 27°F	13.3°C 55.9°F	–6.4°C 20.5°F
🌡	**Average July Temperature**	24°C 75°F	24.7°C 76.5°F	16.7°C 62.1°F	20.7°C 69.3°F
☂	**Average Rainfall per Year**	576.9 mm 22.71 in	1,242 mm 49 in	634.3 mm 25 in	877.7 mm 32.2 in
☕	**Cost of a Cup of Coffee ($US)**	$2.92	$3.00	$1.15	$3.26
🚌	**Cost of a Bus Ticket ($US)**	$1.17	$0.44	$0.35	$1.86

1. Seoul has _____ *the largest* _____ population of all four cities. But Mexico City

(large / small)
   is _____ city in area.

(big / small)

2. Beijing is _____ *the smallest* _____ city in area.

(big / small)

3. Toronto is _____ *the smallest* _____ city in population, but not in area.

(big / small)

4. In winter, _____ *the coldest* _____ city is Toronto.

(warm / cold)

5. Seoul has _____ *the hottest* _____ July temperatures.

(hot / cool)

6. Of all the cities in the chart, Mexico City is _____ in July,

(hot / cool)
   and it is _____ in January. Mexico City definitely has

(warm ∧ cold)
   _____ climate of all.

(comfortable / uncomfortable)

7. _____ city is Seoul. _____

(dry / rainy)   (dry / rainy)
   city is Beijing.

8. You'll find _____ cup of coffee in Mexico City, and you'll find

(cheap / expensive)
   _____ in Toronto.

(cheap / expensive)

9. The city with _____ public buses is Mexico City. Toronto has

(cheap / expensive)
   _____ *the most expensive* _____.

(cheap / expensive)

EXERCISE 3: Superlative Adjectives

(Grammar Notes 1–3)

Read about the CN Tower. Complete the information. Use the superlative form of the correct adjective from the box.

| ~~clear~~ | ~~famous~~ | fast | heavy | ~~long~~ | popular | ~~tall~~ |

The CN Tower / *La Tour CN*

1. At 1,815 feet, 5 inches (553.33 m), the CN Tower is one of ___the tallest___ structures in the world.

2. Everyone recognizes the CN Tower. It is ___the most famous___ building in Canada.

3. At 130,000 tons (117,910 metric tonnes), the impressive CN Tower is one of the ___the heaviest___ buildings in the world.

4. With 2 million visitors every year, it is one of ___the most popular___ tourist attractions in the country.

5. Because of its very high antenna, the tower provides the people of Toronto with some of ___the clearest___ radio and TV reception in North America.

6. Moving at 15 miles (22 km) per hour, the six elevators are among ___the fastest___ in the world. The ride to the Look Out Level takes just 58 seconds.

7. If you don't want to take the elevator, you can try the stairs! The CN Tower has ___the longest___ metal staircase in the world.

EXERCISE 4: *The Most* and *The Least + Ever*

(Grammar Note 3)

Write superlative sentences about your own experiences. Use the words in parentheses with **the most** *or* **the least + ever** *and the present perfect. Write two sentences for each item. Go to Appendix 1, page A-1 for help with the irregular past participles.*

EXAMPLE: Toronto is the most multicultural city I've ever visited.
Meadville is the least multicultural city I've ever visited.

1. (multicultural / city / visit)

_____

_____

(continued on next page)

2. (comfortable / place / stay)

_____

_____

3. (friendly / people / meet)

_____

_____

4. (expensive / trip / take)

_____

_____

5. (attractive / place / see)

_____

_____

6. (exciting / team / watch)

_____

_____

EXERCISE 5: Editing

Read the postcard. There are eight mistakes in the use of superlative adjectives. The first mistake is already corrected. Find and correct seven more.

> _most beautiful_
> Greetings from Toronto—the ~~beautifulest~~ city I've ever visited. Yesterday we went to the CN Tower—the more recognizable structure in all of Canada. From there you get the best view of the city—the different neighborhoods, the harbor, the fast traffic—it made my head spin! This is one of most dynamic places I've ever visited! The restaurant was the most expensivest I've ever seen, so we just enjoyed the view and then went to Kensington Market to eat. This place has the baddest crowds but the cheapest and the goodest food we've had so far. We're staying in East Toronto. It's not the closer place to downtown, but it has some of most historic buildings. In fact, our bed-and-breakfast is called 1871 Historic House. John Lennon slept here!
>
> Love, Marissa

EXERCISE 6: Listening

A | *May and Dan are planning a vacation. Read the sentences. Listen to May and Dan's conversation. Then listen again and complete the sentences.*

1. May and Dan are going to go to _____*Toronto*_____ next summer.

2. They are trying to decide among _____ hotels.

3. The Westin Harbour Castle has a _____ with views of both the lake and the _____.

4. The Hôtel Le Germain is close to the entertainment _____.

5. The rooms at Hôtel Le Germain start at _____.

6. The Delta Chelsea has _____ rooms.

7. Dan says, "This is going to be the _____ vacation we've ever had."

B | *Listen again to the conversation and check (✓) the correct hotel for each feature.*

FEATURES	Westin Harbour Castle	Hôtel Le Germain	Delta Chelsea
the best view	✔		
the most convenient			
the least convenient			
the most comfortable			
the most expensive			
the least expensive			
the biggest			
the smallest			

EXERCISE 7: Pronunciation

A | *Read and listen to the Pronunciation Note.*

> **Pronunciation Note**
>
> In **words that end in -st**, we often **drop the final -t sound** before a word that begins with a **consonant** sound. For example, we drop the *t* in the word **most** and pronounce it "**mos'**" when the following word begins with a consonant sound.
>
> **EXAMPLES:** It's the **most beautiful** city. → "It's the **mos' beautiful** city."
> It's the **safest place**. → "It's the **safes' place**."

B | *Listen to the short conversations. Draw a slash (/) through the final -t when it is not pronounced in the superlative adjectives.*

1. **A:** The view from here is great.

   B: But the **best view** is from the CN Tower.

2. **A:** This restaurant is expensive.

   B: Yes, it's the **most expensive** restaurant in town.

3. **A:** This is an interesting part of town.

   B: It is. But it's not the **most interesting** part.

4. **A:** Toronto's a very safe city.

   B: Yes, it's the **safest city** in Canada.

5. **A:** This hotel is pretty expensive.

   B: Yes, but it's the **least expensive** one in this part of town.

6. **A:** I love Toronto.

   B: Me too. I think it's one of the **nicest places** in the world.

C | *Listen again and repeat each response. Then practice the conversations with a partner.*

EXERCISE 8: What About You?

Work with a partner. Talk about your answers to Exercise 4 on page 301. Keep the conversation going by asking more questions like these:

- Which . . . did you like best?
- Why do you say that?
- Sounds great! What else did you like?
- Who did you meet?

EXAMPLE: **A:** What's the most interesting city you've ever visited?
  B: Toronto. People from all over the world live there. It's very multicultural.
  A: Are there interesting neighborhoods?
  B: Oh, yes. Greektown is one of the most dynamic places I've ever seen.

EXERCISE 9: Discussion

Work in small groups. Discuss cities in your countries. You can use some of the adjectives from the box.

beautiful	crowded	exciting	interesting	multicultural
clean	dynamic	friendly	modern	old

EXAMPLE: **A:** What's the most interesting city in Argentina?

B: I think Buenos Aires is the most interesting city in Argentina. There's so much to do—theater, sports, movies. It's also the most multicultural city in the country. People from all over the world live there.

C: It sounds very exciting. What's the most exciting city in your country, Chen?

EXERCISE 10: Writing

A | *Write a fact sheet for your hometown or city. Use Exercise 1 on page 299 as a model. Include superlatives.*

EXAMPLE: **What to Do and See in Meadville**

- Go to Joe's for the best pizza in town.
- Ride the number 53 bus for one of the cheapest and best ways to see the major sights.

B | *Check your work. Use the Editing Checklist.*

Editing Checklist

Did you . . . ?
- ☐ use superlative adjectives
- ☐ form them correctly
- ☐ use words and expressions such as ***in the city***

21 Review

Check your answers on page UR-5.

Do you need to review anything?

A | Complete each sentence with the superlative form of the correct word from the box.

| big | cheap | dry | expensive | rainy | short |

1. The _____ river in the world is the Roe River in the United States. It's only

   200 feet long.

2. The _____ lake is Lake Superior in North America. It's 32,000 square miles.

3. Calama, Chile, is one of the _____ towns on earth. It gets only .004 inches

   of rain a year.

4. Cherrapunji, India, is one of the _____. It gets around 400 inches.

5. Tokyo, Japan, is one of the _____ cities. A cup of coffee costs $4.00.

6. Johannesburg, South Africa, is one of the _____. A cup of coffee is $1.35.

B | Complete the conversation with the superlative form of the adjectives in parentheses.

A: Welcome back! You just missed _____ week of the year so far.
　　　　　　　　　　　　　　　　　　　　　　1. (cold)

B: But Florida was great! The Magic Kingdom is _____ place.
　　　　　　　　　　　　　　　　　　　　　　　　　　　2. (fantastic)

A: It's _____ amusement park. It's also _____.
　　　　　　　3. (popular)　　　　　　　　　　　　　　　　　　　4. (crowded)

B: True. The long lines were _____ part of the trip.
　　　　　　　　　　　　　　　　　　　　5. (fun)

A: What was _____ part?
　　　　　　　　6. (good)

B: Monsters, Inc. It's not _____ show in the world, but it's quite good.
　　　　　　　　　　　　　　　　7. (funny)

C | Find and correct seven mistakes.

Small towns aren't most dynamic places to visit, and that's just why we love to vacation on

Tangier Island. This tiny island is probably the less popular vacation spot in the United States.

Almost no one comes here. But it's also one of the most safest places to visit. And you'll find some

of the goodest seafood and the beautiful beaches here. It's one of the easiest place to get around

(there are no cars on the island). If you get bored, just hop on the ferry. You're only a few hours

from Washington, D.C., and a few more hours from New York and the excitingest nightlife ever.

22 Adverbs: *As . . . as,* Comparatives, Superlatives

SPORTS

Before You Read

Look at the photo. Discuss the questions.

1. What game are they playing?
2. Which sports do you like to watch?
3. Do you play any sports? Which ones?
4. Why do you like them?

Australia vs France

Read

🎧 *Read the transcript of a TV sports program.*

The Halftime[1] Report

CINDY: What a game! Spero, have you ever seen two teams play **more aggressively**?

SPERO: No, I haven't, Cindy. Folks, we're in Bangkok, Thailand, watching the Australian and French teams battle for the Women's World Basketball Championship. It's halftime, and just listen to that crowd! I think the Australians cheer **the loudest** of any fans in the game!

CINDY: Well, the court really belonged to France for the first few minutes of the game, Spero. But the Australian team recovered quickly. They've scored almost **as frequently as** the French in the first half. The score is now 30-28, France, and no one can predict a winner at this point.

SPERO: I heard that Elizabeth Cambage, Australia's star player, injured her arm yesterday, but you can't tell from the way she's playing today. So far, she's scored **the most** of any player on her team.

CINDY: And with an injury too! Spero, I have to say that's pretty amazing. But Maud Medenou of France isn't that far behind. Did you notice that she's been playing **more and more intensely** in this tournament? You can see that she really wants the ball, and she's getting it **more consistently** in every game.

SPERO: You're right, Cindy. And **the harder** she plays, **the more** she scores.

CINDY: The Australians have really been playing a great defense tonight. They've been blocking Medenou **more effectively than** any other team this season. But can they stop her?

SPERO: We'll find out soon! The second half is ready to begin. See you again after the game.

---

[1] *halftime:* a period of rest between two parts of a game such as football or basketball

After You Read

A | Vocabulary: *Match the sentences on the left with the sentences on the right.*

_____ **1.** Medenou is playing very **aggressively**.

_____ **2.** Farley is playing **consistently**.

_____ **3.** France blocked Cambage **effectively**.

_____ **4.** Thizy gets hurt the most **frequently**.

_____ **5.** Cambage is playing pretty **intensely**.

a. She's got a lot more energy and focus.

b. Cambage wasn't able to score.

c. She's had a lot of injuries.

d. She just pushed Jarry off the court.

e. She's played well in the last five games.

B | Comprehension: *Check (✓) the boxes to complete the sentences.*

1. The teams are competing in _____.
- ☐ Thailand
- ☐ Australia
- ☐ France

2. In the beginning of the game, _____ was losing.
- ☐ France
- ☐ Australia
- ☐ Thailand

3. At halftime, Australia had _____ France.
- ☐ a lower score than
- ☐ a higher score than
- ☐ the same score as

4. Cambage _____ today.
- ☐ can't play
- ☐ injured her arm
- ☐ has scored a lot

5. Medenou is _____ Cambage.
- ☐ almost as good as
- ☐ better than
- ☐ just as good as

6. At halftime, _____ knows which team is going to win.
- ☐ Cindy
- ☐ Spero
- ☐ nobody

ADVERBS: *AS . . . AS*, COMPARATIVES, SUPERLATIVES

As . . . as					
		As	**Adverb**	**As**	
France	played didn't play	**as**	**hard** **well** **aggressively** **consistently**	**as**	Australia.

Comparatives				
		Comparative Adverb Form	**Than**	
France	played	**harder** **better** **more aggressively** **less consistently**	**than**	Australia.

Superlatives			
		Superlative Adverb Form	
The star player	played	**the hardest** **the best** **the most aggressively** **the least consistently**	**of** anyone in the game.

GRAMMAR NOTES

1	Use *as* + **adverb** + *as* to compare actions and show how they are <u>the same or equal</u>.	• Girard plays **as well as** Farley.
	Use *just* to make the comparison stronger.	• Girard plays *just* **as well as** Farley. (*Girard and Farley play equally well.*)
	Use *not as* + **adverb** + *as* to show how the actions are <u>NOT the same or equal</u>.	• Girard did**n't** play **as aggressively as** Kunek. (*Girard and Kunek didn't play the same. Kunek played more aggressively.*)

(continued on next page)

2 Use **comparative adverbs** + *than* to show how the actions of two people or things are <u>different</u>.

Use *even* to make the comparison stronger.

USAGE NOTE: We usually do NOT use *less . . . than* with <u>one syllable adverbs</u>. Instead we use:
- *not as . . . as*
  OR
- another adverb with the <u>opposite meaning</u>

REMEMBER: When the meaning is clear, it's not necessary to mention both parts of a comparison with *as . . . as* or comparative adverbs.

- France played **better than** Australia.
- Cambage played **more skillfully than** Datchy.

- She played *even* **more skillfully than** Datchy.

NOT: Riley runs ~~less fast than~~ Cash.

- Riley does**n't** run **as fast as** Cash.
  OR
- Riley runs **slower than** Cash.

- He played hard. She played just **as hard**.
  (*. . . as hard as he played*)
- Beard shot **more consistently**.
  (*. . . more consistently than King shot*)

3 Use **superlative adverbs** to compare <u>one</u> action with the actions of other people or things in a <u>group</u>.

We often use the superlative with **expressions** beginning with *of*.

- All the players worked hard, but Robins worked **the hardest**.

- She scored **the most frequently** *of any player* on the team.

4 There are several ways of **forming comparative and superlative adverbs**.

a. For most **short adverbs** (one syllable), use:
adverb + *-er* OR *the* + **adverb** + *-est*

Some short adverbs have **irregular** comparative and superlative forms.

b. For **long adverbs** (two or more syllables), use:
more / less + **adverb** OR *the most / the least* + **adverb**

c. **Some adverbs of manner** have <u>two comparative</u> and <u>two superlative</u> forms.

The *-er / -est* forms are more common in <u>spoken English and informal writing</u>.

REMEMBER: Do NOT put an adverb of manner <u>between the verb and the object</u>.

ADVERB	COMPARATIVE	SUPERLATIVE
fast	fast**er**	**the** fast**est**
hard	hard**er**	**the** hard**est**
well	**better**	**the best**
badly	**worse**	**the worst**
far	**farther**	**the farthest**
much/a lot	**more**	**the most**
a little	**less**	**the least**
skillfully	**more / less** skillfully	**the most / the least** skillfully
quickly	**more** quickly	**the most** quickly
	quicker	**the quickest**

MORE COMMON: Davis ran **quicker**.
LESS COMMON: Davis ran **more quickly**.

- She **handled** *the ball* **better** than Farley.
  NOT: She handled ~~better the ball~~ than Farley.

<table>
<tr>
<td>**5**</td>
<td>**Repeat the comparative adverb** to show <u>increase or decrease</u>:

comparative + *and* + **comparative**
    adverb   **adverb**

With long adverbs, repeat only *more* or *less*.</td>
<td>• Kukoc is playing **better and better** as the season continues.
(His performance keeps getting better.)

• He's playing **more and more aggressively**.
NOT: He's playing more ~~aggressively~~ and more aggressively.</td>
</tr>
<tr>
<td>**6**</td>
<td>Use **two comparative adverbs** to show <u>cause and effect</u>:
the + **comparative** + *the* + **comparative**
       adverb   **adverb**</td>
<td>• **The harder** he played, **the better** he got.
(When he played harder, he got better.)</td>
</tr>
</table>

REFERENCE NOTES

For a list of **irregular comparative and superlative adverbs** see Appendix 10 on page A-6.

For more information about **adverbs**, see Unit 19 on page 268.

STEP 3 FOCUSED PRACTICE

EXERCISE 1: Discover the Grammar

Read the story from the sports section of the newspaper. Underline all the comparisons with
(not) as + *adverb* + **as,** *and all the comparative and superlative adverb forms.*

Comets Beat Lions!

In the first basketball game of the season, the Comets beat the Lions, 90 to 83. The Lions played a truly fantastic game, but their defense is still weak. The Comets defended the ball much <u>more aggressively than</u> the Lions did.

Of course, Ace Hernandez certainly helped win the game for the Comets. The Comets' star player was back on the court today to the delight of his many fans. He was hurt badly at the end of the last season, but he has recovered quickly. Although he didn't play as well as people expected, he still handled the ball like the old Ace. He certainly handled it the most skillfully of anyone on the team. He controlled the ball the best, shot the ball the most accurately, and scored the most consistently of any of the players on either team. He played hard and helped the Comets look good. In fact, the harder he played, the better the Comets performed. Watch Ace this season.

And watch the Lions. They have a new coach, and they're training more seriously this year. I think we'll see them play better and better as the season progresses.

EXERCISE 2: Comparisons with *As . . . as*

(Grammar Note 1)

Read the chart comparing several brands of basketball shoes. Complete the sentences. Use
(not) as + *adverb* + **as** *and the words in parentheses.*

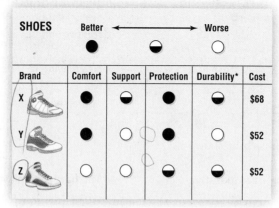

*how long the product lasts

1. Brand X _____ *fits as comfortably as* _____ brand Y.
   (fit / comfortable)

2. Brand Z _____ brand X or Y.
   (fit / comfortable)

3. Brand Y _____ brand Z.
   (support / the ankles / good)

4. Brands Y and Z _____ brand X.
   (support / the ankles / good)

5. Brand Z _____ brand X or Y.
   (protect / the feet / effective)

6. Brand X _____ brand Y.
   (protect / the feet / effective)

7. Brand X _____ brand Z.
   (last / long)

8. Brand Y _____ brand X or Z.
   (last / long)

9. Brands Y and Z _____ brand X.
   (cost / much)

EXERCISE 3: *As . . . as*, Comparative and Superlative Adverbs

(Grammar Notes 1–6)

*Complete the conversation between sports commentator Carla Lobo and player Elena
Bard. Change the adjectives in parentheses to adverbs. Use them with **as . . . as** or with the
comparative or superlative forms. Add **the** or **than,** and choose between **more** or **less** where
necessary.*

LOBO: Why do people still take female basketball players _____ *less seriously than* _____

        1. (serious)

male players? Do women really play _____ men?

        2. (aggressive)

BARD: Absolutely not! We play just _____. And when we fall, we hit

        3. (aggressive)

the floor just _____ the guys do.

        4. (hard)

LOBO: You could sure see that in tonight's game. Jackson played _____

        5. (effective)

of any player I've seen, male or female. She never let Cash anywhere near the basket.

BARD: Yes. And she performs like that much _____ *more* _____ than a lot of the
6. (consistent)

men. Jackson always gets the job done.

LOBO: Some people say women play _____ *more* _____ men.
7. (cooperative)

BARD: I agree. I think we have better teamwork—we play _____ *better* _____
8. (good)

on a team. We're also more patient. I have noticed that most women players are able to wait

_____ for a good chance to shoot.
9. (long)

LOBO: Tickets for women's basketball games cost _____ tickets for
10. (little)

men's games. Does that bother you?

BARD: Sure, but _____ women players attract fans,
11. (fast)

_____ *faster* _____ the women's leagues will make money.
12. (fast)

EXERCISE 4: Comparative and Superlative Adverbs   *(Grammar Notes 2–4)*

Look at the chart. Then complete the sentences. Use the comparative or superlative adverb form of the words from the box. You will use some words more than once.

bad   far   fast   good   high   slow

	Broad Jump (distance)	**Pole Vaulting (height)**	**5-mile Run (speed)**
Nolan	14.3 feet	7 feet, 3 inches	24 minutes
Smith	14.1 feet	7 feet, 2 inches	28 minutes
Diaz	15.2 feet	7 feet, 8 inches	30 minutes
Wang	15.4 feet	8 feet, 2 inches	22 minutes

1. Nolan jumped _____ *farther than* _____ Smith.

2. Wang vaulted _____ *the highest* _____ of all.

3. Diaz ran _____ *the slowest of all* _____.

4. Smith ran _____ *slower than* _____ Wang.

5. Wang jumped _____ *of all* _____.

6. Nolan ran _____ *faster* _____ Smith.

7. Wang vaulted _____ *higher than* _____ Smith.

8. All in all, Wang did _____ *the best of all* _____.

9. All in all, Smith did _____ *worse* _____.

EXERCISE 5: Editing

Read the article from a student newspaper. There are nine mistakes in the use of adverbs.
The first mistake is already corrected. Find and correct eight more.

The Last Game is the Lions' Best

Last night was the last game of the
season, and the Lions played the ~~goodest~~ *best*
they've played for months. Both the Cubs
and Lions play a great offensive game, but
this time the Lions really played defense
much more effectively as the Cubs.
Hernandez, the Cubs' star player, has
been shooting more aggressively and more
aggressively all season. But in last night's
game, the more aggressive he played, the
most closely the Lions guarded him. Then,
in the last two minutes, "Tiny Tim"
O'Connell made the winning shot for the
Lions. "He's less than six feet tall, but he
runs more fastly than anyone else on the
court," the Cubs' coach said. "O'Connell
doesn't shoot as often other players, but
he's a lot more accurately than the bigger
guys." The Cubs played a great game last
night too, but they just didn't play as good
as the Lions. Can the Lions play like this
consistently? If so, they may be this
season's new champions.

EXERCISE 6: Listening

A | *Read the names of the horses in the horse race. Then listen to the sportscasters*
describing the race. Listen again and rank the horses from first place (1) to last place (5).

_____ Exuberant King

_1_ Get Packin'

_____ Inspired Winner

_____ Señor Speedy

_____ Wild Whirl

A fast start to an exciting race

B | *Read the statements about the race. Then listen again to the sportscasters and circle the correct information.*

1. The race was in Sydney / (Dubai).

2. Inspired Winner / Wild Whirl has been winning the most consistently.

3. In the first turn, Inspired Winner and Wild Whirl ran faster / slower than Get Packin'.

4. In the first turn, Señor Speedy and Exuberant King ran the slowest / fastest of all the horses.

5. In the second turn, Señor Speedy and Exuberant King ran slower / faster than in the first turn.

6. In the second turn, Inspired Winner ran better and better / slower and slower.

7. Get Packin' competed the most / least aggressively of all the horses in the race.

EXERCISE 7: Pronunciation

A | *Read and listen to the Pronunciation Note.*

Pronunciation Note

We often **link final consonants to beginning vowels** in *as* + **adverb** + *as* phrases:

Link "s" in *as* to a beginning vowel in the adverb.

EXAMPLE: as easily

For **adverbs** that **end in the letter y**, use the **sound "y"** as in the word *yes* to **link the adverb to** *as*.

EXAMPLE: as easily as

B | *Listen to the short conversations. Notice the pronunciation of* **as** + **adverb** + **as**.

1. **A:** Who scores more easily, Cash or Riley?
   B: Cash can't score **as easily as** Riley.

2. **A:** Our team should play more aggressively.
   B: Nah. We play just **as aggressively as** the other team.

3. **A:** So why do we keep losing this season?
   B: I don't know. Maybe we're not training **as effectively as** we did last year.

4. **A:** Johnson's energy is incredible.
   B: I know. Nobody plays **as intensely as** she does.

5. **A:** I wonder what's wrong with her tonight.
   B: Something is. She's not shooting **as accurately as** usual.

C | *Listen again to the conversations and repeat the responses. Then practice the conversations with a partner.*

EXERCISE 8: Compare and Contrast

Work as a class. Name several famous athletes for one sport. Compare their abilities. Use some of the verbs and adverbs in this list.

Verbs	Adverbs
catch	carefully
hit	defensively
kick	easily
race	fast
run	intensely
play	powerfully
throw	straight
train	successfully

Usain "Lightning" Bolt celebrates a world record in Beijing.

EXAMPLE: Usain Bolt is a runner from Jamaica. He runs faster than anyone else on earth.

EXERCISE 9: Questionnaire: Work and Play

A | *How well do you balance work or study and leisure time? Complete the questionnaire.*

1. How many hours do you work every week? _____

2. How many hours do you study every week? _____

3. How many books have you read for pleasure this month? _____

4. How many hours a week do you watch TV every week? _____

5. How many hours do you spend with your family and friends every week? _____

6. When did you last watch a sports event? _____

7. How many hours a week do you play sports? _____

8. How many days a week do you exercise? _____

9. How many vacation trips have you taken in the last year? _____

B | *Now add your own questions.*

10. _____

11. _____

12. _____

C | *Work in small groups. Compare your answers to questions 1–9 with those of your classmates. Ask the group your own questions (10–12) and compare the answers.*

Find out:

1. Who works the hardest?

2. Who studies the most?

3. Who reads the most?

4. Who has watched a sports event the most recently?

5. Who plays sports the most regularly?

6. Who has traveled the most frequently?

7. Who balances work and play the most effectively?

EXAMPLE: Sharif works the hardest. He works 45 hours every week.

EXERCISE 10: Writing

A | *Write a paragraph comparing two sports figures. Choose two people that you know or two famous athletes. You can use the vocabulary from Exercise 8.*

EXAMPLE: My friends Paul and Nick are both good soccer players, but they have different styles. Nick plays more aggressively than Paul, but Paul runs faster and passes more frequently. Nick scores more often, but Paul plays more cooperatively . . .

B | *Check your work. Use the Editing Checklist.*

Editing Checklist

Did you . . . ?
- [ ] use *as . . . as* to show how two actions are the same or equal
- [ ] use comparative adverbs with *than* to show how actions are different
- [ ] use superlative adverbs to compare one person's actions to actions of a group
- [ ] form comparative and superlative adverbs correctly

A | Circle the correct words to complete the sentences.

1. Chen plays just as <u>good / well</u> as Sanchez.

2. Maya is a slow runner. She <u>runs / doesn't run</u> as fast as her teammates.

3. Dan always shoots the ball <u>more accurately / the most accurately</u> than Will.

4. Inez plays the most aggressively <u>of / than</u> all the other players.

5. Our team didn't play <u>the worst / as well as</u> I expected. I was disappointed.

6. The faster Tranh runs, <u>the more tired he gets / he gets more tired</u>.

7. We need to practice <u>harder / hardly</u> if we want to win.

8. You're playing <u>well / better</u> and better!

B | Complete the sentences with the correct form of the words in parentheses.

1. You play just as _____ as Tomás.
   (good)

2. Olga runs _____ than any of her teammates.
   (fast)

3. Diego shoots the ball _____ of all the players.
   (accurate)

4. He practices _____ of all.
   (hard)

5. Their team played _____ of all the teams.
   (bad)

C | Find and correct seven mistakes.

Last night's game was a very exciting one. The Globes played the best they've played all season. But they still didn't play as good as the Stars. The Stars hit the ball more frequent and ran more fast than the Globes, and their pitcher, Kevin Rodriguez, threw the ball more accurately. Their catcher, Scott Harris, handled better the ball than the Globes' catcher. The Globes are good, but they are less good than the Stars. All in all, the Stars just keep playing good and better. And the better they play, the hardest it is for their fans to get tickets! These games sell out quicker than hotcakes, so go early if you want to get a chance to see the Stars.

From Grammar to Writing
USING DESCRIPTIVE ADJECTIVES

Descriptive adjectives can help your reader better picture what you are writing about.

> **EXAMPLE:** I live in an apartment. →
> I live in a **small comfortable one-bedroom** apartment.

1 | *Read the description of an apartment and the writer's feelings about it. Circle all the adjectives that the writer uses.*

I live in a (small) comfortable one-bedroom apartment with a convenient location close to school. The living room is my favorite room. It's sunny, warm, and peaceful. Its best feature is the old brick fireplace, which I use frequently on cold winter nights. In the corner there's a large soft green couch. I like to sit there and read. Next to it is a small wood table with a charming modern lamp that I bought in town. It's a cozy living room, and I enjoy spending time here. It's an ideal room for a student.

2 | *Complete the word map with the circled words from Exercise 1.*

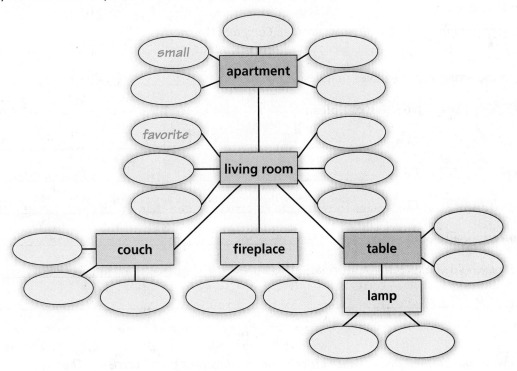

3 | Before you write . . .

1. Work in small groups. Put the adjectives from the box into the correct categories. Brainstorm other adjectives for each category. You can use a dictionary for help.

~~attractive~~	cozy	gorgeous	huge	lovely	~~soft~~
coarse	cute	~~hard~~	~~large~~	rough	tiny
comfortable	enormous	hideous	~~little~~	~~run-down~~	ugly

a. things that are big: _large,_ _____

b. things that are small: _little,_ _____

c. things that look good: _attractive,_ _____

d. things that look bad: _run-down,_ _____

e. things that feel good: _soft,_ _____

f. things that feel bad: _hard,_ _____

2. Think about a room you know. On a separate piece of paper, draw a word map like the one in Exercise 2. Use some of the adjectives in the box above.

3. Discuss your map with a partner. Do you want to add or change any adjectives?

   EXAMPLE: **A:** How small is the dining room?
   B: Oh, it's tiny.

4 | Write a paragraph about the room from Exercise 3. Use your word map.

5 | Exchange paragraphs with a different partner. Complete the chart.

Did the writer use adjectives that describe how things _____?

	Yes	No	Examples
look	☐	☐	_____
feel	☐	☐	_____
smell	☐	☐	_____
sound	☐	☐	_____

What would you like more information about? _____

_____

6 | Work with your partner. Discuss each other's editing questions from Exercise 5. Then rewrite your own paragraph. Answer any questions your partner asked.

GERUNDS AND INFINITIVES

STEP 1 GRAMMAR IN CONTEXT

Before You Read

Look at the cartoon. Discuss the questions.

1. Why are the people standing on the ledge of the building?
2. How do you think they feel about it?
3. How do *you* feel about it?

Read

Read the article about smoking regulations.

NO SMOKING
AROUND THE WORLD FROM A–Z

In the past few decades,[1] life has become more and more difficult for people who **enjoy lighting up**.[2] At the same time, it has become more comfortable for people who don't smoke. And for those who want to **quit smoking**, it has become easier as countries around the world introduce laws that **limit** or **ban smoking** in public, and sometimes even private spaces. Here are some examples, from **A** to **Z**:

⊘ In Austria, the law **prohibits smoking** in many public places, including trains and train stations. It's also banned in offices unless all employees are in favor **of permitting** it. Large restaurants must provide areas for non-smokers, but smaller ones can choose **between permitting smoking** or **being** smoke-free.

⊘ In many provinces of Canada, it's against the law to smoke in a car if there is a child or young adult present.

⊘ In some cities in Japan, it's illegal to smoke on the streets.

⊘ In Mexico, **smoking** is not permitted at all in restaurants. The government has also **banned advertising** tobacco products on TV or radio.

⊘ The United Arab Emirates has recently **started banning** cigarettes in shopping malls and other public places including cafés and nightclubs.

⊘ In Zambia, the law **bans smoking** in all public places. **Not obeying** the law can result in fines and even jail time.

---

[1] **decade:** a ten-year period
[2] **lighting up:** lighting a cigarette

NO SMOKING

Smoking is bad for your health. By now, almost everyone agrees. But, although many people approve of the new laws, not everyone is in favor **of prohibiting** public smoking. "It's one thing to try to discourage the habit **by putting** a high tax on cigarettes," says one smoker, "but some of the new laws go too far." Smokers argue that the laws limit personal freedom. They say everyone today knows the dangers **of lighting up**. So, if someone won't **quit smoking** and wants to smoke outdoors in a park or on the beach, it is that person's choice. Those smokers are only hurting themselves. There are many things that people do that are not good for them, such as **eating** junk food[3] and **not exercising**. But there are no laws that regulate[4] those behaviors.

---

[3] *junk food:* food that is bad for you (usually with a lot of sugar and fat)
[4] *regulate:* to control with rules or laws

After You Read

A | Vocabulary: *Which words can you use to talk about something that is **OK** to do? Something that is **NOT OK** to do? Complete the word maps with the words from the box.*

| approve of | ban | illegal | in favor of | permit | prohibit |

B | Comprehension: *Complete each sentence with the name of the country.*

1. Smoking outside is illegal in some parts of _____.

2. In _____, workers can decide on permitting smoking in the workplace or not.

3. In parts of _____, smoking is sometimes banned on people's own property.

4. Breaking non-smoking laws is a very serious crime in _____.

5. In _____, people can choose between dining in a smoke-free restaurant or in a smaller cigarette-friendly place.

6. You won't see any cigarette ads on TV in _____.

7. _____ has recently started having laws against smoking.

GERUNDS: SUBJECT AND OBJECT

Gerund as Subject		
Gerund (Subject)	**Verb**	
Smoking	causes	health problems.
Not smoking	is	healthier.

Gerund as Object		
Subject	**Verb**	**Gerund (Object)**
You	should quit	**smoking**.
We	suggest	**not smoking**.

Gerund as Object of a Preposition			
	Preposition	**Gerund**	
Are you	**against**	**smoking**	in public?
I plan	**on**	**quitting**	next month.
I'm in favor	**of**	**permitting**	smoking.

GRAMMAR NOTES

1 A **gerund** is the **base form of verb** + **-ing**.

- **Smoking** is bad for your health.
- I enjoy **having** a cigarette in the park.
- She's against **allowing** cigarettes at work.

BE CAREFUL! There are often **spelling changes** when you add **-ing**.

BASE FORM	GERUND
smoke	smok**ing**
permit	permit**ting**
die	d**ying**

Form the **negative** by placing *not* before the gerund.

- **Not exercising** is bad for you.
- The doctor suggested **not drinking** coffee.
- She's happy about **not working** today.

2 A gerund is a verb that we use **like a noun**.

a. A gerund can be the **subject** of a sentence. It is always <u>singular</u>. Use the third-person-singular form of the verb after gerunds.

- **Eating** junk food *makes* me sick.
- **Advertising** cigarettes on TV *is* illegal.

<small>GERUND</small>
- **Drinking** a lot of coffee is unhealthy.

<small>PROGRESSIVE FORM</small>
- He **is drinking** coffee right now.

BE CAREFUL! Do NOT confuse a <u>gerund</u> with the <u>progressive form</u> of the verb.

b. A gerund can be the **object** of certain verbs. Use a gerund **after these verbs**:

admit	consider	keep	resist
advise	deny	like	risk
appreciate	dislike	mind	start
avoid	enjoy	miss	stop
can't stand	finish	quit	suggest

- Jiang *avoids* **hanging out** with smokers.
- Have you ever *considered* **quitting**?
- I *dislike* **sitting** near smokers in cafés.
- We *finished* **studying** and went out.
- Did you *miss* **smoking** after you quit?
- Dr. Ho *suggested* **not staying up** late.

c. We often use *go* + **gerund** to describe <u>activities</u> such as *shopping, fishing, skiing, swimming,* and *camping*.

- Let's *go* **swimming** in the lake.
- I *went* **shopping** for running shoes at the mall.

3 A gerund can also be the **object of a preposition**.

Use a gerund **after prepositions** such as:

about	before	for	on
against	between	in	to
at	by	of	with / without

- It's all *about* **getting** fit.
- I'm *against* **smoking** in public.
- You'll improve your health *by* **quitting**.
- I'm *for* **banning** tobacco ads.

There are many **expressions with prepositions**. You can use a gerund after expressions with:

- **verb + preposition**
  advise *against*   believe *in*   count *on*

- I *believe in* **taking** care of my health.

- **adjective + preposition**
  afraid *of*   bored *with*   excited *about*

- I'm *excited about* **joining** the health club.

BE CAREFUL! Use a **gerund**, not an infinitive (*to* + **base form of verb**), after **expressions with the preposition *to***:
look forward *to*   be opposed *to*   object *to*

- I *look forward to* **seeing** you.
  NOT: I look forward ~~to see~~ you.

REFERENCE NOTES
For **spelling rules for verb + -ing**, see Appendix 21 on page A-10.
For a more complete list of **verbs** that can be **followed by gerunds**, see Appendix 13 on page A-7.
For a list of **adjectives followed by prepositions**, see Appendix 17 on page A-7.
For a list of **verbs followed by prepositions**, see Appendix 18 on page A-8.

EXERCISE 1: Discover the Grammar

Read the online bulletin board about smoking. Underline all the gerunds.

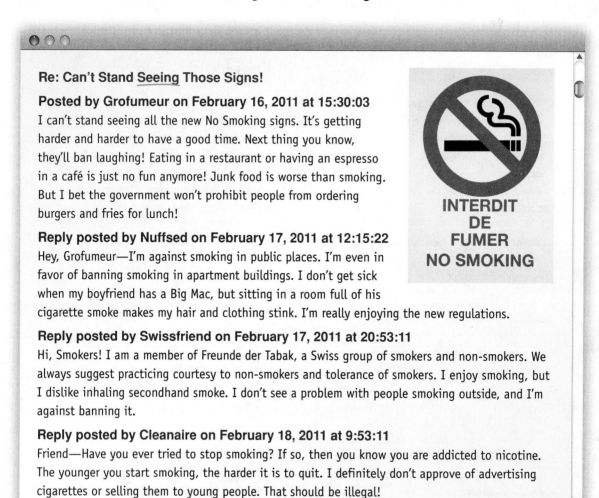

Re: Can't Stand Seeing Those Signs!

Posted by Grofumeur on February 16, 2011 at 15:30:03
I can't stand seeing all the new No Smoking signs. It's getting
harder and harder to have a good time. Next thing you know,
they'll ban laughing! Eating in a restaurant or having an espresso
in a café is just no fun anymore! Junk food is worse than smoking.
But I bet the government won't prohibit people from ordering
burgers and fries for lunch!

Reply posted by Nuffsed on February 17, 2011 at 12:15:22
Hey, Grofumeur—I'm against smoking in public places. I'm even in
favor of banning smoking in apartment buildings. I don't get sick
when my boyfriend has a Big Mac, but sitting in a room full of his
cigarette smoke makes my hair and clothing stink. I'm really enjoying the new regulations.

Reply posted by Swissfriend on February 17, 2011 at 20:53:11
Hi, Smokers! I am a member of Freunde der Tabak, a Swiss group of smokers and non-smokers. We
always suggest practicing courtesy to non-smokers and tolerance of smokers. I enjoy smoking, but
I dislike inhaling secondhand smoke. I don't see a problem with people smoking outside, and I'm
against banning it.

Reply posted by Cleanaire on February 18, 2011 at 9:53:11
Friend—Have you ever tried to stop smoking? If so, then you know you are addicted to nicotine.
The younger you start smoking, the harder it is to quit. I definitely don't approve of advertising
cigarettes or selling them to young people. That should be illegal!

INTERDIT
DE
FUMER
NO SMOKING

EXERCISE 2: Gerunds: Affirmative and Negative   *(Grammar Notes 1–2)*

*Complete the article with gerunds. Use the verbs from the box. You will use one verb more
than once. Choose between affirmative and negative.*

| eat | exercise | go | increase | join | pay | smoke | start | stay |

___*Not paying*___ attention to their health is a mistake a lot of college students make.
1.

_____ healthy will help you do well in school and help you enjoy your college
2.
experience. Here are some tips:

- Smokers have more colds and less energy. Quit _____ now or don't start.
  3.

- _____ regularly reduces stress and brings more oxygen to your brain. If you
  4.

  don't exercise, I suggest _____ every day with a walk or run around campus.
  5.

- _____ breakfast is a common mistake. It's the most important meal of the day.
  6.

- Avoid _____ junk food. Your brain will thank you!
  7.

- Health experts advise _____ the fruits and vegetables in your diet. You need at
  8.

  least four and a half cups a day, but more is better.

- _____ to the doctor when you're sick is another common mistake. Know where
  9.

  your school Health Service is, and use it when you need it.

- Better yet—consider _____ Healthy Campus—a program for staying healthy.
  10.

EXERCISE 3: Gerund as Object

(Grammar Note 2)

*Write a summary sentence for each conversation. Use the correct form of the verbs from the
box and the gerund form of the verbs in parentheses.*

admit	avoid	consider	deny	enjoy	go	mind	~~quit~~

1.   **RALPH:** Would you like a cigarette?

      MARTA: Oh, no, thanks. Since restaurants have banned cigarettes, I don't smoke anymore.

   SUMMARY: Marta _____*quit smoking*_____.
                            (smoke)

2.   **BRIAN:** Where are the cookies I bought? You ate them, didn't you?

      ELLEN: No, I didn't.

   SUMMARY: Ellen _____ the cookies.
                            (eat)

3.   **ANN:** Do you want to go running with me before work?

      TOM: Running? Are you kidding? I hate it!

   SUMMARY: Tom doesn't _____.
                            (run)

4.   **CHEN:** What are you doing after work?

      AN-LING: I'm going to that new swimming pool. Would you like to go with me?

   SUMMARY: An-ling is going to _____.
                            (swim)

(continued on next page)

5.   **IRENE:** You're lazy. You really need to exercise more.

        MIKE: You're right. I *am* lazy.

    SUMMARY: Mike _____ lazy.
                               (be)

6.   **MONICA:** Would you like a piece of chocolate cake?

       PAULO: No, thanks. I try to stay away from sweets.

    SUMMARY: Paulo _____ sweets.
                             (eat)

7.   **CRAIG:** I know exercise is important, but I hate it. What about you?

       VILMA: Well, I don't *love* it, but it's OK.

    SUMMARY: Vilma doesn't _____.
                           (exercise)

8.   **ALICE:** We've been working too hard. Maybe we need a vacation.

       ERIK: A vacation? Hmmm. That's an interesting idea. Do you think we can afford it?

    SUMMARY: Erik and Alice _____ a vacation.
                             (take)

EXERCISE 4: Gerund as Object of a Preposition   *(Grammar Note 3)*

Combine the pairs of sentences to make statements about the Healthy Campus Program. Use the prepositions in parentheses plus a gerund.

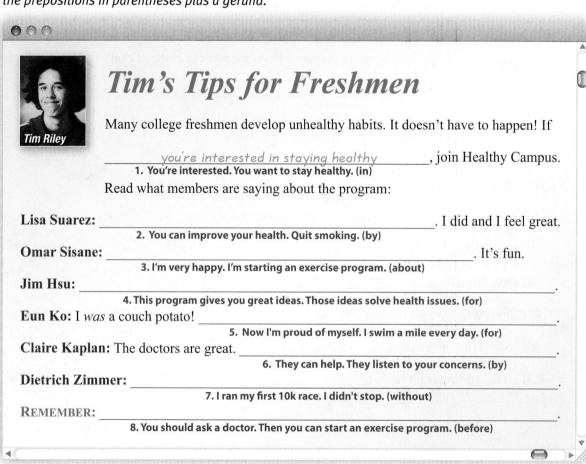

Tim's Tips for Freshmen

Tim Riley

Many college freshmen develop unhealthy habits. It doesn't have to happen! If

_____*you're interested in staying healthy*_____, join Healthy Campus.
      1. You're interested. You want to stay healthy. (in)

Read what members are saying about the program:

Lisa Suarez: _____. I did and I feel great.
      2. You can improve your health. Quit smoking. (by)

Omar Sisane: _____. It's fun.
      3. I'm very happy. I'm starting an exercise program. (about)

Jim Hsu: _____.
      4. This program gives you great ideas. Those ideas solve health issues. (for)

Eun Ko: I *was* a couch potato! _____.
      5. Now I'm proud of myself. I swim a mile every day. (for)

Claire Kaplan: The doctors are great. _____.
      6. They can help. They listen to your concerns. (by)

Dietrich Zimmer: _____.
      7. I ran my first 10k race. I didn't stop. (without)

REMEMBER: _____.
      8. You should ask a doctor. Then you can start an exercise program. (before)

EXERCISE 5: Editing

Read part of an ex-smoker's journal. There are sixteen mistakes in the use of gerunds as subject and object. The first mistake is already corrected. Find and correct fifteen more. Remember to check for spelling mistakes.

>   smoking
> DAY 1 I quit ~~to smoke~~! This was the first day of the rest of my life as a non-smoker. Get through the day wasn't too difficult. I quit drinking coffee today too, and I think that helped. I used to enjoy had a cigarette with a cup of coffee in the morning. But now I'm looking forward to get healthier.
>
> DAY 3 Today was harder. I called Dinah and admitted wanted to smoke. She advised takeing deep breaths and staying busy. That worked. I have to resist eat too much. Gaining 5 pounds aren't a big deal, but I don't want to gain more than that.
>
> DAY 5 I got through the workweek smoke free. My boss definitely approves of the new me. She keeps tells me, "You can do it." I really appreciate to have her support. I miss smoking, but I don't miss to standing outside in the cold just to smoke. I also don't mind don't burning holes in my clothes!
>
> DAY 7 Dinah suggested to go out to dinner, but I can't risk be around smokers. Instead, we went shoping, and I bought a shirt with the money I saved during my first week as a non-smoker. Also, I'm happy about have clothes that smell fresh! Not smoking has advantages.

STEP 4 COMMUNICATION PRACTICE

EXERCISE 6: Listening

A | *A doctor is giving advice to a patient. Some things are **OK to Do** for this patient, but other things are **Not OK to Do**. Read the list. Then listen to the conversation between doctor and patient. Listen again and check (✓) the correct column.*

	OK to Do	Not OK to Do
1. smoking	☐	☑
2. drinking a little coffee	☐	☐
3. losing more weight	☐	☐

(continued on next page)

	OK to Do	Not OK to Do
4. eating more complex carbohydrates	☐	☐
5. running every day	☐	☐
6. riding a bike every day	☐	☐
7. working eight hours a day	☐	☐

B | *Read the statements. Then listen again to the conversation and circle the correct information.*

1. The patient is going to try to stop <u>drinking coffee</u> / (smoking).

2. The doctor says the patient should <u>gain / stay the same</u> weight.

3. The patient thanks the doctor for giving him a list of foods that are high in

   <u>complex carbohydrates / protein</u>.

4. The patient says he enjoys <u>running / cycling</u>.

5. The patient is not going to quit <u>running / working</u> every day.

EXERCISE 7: Pronunciation

A | *Read and listen to the Pronunciation Note.*

> **Pronunciation Note**
>
> Gerunds end in *-ing*. When a word beginning with a vowel sound follows a gerund, we usually **link the -ing with the vowel sound**.
>
> EXAMPLES: **Swimming is** fun.
>
> They shouldn't allow **smoking on** the street.

B | *Listen to the sentences. Draw linking lines (‿) between the gerunds and the words beginning with a vowel.*

1. **Smoking** is bad for your health.

2. **Smoking** causes health problems.

3. **Quitting** is very difficult.

4. He's opposed to **smoking** near other people.

5. He's even opposed to **smoking** outside.

6. She doesn't like **seeing** those signs.

7. She used to enjoy **lighting** up after dinner.

8. She plans on **quitting** in April.

C | *Listen again and repeat the sentences.*

EXERCISE 8: Survey

A | *Take a class survey. How many students agree with the statements? Write the numbers in the appropriate column.*

	Agree	Disagree	No Opinion or Don't Know
Smoking a few cigarettes a day is safe.			
Quitting is very difficult.			
Increasing the price of cigarettes encourages quitting.			
Banning all cigarette ads is a good idea.			
TV programs shouldn't allow scenes with smoking.			
Health insurance should be higher for smokers.			
They should allow smoking on the street.			
Selling cigarettes to teenagers should be illegal.			

B | *Discuss your survey results.*

> EXAMPLE: A: Only three students agree that smoking a few cigarettes a day is safe. Ten students disagree. Three students have no opinion or don't know.
> B: It seems that most students think that smoking is bad for people's health.
> C: Great! . . . Now how do they feel about quitting smoking?

EXERCISE 9: For or Against

Many people agree with laws that prohibit smoking. What is your opinion? Work in small groups. Think of arguments for and against allowing smoking in these places:

- in restaurants
- outside of schools
- at outdoor bus stops
- in parks
- in a car with children under 18
- in elevators
- in outdoor sports arenas
- in indoor shopping malls

> EXAMPLE: A: I'm in favor of banning smoking in restaurants.
> B: I agree. Sitting in a room full of smoke is unhealthy.
> C: But some restaurants have outdoor seating. I'm not against allowing smoking at tables outside.

EXERCISE 10: Writing

A | *Smoking is just one of many topics that people disagree about. Write a two-paragraph opinion essay for or against one of these topics:*

- allowing dogs in restaurants and stores
- texting or talking on cell phones while driving
- riding a motorcycle without wearing a helmet on your head
- forcing drivers over age 75 to pass a road test
- listing calories and fat content on restaurant menus
- eating junk food

EXAMPLE: In the United States, bringing your dog into a restaurant is illegal in most places. Some people don't like dogs. They don't want to eat dinner with one nearby. Other people are afraid of getting sick because a server touched a dog and didn't wash his or her hands . . .

B | *Check your work. Use the Editing Checklist.*

Editing Checklist
Did you use gerunds . . . ?   ☐ as subjects   ☐ as objects after certain verbs   ☐ after prepositions   ☐ with third-person-singular verbs

Check your answers on page UR-6.

Do you need to review anything?

A | *Complete each sentence with the gerund form of the correct verbs from the box. Choose between affirmative and negative.*

| eat | feel | improve | join | like | smoke | swim |

1. I admit _____ exercise. I've never enjoyed it.

2. I'm going to quit _____ on my birthday. This is my last pack.

3. You can count on _____ better as soon as you quit. You'll sleep better too.

4. Are you interested in _____ a gym?

5. Rafe goes _____ almost every day.

6. Sally doesn't mind _____ sweets anymore. She doesn't miss them.

7. I'd like some ideas for _____ my health. I catch too many colds.

B | *Complete the sentences with the correct form of the words in parentheses. Use the correct word order.*

1. _____ good for your health.
   (laugh / be)

2. My doctor _____ funny movies.
   (suggest / watch)

3. _____ jokes _____ your
   (tell / help)
   blood pressure.

4. One expert _____ too much coffee.
   (advise against / drink)

5. We _____ long walks.
   (enjoy / take)

6. What do you _____ in restaurants?
   (think about / smoke)

C | *Find and correct seven mistakes. Remember to check punctuation.*

1. You look great. Buying these bikes were a good idea.

2. I know. I'm happy about lose weight too. Didn't exercising was a bad idea.

3. It always is. Hey, I'm thinking of rent a movie. What do you suggest to see?

4. I've been looking forward to see *Grown Ups*. Have you seen it yet?

5. Not yet. Do you recommend it? You're so good at choose movies.

Infinitives after Certain Verbs
FRIENDS AND FAMILY

STEP 1 GRAMMAR IN CONTEXT

Before You Read

Look at the advice column. Discuss the questions.

1. What kind of questions do you think Annie answers?
2. Do you think this is a good place to get advice? If no, why not?

Read

Read the newspaper advice column, Ask Annie.

Lifestyles	Section 4

ASK ANNIE

Dear Annie,

I've just moved to Seattle and started going to a new school. I **try to meet** people but nothing **seems to work**. A few weeks ago, I **agreed to have** dinner with someone from my English class. Bad idea. Right after we got to the restaurant, he **asked to borrow** money from me for the check. And he also **wanted to correct** my pronunciation (I'm from Louisiana). Obviously, I **decided not to see**[1] him again. Now my roommate **would like** me **to go out** with her brother. I **asked** her **not to arrange** anything because I really **don't want to date** anyone right now. First, I'd just **like to find** some friends to hang out with.[2] Do you have any suggestions?

Lonely in Seattle

Dear Lonely,

You **seem to have** the right idea about making new friends. A lot of people **try to solve** the problem of loneliness by falling in love. I usually **advise** them **to make** friends first. Perhaps you just **need to relax** a bit. Don't **expect to develop** friendships overnight because that takes time. Instead, do things that you'**d like to do** anyway. Join a sports club. **Learn to dance**.

Try not to focus so much on your problem. Just **remember to have** fun with your new activities. You'll interact with people who have similar interests. Even if you **fail to meet** your new best friends immediately, you will at least have a good time!

Don't give up!

Annie

---

[1] **see:** to go out socially with; to date
[2] **hang out with:** to spend free time with people

After You Read

A | Vocabulary: *Match the underlined words with the words in* **blue.**

_____ **1.** <u>It's easy to see that</u> they're going to be great friends.

_____ **2.** They have <u>almost the same</u> interests—dancing, for example.

_____ **3.** At school we <u>talk and work</u> with people from all over the world.

_____ **4.** <u>Keep your attention</u> on your work, and your grades will improve.

_____ **5.** Some people <u>find an answer to</u> their problem by writing to Annie.

a. interact

b. solve

c. obviously

d. similar

e. focus

B | Comprehension: *Check (✓)* **True** *or* **False.** *Correct the false statements.*

	True	False
1. "Lonely" has been successful in meeting people.	☐	☐
2. "Lonely" isn't asking for advice about dating.	☐	☐
3. Annie thinks making friends is a good idea.	☐	☐
4. Annie says that friendships develop quickly.	☐	☐
5. Annie thinks that "Lonely" ought to have some fun.	☐	☐

INFINITIVES AFTER CERTAIN VERBS

Statements				
Subject	Verb	(Object)	Infinitive	
I	**decided**		**(not) to write**	to Annie.
You	**advised**	John	**(not) to borrow**	money.
He	**asked**	(her)	**(not) to arrange**	a date.

GRAMMAR NOTES

1
An **infinitive** is *to* + **base form of the verb**.

Form the **negative** by placing *not* before the infinitive.

An infinitive can **follow certain verbs**.

- She decided **to join** a health club.

- She decided *not* **to join** the math club.

- I *agreed* **to have** dinner.
- He *wants* **to make** new friends.

2
Some **verbs**, such as the ones below, can be **followed directly by an infinitive.** 不定詞

agree	forget	remember
attempt	hope	rush
begin	learn	seem
can't wait	manage	try
decide	plan	volunteer
fail	refuse	wait

VERB + INFINITIVE
- He *decided* **to take** a dance class.
- He *hoped* **to meet** new people.
- She *refused* **to go out** with him.
- She *tried* **not to be** late.

3
Some verbs, such as the ones below, need an **object** (noun or pronoun) **before the infinitive.**

advise	encourage	permit	tell
allow	force	persuade	urge
convince	invite	remind	warn

VERB + OBJECT + INFINITIVE
- I *invited* Mary **to eat** with us.
- I *reminded* her **to come**.
- She *told* me **to call** her.
- They *warned* us **not to forget**.

4
Some verbs, such as the ones below, can be **followed by:**
- **an infinitive**

  OR

- **an object + infinitive**

ask	need	promise
choose	pay	want
expect	prefer	would like

INFINITIVE
- I *asked* **to come** to the meeting.

OBJECT + INFINITIVE
- I *asked* them **to come** to the meeting.

REFERENCE NOTES
For a list of **verbs** that are **followed by infinitives**, see Appendix 14 on page A-7.
For a more complete list of **verbs** that need an **object before the infinitive**, see Appendix 16 on page A-7.

EXERCISE 1: Discover the Grammar

Read the diary entry. Underline all the **verb + infinitive** *and the* **verb + object + infinitive** *combinations. Circle the objects.*

Annie advised me to join a club or take a class, and I finally did it! I decided to join the school's Outdoor Adventure Club, and I went to my first meeting last night. I'm really excited about this. The club is planning a hiking trip next weekend. I can't wait to go. I hope it won't be too hard for my first adventure. Last night they also decided to go rafting in the spring. At first I didn't want to sign up, but the leader was so nice. He urged me not to miss this trip, so I put my name on the list. After the meeting, a group of people asked me to go out with them. We went to a coffee shop and talked for hours. Well, I hoped to make some new friends when I joined this club, but I didn't expect everyone to be so friendly. I'm glad Annie persuaded me not to give up.

EXERCISE 2: Verb (+ Object) + Infinitive   *(Grammar Notes 1–4)*

Complete the article. Use the correct form of the verbs in parentheses. Use the simple present or the imperative form for the first verb.

Most people make careful plans when they _____ decide to take _____
                                              1. (decide / take)
a vacation. But when they _____ attempt to find _____ a mate, they depend on
                              2. (attempt / find)
luck. Edward A. Dreyfus, Ph.D., _____ warn single people not to leave _____ love to chance.
                                    3. (warn / single people / not leave)
He _____ urge them to use _____ his relationship plan when they search for a life partner.
       4. (urge / them / use)
Remember: When you _____ fail to plan _____, you _____ plan to fail _____.
                       5. (fail / plan)   **6. (plan / fail)**

STEP ONE: Make a list. What kind of person would you _____ like to meet _____?
                                                             7. (like / meet)

Someone intelligent? Someone who loves sports? List everything.

STEP TWO: Make another list. What kind of person are *you*? List all your characteristics (don't just

focus on your good points!). _____ ask two friends to read _____ this list and comment on it.
                                 8. (ask / two friends / read)
_____ tell them not to worry _____ about hurting your feelings. The two lists should match.
   9. (tell / them / not worry)

(continued on next page)

STEP THREE: **Increase your chances.** _____ in activities you like.
                                              10. (begin / participate)
That way you'll interact with people who have similar interests.

STEP FOUR: _____ **introductions.** Dr. Dreyfus always
                 11. (ask / friends / arrange)
_____ embarrassed. After all, almost everyone
12. (advise / people / not feel)
_____ a matchmaker!
13. (want / be)

EXERCISE 3: Object or No Object

(Grammar Notes 1–4)

*Write a summary sentence for each conversation. Use the correct form of a verb from the box
followed by an infinitive or an object + infinitive.*

agree	encourage	forget	invite	need	remind	would like

1. **KAREN:** *(yawn)* Don't you have a meeting tomorrow? Maybe you should go home now.

   TOM: It's only nine o'clock. And *Lost* is on in five minutes!

   SUMMARY: Karen _would like Tom to go home_____.

2. **KURT:** Hey, honey, did you get any stamps?

   LILY: Oh, I forgot. I'll stop at the post office on the way home.

   SUMMARY: Kurt _____.

3. **JOHN:** We're going out for coffee. Would you like to join us?

   MARY: I'd love to.

   SUMMARY: John _____.

4. **DAD:** I expect you to come home by 10:30. Do you understand? If you don't, I'm

   grounding you for two weeks—no parties, no friends, no telephone. Understand?

   JASON: OK, OK. Take it easy, Dad. I'll be home by 10:30.

   SUMMARY: Jason _____.

5. **DON:** You didn't go to the staff meeting. We missed you.

   JEFF: Oh, no! The staff meeting!

   SUMMARY: Jeff _____.

6.   **LISA:** I hate to ice skate. I always fall down.

   MOM: Don't be scared, sweetie. Just try once more. You'll love it.

   SUMMARY: Lisa's mom _encourage her daughter to skate_.

7.   **BRAD:** Are you using the car tonight?

   TERRY: Well, I have a lot of shopping to do. And I promised Susan I'd give her a ride.

   SUMMARY: Terry _need to use the car tonight_.

EXERCISE 4: Editing

Read the article from an online how-to site. There are nine mistakes in the use of infinitives.
The first mistake is already corrected. Find and correct eight more.

The things you need to know!

How to Make New Friends

You'd like to ~~making~~ *make* some new friends. Maybe you're at a new school or job, or, possibly, you

have changed and the "new you" wants meet new people. First, I strongly advise to turn off

your computer and TV. "Friending" people on Facebook just isn't the same as making real

friends. And those people on that old show "Friends" aren't YOUR friends. You need go out

and interact with real people. Decide right now to don't refuse invitations. When a classmate

or co-worker invites you for coffee, just say "Yes." Join a club and volunteer to doing

something. That responsibility will force you to attend the meetings. By doing these things, you

will manage meeting a lot of new people. But don't rush to become close friends with

someone right away. Learn to listen. Encourage the person to talks by asking questions. Allow

each relationship develops naturally, and soon you'll have a group of people you're really

comfortable with.

EXERCISE 5: Listening

A | *Read the statements about a blended family.¹ Then listen to a couple talk to a family counselor about their family. Listen again to their conversation and check (✓)* **True** *or* **False.** *Correct the false statements.*

	True	False
first 1. The woman has a daughter from her ~~second~~ marriage.	☐	☑
2. The man finally stopped arguing with his stepdaughter.	☐	☐
3. The woman was surprised about the problems with her daughter.	☐	☐
4. The girl stopped talking to her stepfather for a while.	☐	☐
5. The adults weren't interested in the girl's feelings.	☐	☐
6. The man invited his stepdaughter to go on a family vacation.	☐	☐
7. The family hasn't solved all their problems.	☐	☐

¹ *blended family:* a family that includes children from one parent's or both parents' earlier marriages

B | *Read the pairs of statements. Then listen again to the conversation and circle the letter of the statements you hear.*

1. **a.** I really wanted to discuss their problems.

   (b.) I really wanted them to discuss their problems.

2. **a.** I finally learned to argue with my stepdaughter.

   b. I finally learned not to argue with my stepdaughter.

3. **a.** I expected to have problems with my daughter.

   b. I expected you to have problems with my daughter.

4. **a.** Sometimes I just wanted to leave the house for a few hours.

   b. Sometimes I just wanted her to leave the house for a few hours.

5. **a.** After all, she didn't choose to live with us.

   b. After all, she chose to live with us.

6. **a.** Then one day, Brenda asked to go on a family vacation.

   b. Then one day, Brenda asked me to go on a family vacation.

7. **a.** We wanted to enjoy being together as a family

   b. We wanted her to enjoy being together as a family.

EXERCISE 6: Pronunciation

A | *Read and listen to the Pronunciation Note.*

> **Pronunciation Note**
>
> In sentences with **infinitives**:
> - We usually **stress** the **main verb** and the **base form** of the verb in the infinitive.
> - We do NOT usually stress *to* or a pronoun object.
>
> EXAMPLES: She **expected to go** on vacation.
>
> She **expected me to go** on vacation.

B | *Listen to the sentences. Put a dot (●) over the words or parts of words that are stressed.*

1. She **advised me to stay**.

2. They **prefer to study** at home.

3. Would you **like to leave**?

4. We **encouraged her to join** a club.

5. My parents **expect me to call** them tonight.

6. He **said to park** here.

C | *Listen again and repeat the sentences.*

EXERCISE 7: What About You?

A | *Work in pairs. Tell each other about your childhood relationship with your parents or other adults.*

- What did they encourage you to do?
- How did they encourage you to do that?
- What didn't they allow you to do?
- What did they force you to do?
- What would they like you to do?

- What did they advise you to do?
- Why did they advise you to do that?
- What do they expect you to do?
- What would you prefer to do?
- Why would you prefer to do that?

EXAMPLE: My parents encouraged me to learn other languages.

B | *Add your own questions.*

_____

_____

_____

EXERCISE 8: Cross-Cultural Comparison

As a class, discuss how people in your culture socialize. Do young men and women go out together? If so, do they go out in couples or in groups? What are some ways people meet their future husbands or wives?

EXAMPLE: **A:** In Brazil, young people usually prefer to go out together in groups. They like to go to clubs or to the movies.

B: In Germany, families allow young people to go out on dates.

C: In Thailand . . .

EXERCISE 9: Writing

A | *Write emails to two or three friends and invite them to join you for an event that a group of your friends is going to attend. Remember to use infinitives.*

EXAMPLE: Hi Ari,

Some classmates and I plan to see *Avatar* at the Regis Cineplex on Saturday. Would you like to come with us? We want to go to the 7:00 P.M. show. After the movie, we'll probably go out for pizza. I hope to see you Saturday.

It's going to be fun!

Liv

B | *Check your work. Use the Editing Checklist.*

Editing Checklist

Did you . . . ?

☐ use infinitives after the correct verbs

☐ form the negative with ***not* + infinitive**

☐ use **verb** + **object** + **infinitive** correctly

UNIT **24** **Review**

Check your answers on page UR-6.
Do you need to review anything?

A | Complete each sentence with the infinitive form of the correct verbs from the box.

call	finish	get	go	meet	play

1. Sorry. I forgot _____ milk on the way home.

2. I've heard so much about you. I can't wait _____ you!

3. Did you manage _____ your paper on time?

4. Where did you decide _____ on your next vacation?

5. I love the piano. I want to learn _____ .

6. Remember _____ when you get home.

B | Unscramble the words to complete the sentences.

1. I _____ .
   (visit / Mary / invited / us / to)

2. She _____ .
   (come / to / agreed)

3. She _____ .
   (to / wants / new friends / make)

4. I _____ .
   (early / her / to / told / come)

5. I _____ .
   (Tom / not / decided / invite / to)

6. He _____ .
   (his project / to / needs / finish)

C | Find and correct eight mistakes.

1. **A:** I want invite you to my party.

   B: Thanks. I'd love coming.

2. **A:** I plan to not get there before 8:00.

   B: Remember getting the soda. Don't forget!

3. **A:** Sara asked I to help her.

   B: I agreed helping her too.

4. **A:** I promised pick up some ice cream.

   B: OK. But let's do it early. I prefer don't arrive late.

25 More Uses of Infinitives
SMART PHONES

Before You Read

Look at the photo and the title of the article. Discuss the questions.

1. Why is the article called "The World in Your Pocket"?
2. What can you use a smart phone for?
3. Do you have a smart phone or a cell phone? How do you use it?

Read

Read the article about smart phones.

The World in Your Pocket

What's **smart enough to get** you all the information you'll ever need but **small enough to fit** inside your pocket? A smart phone! And it's getting smarter and smaller all the time. When smart phones first came out, people used them for three major purposes: **to make** calls, **to check** email, and **to connect** to the Internet. Today, people of all ages and walks of life[1] are using them for a lot more. Here's what some happy users report:

"I use my smart phone **to play** games, **listen** to music, and **watch** videos. It's awesome!"
— *Todd Miller, 16, high school student*

"I use it **to translate** words I don't understand."
— *Lian Chang, 21, nurse*

"When I'm considering buying a book in a bookstore, (sounds old-fashioned, doesn't it?) I use it **to look up** reviews."
—*Rosa Ortiz, 56, accountant*

"I travel a lot. When I'm on the road, I use it **to avoid** traffic jams. And if I get lost, I use it **to get** directions."
—*Brad King, 32, reporter*

It's **easy to see** why these multipurpose devices are so popular. They combine the functions of a phone, GPS,[2] camera, computer, calculator, organizer, and much more. But they have a downside too. Although the phones have become cheaper, when you add the monthly service charges, they are still **too expensive** for many people **to afford**. And there's another cost. When you are available 24/7,[3] people expect you to work and be reachable all the time. For a lot of people, that price may be **too high to pay**.

---

[1] *walks of life:* occupations

[2] *GPS:* Global Positioning System, a device that tells you where you are and gives you directions

[3] *24/7:* twenty-four hours a day, seven days a week

After You Read

A | Vocabulary: *Circle the letter of the word or phrase that best completes each sentence.*

1. An **old-fashioned** idea is NOT _____.
   a. good
   b. modern
   c. interesting

2. A **device** is a small _____.
   a. phone
   b. machine
   c. video

3. If something is **multipurpose**, it has many _____.
   a. uses
   b. pieces
   c. meanings

4. If you **combine** several things, you _____.
   a. separate them
   b. clean them
   c. bring them together

5. Another word for **function** is _____.
   a. information
   b. purpose
   c. computer

6. A **major** reason is a reason that is very _____.
   a. popular
   b. expensive
   c. important

B | Comprehension: *Check (✓)* **True** *or* **False**. *Correct the false statements.*

	True	False
1. Today's smart phones are not very big.	☐	☐
2. People mostly use them to make calls.	☐	☐
3. Only young people use them.	☐	☐
4. Todd Miller uses one to have fun.	☐	☐
5. Lian Chang uses one to take pictures.	☐	☐
6. Rosa Ortiz uses one to read books on.	☐	☐
7. Brad King uses one on his way to work.	☐	☐
8. Many people like using them.	☐	☐
9. They are very cheap to own.	☐	☐
10. People are totally happy with them.	☐	☐

INFINITIVES

Infinitives of Purpose

Affirmative	Negative
I use it **to call** my friends.	I left at 9:00 **in order not to be** late.

Infinitives after Adjectives and Adverbs

With *Too*				
	(Too)	Adjective / Adverb	(*For* + Noun / Object Pronoun)	Infinitive
It's	(too)	hard		to use.
It's not		expensive	for Todd	to buy.
She spoke	too	quickly	for him	to understand.
They worked		slowly		to finish.

With *Enough*				
	Adjective / Adverb	*(Enough)*	(*For* + Noun / Object Pronoun)	Infinitive
It's	easy	(enough)		to use.
It's	cheap		for Todd	to buy.
She spoke	slowly	enough	for him	to understand.
They didn't work	quickly			to finish.

GRAMMAR NOTES

1	Use an **infinitive** (*to* + **base form of verb**) to explain the **purpose** of an action. It often answers the question *Why?*	**A:** *Why* did you go to the mall? **B:** I went there **to buy** a new phone.
	USAGE NOTES:	
	a. In conversation, you can answer the question *Why?* with an <u>incomplete sentence</u> beginning with *to*.	**A:** *Why* did you go to the mall? **B:** **To buy** a new camera phone.
	b. We usually <u>do NOT repeat *to*</u> when we give more than one purpose.	• I went to the mall **to buy** a phone, **eat** lunch, and **see** a movie. Not: I went to the mall to buy a phone, ~~to~~ eat lunch, and ~~to~~ see a movie.

2

In **formal writing** we often use:

a. *in order to* + **base form of verb** to explain
a <u>purpose</u>

FORMAL: He acquired it **in order to stay**
connected to the world.
INFORMAL: He got it **to stay** in touch with his friends.

b. *in order not to* + **base form of verb** to explain
a <u>negative purpose</u>

- They use a GPS **in order not to get** lost.

USAGE NOTE: In everyday <u>spoken English</u>, we
often express a negative purpose with
because + **a reason**.

- I use a GPS *because I don't want to get lost*.

3

You can use the infinitive **after adjectives and
adverbs**.

ADJECTIVE
- It's *easy* **to use**.

ADVERB
- We worked *hard* **to finish** on time.

Sometimes we use *for* + **noun / pronoun** <u>before</u>
the infinitive.

- It's *easy for Todd* **to use**.
- It's *easy for him* **to use**.

Use *too* <u>before</u> the adjective or adverb to show
the reason something is **not possible**.

- It was *too expensive* **to buy**.
(It was expensive, so I couldn't buy it.)

Use *enough* <u>after</u> the adjective or adverb to show
the reason something is **possible**.

- It was *cheap enough* **to buy**.
(It was cheap, so I could buy it.)
NOT: It was ~~enough cheap~~ to buy.

Notice the **word order** in sentences with:
- *too* + adj. + *for* + noun/pro. + infinitive
- adj. + *enough* + *for* + noun/pro. + infinitive

- It's **too hard** *for my son* **to understand**.
- It's **easy enough** *for Jana* **to use**.

REMEMBER: We **don't need the infinitive** when the
meaning is clear.

A: Did you buy a smart phone?
B: Yes. It's finally **cheap enough** *for me*!
(It's cheap enough for me to buy.)

EXERCISE 1: Discover the Grammar

Read about changes in the telephone. Underline all the infinitives of purpose and infinitives after adjectives or adverbs.

PHONE TALK

The telephone has really changed a lot in less than a century. From the 1920s through the 1950s, there was the good old-fashioned rotary phone. It had just one function, but it wasn't that convenient to use. Callers had to turn a dial to make a call. And it was too big and heavy to move from place to place. (Besides, there was that annoying cord connecting it to the wall!). The 1960s introduced the touch-tone phone. It was much faster to place a call with it. You just pushed buttons in order to dial. With cordless phones, introduced in the 1970s, callers were free to move around their homes or offices while talking. Then came a really major change—hand-held cell phones. These were small enough to carry with you and you didn't even have to be inside to talk to your friends. But it wasn't until the invention of the camera phone that people began to use the phone to do more than just talk. And, that was nothing compared to today's multipurpose smart phones. People use them to do almost everything. What will the newest technology bring to the phone? It's hard to predict. But one thing is certain: It will be faster and smaller. And, as always, people will find uses for it that are difficult to imagine today.

EXERCISE 2: Affirmative and Negative Purposes

(Grammar Notes 1–2)

A | *Match the actions with their purposes.*

Action	Purpose
_b_ **1.** She bought a smart phone because she	**a.** didn't want to get calls.
____ **2.** He took the bus because he	**b.** wanted to check email.
____ **3.** We turned our phone off because we	**c.** wanted to buy a new phone.
____ **4.** She recorded her favorite TV show because she	**d.** didn't want to be late.
____ **5.** She went to the electronics store because she	**e.** didn't want to miss it.

B | *Now combine the sentences. Use the infinitive of purpose.*

1. _She bought a smart phone to check email._

2. _____

3. _____

4. _____

5. _____

EXERCISE 3: Affirmative Statements

(Grammar Note 1)

On a moblog, you can post pictures, videos, and text from your camera phone directly to the Web for millions of people to see. Look at this moblog. Complete the sentences with the correct words from the box. Use the infinitive of purpose.

buy fruit and vegetables	**pass it**	**exchange money**
communicate with her	**get more gas**	~~**take my own picture**~~
drive to Montreal	**have coffee**	

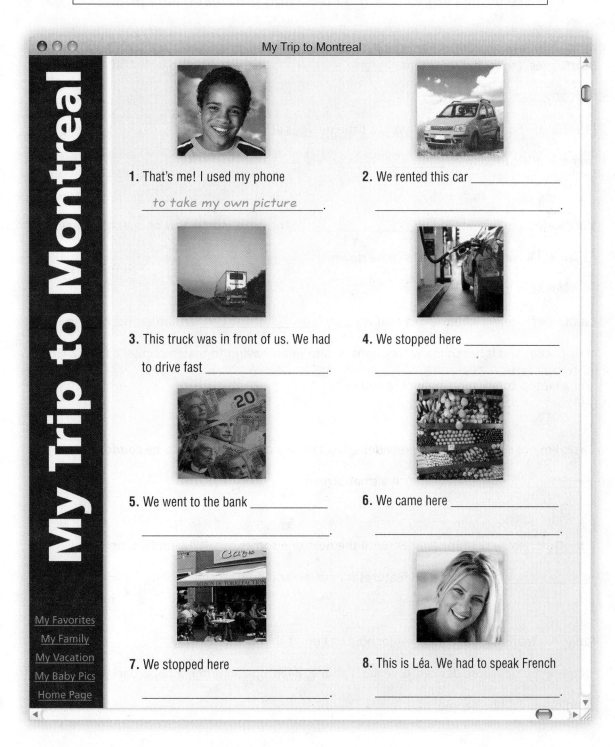

My Trip to Montreal

My Trip to Montreal

1. That's me! I used my phone
   _to take my own picture_____.

2. We rented this car _____
   _____.

3. This truck was in front of us. We had
   to drive fast _____.

4. We stopped here _____
   _____.

5. We went to the bank _____
   _____.

6. We came here _____
   _____.

7. We stopped here _____
   _____.

8. This is Léa. We had to speak French
   _____.

My Favorites
My Family
My Vacation
My Baby Pics
Home Page

EXERCISE 4: Infinitive after Adjectives

(Grammar Note 3)

Complete the responses to an online survey. Use the infinitive form of the verbs from the box.

| carry | find out | ~~have~~ | own | spend | use | watch |

SURVEY

2-10-2012

Are you going to buy the latest and greatest smart phone?

2-10-2012

BobG: Yes. I think it's important _____*to have*_____ the latest technology. And, it's cool!
        1.

2-10-2012

Finefone: I don't know. I'm always a little nervous about buying a new device. I hope it

isn't too difficult for me _____ .
        2.

2-10-2012

YIKES: No. I'm just not ready _____ the money on a new phone. It's a major
        3.

expense. I'll wait until the prices come down.

2-11-2012

LilaX: Definitely! I love the fact that it's easy _____ around. It fits right in
        4.

your pocket and it has so many functions. It sure beats having to take a phone, a PDA, a GPS,

and a laptop computer everywhere you go!

2-11-2012

Cat2: I'm not sure. I want one for videos, but I'm afraid it's not going to be comfortable

_____ them on such a small screen.
        5.

2-11-2012

TimeOut: Not yet. I think I'll wait until the next one comes out. It'll be interesting

_____ what new features it'll have—and how much it'll cost.
        6.

2-12-2012

Rosy: No thanks! Call me old-fashioned, but I don't think it's necessary _____
        7.

all these multipurpose devices. Give me a phone, a laptop computer, a paperback book,

a radio—and I'll be happy.

EXERCISE 5: Infinitive after Adjectives and Adverbs

(Grammar Note 3)

Complete the conversations. Use the words in parentheses and **too** *or* **enough**.

1. **A:** Did you buy the new smart phone?

   B: No. Right now it's still _____ *too expensive for me to buy* OR *too expensive for me* _____.
      (expensive / for me)

2. **A:** Can we call Alicia now?

   B: Sure. It's _____.
      (early)

3. **A:** What did Mrs. Johnson just say? I didn't understand her.

   B: Me neither. She always speaks _____.
      (quickly / for me)

4. **A:** Did Dan ever pass his driving test?

   B: Yes. The last time he drove _____.
      (well)

5. **A:** Does he have enough money to get that used car?

   B: It's only $300. I think it's _____.
      (cheap / for him)

6. **A:** Do you want to go to a movie tonight?

   B: Sorry. I'm _____.
      (busy)

EXERCISE 6: Editing

Read the online bulletin board about smart phones. There are ten mistakes in the use of the infinitive of purpose and infinitives after adjectives. The first mistake is already corrected. Find and correct nine more.

● ○ ○

           to tell

Click here <del>for telling</del> us how you've used your smart phone recently.

I was riding my bike when I saw an accident. A car hit a truck, but it didn't stop. I used my

smart phone take a picture of the car and the license plate number. Then I used it to call the

police. It was so fast and convenient to using!   **Jason Harvey, England**

I was at a great concert in Mexico City. I wanted to share the experience with my best friend

back home. I picked up my smart phone and used it to make a video and sending it to my

friend. Instantly my friend was "there" with me. Awesome!   **Emilia Leale, Italy**

(continued on next page)

I sell houses. I always use my phone in order no waste my customers' time. When I see an interesting house, I immediately send a photo. Then, if they are interested, I make an appointment for them. Without a smart phone, my job would be to hard to do.

Andrea Cook, U.S.

Last night I used it to helping me make dinner. First, I searched online for a recipe. It was in grams, so I used a program to converts it to ounces. Then I used another program to create a shopping list. When I returned home from shopping, I set the phone's timer to reminded me when to take the food out of the oven. While dinner was baking, I used the phone to listen to my favorite songs. I love this thing! It combines functions for work and play, and it's enough smart to do almost everything. Too bad it can't do the dishes too!

Kim Soo-Min, South Korea

STEP 4 COMMUNICATION PRACTICE

EXERCISE 7: Listening

A | *Read the statements. Then listen to a TV ad for a new phone. Listen again and circle the correct information.*

1. The E-phone is (small) / light enough to carry in your pocket.

2. It's easy / fun to use.

3. There are hundreds / thousands of things you can use it to do.

4. The price is affordable / cheap.

5. You can buy the phone at an electronics store / online.

B | *Read the list. Listen again to the ad and check (✓) the things it says you can do with the E-phone.*

The ad says you can . . .

☐ **1.** bank online   ☐ **6.** get driving directions

☑ **2.** search for a restaurant   ☐ **7.** find information in encyclopedias and dictionaries

☐ **3.** find a recipe   ☐ **8.** create a "To Do" list

☐ **4.** create a shopping list   ☐ **9.** put together a clothing outfit

☐ **5.** use a calculator   ☐ **10.** look at newspaper headlines from around the world

EXERCISE 8: Pronunciation

A | *Read and listen to the Pronunciation Note.*

> **Pronunciation Note**
>
> In sentences with **adjective** + **infinitive**, we usually **stress** the **adjective** and the **verb in the infinitive**.
>
> EXAMPLES: It's **nice to know**.   She's **easy to understand**.
>
> It's **too expensive to buy**.   He's **smart enough to learn** it.

B | *Listen to the sentences. Put a dot (●) over the words or parts of words that are stressed.*

1. It's easy to use.

2. It's good to know.

3. It's cheap enough to buy.

4. It's light enough to carry.

5. She's available to work.

6. It's too hard to understand.

C | *Listen again and repeat the sentences.*

EXERCISE 9: Survey

Work in small groups. Complete the sentences with infinitives to give your opinion. Compare your opinions. Give reasons or examples.

1. The smart phones are (not) easy . . .

    EXAMPLE: **A:** The smart phones are easy to use.
    B: I don't agree. They're not easy enough for *me* to use yet!
    C: I only use mine to make calls!
    D: Yes, but, it's easy enough to learn the new features.

2. The price is (not) low enough . . .

3. New technology is important . . .

4. People over age 80 are (not) too old . . .

5. Teens are responsible enough . . .

6. English is (not) difficult . . .

7. Radio and TV broadcasters speak (or don't speak) clearly enough . . .

8. Time goes by too quickly . . .

EXERCISE 10: For or Against

A | *Work in small groups. Look at the cartoon. Do you feel the same as the woman? If yes, which features don't you like? Why? Discuss the pros and cons of new technology.*

> EXAMPLE: **A:** I agree with the woman. Phones with a lot of features are too difficult to use. But everyone should have a cell phone for emergencies.
> **B:** I think people get too involved with their phones. They don't spend enough time with other people.
> **C:** I don't agree with the woman . . .

B | *You've just gotten a new smart phone. What will you use it for? What won't you use it for? Discuss your answers with a partner. Give reasons for your answers.*

> EXAMPLE: **A:** I'll use it to send emails with photos, or to watch videos . . .
> **B:** I won't use it to watch videos! The screen isn't big enough.
> **A:** I disagree. I think . . .

Do you have a phone that doesn't do too much?

EXERCISE 11: Problem Solving

A | *Work in small groups. Think of uses for these everyday objects. Use the infinitive of purpose and your imagination! Share your ideas with other groups.*

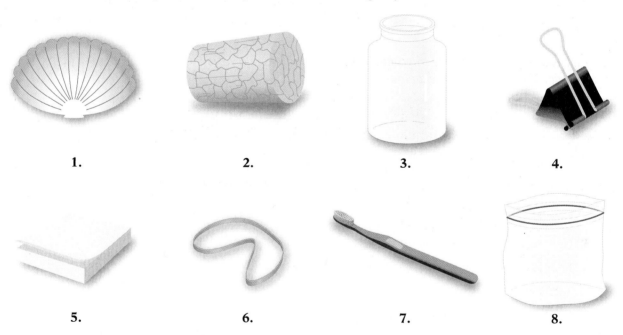

1.   2.   3.   4.

5.   6.   7.   8.

> EXAMPLE: **A:** You can use a shell to hold coins.
> **B:** Right. You can also use it to keep soap in.
> **C:** You can even use it to eat with—like a spoon.

B | *Which item is the most useful? Why?*

EXERCISE 12: Discussion

A | *Read the ad for a smart phone.*

The SMART Phone 1000

Use the Smart Phone 1000 to operate systems in your Smart House. Turn lights on and off, control appliances, and get text messages from your house about what's going on. It's easy and convenient to use. So, get smart, get the Smart Phone 1000.

B | *Work in small groups. Imagine that your smart phone will control everything in your house—not only electronic equipment. What will you use it for?*

> **EXAMPLE:** **A:** I'll use it to turn on the shower.
> **B:** I'll use it to open and close the windows.
> **C:** I think I'll use it to . . .

EXERCISE 13: Writing

A | *Write a post for the online bulletin board in Exercise 6 on page 351. How have you used your phone (or another device) recently?*

> **EXAMPLE:** I was at a family party last week. I used my phone to take a picture of my little nephew and send it to my mother in Argentina. It was great to be able to share the event with her . . .

B | *Check your work. Use the Editing Checklist.*

Editing Checklist

Did you use . . . ?
- ☐ infinitives of purpose
- ☐ **adjective or adverb + infinitive**
- ☐ ***too* or *enough* + adjective or adverb + infinitive**

A | *Circle the correct words to complete the sentences.*

1. Todd uses his smart phone to <u>get / gets</u> directions when he travels.

2. I set the alarm early <u>in order not / not in order</u> to miss my train.

3. In order <u>for taking / to take</u> photographs with your phone, first press this button.

4. It's <u>too / to</u> dark to read in here. Could you turn on a light?

5. It was raining hard. We couldn't see <u>clearly enough / too clearly</u> to drive.

B | *Unscramble the words to complete the conversation. Use the infinitive form of the verbs.*

A: How do you like your new phone? Was it _____?
　　　　　　　　　　　　　　　　　　　1. (enough / easy / figure out)

B: Yes. Luckily, this one isn't _____.
　　　　　　　　　　　　　　　　　2. (hard / too / use / for me)

A: Where's Kim's place? She was talking _____.
　　　　　　　　　　　　　　　　　　3. (fast / too / understand / for me)

B: It's about 20 blocks from here. Is that _____?
　　　　　　　　　　　　　　　　　　4. (too / for us / far / walk)

A: If you're worried, we could take the bus _____.
　　　　　　　　　　　　　　　　　5. (in order / be / late / not)

B: It's only 6:00. I think it's _____.
　　　　　　　　　　　　　　6. (for us / enough / early / walk)

A: Let's cross at the light. The traffic is _____ safely here.
　　　　　　　　　　　　　　　7. (heavy / cross / too / for us)

B: I think we're lost. Let's use _____.
　　　　　　　　　　　　　　8. (get / directions / my phone)

A: You didn't speak _____. Let me try.
　　　　　　　　　9. (clearly / for it / enough / work)

B: We're pretty far away. Let's take _____.
　　　　　　　　　　　　　　10. (save / a taxi / time)

C | *Find and correct five mistakes.*

　　Is 16 too young for drive? It's really hard to saying. Some kids are mature enough to drive at 16, but some aren't. I think most 16-year-olds are still too immature drive with friends in the car, though. It's for them easy to forget to pay attention with a lot of kids in the car. In order preventing accidents, some families have a "no friends" rule for the first year. I think that's a reasonable idea.

Gerunds and Infinitives
PROCRASTINATION

Before You Read

Look at the cartoon and the title of the article. Discuss the questions.

1. What is procrastination?
2. What types of things do you put off doing?
3. Why do people procrastinate?

Read

Read the excerpt from a magazine article about procrastinating.

ST⊙P PR⊙CRASTINATING—N⊙W!

It's a beautiful day. Eva doesn't **feel like spending** it at the library. She goes to the park instead. She **keeps telling** herself she'll work better the next day.

Todd **planned to make** an appointment with the dentist, but he **decided to wait** another week, or maybe two.

Procrastinating—**putting off** until tomorrow things you **need to do** today—is a universal problem. College students are famous **for procrastinating**, but we all do it sometimes. Why do people put off important tasks? Read what the experts say.

UNPLEASANT TASKS • It's not always fun **to do** a lot of the things on our "To Do" lists. Most people **prefer to do** enjoyable things.

POOR TIME MANAGEMENT[1] • **Having** too little time for a task is discouraging. **It's** hard **to get** started on a project when you feel that you can't finish it.

FEAR • An important test can make you feel so anxious that you **put off studying**.

PERFECTIONISM • The belief that you must do a perfect job can prevent you **from starting** or **finishing** a task.

As you can see, people often procrastinate because they **want to avoid** bad feelings. But procrastinators **end up feeling** even worse because of their procrastination. The only solution: **Stop procrastinating**. Now!

Did you **finish writing** your paper on procrastination?

No. I'll do it tomorrow.

---
[1] *time management:* the skills for using your time well when you are trying to reach a goal

After You Read

A | **Vocabulary:** *Complete the sentences with the words from the box.*

anxious	discouraging	project	put off	task	universal

1. Have you finished your class _____ yet?

2. The problem is _____. People all over the world experience it.

3. I get very _____ before a test.

4. Don't _____ writing your essay. Do it today!

5. Shopping for dinner is my least favorite _____.

6. It's _____, but I won't give up hope!

B | **Comprehension:** *Check (✓) the reasons the article gives for procrastination.*

☐ **1.** being lazy

☐ **2.** not enjoying the task

☐ **3.** not understanding something

☐ **4.** feeling anxious about the task

☐ **5.** not having enough time

☐ **6.** not getting enough sleep

☐ **7.** feeling depressed

☐ **8.** thinking your work has to be perfect

STEP 2 GRAMMAR PRESENTATION

GERUNDS AND INFINITIVES

Gerunds	Infinitives
Eva **enjoys going** to the park.	Eva **wants to go** to the park.
She **prefers taking** long breaks.	She **prefers to take** long breaks.
She **stopped studying**.	She **stopped to study**.
Starting a project is hard.	It's hard **to start** a project.
She's worried **about finishing** her paper.	

GRAMMAR NOTES

1	Some **verbs**, such as the ones below, are **followed by a gerund** (base form + *-ing*). avoid · deny · keep consider · enjoy · postpone delay · finish · quit	• Eva *avoids* **doing** her work. • She *doesn't enjoy* **studying**. • She *keeps* **making** excuses.
2	Some **verbs**, such as the ones below, are **followed by an infinitive** (*to* + base form). agree · expect* · plan arrange · fail · promise* choose* · need* · want* decide · offer · would like* *These verbs can also be **followed by**: **object** + **infinitive** **USAGE NOTE:** We usually <u>do NOT repeat</u> *to* when there is more than one infinitive.	• Todd *arranged* **to leave** work early. • He *decided* **not to keep** his appointment. • He *plans* **to make** another one next week. • We **expect to start** the project soon. • We **expect** *them* **to start** the project soon. • He *plans* **to watch** TV, **read** the paper, and **call** his friends. Nᴏᴛ: He plans to watch TV, ~~to~~ read the paper, and ~~to~~ call his friends.
3	Some **verbs**, such as the ones below, can be **followed by a gerund or an infinitive**. They have the <u>same meaning</u>. begin · hate · prefer can't stand · like · start continue · love	• Jeff *hates* **studying**. ᴏʀ • Jeff *hates* **to study**.
4	**BE CAREFUL!** Some **verbs**, such as the ones below, can be **followed by a gerund or an infinitive**, but they have a very <u>different meaning</u>. stop · remember · forget	• Eva *stopped* **taking** breaks. *(She doesn't take breaks anymore.)* • Eva *stopped* **to take** a break. *(She stopped an activity in order to take a break.)* • Todd *remembered* **reading** the story. *(First he read the story. Then he remembered that he did it.)* • Todd *remembered* **to read** the story. *(First he remembered. Then he read the story. He didn't forget.)* • Jeff *forgot* **meeting** Dana. *(Jeff met Dana, but afterwards he didn't remember the event.)* • Jeff *forgot* **to meet** Dana. *(Jeff had plans to meet Dana, but he didn't meet her because he forgot about the plans.)*

(continued on next page)

5 A **gerund** is the only verb form that can **follow a preposition or a phrasal verb.**

PREPOSITION
- He's worried *about* **writing** it.

PREPOSITION
- He's looking forward *to* **finishing** it.

PREPOSITION
- Jeff doesn't feel *like* **working** on his paper.

PHRASAL VERB
- He won't *put off* **starting** it anymore.

6 To make **general statements**, you can use:

- **gerund as subject**

  OR

- *it* + **infinitive**

They have <u>the same</u> meaning.

- **Writing** a paper is hard.

  OR

- *It*'s hard **to write** a paper.

REFERENCE NOTES

For a more complete list of **verbs followed by a gerund**, see Appendix 13 on page A-7.

For a more complete list of **verbs followed by an infinitive**, see Appendix 14 on page A-7.

For a more complete list of **verbs followed by a gerund or an infinitive**, see Appendix 15 on page A-7.

For more on **gerunds after prepositions**, see Unit 23 on page 324, and Appendices 17 and 18 on pages A-7 and A-8.

For a list of **transitive phrasal verbs**, see Appendix 4 on page A-3.

STEP 3 FOCUSED PRACTICE

EXERCISE 1: Discover the Grammar

A | *Read the paragraph. Circle the gerunds. Underline the infinitives.*

Like many students, Eva is a procrastinator. She keeps (putting off) her schoolwork. When she studies, she often stops <u>to go</u> for a walk in the park. She wants to improve her study habits, but she isn't sure how. Eva decided to make a list every day of tasks she needs to do. She always remembers to make her list, but she often forgets to read it. It's very discouraging, and Eva is worried about getting bad grades. Last night Eva remembered reading an article in the school newspaper about a support group for procrastinators. She thinks being in a group is a good idea. She likes sharing ideas with other students. Maybe it will help.

B | *Now read the statements. Check (✓)* **True** *or* **False**. *Correct the false statements.*

	True	False

puts off doing
1. Eva ~~never does~~ her school work. ☐ ☑

2. She quit going for walks in the park. ☐ ☐

3. She'd like to be a better student. ☐ ☐

4. Eva makes a list every day. ☐ ☐

5. She always reads her list. ☐ ☐

6. She read about a support group. ☐ ☐

7. She thinks it's good to be in a group. ☐ ☐

8. She likes to share ideas with others. ☐ ☐

EXERCISE 2: Gerund or Infinitive

(Grammar Notes 1–5)

Read the quiz. Circle the correct form of the verbs. In some cases, both forms are correct.

Are You a Procrastinator?

☐ When I don't feel like to do / (doing) something, I often put off to start / starting it.
    1.   **2.**

☐ I sometimes start to study / studying the night before a test.
    3.

☐ I sometimes start a job but then postpone to finish / finishing it.
    4.

☐ I often delay to make / making difficult decisions.
    5.

☐ I find excuses for not to do / doing things I dislike.
    6.

☐ When a task seems too difficult, I often avoid to work / working on it.
    7.

☐ I prefer to do / doing easy tasks first.
    8.

☐ I often promise myself to work / working on a project but then fail to do / doing it.
    9.   **10.**

☐ I worry about to make / making mistakes or about not to be / being perfect.
    11.   **12.**

☐ I often choose to do / doing other tasks instead of the most important one.
    13.

☐ I want to improve / improving, but I keep to put / putting it off.
    14.   **15.**

EXERCISE 3: Gerund or Infinitive

(Grammar Notes 1–5)

Complete the tips from a website. Use the correct form of the verbs in parentheses.

Some Tips for _____Stopping_____ Procrastination
1. (stop)

● If you have a large project to work on, break it into small tasks. Finish

_____ one small task before _____ the next.
2. (do) **3. (start)**

● Choose _____ the hardest task first. You'll get it out of the way, and
4. (do)

you'll feel better about yourself.

● Promise yourself _____ at least 15 minutes on a task even if you don't
5. (spend)

really feel like _____ it. You'll be surprised. You can get a lot done in
6. (do)

15 minutes—and you'll often keep _____ even longer.
7. (work)

● Stop _____ short breaks—but for no longer than 10 minutes at a time.
8. (take)

● Arrange _____ yourself a reward when you succeed in _____
9. (give) **10. (finish)**

a task. Do something you enjoy _____.
11. (do)

● Consider _____ a support group for procrastinators.
12. (join)

EXERCISE 4: General Statements: Gerund and Infinitive

(Grammar Note 6)

Eva and Todd are talking. They agree on everything. Read one person's opinion and write the other's. If the first person uses the gerund, use the infinitive. If the first person uses the infinitive, use the gerund.

1. **Eva:** It's hard to start a new project.

   Todd: I agree. *Starting a new project is hard.* _____

2. **Todd:** Taking short breaks is helpful.

   Eva: You're right. *It's helpful to take short breaks.* _____

3. **Eva:** It's difficult to work on a long project.

   Todd: That's true. _____

4. **Todd:** Completing a job on time feels great.

   Eva: You're right. _____

5. **Todd:** Rewarding yourself for finishing a project is a good idea.

   Eva: I agree. _____

6. **Eva:** Being in a support group is very helpful.

   Todd: Yes. _____

7. **Eva:** It's good to meet people with the same problem.

   Todd: I feel the same way. _____

EXERCISE 5: Gerund or Infinitive   *(Grammar Notes 1–4)*

Read the conversations that took place at a procrastinators' support group meeting.
Complete the summary statements. Use the gerund or the infinitive.

1.   **Jeff:** Hi, Todd. Did you bring the soda?

   Todd: Yes. Here it is.

   SUMMARY: Todd remembered *to bring the soda* _____.

2.   **Lee:** Eva, do you remember Todd?

   Eva: Oh, yes. We met last year.

   SUMMARY: Eva remembers _____.

3.   **Eva:** Todd, will Miriam be here tonight? I haven't seen her in ages!

   Todd: Yes, she's coming later.

   SUMMARY: Todd expects Miriam _____.

4.   **Jeff:** You take too many breaks.

   Todd: No, I don't!

   SUMMARY: Todd denied _____.

5.   **Eva:** What do you do in your free time, Kay?

   Kay: I listen to music a lot.

   SUMMARY: Kay likes _____.

6.   **Uta:** I'm tired. Let's go home.

   Kay: OK. Just five more minutes.

   SUMMARY: Uta wants _____.

(continued on next page)

7.   UTA: Eva, can we give you a ride home?

   EVA: Thanks, but I think I'll stay a little longer.

SUMMARY: Uta offered _____.

   Eva decided _____.

8.   PAT: Good night. Please drive carefully.

   UTA: Don't worry. I will.

SUMMARY: Uta promised Pat _____.

EXERCISE 6: Editing

Read Eva's blog entry. There are eight mistakes in the use of the gerund and infinitive. The first mistake is already corrected. Find and correct seven more.

---

000   Eva's Blog

The Test of Time

going

For months I was thinking about ~~to go~~ to a support group for procrastinators, but

I kept putting it off! Last night I finally decided going, and I'm glad I did. I'm not alone!

There were a lot of people there with the same problem as me. I expected them being

boring, but they were really quite interesting—and helpful. I even knew some of the

other students there. I remembered to meet a few of them at a school party last year.

I really enjoyed to talk to Todd, and before I left I promised coming again.

   I have a math test tomorrow, so I really should stop to write now and start studying.

See, I've already learned something from to be in this group! I have to stop making

excuses and start my work! NOW!

EXERCISE 7: Listening

A | *The school newspaper is interviewing Eva about her study habits. Read the statements. Then listen to the interview. Listen again and check (✓)* **True** *or* **False.** *Correct the false statements.*

	True	False
1. Eva ~~is trying to find a solution to the problem on her own.~~ *has joined a support group*	☐	☑
2. She has had a problem with procrastination.	☐	☐
3. Eva says the problem was discouraging.	☐	☐
4. She feels very anxious before tests.	☐	☐
5. The interviewer says Eva has good time management skills.	☐	☐
6. Eva gets good grades.	☐	☐

B | *Read the list of activities. Then listen again to the interview and check (✓) the things Eva does and doesn't do now when she is studying for a test.*

	Things Eva Does	Things Eva Doesn't Do
1. clean her work area	☑	☐
2. start the night before the test	☐	☐
3. study the hardest thing first	☐	☐
4. make a "To Do" list	☐	☐
5. take long breaks	☐	☐
6. do relaxation exercises	☐	☐
7. reward herself for finishing	☐	☐

EXERCISE 8: Pronunciation

🎧 **A |** *Read and listen to the Pronunciation Note.*

Pronunciation Note

In **conversation**:

We usually pronounce the preposition **to** and the **to** in the infinitive /tə/.

EXAMPLES: She looks forward **to** taking a break.   We plan **to** meet after class today.
   We're used **to** studying late.   I'd like you **to** help me with this paper.

We pronounce the prepositions **for** /fɚ/ and **on** /ən/.

EXAMPLES: I'm sorry **for** not calling today.   She plans **on** going to college.
   She has a good excuse **for** being late.   Can we count **on** seeing you next week?

🎧 **B |** *Listen to the short conversations. Notice the pronunciation of* **to,** **for,** *and* **on.**

1. **A:** Would you like **to** walk in the park today?
   B: I can't. I need **to** study.

2. **A:** You need **to** take a break.
   B: I plan **on** going **to** the movie at school tonight.
   A: Good. I look forward **to** seeing you there.

3. **A:** Thanks **for** lending me that book.
   B: It helped me. It's hard **to** change, but it's possible.

4. **A:** I'm sorry **for** being late today.
   B: It's OK, but I insist **on** starting class at 9:00.

🎧 **C |** *Listen again. Then practice the conversations with a partner.*

EXERCISE 9: Brainstorming

A | *Taking short breaks can help you work more effectively. Work in small groups. Brainstorm ideas for 10-minute work breaks.*

EXAMPLE: **A:** I enjoy . . .
   B: It's relaxing . . .
   C: You could consider . . .
   D: I recommend . . .

B | *Share your ideas with the rest of your classmates.*

EXERCISE 10: Information Gap: At the Support Group

Work in pairs (A and B). **Student A,** *follow the instructions on this page.* **Student B,** *turn to page 370 and follow the instructions there.*

1. Look at the picture below. Ask your partner questions to complete what people said at the support group meeting.

   EXAMPLE: **A:** What does Eva remember doing?
   B: She remembers meeting Todd.

2. Answer your partner's questions.

   EXAMPLE: **B:** What does Todd hope to do?
   A: He hopes to see Eva again.

When you are done, compare your pictures. Are they the same?

EXERCISE 11: Quotable Quotes

Read the quotes about procrastination. Discuss them with a partner. What do they mean? Do you agree with them?

1. Never put off till tomorrow what you can do today.
   —*Lord Chesterfield (British politician, 1694–1773)*

   EXAMPLE: **A:** Lord Chesterfield advises doing things right away.
   B: I think that's not always possible because . . .

2. Procrastination is the art of keeping up with yesterday.
   —*Don Marquis (U.S. author, 1878–1937)*

3. Procrastination is the thief of time.
   —*Edward Young (British poet, 1683–1765)*

4. When there is a hill to climb, don't think that waiting will make it smaller.
   —*Anonymous[1]*

5. Putting off an easy thing makes it hard, and putting off a hard one makes it impossible.
   —*George H. Lorimer (U.S. magazine editor, 1868–1937)*

6. Procrastination is like a credit card: It's a lot of fun until you get the bill.
   —*Christopher Parker (British actor, 1983–)*

---

[1] ***anonymous:*** The writer's name is not known

EXERCISE 12: Problem Solving

A | *Look at the picture. Like procrastination, clutter is a universal problem. What are some solutions to the problem? Work in groups. Brainstorm ways of stopping clutter. You can use the verbs from the box.*

avoid   decide   don't forget   keep   need   plan   remember   start   stop

EXAMPLE: **A:** You need to put away your things every night.
B: Plan on . . .
C: Remember to . . .

B | *Compare your ideas with the rest of the class.*

EXERCISE 13: Writing

A | *Writing a goals worksheet is a good way to help prevent procrastination. First, complete the worksheet. List three goals for this month in order of importance (1 = the most important goal).*

This Month's Goals	
Goal 1:	Complete by:
Goal 2:	Complete by:
Goal 3:	Complete by:

B | *Write three paragraphs (one for each goal) on how you plan to accomplish your goals.*

> EXAMPLE: I want to finish writing my English paper by March 28. First, I plan to . . .

C | *Check your work. Use the Editing Checklist.*

Editing Checklist

Did you use . . . ?
- ☐ correct **verbs + gerunds**
- ☐ correct **verbs + infinitives**
- ☐ **prepositions + gerunds**
- ☐ gerunds as subjects
- ☐ *it* + **infinitive**

1. Look at the picture below. Answer your partner's questions.

    EXAMPLE: **A:** What does Eva remember doing?
                       B: She remembers meeting Todd.

2. Ask your partner questions to complete what people said at the support group meeting.

    EXAMPLE: **B:** What does Todd hope to do?
                       A: He hopes to see Eva again.

When you are done, compare your pictures. Are they the same?

Check your answers on page UR-7.
Do you need to review anything?

A | Circle the correct words to complete the sentences.

1. Don't put off <u>to start / starting</u> your project.

2. I expect you <u>to finish / finishing</u> on time.

3. I keep <u>to try / trying</u> to improve my study habits.

4. Did you decide <u>to join / joining</u> our study group?

5. I look forward to <u>see / seeing</u> you there.

6. Don't forget <u>to call /calling</u> me the night before.

7. <u>To study / Studying</u> together can help.

B | Complete the conversation with the correct form of the verbs in parentheses.

A: Have you finished _____ your homework?
                     1. (do)

B: No, not yet. I decided _____ a break.
                        2. (take)

A: Already? You just started _____.
                        3. (work)

B: I know. But I'm tired of _____ at my desk.
                        4. (sit)

A: Well, _____ a short break is OK, I guess.
              5. (take)

B: Don't worry. I promise _____ it done before dinner.
                    6. (get)

A: OK. I know you hate _____, but it's important.
                   7. (study)

B: I agree.

C | Find and correct six mistakes.

It's difficult to study in a foreign country, so students need preparing for the experience. Most people look forward to living abroad, but they worry about don't feel at home. They're afraid of not understanding the culture, and they don't want making mistakes. It's impossible to avoid to have some problems at the beginning. No one escapes from feeling some culture shock, and it's important realizing this fact. But soon most people stop to feel uncomfortable and start to feel more at home in the new culture.

Part VII

From Grammar to Writing

COMBINING SENTENCES WITH *AND, BUT, SO, OR*

You can combine two sentences with **and**, **but**, **so**, and **or**. The new longer sentence is made up of **two main clauses**.

EXAMPLE: Commuting to school is hard. I prefer to live in the dorm. ➔

MAIN CLAUSE   MAIN CLAUSE
Commuting to school is hard, **so** I prefer to live in the dorm.

The clause starting with **and**, **but**, **so**, or **or** always comes second. Notice that a **comma** comes after the first clause.

1 | *Circle the correct words to complete the email.*

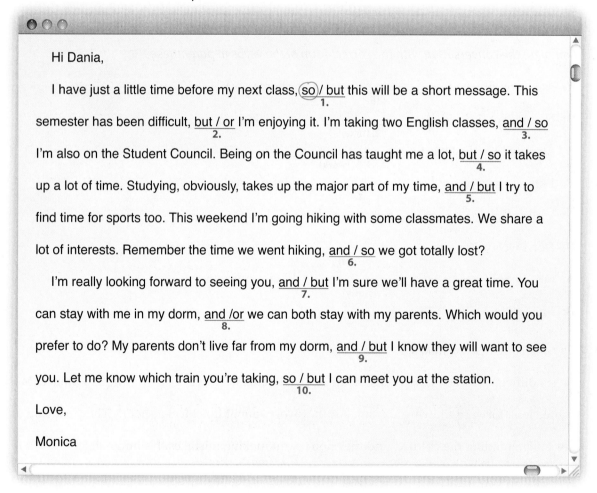

Hi Dania,

I have just a little time before my next class, (so)/ but this will be a short message. This
1.
semester has been difficult, but / or I'm enjoying it. I'm taking two English classes, and / so
2.   3.
I'm also on the Student Council. Being on the Council has taught me a lot, but / so it takes
4.
up a lot of time. Studying, obviously, takes up the major part of my time, and / but I try to
5.
find time for sports too. This weekend I'm going hiking with some classmates. We share a

lot of interests. Remember the time we went hiking, and / so we got totally lost?
6.
    I'm really looking forward to seeing you, and / but I'm sure we'll have a great time. You
7.
can stay with me in my dorm, and /or we can both stay with my parents. Which would you
8.
prefer to do? My parents don't live far from my dorm, and / but I know they will want to see
9.
you. Let me know which train you're taking, so / but I can meet you at the station.
10.
Love,

Monica

There are many ways to close a personal email. Here are a few popular choices.

- *Love* or *Love you*, for family and close friends
- *Bye for now* or *Take care*, for friends
- *Best*, *Best wishes*, or *Best regards*, for colleagues and acquaintances

2 | *Complete the rules for using* **and, but, so,** *and* **or.** *Look at the email in Exercise 1 for help.*

1. Use _____*and*_____ when the second sentence adds information.

2. Use _____ when the second sentence gives a choice.

3. Use _____when the second sentence gives a contrasting idea.

4. Use _____ when the information in the second sentence is a result of the

   information in the first sentence.

3 | *Complete the sentences with your own ideas.*

1. It has started to rain, but _____.

2. I don't really want to study tonight, so _____.

3. This weekend my friends and I will go to a movie, or _____.

4. I'm reading a lot of books in English, and _____.

5. After class I'm going shopping, so _____.

6. I used to go dancing a lot, but _____.

7. I'm looking forward to graduating, and _____.

8. Ed is too young to vote, but _____.

9. We can take a train, or _____.

10. Dan is tired of staying home evenings, so _____.

4 | *Before you write . . .*

Talk to a partner about your life these days. Answer some of these questions.
- What are you doing these days?
- What do you enjoy doing?
- What can't you stand?
- What do you plan to do next semester?
- What are you looking forward to?

5 | *Write an email to a friend describing your present life. Use the email in Exercise 1 as a model. Include some of your ideas from Exercise 4. Use* **and, but, so,** *and* **or.**

6 | *Exchange emails with a new partner. Answer your partner's email.*

VIII

PRONOUNS AND PHRASAL VERBS

UNIT	GRAMMAR FOCUS	THEME
27	Reflexive and Reciprocal Pronouns	Self-Talk
28	Phrasal Verbs	Animal Intelligence

Reflexive and Reciprocal Pronouns
SELF-TALK

STEP 1 GRAMMAR IN CONTEXT

Before You Read

What do you think self-talk *is? Look at the examples of self-talk in the photos. Discuss the questions.*

1. Which examples are positive?
2. Which examples are negative?
3. What are some other examples of positive and negative self-talk?

Read

Read the article from a psychology magazine.

S elf-talk is the way we explain a problem to **ourselves**. It can impact how we feel and how we act. Take the case of Tom and Sara. They both got laid off[1] from their jobs at the same company, but their reactions were totally different. Sara maintained her normal life. She frequently talked on the phone with her friends, continued her usual activities, and kept **herself** fit.

Tom, on the other hand, spent all of his time at home **by himself**, didn't allow **himself** to have a good time, and gained 10 pounds.

Why were their reactions so very different from **one another**? They both lost their jobs, so the situation **itself** can't explain Tom's problems. The main difference was the way Tom and Sara explained the problem to **themselves**.

[1] *get laid off:* to lose your job, usually because your employer doesn't have enough money to keep you or because there isn't enough work

SELF-TALK

Sara told **herself** that the problem was temporary and that she herself could change it. Tom saw **himself** as completely helpless and likely to be unemployed forever.

Tom and Sara both got their jobs back. Their reactions when they talked to **each other** were, again, very different. For his part, Tom grumbled, "Oh, I guess they were really desperate." Sara, on the other hand, smiled and said, "Well! They finally realized that they need me!"

After You Read

A | Vocabulary: *Complete the sentences with the words from the box.*

fault	finally	impact	maintain	reaction	realize

1. I waited for more than an hour before I _____ got the call.

2. What was your _____ when you heard the news? Were you surprised?

3. At first, I didn't _____ that the problem was serious.

4. Everyone needs exercise and sleep in order to _____ good health.

5. It wasn't your _____. You didn't do anything wrong.

6. The company had to lay off 50 employees, but that didn't _____ John's job.

   He still works there.

B | Comprehension: *Check (✓) the correct answers.*

Who . . . ?	Tom	Sara	Tom and Sara
1. stayed in good physical condition	☐	☐	☐
2. spent a lot of time alone	☐	☐	☐
3. thought the problem was temporary	☐	☐	☐
4. felt helpless	☐	☐	☐
5. had a conversation back at work	☐	☐	☐

REFLEXIVE AND RECIPROCAL PRONOUNS

Reflexive Prounouns				
Subject Pronoun		**Reflexive Pronoun**		
I		**myself**		
You		**yourself**		
He		**himself**		
She	looked at	**herself**	in the mirror.	
It		**itself**		
We		**ourselves**		
You		**yourselves**		
They		**themselves**		

Reciprocal Pronouns		
Subject Pronoun		**Reciprocal Pronoun**
We You They	looked at	**each other**. **one another**.

GRAMMAR NOTES

1 Use a **reflexive pronoun** when the subject and object refer to the <u>same people or things</u>.

SUBJECT = OBJECT
- **Sara** looked at **herself** in the mirror.
  (*Sara looked at her own face.*)

SUBJECT = OBJECT
- **They** felt proud of **themselves**.
  (*They were proud of their own actions.*)

SUBJECT = OBJECT
- My **office light** turns **itself** off.
  (*It turns off automatically.*)

2 In **imperative sentences** with reflexive pronouns, use:

- *yourself* when the subject is <u>singular</u>

- *yourselves* when the subject is <u>plural</u>

REMEMBER: In imperative sentences, the subject is *you*, and *you* can be either singular or plural.

- "Don't push **yourself** so hard, **Tom**," Sara said. (*talking to one friend*)

- "Don't push **yourselves** so hard, **guys**," Sara said. (*talking to several friends*)

3 Use a reflexive pronoun to **emphasize a noun**. The reflexive pronoun usually <u>follows the noun</u> directly.

- Tom was upset when he lost his job. The **job itself** wasn't important to him, but he needed the money.

- **Sara herself** didn't get depressed, but her co-workers felt terrible.

4	*By* + **a reflexive pronoun** means *alone* or *without any help*.	• Sara lives **by herself**. *(Sara lives alone.)* • We finished the job **by ourselves**. *(No one helped us.)*
	Be + **a reflexive pronoun** means *act in the usual way*.	• Just **be yourself** at your interview.

5	Use a **reciprocal pronoun** when the subject and object of a sentence refer to the <u>same people</u>, and these people have a <u>two-way</u> relationship.	
	• Use *each other* for <u>two</u> people.	SUBJECT = OBJECT • **Tom and Sara** met **each other** at work. *(Tom met Sara, and Sara met Tom.)*
	• Use *one another* for <u>more than two</u> people.	SUBJECT = OBJECT • **We all** told **one another** about our jobs. *(Each person exchanged news with every other person.)*
	USAGE NOTE: Many people use *each other* and *one another* in the **same way**.	• **Sara and Tom** talked to **each other**. OR • **Sara and Tom** talked to **one another**.
	BE CAREFUL! Reciprocal pronouns and plural reflexive pronouns have **different meanings**.	• Fred and Jane blamed **each other**. *(Fred blamed Jane, and Jane blamed Fred.)* • Fred and Jane blamed **themselves**. *(Fred blamed himself, and Jane blamed herself.)*
	Reciprocal pronouns have **possessive forms**: *each other's*, *one another's*	• Tom and Sara took **each other's** number. *(Tom took Sara's number, and Sara took Tom's.)*

REFERENCE NOTE

For a list of **verbs and expressions that often take reflexive pronouns**, see Appendix 3 on page A-2.

EXERCISE 1: Discover the Grammar

Read the rest of the article about self-talk. Underline the reflexive pronouns once and the reciprocal pronouns twice. Draw an arrow to the words that the pronouns refer to.

SELF-TALK *(continued)*

Positive self-talk can affect our thoughts, feelings, and actions. It can even make the difference between winning and losing. Top athletes not only compete against one another, they also compete against themselves when they try to improve their performances. Many athletes use self-talk to maintain their self-confidence and help themselves reach new goals. If you've asked yourself how Korean Olympic gold winner Kim Yu-Na can do those perfect jumps under so much stress, now you know it's probably because she's telling herself, "I can, I will, I am."

Kim Yu-Na

One sports psychologist believes that Olympic athletes are not very different from one another —they are all the best in their sports. When two top athletes compete against each other, the winner is the one with the most powerful positive "mental movies."

According to psychologists, ordinary people themselves can use these techniques too. We can create "mental movies" to help ourselves succeed in difficult situations.

EXERCISE 2: Reflexive or Reciprocal Pronouns

(Grammar Notes 1–5)

Tom and Sara's company had an office party. Choose the correct reflexive or reciprocal pronouns to complete the conversations.

1. **A:** Listen, guys! The food and drinks are over here. Don't be shy. Please come and help

   _____ *yourselves* _____.
   (yourselves / themselves)

   B: Thanks. We will.

2. **A:** Isn't that the new head of the accounting department over there?

   B: I think so. Let's go over and introduce _____.
   (himself / ourselves)

3. **A:** I'm really nervous about my date with Nicole after the party. I actually cut

   _____ twice while shaving, and then I lost my car keys.
   (herself / myself)

   B: Come on. This is a party. Just relax and be _____.
   (yourself / yourselves)

   You'll do just fine.

4. A: What are you giving your boss for the holidays this year?

    B: We always give _____ the same holiday gifts. Every
                                         (ourselves / each other)

        year I give him a book, and he gives me a box of candy. I realize that this doesn't sound

        very exciting, but I _____ am quite happy with the
                                 (myself / ourselves)

        arrangement. It makes things easy that way.

5. A: What's your department's reaction to the new computer program?

    B: I'm not sure. We're still teaching _____ how to use it.
                                      (ourselves / themselves)

6. A: Jessica looks upset. Didn't she get a promotion?

    B: No, and she keeps blaming _____. She thinks it's all her
                                (herself / himself)

        fault. Of course it isn't.

7. A: The Aguayos are finally going to Japan on vacation this year.

    B: That's wonderful. They really need one. Are they going by _____
                                                   (each other / themselves)

        or with a tour group?

8. A: This was a great party.

    B: Yeah. We really enjoyed _____.
                              (ourselves / myself)

EXERCISE 3: Reflexive or Reciprocal Pronouns
(Grammar Notes 1–5)

Read the interview with George Prudeau, a high school French teacher. Complete the interview. Use the correct reflexive or reciprocal pronouns.

INTERVIEWER: How did you become a teacher?

GEORGE: When I got laid off from my 9:00 to 5:00 job, I told _____*myself*_____, "Here's my
                                                  1.

        chance to finally do what I really want." One of the great things about teaching is the

        freedom I have. I run the class by _____—just the way I want to. I also
                                          2.

        like the way my students and I learn from _____. My teaching impacts
                                         3.

        my students' lives, but they teach me a lot too.

INTERVIEWER: What about maintaining discipline? Is that a problem?

GEORGE: We have just a few rules. I tell my students, "Keep _____ busy. Discuss
                                                 4.

        the lessons, but don't interfere with _____'s work."
                                          5.

(continued on next page)

INTERVIEWER: What do you like to teach best?

GEORGE: I love French, but the subject _____ really isn't all that important. A
                                                                    6.
good teacher helps students learn by _____ and encourages them not to
                                                                    7.
give up when they have problems. For instance, John, one of my students, just taught

_____ how to bake French bread. The first few loaves were failures. His
            8.
first reaction was to give up, but I encouraged him to use positive self-talk, and in the

end he succeeded.

INTERVIEWER: What teaching materials do you use?

GEORGE: Very simple ones. I pride _____ on the fact that I can teach anywhere,
                                                    9.
even on a street corner.

INTERVIEWER: What do you like least about your job?

GEORGE: The salary. I teach French culture, but I can't afford to travel to France. I have to

satisfy _____ with trips to French restaurants!
            10.

EXERCISE 4: Verbs with Reflexive or Reciprocal Pronouns   *(Grammar Notes 1, 4–5)*

*Sara and Tom went to an office party. Look at each picture and write a sentence describing
what happened. Use the correct form of a verb from the box with a reflexive or reciprocal
pronoun. You will use one verb more than once.*

buy	cut	drive	greet	introduce	smile at	talk to

1. _Sara bought herself a new dress._   2. _____

3. _____

4. _____

5. _____

6. _____

7. _____

8. _____

EXERCISE 5: Editing

Read the woman's diary. There are seven mistakes in the use of reflexive and reciprocal pronouns. The first mistake is already corrected. Find and correct six more.

>   *myself*
>
> Jan's birthday was Wednesday, and I forgot to call him. I reminded ~~me~~ all day, and then
>
> I forgot anyway! I felt terrible. My sister Anna said, "Don't be so hard on yourselves."
>
> But I myself didn't believe her. She prides herself on remembering everything. Then I
>
> finally remembered the article on self-talk. It said that people can change the way they
>
> explain problems to theirselves. Well, I listened to the way I talked to me, and I realized
>
> it sounded really insulting — like the way our high school math teacher used to talk to
>
> us. I thought, Jan and I are good friends, and we treat each other's well. One mistake
>
> shouldn't impact our friendship that much. In fact, he forgave myself for my mistake
>
> right away. And I forgave him for forgetting our dinner date two weeks ago. Friends
>
> can forgive themselves, so I guess I can forgive myself.

EXERCISE 6: Listening

A | *Employees are at an office party. Read the sentences. Then listen to the conversations. Then listen again and circle the pronouns that you hear.*

1. They should be really proud of <u>themselves</u> / (<u>each other</u>).

2. You know Ed blames <u>him / himself</u> for everything.

3. Are you going by <u>yourself / yourselves</u> or with a tour?

4. The doctor <u>herself / himself</u> called me this morning.

5. Megan keeps asking <u>herself / her</u> if she can do the job.

6. In our department, we're still teaching <u>each other / ourselves</u> how to use it.

7. I'm glad you enjoyed <u>yourself / yourselves</u>.

1. The people in Mark's department probably work _____ a lot.

   a. alone   **(b.)** together

2. Ed blames _____ for everything.

   a. himself   **b.** Jeff

3. The woman plans to travel _____.

   a. alone   **b.** with other people

4. The doctor called _____.

   a. the woman   **b.** the man

5. Megan isn't sure if _____ can do the job.

   a. Jennifer   **b.** she herself

6. The man _____ new computer system.

   a. wants to buy a   **b.** is still learning to use the

7. The woman went to the party _____.

   a. by herself   **b.** with other people

EXERCISE 7: Pronunciation

A | *Read and listen to the Pronunciation Note.*

> **Pronunciation Note**
>
> We usually **stress -self** or **-selves** in reflexive pronouns.
>
> **EXAMPLE:** Did you enjoy **yourselves** at the party?
>
> We **stress other** or **another** in reciprocal pronouns.
>
> **EXAMPLE:** Yes. We spoke to **each other** for hours.

B | *Listen to the sentences. Put a dot (●) over the parts of the reflexive and reciprocal pronouns that are stressed.*

1. Sara looked at herself in the mirror.

2. They felt proud of themselves.

3. The job itself wasn't important to him.

4. They met each other at work.

5. We all told one another about our jobs.

6. Tom helped himself to the food.

C | *Listen again and repeat the sentences.*

EXERCISE 8: Questionnaire

A | *Test yourself by completing the questionnaire.*

Are you an optimist or a pessimist?

Optimists see bad situations as temporary or limited. Pessimists see them as permanent. What's *your* reaction when things go wrong? What do you tell yourself? Check (✓) your most likely self-talk for each situation below. Then find out if you're an optimist or a pessimist.

1. Your boss doesn't say good morning to you.
- ☐ **a.** She isn't herself today.
- ☐ **b.** She doesn't like me.

2. Your family forgets your birthday.
- ☐ **a.** Next year we should keep in touch with one another more.
- ☐ **b.** They only think about themselves.

3. You gain 10 pounds.
- ☐ **a.** I promise myself to eat properly from now on.
- ☐ **b.** Diets never work for me. I'll never maintain a healthy weight.

4. Your boyfriend or girlfriend decides to go out with other people.
- ☐ **a.** We didn't spend enough time with each other.
- ☐ **b.** We're wrong for each other.

5. You're feeling tired lately.
- ☐ **a.** I pushed myself too hard this week.
- ☐ **b.** I never take care of myself.

6. Your friend forgets an appointment with you.
- ☐ **a.** He sometimes forgets to read his appointment book.
- ☐ **b.** He never reminds himself about important things.

Score your questionnaire

All the **a** answers are optimistic, and all the **b** answers are pessimistic. Give yourself **0** for every **a** answer and **1** for every **b** answer.

If You Scored	You Are
0–2	very optimistic
3–4	somewhat optimistic
5–6	pessimistic

B | *Discuss your questionnaire with a partner. Which is more useful—optimistic or pessimistic self-talk? Why?*

C | *Now interview five classmates and find out how they answered the questions. Report the results to another group.*

> **EXAMPLE:** For question 1, three people checked "She isn't herself today."
> Two people checked "She doesn't like me."

EXERCISE 9: Game: Who remembers more?

A | *Work with a partner. First look at the picture carefully for 30 seconds. Then shut your books and do the following.*

1. Write down as many things as you can remember about what the people are doing.

2. Then compare your notes. Use reciprocal and reflexive pronouns in your description.

   EXAMPLE: **A:** Two men are waving at each other.
                 B: No, I think two women are waving at each other.

B | *When you are finished, open your books and check your answers. Who remembered the most? What did you leave out?*

EXERCISE 10: Picture Discussion

Look at the picture again. With your partner, imagine the self-talk of some of the people at the party.

  EXAMPLES: The man at the mirror: "I'll never give myself a haircut again."
                   The woman on the couch: "I don't know many people here.
                   Should I introduce myself to that couple?"

EXERCISE 11: Problem Solving

A | *Work in small groups. Discuss two or three of the situations in the list below. How do you make yourself feel better?*

- You're going to take a big test.
- You're stuck in traffic.
- You have a roommate you don't like.
- You're going to compete in a sports event.
- You're having an argument with a friend or relative.
- You forgot something important, and you're very angry at yourself.

  EXAMPLE: **A:** When I'm going to take a big test, I tell myself that I usually get a good grade.
  B: Me too. I tell myself that I've studied enough to do well.
  C: I remind myself that . . .

B | *Report to the class. Make a class list of some of the best self-talk for each situation.*

  EXAMPLES: When they're going to take a big test, Donna and Yuri remind themselves that they usually get very good grades.

  When she's having an argument with a friend or a relative, Jana tells herself that the situation is temporary. Nobody stays angry forever.

  When Javier is upset with his roommate, he always talks to his brother, and they cheer each other up.

EXERCISE 12: Writing

A | *Imagine that you write an Internet advice column called "Help Yourself with Self-Talk." A reader writes that he or she is not doing well at school and is having problems with a boyfriend or a girlfriend. Complete the advice column. You can use some of these phrases:*

- Some people tell themselves . . .
- One person I know tells herself/himself . . .
- Friends can remind each other that . . .
- I never tell myself . . .

Help Yourself with Self-Talk

Dear _____,

    I'm sorry you're having trouble at school. The best advice I can give you is to change your self-talk! What positive things can you say to yourself in this situation? What negative self-talk can you avoid? For example, some people tell themselves . . .

B | *Check your work. Use the Editing Checklist.*

Editing Checklist

Did you use . . . ?

☐ correct reflexive pronouns when the subject and object refer to the same people or things

☐ reciprocal pronouns to show a two-way relationship

☐ *by* + **reflexive pronoun** to mean *alone* or *without any help*

Check your answers on page UR-7.
Do you need to review anything?

A | *Circle the correct pronouns to complete the sentences.*

1. Emily and I see <u>each other / ourselves</u> at the gym every week.

2. My friend Lan teaches an exercise class there. He <u>itself / himself</u> is very fit.

3. The people in his class all know <u>themselves / one another</u>. They've been in his class for years.

4. Emily likes to exercise alone. She works out by <u>herself / oneself</u> every day.

5. I told her about Lan's class. I <u>myself / ourselves</u> wasn't attending his class, but I knew about it.

6. We decided to try it out <u>themselves / ourselves</u>, so we went to Lan's class together.

7. Lan told both of us, "You're pushing <u>yourself / yourselves</u> too hard. Slow down a little."

8. The class <u>itself / himself</u> isn't so different from other classes, but we like how Lan teaches.

B | *Complete the sentences with the correct form of the verbs in parentheses and the correct pronouns.*

1. Karl and Ana are good friends. They _____ every day.
   (talk to)

2. Ina and Eva always _____ with a kiss.
   (greet)

3. Lee, please _____ to some more cake.
   (help)

4. Rita and Tom are reading in the library. They're really _____.
   (enjoy)

5. Tania _____ to the party last night.
   (drive)

C | *Find and correct seven mistakes.*

When I first met Nicole, I told myself, "I'm not going to like working with herself." I was really wrong. Nicole has helped myself out with so many things. When she oneself didn't know something, she always found out for me. That way, both of ourselves learned something. After I learned the job better, we helped each other's out. Now the job themselves isn't that challenging, but I'm really enjoying myself. Everyone here likes each another. That makes it a great place to work. I feel lucky to be here.

STEP 1 GRAMMAR IN CONTEXT

Before You Read

Look at the picture. Discuss the questions.

1. Do you know who the man is?
2. What do you think he is famous for?
3. Why do you think people call him "The Dog Whisperer"?
4. Do people in your country have pets? If so, what kinds?

Read

Read the article about Cesar Millan.

When He Whispers, They Tune In[1]

What do you do when your dog **takes over** the dog park and attacks other dogs? Or when it gets lazy and won't **get up** and take a walk? When pet owners are ready to **give up**, many of them call Cesar Millan, the Dog Whisperer.

Millan is famous for **helping out** celebrities[2] like Oprah when they have problems with their pets. He also works with the problem pets of ordinary people. He usually goes into their homes to **figure out** the problem. Sometimes he can't help the dog at its home, so he brings it to his ranch outside Los Angeles. There, Millan works with animals with more serious problems. His training **turns** their lives **around**.

But what if you don't live in LA? No problem! Just **turn on** the TV. Fans of Millan's show *The Dog Whisperer* watch every week as Millan **straightens out** a "bad" dog and its owner.

When Millan rings the doorbell, he learns about the dog and its family for the first time. By the end of the show, a miracle[3] has happened: the angry or frightened dog now obeys its owner's commands to **get off** the couch, walk quietly, and **sit down**.

Not everybody admires Millan. Some believe that his ideas about dog psychology[4] are too simple. Others say that real change doesn't happen in an hour. These critics haven't stopped Millan's fans, however. They **keep on tuning in** for the weekly miracles.

---

[1] ***When he whispers, they tune in:*** When he speaks very quietly, the dogs listen.
[2] ***celebrity:*** a famous person, usually someone in movies or on TV
[3] ***miracle:*** a very positive, surprising event
[4] ***psychology:*** the study of the mind and how it works

A | **Vocabulary:** *Match the phrasal verbs with their meanings.*

_____ 1. figure out   **a.** to change bad behavior

_____ 2. turn on   **b.** to quit

_____ 3. give up   **c.** to solve

_____ 4. keep on   **d.** to get control

_____ 5. straighten out   **e.** to start (a machine)

_____ 6. take over   **f.** to continue

B | **Comprehension:** *Check (✓) the boxes to complete the sentences. Check **all** the true information from the reading.*

1. Owners get upset when their dogs _____.
- ☐ attack other dogs
- ☐ won't leave the dog park
- ☐ get lazy

2. In his business, Millan helps dogs _____.
- ☐ of celebrities
- ☐ with serious problems
- ☐ only in people's homes

3. Millan helps dogs _____.
- ☐ in their homes
- ☐ on his ranch
- ☐ on his TV program

4. On his show, Millan works with _____.
- ☐ dogs he already knows
- ☐ frightened dogs
- ☐ the dogs' owners

5. People who disagree with Millan think that _____.
- ☐ dog psychology is complicated
- ☐ change takes time
- ☐ Millan makes miracles happen

PHRASAL VERBS: TRANSITIVE AND INTRANSITIVE

Transitive Phrasal Verbs

Subject	Verb	Particle	Object (Noun)
He	figured	out	the problem.
	helped	out	the owners.

Subject	Verb	Object (Noun / Pronoun)	Particle
He	figured	the problem	out.
		it	
	helped	the owners	out.
		them	

Intransitive Phrasal Verbs

Subject	Verb	Particle	
She	gave	up.	
He	sat	down	quickly.
They	get	up	early.

GRAMMAR NOTES

1 **Phrasal verbs** (also called *two-word verbs*) are made up of a **verb** + **particle**.

On, *off*, *up*, *down*, *in*, and *out* are common particles.

Particles and prepositions look the same. However, particles are part of the verb phrase, and they often <u>change the meaning</u> of the verb.

VERB + PARTICLE
• He **turned on** the TV.

VERB + PARTICLE
• Cesar **helps out** pet owners.

VERB + PREPOSITION
• She's **looking up** at the sky.
(She's looking in the direction of the sky.)

VERB + PARTICLE
• She's **looking up** the word.
(She's searching for the word in the dictionary.)

2 Many **phrasal verbs** and **one-word verbs** have <u>similar meanings</u>.

USAGE NOTE: Phrasal verbs are often <u>less formal</u>, and they are <u>more common</u> in everyday speech.

PHRASAL VERB (less formal)	ONE-WORD VERB (more formal)
figure out	solve
give up	quit
hand in	submit
help out	assist
keep on	continue

(continued on next page)

3 Phrasal verbs can be **transitive or intransitive**.

a. Transitive phrasal verbs have objects.

Most transitive phrasal verbs are **separable**. This means that the object can come:

- after the verb + particle

OR

- between the verb and its particle

BE CAREFUL! When the object is a **pronoun**, it must come between the verb and the particle.

b. Intransitive phrasal verbs do NOT have objects.

PHRASAL VERB + OBJECT
- He **turned on** *the TV*.

VERB + PARTICLE + OBJECT
- He **helped out** *the students*.

OR

VERB + OBJECT + PARTICLE
- He **helped** *the students* **out**.

OBJECT
- He **helped** *them* **out**.
  Not: He helped out them.

- Cesar Millan **grew up** in Mexico.
- He never **gives up**.

REFERENCE NOTES

For a list of **transitive phrasal verbs** and their meanings, see Appendix 4 on page A-3.
For a list of **intransitive phrasal verbs** and their meanings, see Appendix 5 on page A-4.

STEP 3 FOCUSED PRACTICE

EXERCISE 1: Discover the Grammar

A | *Read the article. Underline the phrasal verbs. Circle the objects of the transitive phrasal verbs.*

Cesar Millan puts his running shoes on as soon as he gets up in the morning. Then he wakes his dogs up, and they all set out on their daily four-hour walk. The exercise is part of Millan's dog therapy.[1] Most of these dogs were once dangerous, but now they are a "family" that teaches problem dogs how to fit in and get along in a group.

Millan's dream began on the farm in Mexico where he grew up. There, he found out he had a special ability with animals (his family called him "El Perrero"[2]). When Millan was 13, he told his mother, "I'm going to be the best dog trainer in the world." A few years later, Millan went to the United States. He was homeless for a while, but he never gave up his dream. Finally, he found a job as a dog groomer.[3] On the job, Millan showed owners some ways to calm their dogs down. Jada Pinkett (wife of actor Will Smith) hired him and also paid for his English lessons. After that, he was able to set up his own business. Today the Dog Whisperer lives and works on a 40-acre ranch with his pack of around 50 dogs and many other kinds of animals.

[1] *therapy:* the treatment of an illness or mental problem over a fairly long period of time
[2] *"El Perrero":* (*Spanish*) The Dog Boy
[3] *dog groomer:* someone who washes dogs and cuts their hair and nails

B | Match the underlined words with the phrasal verbs.

_f_ **1.** Millan and his dogs <u>start</u> on their walk early in the morning.   **a.** found out

____ **2.** The dogs never fight because they all <u>have a good relationship</u>.   **b.** calm down

____ **3.** Millan <u>became an adult</u> in Mexico.   **c.** grew up

____ **4.** On the farm, he first <u>discovered</u> that he had a special ability.   **d.** set up

____ **5.** He showed owners how to help their dogs <u>become less excited</u>.   **e.** get along

____ **6.** Millan <u>started</u> his business after he learned English.   **f.** set out

EXERCISE 2: Particles

(Grammar Notes 1–2)

Circle the correct particle to complete each phrasal verb. Go to Appendices 4 and 5 on pages A-3 and A-4 for help.

Vicky: Hi. Carla? I'm Vicky Chang, the dog trainer.

Carla: Come <u>back</u> /(in), Vicky! Please call me Carla. And say hello to Mitzi.
        1.

Vicky: She's really excited! I'll greet her when she calms <u>up</u> / <u>down</u>, OK?
                                                2.

Carla: Come <u>on</u> / <u>by</u>, Mitzi! Stop jumping!
        3.

Vicky: Do you mind if I sit <u>into</u> / <u>down</u> here next to Mitzi?
                        4.

Carla: Please go <u>ahead</u> / <u>through</u>. Sorry, she always takes <u>on</u> / <u>over</u> the couch.
               5.   **6.**

Vicky: Thanks. Today, I'd like to find <u>up</u> / <u>out</u> what problems you're having.
                                    7.

Carla: Well, Mitzi jumps on people. Also, sometimes she doesn't get <u>along</u> / <u>away</u> with other dogs,
                                                                           8.

but sometimes she does. I can't figure it <u>up</u> / <u>out</u>.
                                    9.

Vicky: Maybe she's frightened. At the park, pick <u>out</u> / <u>up</u> small dogs for her to play with.
                                            10.

Carla: Good idea. I'll try that <u>out</u> / <u>over</u> the next time we're there. Anything else?
                             11.

Vicky: Exercise always helps behavior. Do you walk her when you get <u>up</u> / <u>by</u> in the morning?
                                              12.

Carla: Every day. But sometimes I'm too tired when I get <u>back</u> / <u>over</u> from work.
                                    13.

Vicky: Don't worry. We'll straighten <u>out</u> / <u>down</u> Mitzi's problems. She's a very smart dog.
                                  14.

Carla: Thanks. We're going to take her to my company picnic tomorrow. I hope it works <u>by</u> / <u>out</u>!
                                                    15.

Vicky: She'll love that. She'll probably fit <u>in</u> / <u>up</u> very well.
                              16.

EXERCISE 3: Transitive Phrasal Verbs and Pronouns   *(Grammar Note 3)*

Complete the conversations. Use phrasal verbs and pronouns.

1. **BEN:** It looks like rain. I hope they don't call off the picnic.

    CARLA: Well, if they _____ *call it off* _____, we can go for a ride in the car.

2. **BEN:** Remember to put on Mitzi's leash.

    CARLA: OK. I'll _____ now.

3. **BEN:** The car's really hot. How do you turn on the air conditioner?

    CARLA: You _____ with this knob.

4. **BEN:** That breeze feels good. I'm going to take off my hat.

    CARLA: Don't _____ yet. It'll help protect you from this hot sun.

5. **CARLA:** Uh-oh. Here comes another dog. I'll pick up Mitzi.

    BEN: She can handle it. Don't _____.

6. **CARLA:** Could someone wake up Ben and Mitzi? They're taking a nap under that tree.

    TRISH: No problem. I'll _____.

EXERCISE 4: Transitive and Intransitive Phrasal Verbs: Word Order   *(Grammar Note 3)*

Unscramble the words to make sentences. If more than one answer is possible, give both.

1. on / put / your lab coats   _Put your lab coats on._ **OR** _Put on your lab coats._ _____

2. the experiment / set / up   _____

3. out / it / carry   _____

4. down / sit / when you're done   _____

5. to page 26 / on / go   _____

6. up / your reports / write   _____

7. in / them / hand   _____

8. off / take / your lab coats   _____

9. them / put / away   _____

10. the lab / clean / up   _____

EXERCISE 5: Meaning of Phrasal Verbs

(Grammar Note 2)

Complete the article. Choose the phrasal verb from the box that is closest in meaning to the verbs in parentheses. Use the correct form of the phrasal verb. Go to Appendices 4 and 5 on pages A-3 and A-4 for help.

calm down	find out	go away	keep on	make up	pass on
carry out	get along	~~grow up~~	look up	pass away	turn on

Bird Brains
(They're Smarter Than You Think)

Some children grow up with dogs and cats. Irene

Pepperberg _____*grew up*_____ with birds. Like many
     1. (became an adult)

shy people, she sometimes _____
     2. (had a good relationship)

Irene Pepperberg with Alex and friends

with her pets better than with people. Pepperberg got a Ph.D. in chemistry from

Harvard, but she never lost her interest in animal intelligence. One day at home, she

_____ the TV and saw a show about communicating with dolphins.
     3. (started)

Why not birds? she thought. She _____ information about talking birds
     4. (searched books)

and _____ about African gray parrots. In 1977, she bought Alex. For 30
     5. (discovered information)

years Pepperberg _____ experiments with Alex in a lab full of colorful
     6. (conducted)

toys. Alex didn't just "parrot"[1] words. He learned the meaning of more than 100 words

and could understand ideas such as "different," "smaller," and "_____."
                                                      7. (relax)

He even _____ words such as "yummy bread" for cake. When he got
     8. (created)

bored with an experiment, he'd say "I'm gonna _____ now."
                                                     9. (leave)

    In September 1999, Alex _____. It was a terrible loss for Pepperberg,
                                          10. (died)

but today she _____ working with her other parrots. To her students at
     11. (continues)

Harvard and Brandeis, she is _____ her love and respect for these
     12. (giving to others)

intelligent birds.

_____

[1] **parrot:** to repeat someone else's words or ideas without understanding them

EXERCISE 6: Editing

Service dogs help out people with disabilities. Read the entry from a website about service dogs. There are ten mistakes in the use of phrasal verbs. The first mistake is already corrected. Find and correct nine more. Go to Appendices 4 and 5 on pages A-3 and A-4 for help.

A Good Match

               for

For a long time, I looked ˄ the right service dog ~~for~~. I almost gave on, but as soon as I met Barnie, I knew he was the one. The trainer had four puppies, and I picked out Barnie right away. Actually, he picked out me. He walked over to my wheelchair and sat down next to me. After that, I didn't have to think it down at all. I just said, "Come by, Barnie, let's go home."

When I started to train him, I was surprised at how fast he caught back. He learned to pick my keys up from the floor when he was only nine weeks old. Once I fell out of bed, so he started to wake on before me. Now he stands next to me while I get up and get into my chair.

When we started school, he figured my schedule through right away. After the first week, he would go to the right classroom and lie down. He stands up just before the bell rings. (How does he know how to do that?) When I need a book, he opens my book bag and takes out it for me! He really loves to take care of me.

Today, the famous Dr. Pepperberg dropped into my animal behavior class and brought an African gray parrot. At first, Barnie looked a little excited, but he calmed back right away. I know I can always count on him.

STEP 4 COMMUNICATION PRACTICE

EXERCISE 7: Listening

A | *Some college students are taking a science class. Read the conversations. Then listen and circle the phrasal verbs that you hear. Listen again and check your answers.*

1. **A:** Did you see Dr. Pepperberg in class today?

   B: Yes. She (brought up) / brought back that DVD about Alex. Very interesting.

2. **A:** What's Terry doing?

   B: She's handing in / handing out some lab reports.

3. **A:** Are you done with your report, Rea?

   B: Almost. I just have to look up / look over some information.

4. **A:** Hey, guys. That music is disturbing us.

   B: Sorry. We'll turn it down / turn it off.

5. **A:** Jason is discouraged.

   B: I know. He says he can't keep on / keep up with the class.

6. **A:** Did you hear about Lila?

   B: Yes, we were all surprised when she dropped in / dropped out yesterday.

7. **A:** OK, class. It's time to take back / take off your lab coats.

   B: Oh, could we have a few more minutes? We're almost done.

8. **A:** Hi. Can I help you?

   B: Yes, thanks. I need to pick up / pick out a book for my biology report.

B | *Listen again and check (✓)* **True** *or* **False**. *Correct the false statements.*

	True	False
1. Professor Pepperberg ~~brought in~~ a DVD. *(talked about)*	☐	☑
2. Terry is giving some reports to the teacher.	☐	☐
3. Rea is going to look for some information in a reference book.	☐	☐
4. They're going to make the music lower.	☐	☐
5. Jason feels that the class is going too fast for him.	☐	☐
6. Lila visited the class yesterday.	☐	☐
7. It's time to return the lab coats.	☐	☐
8. He needs to choose a book for his report.	☐	☐

EXERCISE 8: Pronunciation

🎧 **A** | *Read and listen to the Pronunciation Note.*

> **Pronunciation Note**
>
> When the **object of a phrasal verb** is a **noun** that comes between the verb and its particle, **all three words** are usually **stressed**.
>
> EXAMPLE: Could you **turn the lights off**?
>
> When the object is a **pronoun**, the **particle** usually receives **stronger stress** than the verb. The pronoun is not stressed.
>
> EXAMPLE: Sure. I'll **turn them off** in a minute.

🎧 **B** | *Listen to the short conversations. Put dots (• or ●) over the phrasal verbs and their objects to show the stress on each part.*

1. **A:** What happens if you drop your keys?

   B: My service dog **picks them up**.

2. **A:** What are you doing?

   B: I'm **cleaning the lab up**.

3. **A:** How did Alex learn all those words?

   B: I can't **figure it out**. He was a genius, I guess.

4. **A:** I don't have your email address.

   B: I'll **write it down** for you.

5. **A:** I need some help planning the class party.

   B: OK. I'll **pick the music out**.

6. **A:** I failed the quiz today. I'm really upset.

   B: When that happens, I take my dog for a walk. It always **calms me down**.

🎧 **C** | *Listen again to the conversations and repeat the responses. Then practice the conversations with a partner.*

EXERCISE 9: Making Plans

Work in groups. Imagine that you are going to take a class field trip. Decide where to go—for example, the zoo, a museum, a park. Then assign tasks and make a list. Try to include some of the phrasal verbs from the box. Go to Appendices 4 and 5 on pages A-3 and A-4 for help.

call up	figure out	look over	make up	pick out	talk over
clean up	hand out	look up	pass out	pick up	write down

EXAMPLE: **A:** I'll write down the "To Do" list.
B: Good idea. I'll call the zoo up to find out the hours.
C: I can pick up a bus schedule.

EXERCISE 10: For or Against

What are some reasons for and against owning a pet? Work in groups to discuss the question. Use some of the phrasal verbs from the box. Go to Appendices 4 and 5 on pages A-3 and A-4 for help.

calm down	chew up	get along	get up	play around
cheer up	clean up	get off	go away	wake up

EXAMPLE: **A:** A pet can calm you down when you're upset.
B: But what do you do with your pet when you go away on vacation?

EXERCISE 11: Writing

A | *How intelligent are animals? Write a paragraph about a pet or an animal you've read about or observed in a zoo or on a TV show. Use phrasal verbs.*

EXAMPLE: I think animals have a lot of intelligence. They can figure out how to solve problems and some of them even use tools. For example, my cat always sleeps on top of the TV. She can turn it on so that it heats up and keeps her warm . . .

B | *Check your work. Use the Editing Checklist.*

Editing Checklist

Did you . . . ?
☐ use phrasal verbs
☐ use the correct particles
☐ put pronoun objects between the verb and the particle

A | Circle the correct words to complete the sentences.

1. Have you figured <u>in / out</u> the homework problem yet?

2. Not yet, but I won't give <u>up / back</u>.

3. I'm going to keep <u>away / on</u> trying.

4. Let me know if I can help you <u>out / over</u>.

5. I need to look <u>down / up</u> some information.

6. Maybe you can look <u>out / over</u> my answers when I'm finished.

B | Unscramble the words to make sentences. Give two answers when possible.

1. _____
   (early / Joe / up / gets)

2. _____
   (on / the TV / turns / he)

3. _____
   (he / down / with Ana / sits)

4. _____
   (get / well / they / along)

5. _____
   (his schedule / over / they / look)

6. _____
   (talk / over / they / it)

7. _____
   (they / put / away / it)

8. _____
   (put / on / their coats / they)

C | Find and correct six mistakes.

As soon as Ina wakes up, she finds Abby's leash and puts it away her. Then the two of them set

for their morning walk out. They keep up walking until they get to the park, where there are a lot

of other dogs and their owners. Abby is a very friendly animal, and she gets well along with other

dogs. Ina loves dogs and always had one when she was growing over. There is a saying that "A

dog is a man's best friend," but Ina knows it's a woman's best friend too. "I enjoy playing with

Abby," she says, "and just being with her cheers up me." Abby obviously enjoys being with Ina

too. The two have become really good friends and have improved each other's lives a lot.

From Grammar to Writing
USING PRONOUNS FOR COHERENCE

When you write a paragraph, it is usually better to use **pronouns** than to repeat the same noun. Pronouns can make your writing smoother and more connected.

> EXAMPLE: **My apartment** is pretty cozy. I hope you enjoy staying in **my apartment**. ➔
> **My apartment** is pretty cozy. I hope you enjoy staying in **it**.

1 | *Read the email from Ted, thanking Felicia in advance for house-sitting. Circle all the pronouns. Above each pronoun, write the noun that it refers to.*

⬤ ⬤ ⬤

Dear Felicia,

Thanks for staying in my apartment next weekend and taking care of the dog. Help

Felicia
(yourself) to the food in the fridge—you can use it all up if you want. I rented some DVDs

for you. They're on top of the TV. I picked out some action movies. I hope you like them.

The DVD player is easy to figure out. Just turn it on with the remote control. But please

remember to turn it down at 11:00 P.M. My upstairs neighbor is very touchy about noise.

There are just a few other things to remember. Red's friendly, but please keep her away

from my neighbor's poodle. They don't like each other. Her bowl is on the kitchen

counter. Fill it up once a day with dry food. Please walk her twice a day. When you go out,

remember to turn on the answering machine. It's in the living room. The Sunday

newspaper arrives at about 8:00 A.M. Pick it up early—sometimes it disappears! Finally,

when you leave for work Monday, just leave the keys with Mrs. Delgado next door. I'll get

them from her when I get back.

Thanks again!

Ted

Dear Dara,

Welcome! I hope you enjoy staying here this week. Here are a few things to keep in mind:

- The mail is delivered every day around noon. You'll find ~~the mail~~ *it* in the mailbox on the ground floor. Please pick up the mail and put the mail on the dining room table.

- Feel free to use the air conditioner, but please turn off the air conditioner when you leave the house.

- There's plenty of food in the refrigerator! Please feel free to use up the food.

- I'm expecting a few phone calls. If you're home, could you please take a message? Just write down the message on the yellow pad in the top left desk drawer.

I think you'll find that the apartment is pretty comfortable. Enjoy the apartment and make yourself at home!

See you in a week.

Rachel

3 | *Before you write . . .*

1. Imagine that a friend is going to take care of your home while you are away. What will your friend's responsibilities be? What special things do you need to tell him or her about your home or neighborhood? Make a list.

2. Exchange lists with a partner. Ask questions about your partner's list. Answer your partner's questions.

    EXAMPLE: **A:** How often should I take out the garbage?
                     B: Oh, you can take it out every other day.
                     A: Where do you keep the dog food?
                     B: It's in the cupboard under the kitchen sink.

4 | *Write a note to your friend. Use your own paper. Give instructions about taking care of your home. Include answers to your partner's questions in Exercise 3. Use pronouns and phrasal verbs.*

5 | *Exchange notes with a different partner. Complete the chart.*

---

1. Did the writer use pronouns where necessary?   **Yes** ☐   **No** ☐

2. Put a question mark **(?)** over each pronoun you think is in the wrong place.

3. Complete this chart of daily tasks with information from your partner's note. If you have a question ask your partner, and write the answer on the chart.

   EXAMPLES: Sunday: water the plants, feed the pets, pick up the newspaper
   Monday: feed the pets, pick up the mail and put it on the hall table

   Day   **Tasks**

   _____   _____

   _____   _____

   _____   _____

   _____   _____

   _____   _____

   _____   _____

   _____   _____

---

6 | *Work with your partner. Discuss each other's editing questions from Exercise 5. Then rewrite your note. Make any necessary changes in your use of pronouns. Add information that your partner requested.*

MORE MODALS
AND SIMILAR EXPRESSIONS

World Weather Channel

Stockholm 1/-3

London 2/-4

Berlin 6/3

Warsaw 9/3

Paris 8/2

Budapest 15/1

Madrid 19/6

Rome 20/10

Athens

HOLMES

UNIT	GRAMMAR FOCUS	THEME
29	Necessity: *Have (got) to, Must, Don't have to, Must not, Can't*	Transportation
30	Expectations: *Be supposed to*	Wedding Customs
31	Future Possibility: *May, Might, Could*	Weather
32	Conclusions: *Must, Have (got) to, May, Might, Could, Can't*	Mysteries

STEP 1 GRAMMAR IN CONTEXT

Before You Read

Look at the title and the illustration. Discuss the questions.

1. Have you ever traveled to a different country?
2. How did you prepare for your trip?
3. What did you need to know?

Read

Read the article about some rules for international travel.

KNOW BEFORE YOU GO

What do international travelers **have to know** before they go? This week's column answers some questions from our readers.

Q: **Do** I **have to put** my computer and digital camera through the X-ray machine at airport security?[1] I'm worried that the machine will damage them.

A: It probably won't, but you **don't have to put** them through the X-ray equipment. An agent **must inspect** them, though. Ask for someone to inspect them by hand.

Q: My passport is going to expire in three months. Can I use it for a short trip to Asia next month?

A: For many countries, your passport **must be** valid for at least six months after you enter the country. Renew your passport before you leave, or you**'ll have to check** the rules of each country you plan to visit.

Q: I'm a French citizen. Last month I visited the United States, and I brought some gifts for friends. Why did U.S. Customs take the cheese?

A: You **can't bring** most types of cheese into the U.S. without a special permit. Many governments have strict rules about bringing food into their countries. To avoid problems, don't bring gifts of fresh food, and eat your snacks on the plane.

Q: I'm from Australia. My family and I are planning a trip to Europe and North America. We'd like to rent cars in a few places. **Do** I **have to get** an International Driver's Permit (IDP)?

A: Regulations differ: In Germany you **must not drive** without an IDP (unless you have a European Union driving license); in Canada you **don't have to have** one, but it's recommended. For a world tour, you really should get an IDP to avoid problems and disappointment.

[1] ***airport security:*** the area at the airport where they inspect your carry-on bags to make sure they are safe

KNOW BEFORE YOU GO

Q: I'm planning a trip from Toronto to New Delhi. There's a new nonstop flight, but it's more expensive, and it's about 14 hours long! What do you recommend?

A: Several airlines are now offering super-long flights. They provide more comfortable seats, wireless computers, and lots of entertainment. They cost a bit more, but you **won't have to make** as many connecting flights. That saves you time and hassles. But remember: To stay healthy on long flights you**'ve got to get up** and **move** around. You also **must drink** plenty of water. On a long flight these are "musts," not "shoulds"!

After You Read

A | Vocabulary: *Cross out the one word that does NOT belong in each category.*

1.	They must be **valid**:	passports	licenses	computers
2.	Agents **inspect** them at airports:	teeth	luggage	tickets
3.	They can be **hassles**:	cars	flights	movies
4.	There are **regulations** for them:	sleeping	driving	traveling
5.	They can be **strict**:	books	laws	parents
6.	They are **equipment**:	cameras	X-ray machines	bottles

B | Comprehension: *Check (✓)* **True** *or* **False**. *Correct the false statements.*

	True	**False**
1. Passengers must put computers and cameras through security X-ray equipment.	☐	☐
2. A passport is always valid.	☐	☐
3. Travelers are not allowed to bring cheese into the United States without permission.	☐	☐
4. You can't eat cheese on the plane.	☐	☐
5. Most international visitors need an IDP to drive in Germany.	☐	☐
6. You must have an IDP to drive in Canada.	☐	☐
7. To stay healthy on long flights, passengers must stay in their seats.	☐	☐

NECESSITY: *HAVE (GOT) TO, DON'T HAVE TO*

Affirmative Statements

Subject	Have to / Have got to	Base Form of Verb	
I You We They	**have to** **have got to**	**leave**	now.
He She It	**has to** **has got to**		

Negative Statements*

Subject	Do not	Have to	Base Form of Verb	
I You We They	**don't**	**have to**	**leave**	now.
He She It	**doesn't**			

*There is no negative form for *have got to.*

Contractions*

have got to	=	**'ve got to**
has got to	=	**'s got to**

*There are no contractions for *have to* and *has to.*

Yes / No Questions

Do	Subject	Have to	Base Form of Verb
Do	I you we they	**have to**	**leave?**
Does	he she it		

Short Answers

Affirmative			Negative		
Yes,	you I / we you they	**do.**	**No,**	you I / we you they	**don't.**
	he she it	**does.**		he she it	**doesn't.**

Wh- Questions

Wh- Word	Do	Subject	Have to	Base Form of Verb
When	**do**	I you we they	**have to**	**leave?**
	does	he she it		

NECESSITY: *MUST, MUST NOT, CAN'T*

Must*			
Subject	***Must (not)***	**Base Form of Verb**	
I You He She It We They	**must**	**leave**	very early.
	must not	**arrive**	too late.

Can't*			
Subject	***Can't***	**Base Form of Verb**	
You He They	**can't**	**sit**	over there.

*Must and *can't* are modals. Modals have only one form. They do not have *-s* in the third-person singular.

GRAMMAR NOTES

1 Use **have to**, **have got to**, or the modal **must** to show that something is **necessary**.

a. **Have to** is the most common expression in <u>everyday speaking and writing</u>.

b. You can also use **have got to** in <u>conversation</u> and <u>informal writing</u>.

c. **Must** is not very common in conversation. You will see **must** in <u>formal writing</u> and in official forms, signs, and notices. People also use it when they talk about laws and regulations.

USAGE NOTE: *Must* is much **stronger** than *have to*. In <u>conversation</u>, usually only people with power use it (parents, police, teachers, government leaders).

- You **have to carry** your passport when you travel to most countries.

- I**'ve got to apply** for a new passport right away!

- All passengers **must show** their passports when they check in.

MOTHER: Jess, you really **must pack** tonight.
JESSICA: OK, Mom.

(continued on next page)

2	You can use a form of *have to* for **past**, **present**, and **future** time.	• She **had to travel** a lot last year. *(past)* • He **has to travel** a lot for his job. *(present)* • We**'ll have to visit** them soon. *(future)*
	You can also use it with the **present perfect**.	• I **haven't had to drive**. *(present perfect)*
	Have got to and *must* have no past forms. Use *had to* for the **past**.	• We **had to work** last night. *(past)* Not: We ~~had got to~~ work last night. Not: We ~~must~~ work last night.
	Use *have got to* and *must* only for the **present** and the **future**.	• I**'ve got to turn off** my phone now. *(present)* • We **must be** at the airport an hour before tomorrow's flight. *(future)*

3	Use *have to* for most **questions**.	• **Did** you **have to renew** your passport? • **Do** you **have to leave** now?
	USAGE NOTE: We <u>almost never</u> use *must* in questions, and we do NOT use *have got to*.	Not Common: Must I leave now? Not: ~~Have I got to leave~~ right now?

4	**BE CAREFUL!** *Have (got) to* and *must* have similar meanings. However, *don't have to* and *must not* have very **different meanings**.	
	a. Use *don't have to* to show that something is **not necessary**. There is a <u>choice</u>.	• Tourists **don't have to have** an IDP in Canada. They can drive without one. • We **didn't have to show** our passports. • You **won't have to go** through customs.
	There is NO negative form of *have got to*.	Not: Tourists ~~haven't got to have~~ an IDP in Canada.
	b. Use *must not* to show that something is **against the rules**. There is <u>no choice</u>.	• You **must not drive** without a license. It's against the law.
	USAGE NOTE: We often use *can't* instead of *must not* to express prohibition in spoken English.	• Very Common: You **can't drive** without a license.

5	We sometimes use "**hafta**," "**hasta**," and "**gotta**" in <u>very informal</u> notes, emails, and text messages.	• **Gotta** go now. I **hafta** be at the dentist's office in five minutes. *(informal email)*
	BE CAREFUL! Do NOT use these forms in more <u>formal</u> writing.	Not: Dear Mr. Smith, I ~~hafta~~ go to the dentist's office today, so I'll be late for class. *(formal note)*

REFERENCE NOTES

For general information on **modals**, see Unit 13, Grammar Note 2, on page 179.

Have (got) to, *must*, and *can't* are also used for **conclusions** (see Unit 32).

Can't is also used for **ability** (see Unit 13), **permission** (see Unit 14) or **requests** (see Unit 15).

For a list of **modals and their functions**, see Appendix 19 on page A-8.

EXERCISE 1: Discover the Grammar

A | *Read Ben Leonard's telephone conversation with a clerk from the Italian consulate. Underline the words in their conversation that show that something is **necessary**, **not necessary**, or **against the rules**.*

BEN: Hello. I'm Australian, and I'm planning to spend several weeks in Europe with my family. I have some questions. First, <u>do we have to get</u> visas to visit Italy?

CLERK: Not for a short visit. But you can't stay for longer than 90 days without a visa. Australians also have to have a Permit to Stay for visits in Italy longer than eight days. You must apply for the permit at a local police station within eight days of your arrival. It's a hassle, but you've got to do it.

BEN: Can my wife and I use our Australian driver's licenses in Italy?

CLERK: You have to carry your Australian license, but you must also have a valid International Driver's Permit. And you've got to be at least 18 years old.

BEN: When do we have to get the IDPs? Is it possible to apply for them when we get to Europe?

CLERK: No, you must apply before you leave. The Australian Automobile Association can help you. You'll also have to get an International Insurance Certificate to show you have insurance. They're very strict about this, but you'll be able to get one at the car rental agency.

BEN: We'll be in Italy in January. We don't have a set schedule, so we haven't made any reservations. Is that going to be a problem?

CLERK: Yes. You've got to have reservations, even in January—especially in major cities like Rome, Florence, or Venice.

BEN: OK. Thanks a lot. You've been very helpful.

B | *Check (✓) the appropriate box for each instruction.*

	Necessary	Not Necessary	Against the Rules
1. Get a visa for a two-week visit.	☐	☑	☐
2. Get a Permit to Stay for visits longer than eight days.	☐	☐	☐
3. Apply for a Permit to Stay 10 days after arrival.	☐	☐	☐
4. Get a visa for a one-month visit.	☐	☐	☐
5. Use only an Australian driver's license.	☐	☐	☐
6. Apply for an IDP in Europe.	☐	☐	☐
7. Make hotel reservations.	☐	☐	☐

EXERCISE 2: Affirmative and Negative Statements: *Have to*   (Grammar Notes 1, 4)

*The Leonards have checked off the things they've already done to get ready for their trip. Read the lists and write sentences about what the Leonards still **have to do** and what they **don't have to do.***

BEN
✔ make copies of passports and IDPs
buy euros
give the house keys to Nora

ANN
buy phone cards online
✔ call Pet Care
buy batteries for the digital camera
✔ stop the mail for two weeks

Sean and Maya
✔ pack clothes
choose DVDs and CDs for the trip
say good-bye to friends

Ben doesn't have to make copies of passports and IDPs.

He has to buy euros, and he . . .

Ann . . .

EXERCISE 3: Questions and Statements: *Have (got) to* and *Can't*   (Grammar Notes 1–4)

Ben's family is traveling from Australia to Italy. Complete the conversations. Use the correct form of **have to**, **have got to**, *or* **can't** *and the verbs in parentheses. Use short answers.*

1. **BEN:** What time ___*do*___ we ___*have to leave*___ tomorrow?
                                          a. (leave)

   ANN: We _____ later than 5:30. We _____
                          b. (start)   c. (check in)
   with the airline by 7:00.

   SEAN: _____ we really _____ there so early? Our flight leaves at
                                              d. (get)
   10:00. We've got plenty of time.

   ANN: Yes, _____. It takes a long time to check in and get through
                              e.
   airport security these days. They're very strict, and they inspect everything. It's a hassle,

   but they _____ it!
                      f. (do)

   MAYA: And Mom _____ the car. That takes some time too!
                              g. (park)

2. **BEN:** Maya, this bag _____ over 50 pounds, or we
                                      a. (weigh)

   _____ extra. _____ you _____
              b. (pay)   c. (bring)
   so many clothes?

   MAYA: Yes, _____. I _____ all my stuff! We'll
                              d.   e. (have)
   be gone for weeks.

   ANN: Put some in my bag. And hurry. We _____!
                                                              f. (go)

3. **BEN:** We _____ never _____ this long to check in before.
                                      a. (wait)

   ANN: I know. But we _____ much longer. We're next.
                                  b. (not wait)

4. **SEAN:** Look! They have computers and TV screens! I _____ Randy!
                                                                      a. (call)

   BEN: We _____ our cell phone on the plane. Send an email.
                          b. (use)

5. **ANN:** We _____ around again. Come on, everybody, let's go.
                          a. (walk)

   SEAN: Why _____ we _____ up all the time?
                                      b. (get)

   BEN: Remember our rules? We _____ for more than three hours.
                                              c. (sit)

   It's unhealthy.

6. **MAYA:** Are we there yet? This flight is endless!

   ANN: We _____ in here much longer. We're landing in an hour.
                          a. (not be)

EXERCISE 4: Affirmative and Negative Statements: *Must* (Grammar Notes 1, 4)

Complete the rules for airline travel. Use **must** or **must not**.

1. Passengers _____ *must* _____ arrive three hours before an international flight.

2. They _____ keep their bags with them at all times.

3. Carry-on bags _____ be bigger than 45 inches (115 cm).

4. They _____ fit under the seat or in the overhead compartment of the airplane.

5. They _____ contain knives, scissors, or other dangerous items.

6. Checked bags _____ have labels with the passenger's name.

7. They _____ weigh more than 50 pounds, or there will be additional charges.

8. Travelers _____ show identification when they check in with the airline.

9. Everyone _____ have a ticket in order to go through security.

10. On board, passengers _____ get up when the seat belt sign is on.

11. On many flights, passengers _____ use cell phones when the plane is in the air.

EXERCISE 5: Negative Statements: *Must not* or *Don't have to* (Grammar Note 4)

Read the sign at the Casa Luciani swimming pool. Complete each statement. Use **must not** or **don't have to**.

Swimming Pool Rules and Regulations
Pool Hours 10:00 A.M. – 10:00 P.M.
Children under 12 years NOT ALLOWED
in pool without an adult.
Towels available at front desk.

- NO radio
- NO diving
- NO ball playing
- NO glass bottles
- NO alcoholic beverages

1. Children under age 12 ___ *must not swim* ___
   (swim)
   without an adult.

2. You _____ your own towel.
   (bring)

3. You _____ ball in or around
   (play)
   the pool.

4. You _____ into the pool.
   (dive)

5. Teenagers _____ with an adult.
   (swim)

6. You _____ the pool before
   (enter)
   10:00 A.M.

7. You _____ the swimming pool
   (leave)
   at 8:00 P.M.

8. You _____ in the pool past
   (stay)
   10:00 P.M.

EXERCISE 6: Editing

Read Sean's email to his friend. There are seven mistakes in expressing necessity. The first mistake is already corrected. Find and correct six more.

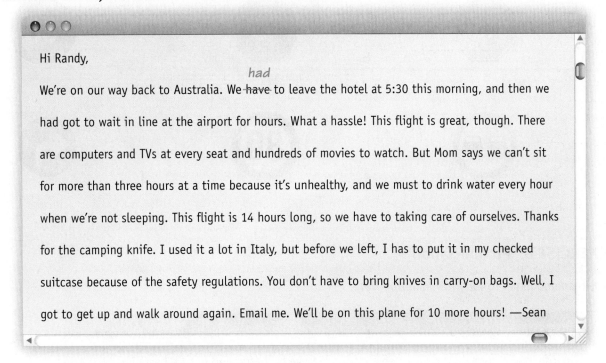

Hi Randy,

> *had*

We're on our way back to Australia. We ~~have~~ to leave the hotel at 5:30 this morning, and then we

had got to wait in line at the airport for hours. What a hassle! This flight is great, though. There

are computers and TVs at every seat and hundreds of movies to watch. But Mom says we can't sit

for more than three hours at a time because it's unhealthy, and we must to drink water every hour

when we're not sleeping. This flight is 14 hours long, so we have to taking care of ourselves. Thanks

for the camping knife. I used it a lot in Italy, but before we left, I has to put it in my checked

suitcase because of the safety regulations. You don't have to bring knives in carry-on bags. Well, I

got to get up and walk around again. Email me. We'll be on this plane for 10 more hours! —Sean

---

STEP 4 COMMUNICATION PRACTICE

EXERCISE 7: Listening

A | *Read the statements. Then listen to the conversations. Listen again and mark each statement **True** or **False**. Correct the false statements.*

		True	False
1.	The young man has to turn ~~right~~. *(left)*	☐	☑
2.	The young woman must drive slower.	☐	☐
3.	The woman has to stop.	☐	☐
4.	The man is driving too fast.	☐	☐
5.	The young woman was not preparing to stop.	☐	☐
6.	The woman has to pass.	☐	☐

B | *Listen again to the conversations and write the number of each conversation next to the appropriate sign.*

a. ____

b. ____

c. ____

d. ____

e. ____

f. _1_

EXERCISE 8: Pronunciation

A | *Read and listen to the Pronunciation Note.*

> **Pronunciation Note**
>
> In **informal conversation**, we often pronounce **have to** "hafta" and **has to** "hasta."
>
> **EXAMPLES:** I **have to** drive Bob to the airport. → "I **hafta** drive Bob to the airport."
> He **has to** be there by 5:00. → "He **hasta** be there by 5:00."
>
> For **have got to**, we often pronounce **got to** "gotta," and we sometimes leave out **have**.
>
> **EXAMPLE:** You **have got to** turn left here. → "You**'ve gotta** turn left here." OR
> "You **gotta** turn left here."

B | *Listen to the short conversations. Notice the pronunciation of* **have/has to,** *and* **have/has got to.**

1. **A:** John **has to** renew his passport. What about you?
   B: I don't **have to** renew mine yet. It's valid for another year.

2. **A:** When does he **have to** be at the airport?
   B: He **has to** be there by 8:00.

3. **A:** He**'s got to** leave now. Is he ready?
   B: Almost. He**'s got to** bring his bags downstairs, that's all.

4. **A:** Will we **have to** show our tickets before we board?
   B: Yes. And we'll **have to** show our passports too.

5. **A:** I**'ve got to** turn right here.
   B: No. You**'ve got to** turn left. You can't turn right here.

C | *Listen again. Then practice the conversations with a partner.*

EXERCISE 9: Picture Discussion

Work in pairs. Where can you find these signs? What do they mean? What do you have to do when you see each one? What can't you do? What do you think of the rules?

> **EXAMPLE:** **A:** You can find this sign near train tracks.
>
> **B:** Right. It means drivers have to slow down and look both ways before they continue . . .

EXERCISE 10: Game: Invent a Sign

Draw your own sign to illustrate something people **have to do** *or* **must not do.** *Show it to your classmates. See if they can guess the meaning. Decide where the sign belongs.*

> **EXAMPLE:** **A:** I think that means you have to wear shoes.
>
> **B:** Right! And where can you find a sign like this?
>
> **A:** Near some poolside restaurants.
>
> **C:** You can also find it . . .

EXERCISE 11: What About You?

A | *Work in small groups. Make a list of your most important tasks for this week. Check (✓) the things you've already done. Tell a partner what you still* **have to do** *and what you* **don't have to do.**

> **EXAMPLE:** **Hamed:** I don't have to renew my driver's license. I've already done it.

B | *Report to the group.*

> **EXAMPLE:** **Nadia:** Hamed doesn't have to renew his driver's license. He's already done it.

EXERCISE 12: Discussion: Rules and Regulations

A | *Work in small groups. Discuss your school's rules and regulations. What do you have to do? What don't you have to do? What can't you do?*

Some topics to consider:

- student cars and parking
- clothing
- cell or smart phones
- calculators
- class hours
- homework
- cigarettes
- food
- music

EXAMPLES: **A:** Our cars have to have a sticker for the student parking lot.
B: But we don't have to pay for parking.
C: We can't leave our cars in the parking lot overnight.

B | *Compare answers with your classmates. Complete a chart on the board like the one below.*

Things we have to do | Things we don't have to do | Things we can't do
have a parking sticker | pay for parking | leave cars in the parking lot overnight

EXERCISE 13: Writing

A | *Write about the application procedure for getting a driver's license, a passport, a work permit, citizenship, school admission, or a new job. What do you have to do? What don't you have to do? Use* **have to, don't have to, must, must not,** *or* **can't.**

EXAMPLE: To get a driver's license in my state, you must be at least 16 years and 3 months old. Drivers under the age of 19 also have to take a driver's education course. Then . . .

B | *Check your work. Use the Editing Checklist.*

Editing Checklist

Did you use . . . ?
- ☐ *must* or *have to* to show that something is necessary
- ☐ *don't have to* to show that something is not necessary
- ☐ *must not* or *can't* to show that something is against the rules.

29 Review

Check your answers on page UR-7.

Do you need to review anything?

A | *Circle the correct words to complete the sentences.*

1. You <u>don't have to / must not</u> buy euros for the trip. I've already done it.

2. <u>Do / Does</u> Ken have to leave already? It's still early.

3. They said we <u>can't / don't have to</u> carry scissors onto the airplane.

4. We<u>'ve got to / can't</u> arrive at the airport by 9:00, or we won't be able to board.

5. Jake <u>has / had</u> to renew his passport before he left for Italy.

6. Tomorrow, Tara will <u>have / got</u> to take her driving test again. She failed the last time.

B | *Complete the sentences with* **can't** *or the correct form of* **have to** *and the verbs in parentheses.*

1. I've already downloaded several movies, so I _____ it before we leave.
   (do)

2. We forgot to get a gift for Uncle Fred. We _____ something at the airport.
   (pick up)

3. I _____ never _____ in line this long in my entire life.
   (stand)

4. Relax. We're next. We _____ much longer.
   (wait)

5. Sir, you _____ on any part of the plane, not even in the bathrooms.
   (smoke)

6. The passenger in 23B _____. She's in the wrong seat.
   (move)

7. Sorry. You _____ here. May I see the seat number on your boarding pass?
   (sit)

8. We _____ some French cheese at dinner tonight. I can't wait to try it.
   (have)

9. We _____ the cheese before landing. It isn't allowed into the country.
   (eat)

C | *Find and correct five mistakes.*

1. He can't boards the plane yet.

2. Passengers must not stay in their seats when the seat belt light is off.

3. Passengers: Please note that you gotta pay extra for luggage over 50 pounds.

4. You don't have got to show your passport right now, but please have it ready.

5. Paul will has to unpack some of his stuff. His suitcase is much too heavy.

Expectations: *Be supposed to*
WEDDING CUSTOMS

STEP 1 GRAMMAR IN CONTEXT

Before You Read

Look at the photo and the title of the book excerpt. Discuss the questions.

1. What do you think the letter to Ms. Etiquette is about?
2. Have you ever been to a wedding or been part of a wedding?
3. If yes, what special clothing did people wear? What special customs did they follow?

Read

🎧 *Read the page from Ms. Etiquette's book,* The Right Thing.

Wedding Wisdom

Dear Ms. Etiquette:

What **is** the maid of honor **supposed to do** in a wedding ceremony? My best friend is getting married soon. She has invited me to be her maid of honor. I was planning to buy a new dress to wear, but someone told me that the bride **is supposed to select** my dress. This surprised me. I'm new in this country, and I'm not sure what my friend expects of me.

Dear Reader:

First, you should be very proud. In the past, the bride's sister **was supposed to serve** as her maid of honor, and the groom's brother **was supposed to be** his best man. Today, however, the bride and groom can ask anyone they want. Your friend's invitation means that she values your friendship very highly.

You and the best man will play important roles before, during, and after the ceremony. The maid of honor is the bride's assistant, and the best man is the groom's. Before the wedding, these two **are supposed to help** the couple prepare for the ceremony. You might help the bride choose the bridesmaids' dresses and send the wedding invitations, for example. The day of the wedding, the best man **is supposed to drive** the groom to the ceremony. During the ceremony, the maid of honor holds the bride's flowers. After the wedding, the maid of honor and the best man **are** both **supposed to sign** the marriage certificate as witnesses.

🔔 🔔 🔔

After You Read

A | Vocabulary: *Circle the letter of the word or phrase that best completes each sentence.*

1. An **assistant** is someone who _____ you.
   a. helps
   b. teaches
   c. protects

2. A _____ is an example of a **ceremony**.
   a. new job
   b. graduation
   c. math test

3. A **certificate** will NOT show facts about your _____.
   a. birth
   b. marriage
   c. phone bill

4. If you know wedding **etiquette**, you can _____ at a wedding.
   a. behave correctly
   b. take good photos
   c. hold the bride's flowers

5. The best man's **role** is the _____ for the wedding.
   a. suit he wears
   b. job he does
   c. car he uses

6. If you **select** flowers for an event, you _____ them.
   a. choose
   b. water
   c. pay for

B | Comprehension: *Check (✓) the maid of honor's responsibilities.*

She has to . . .

☐ **1.** choose her own dress for the wedding

☐ **2.** help send wedding invitations

☐ **3.** choose the best man

☐ **4.** drive the groom to the ceremony

☐ **5.** hold the bride's flowers during the ceremony

☐ **6.** sign the marriage certificate as a witness

EXPECTATIONS: *BE SUPPOSED TO*

Statements					
Subject	*Be*	*(Not)*	*Supposed to*	**Base Form of Verb**	
I	am was				
You We They	are were	(not)	supposed to	sign	the marriage certificate.
He She	is was				
It				be	a small wedding.

Yes / No Questions			
Be	**Subject**	*Supposed to*	**Base Form of Verb**
Am **Was**	I		
Are **Were**	you	supposed to	stand?
Is **Was**	she		

Short Answers						
Affirmative			**Negative**			
Yes,	you	are. were.	No,	you	aren't. weren't.
	I	am. was.		I	'm not. wasn't.
	she	is. was.		she	isn't. wasn't.

Wh- Questions				
Wh- Word	*Be*	**Subject**	*Supposed to*	**Base Form of Verb**
Where	am was	I		
	are were	you	supposed to	stand?
	is was	she		

GRAMMAR NOTES

1 Use the expression **be supposed to** + **base form** of the verb to talk about different kinds of expectations:

- **rules**

  - You**'re not supposed to park** over here. There's a No Parking sign.

- **customs** (usual ways of doing things)

  - The groom **is supposed to arrive** at the ceremony early.

- **predictions**

  - The weather forecast says it**'s supposed to rain** tomorrow morning.

- **hearsay** (what everyone says)

  - The beaches in Aruba **are supposed to be** beautiful. Everyone says so.

- **plans** or **arrangements**

  - Let's hurry. We**'re supposed to pick up** the Smiths at 6:00. They're expecting us.

2 Use **be supposed to** only in the **simple present** or the **simple past**.

- **a.** Use the **simple present** for the present or the future.

  - The bride **is supposed to be** here *now*.
  - I**'m supposed to be** at the wedding rehearsal *tomorrow evening*.
    Not: I ~~will be~~ supposed to be . . .

- **b.** Use the **simple past** for past expectations.

  - They **were supposed to get** there by 6:00, so they took a taxi.

USAGE NOTES:

Was/were supposed to and **was/were going to** can have similar meanings.

  - The ceremony **was supposed to start** at 8:00.
  - The ceremony **was going to start** at 8:00.

We often use **was/were supposed to** or **was/were going to** when something we expected to happen did not happen.

  - Nathaniel **was supposed to get** here at noon, **but** his train was late.
  - Nathaniel **was going to get** here at noon, **but** his train was late.

EXERCISE 1: Discover the Grammar

A | *Read the article. Underline the phrases that express expectations.*

Wheel2Wheel: A blog for cyclists

It <u>wasn't supposed to</u> be a big wedding.

For people who believe that serious cyclists only think about the newest equipment, here's a romantic story about my friends Bill and Beth Strickland.

The Stricklands wanted a small, quiet wedding—that's why they eloped[1] to Block Island, off the Atlantic Coast of the United States.

The ferry they took to their wedding site doesn't carry cars, so the Stricklands packed their bikes for the trip.

The couple found a lonely hill overlooking the ocean. The weather was supposed to be beautiful, so they asked the town mayor to marry them on the hill the next afternoon. They were going to have a small private ceremony in this romantic setting.

"When we got there, we found a crowd of cyclists admiring the view," laughed Beth Strickland.

When Bill kissed his bride, the audience burst into loud applause and rang their bicycle bells. "We weren't supposed to have 50 wedding guests, but we love biking, and we're not sorry," Bill said.

When they packed to leave the island the next day, Beth left her wedding bouquet at the hotel. She remembered it minutes before the ferry was going to leave. Bill jumped on his bike, recovered the flowers, and made it back to the ferry before it left.

"Cyclists are supposed to stay fast and fit," he said. "Now I know why."

---

[1] *elope:* to go away and get married secretly

B | *Read the article again. Check (✓)* **True** *or* **False** *for each statement. Correct the false statements.*

	True	False
1. The Stricklands planned a ~~big~~ *small* wedding.	☐	☑
2. The weather forecaster predicted rain.	☐	☐
3. The Stricklands wanted an outdoor wedding.	☐	☐
4. They didn't expect 50 guests.	☐	☐
5. Beth remembered her bouquet after the ferry left.	☐	☐
6. People expect cyclists to be in good shape.	☐	☐

426 UNIT 30

EXERCISE 2: Questions and Statements

(Grammar Notes 1–2)

Complete the conversations. Use the verbs in parentheses and a form of **be supposed to.**

1. **SOPHIE:** Netta, Gary called while you were out.

   NETTA: _____Am_____ I _____supposed to call_____ him back?

a. (call)

   SOPHIE: No, he'll call you later in the afternoon.

2. **SOPHIE:** The dress store called too. They delivered your wedding dress to your office this

   morning. _____ they _____ that?

a. (do)

   NETTA: No, they weren't! They _____ it here. That's why I

b. (deliver)

   stayed home today.

3. **SOPHIE:** Let's get in line. The rehearsal _____ in a few minutes.

a. (start)

   JULIA: We're bridesmaids. Where _____ we _____?

b. (stand)

   SOPHIE: Right here, behind Netta.

4. **GARY:** Hi. Where's Netta?

   SOPHIE: Gary! You _____ here!

a. (not be)

   GARY: Why not?

   SOPHIE: The groom _____ the bride on the day of the wedding

b. (not see)

   until the ceremony. It's bad luck.

5. **NETTA:** Sophie, could I borrow your handkerchief, please?

   SOPHIE: Sure, but why?

   NETTA: I _____ something old, something new, something

a. (wear)

   borrowed, and something blue. I don't have anything borrowed.

   SOPHIE: It _____ this afternoon. Maybe I should lend you my

b. (rain)

   umbrella instead.

6. **JULIA:** Where are Gary and Netta going on their honeymoon?

   SOPHIE: Aruba.

   JULIA: Oh, that _____ a really nice island.

a. (be)

7. **JULIA:** How long are they going to be away?

   SOPHIE: They _____ 10 days, but they decided to stay two

a. (stay)

   weeks instead.

EXERCISE 3: *Was* or *Were going to* (Grammar Note 2)

Look at the list of wedding plans. Write sentences describing the changes. Use **was/were going to**.

TASK	WHO	COMPLETED
1. select the bridesmaids' dresses	Sophie ~~Netta~~	✓
2. mail ~~180~~ 210 invitations	Netta's parents	✓
3. order a ~~vanilla~~ chocolate! cake	Netta	✓
4. hire a ~~rock~~ jazz band	Gary's parents	✓
5. give the bridal shower May ~~10~~ 20	Sophie	✓
6. plan the rehearsal dinner	Gary's parents ~~Gary~~	✓
7. find a photographer	Jack ~~Netta~~	✓
8. rent a ~~limo~~ red sports car	Jack	✓
9. order flowers by ~~April 1~~ April 15	Sophie	✓
10. Buy ~~candles~~ clocks as bridesmaids' gifts	Netta's parents	✓
11. Send the wedding announcement to the newspaper	Jack ~~Gary~~	✓

1. _Netta was going to select the bridesmaids' dresses, but instead, Sophie selected them._

2. _____

3. _____

4. _____

5. _____

6. _____

7. _____

8. _____

9. _____

10. _____

11. _____

EXERCISE 4: Editing

Read Jack's email to a friend. There are eight mistakes in the use of **be supposed to** *and* **was/were going to.** *The first mistake is already corrected. Find and correct seven more.*

Hi Cesar!

Remember my old college roommate Gary? He's getting married tomorrow, and I'm the best man!

He and his fiancée ~~supposed~~ *were* to have a small wedding, but they ended up inviting more than 200 people! As best man, my role is mostly to be Gary's assistant. For one thing, I'm supposing to make sure Gary gets to the wedding ceremony on time—not an easy job for me. At first we was going to hire a limousine and driver, but I decided to drive him there myself in a rented red sports car. I'm also supposed to hold the wedding rings during the ceremony. Then, at the end of the reception party, I'm supposed to helping the newlyweds leave quickly for their honeymoon. They're going straight to the airport. (I'm also suppose to hold the plane tickets for them.) They are going to go to Hawaii, but they changed their minds and are going to Aruba instead. Oh! I just looked at the clock. I'd better sign off now, or I'll be late for the rehearsal dinner. I going to leave five minutes ago! By the way, Sophie, the maid of honor, will be there too. I've never met her, but she supposes to be very nice. I'll let you know how it goes! —Jack

The bride and groom with their
maid of honor and best man

EXERCISE 5: Listening

🎧 **A** | *It's the day of the wedding. Read the statements. Then listen to the conversations. Listen again and check (✓)* **True** *or* **False** *for each statement. Correct the false statements.*

	True	False
isn't **1.** Netta ~~is~~ late.	☐	☑
2. Netta decided to walk to the ceremony.	☐	☐
3. The photographer isn't taking pictures.	☐	☐
4. The families of the bride and groom don't sit together during the ceremony.	☐	☐
5. The bridesmaids aren't wearing pink.	☐	☐
6. The maid of honor comes in before the bride.	☐	☐
7. Guests should say "congratulations" to the bride.	☐	☐
8. Gary and Netta are signing the marriage certificate before the reception.	☐	☐
9. Some people don't throw rice at weddings anymore.	☐	☐

🎧 **B** | *Listen again to the conversations and circle the correct information.*

1. Netta is / (isn't) supposed to be at the church by 2:00.

2. Netta <u>was</u> / <u>wasn't</u> going to walk to the wedding.

3. The photographer <u>is</u> / <u>isn't</u> supposed to take pictures during the ceremony.

4. Members of the bride's family <u>are</u> / <u>aren't</u> supposed to sit on the right.

5. The bridesmaids <u>were</u> / <u>weren't</u> going to wear pink.

6. The maid of honor <u>is</u> / <u>isn't</u> supposed to walk behind the bride.

7. Guests <u>are</u> / <u>aren't</u> supposed to say "congratulations" to the groom.

8. Gary and Netta <u>are</u> / <u>aren't</u> supposed to sign the marriage certificate after the ceremony.

9. Guests <u>are</u> / <u>aren't</u> supposed to throw rice at the bride and groom these days.

EXERCISE 6: Pronunciation

🎧 **A |** *Read and listen to the Pronunciation Note.*

> **Pronunciation Note**
>
> We often pronounce ***supposed to*** "supposta" and ***going to*** "gonna."
>
> **EXAMPLES:** The bride is **supposed to** be here. → "The bride is **supposta** be here."
>
> I was **going to** walk, but it rained. → "I was **gonna** walk, but it rained."

🎧 **B |** *Listen to the short conversations. Notice the pronunciation of* **supposed to** *and* **going to.**

1. **A:** What time is the ceremony **supposed to** start?
   B: The invitation said 4:30.

2. **A:** I think the groom is **supposed to** arrive early.
   B: I've heard that too.

3. **A:** The weather was **supposed to** be great.
   B: Well, the ceremony will be indoors, so the rain won't matter.

4. **A:** I thought Rob was **going to** be the photographer.
   B: He was **supposed to** be, but he got sick.

5. **A:** We were **going to** go, but I had to work.
   B: That's too bad.

🎧 **C |** *Listen again to the conversations and repeat each question or statement with* **supposed to** *or* **going to.** *Then practice the conversations with a partner.*

EXERCISE 7: Discussion

Work with a partner. Discuss important plans that you had that changed. Were you happy or disappointed about the changes in your plans? What did you do instead? What was the result? Use **was/were supposed to** *and* **was/were going to.**

Use these ideas or your own:

- get married
- move to a different town or country
- attend a particular school or take a particular course
- go to or have a party or a celebration
- buy something (some new clothing, a camera, a car . . .)

EXAMPLE: **A:** We were going to get married in Mexico City because my family lives there, but my whole family ended up coming here instead.
B: So I guess it was a big wedding!

EXERCISE 8: Cross-Cultural Comparison

Work in small groups. Discuss these important events. What are people in your culture supposed to do and say at these times? Is there a ceremony? Are people expected to give certain gifts? Wear special clothing? What roles do certain family members and friends play? Report to the class.

- a wedding

- an important birthday

- a school graduation

- an engagement to be married

- an anniversary

- a birth

- a funeral

    EXAMPLE: In traditional Japanese weddings, the bride and groom are supposed to wear kimonos.

EXERCISE 9: Writing

A | *Write a short essay about one of the events listed in Exercise 8. Use* **be supposed to** *for customs and plans or arrangements.*

   EXAMPLE: In Mexico, a girl's 15th birthday is called the *quinceañera*. The quinceañera celebration is very special. The girl is supposed to wear a pink or white dress . . .

B | *Check your work. Use the Editing Checklist.*

Editing Checklist

Did you use . . . ?
- ☐ ***be supposed to*** for customs, rules, and plans
- ☐ only the present or past of ***be*** in ***be supposed to***
- ☐ ***was/were going to*** or ***was/were supposed to*** for things that people expected to happen but did not happen at a particular event

Check your answers on page UR-8.

Do you need to review anything?

A | Circle the letter of the correct answer to complete each sentence.

1. Tomorrow is graduation, and we _____ supposed to be at school at 10:00.

   a. 're   **b.** 'll   **c.** do

2. The weather is _____ to be very nice.

   a. suppose   **b.** supposed   **c.** supposing

3. Jan and Stu _____ going to drive me, but they can't.

   a. are   **b.** was   **c.** were

4. The ceremony was _____ supposed to be outside, but it's going to be in the park.

   a. not   **b.** no   **c.** didn't

5. What time are we supposed _____?

   a. leave   **b.** leaving   **c.** to leave

B | Complete the conversations with the correct form of **be supposed to** and the verbs in parentheses.

- **A:** Hurry up! We _____ there in 10 minutes.

  1. (be)

  B: Don't worry. The ceremony _____ until 10:15.

  2. (not / start)

- **A:** Where _____ we _____?

  3. (sit)

  B: I think we _____ over there, on the right side.

  4. (go)

- **A:** Oh, no. Most men are wearing ties. _____ I _____ one?

  5. (wear)

  B: I think you _____ a jacket, but ties are optional. So, you're fine.

  6. (wear)

- **A:** It _____, but look at those clouds!

  7. (not / rain)

  B: I know. It _____ a beautiful day.

  8. (be)

C | Find and correct seven mistakes.

1. Dahlia was suppose to drive. She was supposed not to fly.

2. She is going to wear her blue dress, but she changed her mind.

3. What are we supposed to doing after the ceremony?

4. My parents will supposed to fly home tomorrow, but they're staying another day.

5. It was no supposed to be this cold, and it didn't suppose to rain.

Unit 30 Review: Expectations: *Be supposed to*   **433**

Before You Read

Look at the map that forecasts weather for European cities. Discuss the questions.

1. Are the temperatures in Celsius or Fahrenheit?
2. What are the possible high and low temperatures for Ankara?
3. What's the weather forecast for Moscow? For London?

Read

🎧 *Read the transcript of a weather report on British TV.*

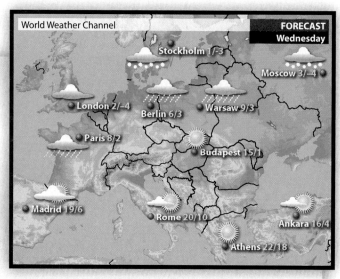

WEATHER WATCH

CAROL: Good morning. I'm Carol Johnson, and here's the local forecast for tomorrow, Wednesday, January 10. The cold front that has been affecting much of northern Europe is moving quickly toward Great Britain. Temperatures **may drop** as much as 11 degrees by late tomorrow afternoon. In London, expect a high of only 2 and a low of –4 degrees. We **might** even **see** some snow flurries[1] later on in the day. By evening, winds **could exceed** 40 miles per hour. So, bundle up; it's going to be a cold one! And now it's time for our travelers' forecast with Ethan Harvey. Ethan?

ETHAN: Thank you, Carol. Take your umbrella if you're traveling to Paris. Stormy conditions **may move** into France by tomorrow morning. Rain **could turn** into snow by evening when temperatures fall to near or below freezing. But look at the forecast for Italy! You **may not need** your coat at all if you plan to be in Rome, where we'll see partly cloudy skies with early morning temperatures around only 10 degrees on Wednesday. But later in the day, temperatures **could climb** to above 20 as skies clear up in the afternoon. The warming trend **could reach** the rest of western Europe by Thursday. But if not, it still looks like it will turn out to be a beautiful, sunny weekend in central Italy, Carol.

CAROL: Italy sounds great! Will you join me on a Roman holiday, Ethan?

ETHAN: I **might!**

---
[1] *flurries:* small amounts of light snow that fall and blow around

After You Read

A | Vocabulary: *Circle the letter of the word or phrase that best completes each sentence.*

1. A **forecast** tells you about _____ weather.

   a. foreign

   b. yesterday's

   c. tomorrow's

2. **Local** news gives you information about places that are _____ you.

   a. near

   b. far from

   c. interesting to

3. When the weather **affects** people, they always feel _____.

   a. better

   b. worse

   c. different

4. If you **bundle up**, you wear a lot of _____ clothes.

   a. warm

   b. new

   c. expensive

5. A **trend** is the way a situation _____.

   a. stays the same

   b. changes with time

   c. is right now

6. If winds **exceed** 30 miles per hour, they will be _____ 30 miles per hour.

   a. exactly

   b. less than

   c. more than

B | Comprehension: *Check (✓)* **True** *or* **False**. *Correct the false statements.*

	True	False
1. Temperatures will definitely drop 11 degrees in Great Britain.	☐	☐
2. Snow is possible in London.	☐	☐
3. There will definitely be stormy weather in France.	☐	☐
4. Snow is possible in Paris.	☐	☐
5. Western Europe is going to get colder.	☐	☐
6. Temperatures will definitely be above 20 degrees Celsius in Rome.	☐	☐

FUTURE POSSIBILITY: *MAY, MIGHT, COULD*

Statements			
Subject	**Modal***	**Base Form of Verb**	
You It They	**may (not) might (not) could**	**get**	cold.

May, *might*, and *could* are modals. Modals have only one form. They do not have -*s* in the third-person singular.

Yes / No Questions			
Are you going to fly to Paris? Are you leaving on Monday?			
Are you going to Will you Is it possible you'll	**be**	there long?	

Short Answers			
I	**may (not).*** **might (not).*** **could.**		
We	**may (not)*** **might (not)*** **could**	(be).	

May not and *might not* are not contracted.

Wh- Questions
When are you **going** to Paris?
How long are you going to **be** there?

Answers			
I	**may**	**go**	next week.
We	**could**	**be**	there a week.

GRAMMAR NOTES

1 Use the modals **may**, **might**, and **could** to talk about the **possibility** that something will happen in the **future**. The three modals have very similar meanings. You can use any one to talk about future possibility.

BE CAREFUL! *May be* and *maybe* both express possibility. Notice these differences:

- *May be* is a modal + be. It is always two words.

- *Maybe* is not a modal. It is an adverb. It is always one word, and it comes at the beginning of the sentence.

REMEMBER: Use a form of the **future** when you are certain that something will happen.

- It **may get** windy *tomorrow*.
- It **might get** windy *tomorrow*.
- It **could get** windy *tomorrow*.
  (*It's possible that it will be windy, but we're not certain.*)

- Demetrios **may be** late today.

- **Maybe** he'll take the train.
  NOT: He maybe take the train.

- It**'s going to rain** tonight.
  (*I'm certain that it will rain.*)

2

Use *may not* and *might not* to express the **possibility** that something will not happen.

BE CAREFUL! We usually do NOT contract *might not*, and we never contract *may not*.

REMEMBER: Use a form of the **future** when you are certain that something will not happen.

- There are a lot of clouds, but it **might not rain**.

- You **may not** need a coat.
  NOT: You mayn't need a coat.

- You **won't need** a coat.
  (*I'm certain that you will not need a coat.*)

3

Questions about possibility usually use the **future** (*will*, *be going to*, the present progressive, the simple present). They usually do not use *may*, *might*, or *could*.

You can also use phrases such as *Do you think . . . ?* or *Is it possible that . . . ?* with the **future** or with *may*, *might*, or *could*.

The **answers** to these questions often use *may*, *might*, or *could*.

In **short answers** to *yes / no* questions, we usually use *may*, *might*, or *could* alone.

USAGE NOTE: If *be* is the main verb, it is common to include *be* in the short answer.

- When *will* it *start* snowing?
  NOT COMMON: When might it start snowing?

- *Do you think* it **will start** snowing?
  OR
- *Do you think* it **could start** snowing?

A: *Are* you *going to drive* to work?
B: I don't know. I **may take** the bus.

A: When *are* you *leaving*?
B: I **might leave** in a few minutes.

A: *Do you think* it**'ll snow** tomorrow?
B: It **could stop** tonight.

A: Will your office close early?
B: It **may**. OR It **may not**.
  NOT: It may not close.

A: Will our flight *be* on time?
B: It **might be**. OR It **might**.
  It **might not be**. OR It **might not**.

REFERENCE NOTES
For general information on **modals**, see Unit 13, Grammar Note 2, on page 179.
May is also used for **permission** (see Unit 14).
Might is also used for **conclusions** (see Unit 32).
Could is also used for **ability** (see Unit 13), **permission** (see Unit 14), **requests** (see Unit 15), and **conclusions** (see Unit 32).
For a list of **modals and their functions**, see Appendix 19 on page A-8.

EXERCISE 1: Discover the Grammar

A | *Anna is a college student who works part-time; Cody is her husband. Read their conversation. Underline the words that express future possibility.*

ANNA: Are you going to drive to work tomorrow?

CODY: I don't know. I might take the car. Why?

ANNA: I just heard the local weather report. It may snow tonight.

CODY: Oh, then I may have to shovel snow before I leave. You know, I might just take the 7:30 train instead of driving. I have a 9:00 meeting, and I don't want to miss it. Do you have a class tomorrow morning?

ANNA: No, but I'm going to the library to work on my paper. Maybe I'll bundle up and take the train with you in the morning. And let's try to go home together too. Maybe we could meet at the train station at 6:00, OK? I'm taking the 6:30 train home.

CODY: I might not be able to catch the 6:30 train. My boss said something about working late tomorrow. I may be stuck there until 8:00. I'll call you tomorrow afternoon and let you know what I'm doing.

ANNA: OK. I'll get some takeout on the way home. Do you mind eating late?

CODY: No. I definitely want to have dinner together.

ANNA: Me too. Definitely.

B | *Read the conversation again. Check (✓) the appropriate box for each activity that they discuss.*

CODY	Certain	Possible
1. take car to work		✓
2. shovel snow		
3. take 7:30 A.M. train		
4. 9:00 meeting		
5. work until 8:00 P.M.		
6. call Anna		
7. dinner with Anna		

ANNA	Certain	Possible
1. go to library	✓	
2. work on paper		
3. ride train with Cody		
4. 6:00 P.M.—meet Cody		
5. take 6:30 train home		
6. buy takeout for dinner		
7. dinner with Cody		

EXERCISE 2: Affirmative and Negative Statements

(Grammar Notes 1–2)

Anna is graduating from college with a degree in meteorology.[1] Complete this entry in her diary. Choose the appropriate words in parentheses.

I just got the notice from my school. I _____ *'m going to* _____ graduate in June, but I still don't

                        1. (might not / 'm going to)

have plans. Some TV stations hire students to help out their meteorologists, so I _____

                                             2. (could / may not)

apply for a job next month. On the other hand, I _____ apply to graduate school and

                              3. (might / might not)

get my master's degree in atmospheric science. I'm just not sure, though—these past two years have

been really hard, and I _____ be ready to study for two more years. At least I *am* sure

                 4. (may / may not)

about my career. I _____ forecast the weather—that's certain. I made an appointment

            5. ('m going to / might)

to discuss my grades with my advisor, Mrs. Humphrey, tomorrow. I _____ talk about

                                           6. (maybe / may)

my plans with her. She _____ have an idea about what I should do.

                   7. (won't / might)

[1] *meteorology:* the scientific study of weather

EXERCISE 3: Statements: *May, Might, Be going to*

(Grammar Note 1)

*Look at Anna's schedule for Monday. She put a question mark (?) next to each item she wasn't sure about. Write sentences about Anna's plans for Monday. Use **may** or **might** (for things that are possible) and **be going to** (for things that are certain).*

MONDAY
1. call Cody at 9:00
2. buy some notebooks before class ?
3. go to the meeting with Mrs. Humphrey at 11:00
4. have coffee with Sue after class ?
5. go to work at 1:00
6. go shopping for snow boots ?
7. take the 7:00 train ?

1. *Anna is going to call Cody at 9:00.* _____

2. _____

3. _____

4. _____

5. _____

6. _____

7. _____

EXERCISE 4: Short Answers

(Grammar Note 3)

Read the questions. Write short answers. Use **could** *(for things that are possible) or* **won't** *(for things that are certain). Use* **be** *when possible.*

1. **A:** Do you think the roads will be dangerous? It's snowing really hard.

   B: _____They could be_____. It's a big storm.

2. **A:** Will the schools stay open?

   B: I'm sure _____. It's too dangerous for school buses.

3. **A:** Will it be very windy?

   B: _____. The winds are very strong already. They might even exceed 40 miles

   per hour. So, bundle up!

4. **A:** Will it get very cold?

   B: _____. The temperature in Centerville is already below zero.

5. **A:** Is it possible that the storm will be over by tomorrow?

   B: _____. It's moving pretty quickly now.

6. **A:** Do you think it will be warmer on Tuesday?

   B: _____. There seems to be a warming trend. It's stopped snowing already.

EXERCISE 5: Editing

Read the student's report about El Niño. There are seven mistakes in the use of **may, might,** *and* **could.** *The first mistake is already corrected. Find and correct six more.*

Every few years, the ocean near Peru becomes warmer. This change is called El Niño. An El Niño
~~maybe~~ *may* cause big weather changes all over the world. The west coasts of North and South America
might have very heavy rains. On the other side of the Pacific, New Guinea might becomes very
dry. Northern areas could have warmer, wetter winters, and southern areas maybe become much
colder. These weather changes affect plants and animals. Some fish mayn't survive in warmer
waters. They may die or swim to colder places. In addition, dry conditions could causing crops to
die. When that happens, food may get very expensive. El Niño does not happen regularly. It may
happen every two years, or it might not come for seven years. Will El Niños get worse in the
future? They could be. Pollution will increase the effects of El Niño, but no one is sure yet.

EXERCISE 6: Listening

A | *Read the statements. Then listen to the weather forecast. Listen again and circle the correct information.*

1. This weather forecast is for the (weekend) / week.

2. The report is <u>local / international</u>.

3. The weather is going to get <u>colder / warmer</u>.

4. On Saturday, you need to <u>bring a jacket / bundle up</u>.

5. On Sunday evening, the weather could affect <u>shopping / driving</u>.

6. The best day will probably be <u>Friday / Saturday / Sunday</u>.

B | *Look at the charts. Then listen again to the forecast and check (✓)* **Certain** *or* **Possible** *for each day.*

Friday

	Certain	Possible
Dry	✓	
Sunny		
Low 50s		

Saturday

	Certain	Possible
Sunny		
62°		
Windy		

Sunday

	Certain	Possible
Cold		
Windy		
Snow flurries		

EXERCISE 7: Pronunciation

A | *Read and listen to the Pronunciation Note.*

Pronunciation Note

In **affirmative short answers** with *may*, *might*, or *could*, the **most stress** is on the **modal**.

EXAMPLE: **A:** Will you be home at 8:00?

                     •

        B: I **might** be.

In **negative short answers** with *may*, *might*, or *could*, the **most stress** is on *not*.

EXAMPLE: **A:** Will it stop raining this afternoon?

                  •

        B: It **might not**.

B | *Listen to the short conversations. Notice the word that has the most stress in each short answer. Put a dot (•) over it.*

1. **A:** Is it going to snow tomorrow?

   B: It could.

2. **A:** Do you think the roads will be dangerous?

   B: They could be.

3. **A:** Are you going to drive?

   B: I might not.

4. **A:** Are schools going to be open?

   B: They may not be.

5. **A:** Will you be able to catch the 8:00 train?

   B: I might be.

6. **A:** Will the train be late?

   B: It could be.

C | *Listen again to the conversations and repeat the short answers. Then practice the conversations with a partner.*

EXERCISE 8: Conversation

Work with a partner. Talk about your weekend plans. Use **be going to** *or* **will** *for plans that are certain. Use* **may, might,** *or* **could** *for plans that are possible. Will the weather affect your plans?*

Example:　**A:** What are you doing this weekend?
　　　　　B: I'm not sure. I might go to the park with some friends on Saturday.
　　　　　A: The forecast says it may rain.
　　　　　B: Well, in that case, I guess we could go to the movies instead. What about you?

EXERCISE 9: Problem Solving

A | *Look at the student profiles from a school newspaper. Work in small groups. Talk about what the students might do in the future. Use the information from the box or your own ideas.*

About Your Classmates

Name:　　Nick Vanek
Major:　　TV broadcasting
Activities: Speakers Club, Sailing Club
Likes:　　learning something new
Dislikes:　crowded places
Plans:　　go to a four-year college
Dreams:　be a TV weather forecaster

Name:　　Marta Rivera
Major:　　Early Childhood Education
Activities: Students' Association, school newspaper
Likes:　　adventure, meeting new people
Dislikes:　snow, boring routines
Plans:　　teach in a preschool
Dreams:　travel around the world

FUTURE POSSIBILITIES		
Occupations	**Hobbies**	**Achievements**
• weather forecaster	• dancing	• fly on space shuttle
• teacher	• skiing	• teach in Alaska
• manager, day-care center	• creative writing	• develop a new weather satellite

Example:　**A:** Marta is on the school newspaper. She might do creative writing as a hobby.
　　　　　B: Nick dislikes crowded places. He might not be happy on the space shuttle.

B | *Now write your own profile. Discuss your future possibilities with your group.*

Future Possibility: *May, Might, Could* **443**

EXERCISE 10: Writing

A | *Think about your conversation in Exercise 8. Write an email to a friend about your weekend plans. What are you certain about? What things do you think are possible? How will the weather affect your plans?*

EXAMPLE: Hi, Erik. What are you doing this weekend? I'm afraid my plans aren't very exciting. I'm going to stay home and study for my science test. If the weather is nice, I might go for a bike ride. If I do that, maybe you could join me . . .

B | *Check your work. Use the Editing Checklist.*

Editing Checklist

Did you use . . . ?

☐ *will*, *be going to*, or the present progressive for things you are certain about or for questions about possibility

☐ *may*, *might*, or *could* for things you think are possible

---

A | Circle the correct words to complete the sentences.

1. Does / Will it rain tomorrow?

2. It might / might be. I'm not sure.

3. When is Ileana might / going to leave for work?

4. She maybe / may not go to work today. She hasn't decided.

5. It could get / gets very cold tonight. Bundle up!

6. The train will / could be late because of bad weather. It's possible, but it doesn't happen often.

7. Maybe / May be I'll take the train with you this evening.

B | Complete the conversations with the correct form of **may, might, could,** or **be going to** and the verbs in parentheses. Choose between affirmative and negative. Use short answers.

- **A:** _____ you _____ to the game with us on Sunday?
    1. (go)
  B: I _____. There's a good chance. I just have to finish this paper.
    2.
- **A:** _____ Marta _____ at Trish's wedding on Saturday?
    3. (be)
  B: She _____. She and Trish had a big argument about something.
    4.
- **A:** How late _____ you _____ this evening?
    5. (work)
  B: I _____ until 6:00. I'll call and let you know, OK?
    6. (stay)
- **A:** Schools _____ tomorrow. They're predicting a lot of snow tonight.
    7. (open)
  B: Or they _____ late. They do that sometimes.
    8. (open)

C | Read this review of the movie Day After Tomorrow. *Find and correct five mistakes.*

> Suddenly, weather forecasts all over the world are predicting terrible storms. Climatologist Jack Hall understands weather trends, and he thinks that a new ice age could to begin very quickly. His son Sam is in New York with his high school class. One student is sick and mayn't live without medicine. May those kids survive by themselves? They maybe not. Jack bundles up and starts walking to New York to save them. There might could be a happy ending. Or the world could end. You'll have to watch to find out!

32 Conclusions: *Must, Have (got) to, May, Might, Could, Can't*

MYSTERIES

STEP 1 GRAMMAR IN CONTEXT

Before You Read

Look at the photograph. Discuss the questions.

1. Who is Sherlock Holmes?
2. Have you ever read or watched a Sherlock Holmes mystery?
3. Do you like mystery stories? Why?
4. Who is your favorite detective?

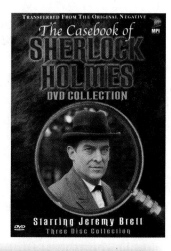

Read

Read the first part of the Sherlock Holmes story.

THE RED-HEADED LEAGUE[1]

Adapted from a story by Sir Arthur Conan Doyle

When Dr. Watson arrived, Sherlock Holmes was with a visitor.

"Dr. Watson, this is Mr. Jabez Wilson," said Holmes. Watson shook hands with a fat man with red hair.

"Mr. Wilson **must write** a lot," Dr. Watson said immediately.

Holmes smiled. "You **could be** right. But why do you think so?"

"His right shirt cuff[2] looks very old and worn. And he has a small hole in the left elbow of his jacket. He probably rests his left elbow on the desk when he writes."

Wilson looked amazed. "Dr. Watson is correct," he told Holmes. "Your methods **may be** useful after all."

"Please tell Dr. Watson your story," said Holmes. Dr. Watson looked very interested.

"I have a small shop," began the red-headed man.

"I don't have many customers, so I was very interested in this advertisement. My clerk, Vincent, showed it to me." He showed Watson a newspaper ad that said:

> An American millionaire started the Red-Headed League to help red-headed men. The League now has one position open. The salary is £4 per week for four hours of work every day. The job is to copy the encyclopedia in our offices.

"They **couldn't pay** someone just for having red hair and copying the encyclopedia," Watson laughed. "This **has to be** a joke."

"It **might not be**," said Holmes. "Listen to Wilson tell the rest of his story."

"I got the job, and I worked at the League for two months. Then this morning I found a note on the door." Wilson gave Holmes the note . . .

(to be continued)

---

[1] *league:* a group of people with the same goal   [2] *cuff:* the end of a shirt sleeve, near the hand

After You Read

A | Vocabulary: *Complete the conversations with the words from the box.*

> advertisement amazed encyclopedia method millionaire position salary

1. **A:** Your English is great—and you've only been studying a year. I'm _____!

   B: Well, I have a good teacher. His teaching _____ really works.

2. **A:** The bank has a(n) _____ available for a clerk. Why don't you apply?

   B: Do you know how much the _____ is?

   A: Here's the _____ in the newspaper. Check it out yourself.

3. **A:** You won the quiz show! You're a(n) _____! How did you do it?

   B: I studied the entire _____, from A to Z.

B | Comprehension: *Circle the letter of the word or phrase that best completes each sentence.*

1. Dr. Watson is probably Sherlock Holmes's _____.
   - **a.** clerk
   - **b.** dentist
   - **c.** friend

2. _____ is heavy and has red hair.
   - **a.** Holmes
   - **b.** Wilson
   - **c.** Watson

3. Watson thinks that Wilson writes a lot because of Wilson's _____.
   - **a.** clothing
   - **b.** shop
   - **c.** red hair

4. Watson helps to solve crimes by _____.
   - **a.** asking questions
   - **b.** looking at details
   - **c.** reading the encyclopedia

5. Wilson learned about the job from _____.
   - **a.** Watson
   - **b.** his clerk Vincent
   - **c.** a note on his door

6. Wilson copied the encyclopedia in _____.
   - **a.** his shop
   - **b.** Holmes's house
   - **c.** the Red-Headed League's office

CONCLUSIONS: *MUST, HAVE (GOT) TO, MAY, MIGHT, COULD, CAN'T*

Affirmative Statements

Subject	Modal*	Base Form of Verb	
I You He They	must may might could	be	wrong.

Negative Statements

Subject	Modal + *Not*	Base Form of Verb	
I You He They	must not may not might not couldn't can't	be	right.

*Must, may, might, could, and *can't* are modals. Modals have only one form.
They do not have -s in the third-person singular.

Affirmative Statements with *Have (got) to*

Subject	*Have (got) to*	Base Form	
I You They	have (got) to	be	right.
He	has (got) to		

Yes / No Questions

Can / Could	Subject	Base Form	
Could Can	he	know	that?

Do	Subject	Base Form	
Does	he	know	that?

Short Answers

Subject	Modal
He	must (not). may (not). might (not). could(n't). has (got) to. can't.

Yes / No Questions with *Be*

Can / Could	Subject	*Be*	
Could Can	he	be	a detective?

Be	Subject	
Is	he	a detective?

Short Answers

Subject	Modal	*Be*
He	must (not) may (not) might (not) could(n't) has (got) to can't	be.

Wh- Questions with *Can* and *Could*

Wh- Word	*Can / Could*	Subject	Base Form
Who What	can could	it they	be? want?

GRAMMAR NOTES

1	We often make guesses and come to **conclusions** about present situations using the facts we have. We use **modals** and similar expressions to show <u>how certain or uncertain</u> we are about our conclusions.		

MORE CERTAIN ↑

AFFIRMATIVE	NEGATIVE
must	**can't, couldn't**
have (got) to	**must not**
may, might, could	**may not, might not**

↓ LESS CERTAIN

2	For **affirmative conclusions**, use these modals:		

a. *must*, *have to*, or *have got to* if you are <u>very certain</u> about your conclusions

b. *may*, *might*, or *could* if you are <u>less certain</u> about your conclusions and you think something is **possible**

FACT	CONCLUSION
Wilson has only one clerk.	• His shop **must be** quite small.
Wilson applied for a position.	• He **has to need** money.
They pay men for having red hair.	• It **'s got to be** a joke.
Wilson has a hole in his sleeve.	• He **may write** a lot.
Vincent knows a lot about cameras.	• He **might be** a photographer.
Holmes solves a lot of crimes.	• His method **could be** a good one.

3	For **negative conclusions**, use these modals:		

a. *can't* and *couldn't* when you are <u>almost 100 percent certain</u> that something is **impossible**

- He **can't be** dead! I just saw him!
- Vincent **couldn't be** dishonest. I trust him completely.

b. *must not* when you are <u>slightly less certain</u>

- He **must not earn** a good salary. He always needs money.

c. *may not* and *might not* when you are <u>even less certain</u>

- He **may not know** about the plan.
- His boss **might not tell** him everything. I don't think his boss trusts him.

BE CAREFUL! Do NOT use *have to* and *have got to* for negative conclusions.

- It **can't be** true!
  NOT: It ~~doesn't have to be~~ true!

(continued on next page)

4 | Use *can* and *could* in **questions**.

- Someone's coming. Who **can** it **be**?
- **Could** Vincent **be** in the shop?

In **short answers**, use a <u>modal alone</u>.

A: Does she still work at Wilson's?
B: She **may not**. I saw a new clerk there.
Not: She may not ~~work~~.

BE CAREFUL! Use *be* in short answers to questions with *be*.

A: *Is* Ron still with City Bank?
B: I'm not sure. He **might not be**.

REFERENCE NOTES

May, *can*, and *could* are also used for **permission** (see Unit 14).
Must, *have to*, and *have got to* are also used for **necessity** (see Unit 29).
May, *might*, and *could* are also used for **future possibility** (see Unit 31).
For a list of **modals and their functions**, see Appendix 19 on page A-8.
For information about the **pronunciation and usage** of *have to* and *have got to*, see Unit 29.

STEP 3 FOCUSED PRACTICE

EXERCISE 1: Discover the Grammar

A | *Read the next part of "The Red-Headed League." Underline the verbs that express conclusions.*

THE RED-HEADED LEAGUE *(continued)*

Sherlock Holmes studied the note: *The Red-Headed League does not exist anymore.*

"This <u>could be</u> serious," Holmes told Wilson. "What can you tell us about your clerk Vincent?"

"Vincent couldn't be dishonest," replied Wilson. "In fact, he took this job for half the usual salary because he wanted to learn the business. His only fault is photography."

"Photography?" Holmes and Watson asked together.

"Yes," replied Wilson. "He's always running down to the basement to work with his cameras."

Wilson left soon after that.

"Wilson's clerk might be the key to this mystery," Holmes told Watson. "Let's go see him." An hour later, Holmes and Watson walked into Wilson's shop. The clerk was a man of about 30, with a scar on his forehead.

Holmes asked him for directions. Then he and Watson left the shop.

"My dear Watson," Holmes began. "It's very unusual for a 30-year-old man to work for half-pay. This clerk has to have a very special reason for working here."

"Something to do with the Red-Headed League?" Watson asked.

"Yes. Perhaps the clerk placed that ad in the newspaper. He may want to be alone in the shop. Did you look at his legs?"

"No, I didn't."

"He has holes in his trouser knees. He must spend his time digging a tunnel from Wilson's basement. But where is it?"

Holmes hit the ground sharply with his walking stick. "The ground isn't hollow, so the tunnel must not be here in front of the shop. Let's walk to the street in back of Wilson's shop."

B | *Read the second part of the story again. What does Sherlock Holmes believe about each of the statements? Check (✓) Possible or Almost Certain for each statement.*

	Possible	Almost Certain
1. Something serious is happening.	✓	☐
2. The clerk is the key to the mystery.	☐	☐
3. The clerk has a special reason for working in Mr. Wilson's shop.	☐	☐
4. He wants to be alone in the shop.	☐	☐
5. He's digging a tunnel from Wilson's basement.	☐	☐
6. The tunnel isn't in front of the shop.	☐	☐

EXERCISE 2: Affirmative and Negative Statements
(Grammar Notes 1–3)

Look at the illustration for the story "The Red-Headed League." Come to conclusions and circle the appropriate words.

1. It **must** / could be nighttime.

2. It <u>must / must not</u> be hot outside.

3. Number 27 <u>might / can't</u> be a bank.

4. The delivery <u>couldn't / might</u> be for the bank.

5. The box <u>could / must not</u> contain gold.

6. The two men on the sidewalk <u>must not / could</u> notice the delivery.

7. The manager <u>might not / must</u> want people to know about this delivery.

8. Robbers <u>may / can't</u> know about it.

EXERCISE 3: *Must* and *Must Not*

(Grammar Notes 1–3)

Look at the poster and the map of Mr. Wilson's neighborhood. Write conclusions. Use the evidence and the words in parentheses with **must** and **must not**.

1. Wilson's clerk is the man on the poster.

He must be a criminal.
_____
(he / be a criminal)

2. The man on the poster is named John Clay.

_____
(Vincent / be the clerk's real name)

3. Wilson trusts Vincent.

_____
(he / know about the poster)

4. Clay has committed a lot of crimes, but the police haven't caught him.

_____
(he / be very clever)

5. The address of the bank on the map and the address in the picture for Exercise 2 are the same.

_____
(number 27 Carlisle Street / be City Bank)

6. The hat shop and the drugstore don't make much money.

_____
(Vincent's tunnel / lead to those shops)

7. There's a lot of money in the bank, and it's very close to Wilson's shop.

_____
(Vincent's tunnel / lead to the bank)

8. The bank is expecting a shipment of gold.

_____
(the tunnel / be almost finished)

EXERCISE 4: *Have got to* and *Can't*

(Grammar Notes 1–3)

Ann and Marie are buying hats in the shop on Carlisle Street. Read the conversation.
*Rewrite the underlined sentences another way. Use **have got to** or **can't** and the word in*
parentheses. Use contractions.

ANN: Look at this hat, Marie. What do you think?

MARIE: Oh, come on. <u>That's got to be a joke.</u>

You can't be serious.
_____
1. (serious)

Anyway, it's much too expensive. Look at the price tag. I mean, I'm not a millionaire!

ANN: It's $100! <u>That can't be right.</u>

_____
2. (wrong)

MARIE: I know. <u>It can't cost more than $50.</u>

_____
3. (less)

Anyway, let's talk about it over lunch. I'm getting hungry.

ANN: It's too early for lunch. <u>It has to be before 11:00.</u>

_____
4. (after)

MARIE: Look at the time. I'm amazed! It's already 12:30.

ANN: Then let's go to the café on Jones Street. <u>It can't be far.</u>

_____
5. (nearby)

MARIE: Let's go home after lunch. I need a nap.

ANN: Oh, come on. <u>You're fine.</u> You must be hungry.

_____
6. (tired)

EXERCISE 5: Short Answers: *Might (not)* or *Must (not)*

(Grammar Note 4)

Sherlock Holmes and Dr. Watson have been discussing the mystery all evening. Write a short
*answer to each question. Use **might (not)** or **must (not)** and include **be** where necessary.*

WATSON: You sound terrible, Holmes. Are you sick?

HOLMES: I _____*must be*_____. I have a headache, and my throat is starting to hurt.
              1.

WATSON: Hmm. This bottle is empty. Do you have more cough syrup?

HOLMES: I _____. I *think* it's the last bottle.
              2.

(continued on next page)

WATSON: I'll have to go get some. My patients like Pure Drops Cough Medicine. Does that work for you, Holmes?

HOLMES: It _____. It's worth a try.
                        3.

WATSON: I forgot to go to the bank today. Do you have any money?

HOLMES: I _____. Look in my wallet. It's on the table downstairs.
                       4.

WATSON: I found it. It's 6:45. Is Drake Drugstore still open?

HOLMES: It _____. Their advertisement says "Open 'til 7."
                       5.

WATSON: Do you think they sell chicken soup? Some drugstores carry food.

HOLMES: They _____. It's a very small store.
                         6.

WATSON: What about the café on Jones Street? Do they have soup?

HOLMES: They _____. They've got everything.
                         7.

EXERCISE 6: Questions and Statements With *Be*   *(Grammar Notes 1-4)*

Mr. and Mrs. Wilson are trying to get to sleep. Write questions and answers. Use **could be,** **couldn't be,** *or* **can't be.** *Choose between affirmative and negative .*

MRS. WILSON: Shh! I hear someone at the door. It's 9:30. Who _____*could*_____ it __*be*__ ?
                                                                                      1.

MR. WILSON: It _____ a late customer. Mrs. Simms said she was going to stop by
                            2.
this evening.

MRS. WILSON: No, it _____ her. It's much too late. Maybe it's the cat.
                                3.

MR. WILSON: It _____. I put the cat out before we went to bed.
                            4.

MRS. WILSON: _____ it _____ Vincent? He's always down in the basement with
                                            5.
his camera.

MR. WILSON: No, Vincent went out an hour ago. He _____ back this early. Wait a
                                                              6.
minute. It _____ Sherlock Holmes and Dr. Watson. They said they
                       7.
wanted to talk to me.

MRS. WILSON: _____ they really _____ here so late?
                                                 8.

MR. WILSON: No. You're right. It _____ them.
                                        9.

MRS. WILSON: What _____ it _____ then?
                                          10.

MR. WILSON: That door rattles whenever the wind blows. It _____ the wind.
                                                                       11.

MRS. WILSON: That must be it. Let's go to sleep.

EXERCISE 7: Editing

Read the student's reading journal for a mystery novel. There are six mistakes in the use of
must, have (got) to, may, might, could, *and* **can't.** *The first mistake is already corrected.*
Find and correct five more.

> The main character, Molly Smith, is a college ESL teacher. She is trying to
> be
> find her dead grandparents' first home in the United States. It may ~~being~~
> in a nearby town. The townspeople there seem scared. They could be have a
> secret, or they must just hate strangers. Molly found some letters hidden in
> an old encyclopedia that might lead her to the place. They are in Armenian,
> but one of her students mights translate them for her. They got to be
> important because the author mentions them right away. The letters must
> contain family secrets. I'm sure of it. Who is the bad guy? It couldn't be
> the student because he wants to help. It must be the newspaper editor in
> the town. That's a possibility.

STEP 4 COMMUNICATION PRACTICE

EXERCISE 8: Listening

A | *The Red-Headed League mystery continues. . . . Sherlock Holmes, Dr. Watson, and*
Captain Rogers meet in front of City Bank. Read the sentences. Then listen to their
conversation. Listen again and number the sentences in order from what happens
first (1) to what happens last (6).

_____ **a.** John Clay arrives.

__1__ **b.** Holmes introduces Watson to Rogers.

_____ **c.** Rogers arrests Clay.

_____ **d.** Watson sits on a box of gold coins.

_____ **e.** Rogers finds Clay's tunnel.

_____ **f.** Holmes, Watson, and Rogers go to the storeroom.

B | Read the statements. Then listen again to the conversation. How certain is each speaker? Check (✓) Possible, Almost Certain, or Fact for each statement.

The speaker believes the statement is . . .	Possible	Almost Certain	Fact
1. Captain Rogers is from the police department.	☐	☐	☑
2. It's 10:00.	☐	☐	☐
3. There are 2,000 gold coins in one of the boxes.	☐	☐	☐
4. John Clay knows about the gold.	☐	☐	☐
5. An American millionaire didn't start the Red-Headed League.	☐	☐	☐
6. Clay ended the Red-Headed League.	☐	☐	☐
7. Clay's tunnel is finished.	☐	☐	☐
8. The tunnel is under the bank floor.	☐	☐	☐
9. Clay is dangerous.	☐	☐	☐
10. Clay is in the tunnel.	☐	☐	☐

EXERCISE 9: Pronunciation

A | Read and listen to the Pronunciation Note.

> **Pronunciation Note**
>
> When we express **conclusions**, we often **stress** the modals **must**, **may**, **might**, **can't**, and **could**.
>
> **EXAMPLE:** That **must** be George Clooney! He looks just like him.
>
> We also stress **have** and **has** in **have/has to** and **got** in **have/has got to**.
>
> **EXAMPLES:** The store **has to** be open. It's only 5:00.
>
> They**'ve got to** sell soup. They have everything.

B | Listen to the short conversations. Notice the stressed modals. Then listen again and complete the conversations with the modals you hear.

1. **A:** Look at the crowds!

   B: This _____ be a really popular movie.

2. **A:** Do you have the tickets?

   B: Yeah, I'm sure I put them in my pocket. They _____ be here somewhere.

3. A: This _____ be the best movie I've seen this year.

   B: Me too. George Clooney is so funny.

4. A: He _____ be the thief. He's already committed a lot of crimes.

   B: He _____ be. He's the star!

5. A: You _____ be right.

   B: I guess we'll know in a few minutes. It _____ be over soon.

6. A: That was a long movie. It _____ be after 10:00 by now.

   B: You're right. It's almost 10:30.

C | *Practice the conversations with a partner.*

EXERCISE 10: Picture Discussion

Work in small groups. Look at the pictures of Sandra Diaz and some things that she and her family own. Make guesses about the Diaz family. Give reasons for your guesses.

   EXAMPLE: **A:** Sandra might be a construction worker. She's wearing a hard hat.
                  B: Or she could be . . .
                  C: She couldn't . . .

EXERCISE 11: Problem Solving

Read the situations. In pairs, discuss possible explanations for each situation. Then come to a conclusion. Discuss your explanations with the rest of the class. Use your imagination!

1. Yolanda lives alone, but she hears a noise in the house.

   EXAMPLE: **A:** It might be an open window. Maybe the wind is blowing.
   B: It couldn't be. She closed all the windows five minutes ago.
   A: Well, then, it could be the cat . . .

2. Stefan has been calling his sister on the phone for three days. She hasn't returned any of his messages.

3. Allan is on the street. He's asked a woman three times for the time. She hasn't answered.

4. Lili sees a neighbor with a 10-year-old. She's never seen the child before.

5. Julia and Claudio went on a picnic in the park. They ate strawberries and cheese. Now they are sneezing and their eyes are watering.

EXERCISE 12: Writing

A | *Agatha James, the mystery writer, starts a new novel by writing story outlines about each one of her characters. Read about the murder suspect's activities on the day of the crime.*

MARCH 1	MURDER SUSPECT'S ACTIVITIES
7:00–8:00	gym—aerobics class—talks to exercise instructor!
9:30	calls Dr. Lorenzo
11:00–1:00	hairdresser—changes hair color
1:30	pharmacy—picks up prescription
2:00	bank—withdraws $10,000
3:00	Mr. Jordan
4:30	calls travel agency—vegetarian meal?

B | *Work in small groups to make guesses and come to conclusions about the story and the characters. Consider questions like these:*

• Is the murder suspect a man or a woman?

• Who is Dr. Lorenzo?

• Why does the suspect need $10,000?

• Who is Mr. Jordan? What is his relationship with the suspect?

EXAMPLE: **A:** The suspect must be a woman. She's going to the hairdresser.
B: It could be a man. Men go to hairdressers too.

C | *Now write possibilities and conclusions about the story and the characters.*

    EXAMPLE: The suspect must be a woman. Very few men take aerobics classes. She talked
                    to the aerobics instructor, so she might . . .

D | *Check your work. Use the Editing Checklist.*

Editing Checklist

Did you use . . . ?

☐ modals that show how certain or uncertain you are of your conclusions

☐ *must*, *have (got) to*, *may*, *might*, and *could* for affirmative statements

☐ *can't*, *couldn't*, *must not*, *may not*, and *might not* for negative statements

---

UNIT 32 Review

Check your answers on page UR-8.
Do you need to review anything?

A | *Circle the correct words to complete the sentences.*

1. Rosa got 100 on her test. She <u>may / must</u> be a good student.

2. It's a gold ring with a very large diamond. It <u>has got to / might</u> cost a lot of money.

3. I'm really not sure how old he is. He <u>has to / could</u> be 21.

4. Doug <u>can't / doesn't have to</u> be married. He's much too young!

5. <u>Could / May</u> Doug know Rosa?

6. The phone is ringing. It <u>must not / could</u> be Alexis. She sometimes calls at this time.

B | *Complete the conversations with the verbs in parentheses. Choose between affirmative and negative.*

- **A:** That _____ George's brother. He looks nothing like George.
  1. (could / be)
  B: He _____. Sometimes brothers don't look at all alike.
  2. (could / be)
- **A:** Someone's at the door. What _____ they _____ at this hour?
  3. (could / want)
  B: I don't know. _____ it _____ Leon?
  4. (could / be)
  A: No. It _____ Leon. Leon's in Spain.
  5. (can / be)
- **A:** _____ this road _____ to Greenville?
  6. (could / lead)
  B: I'm not sure. Ask Talia. She _____.
  7. (might / know)

C | *Find and correct seven mistakes.*

1. Jason has been coughing all morning. He might having a cold.

2. Diana must not likes fish. She left most of it on her plate.

3. May the package be from your parents?

4. That's impossible! It might not be true.

5. Is the bank still open? That's a good question. I don't know. It might.

6. She could be a thief! I trust her completely!

7. It's got be a joke. I don't believe it's serious.

From Grammar to Writing

COMBINING SENTENCES WITH
BECAUSE, ALTHOUGH, EVEN THOUGH

You can combine two sentences with *because*, *although*, and *even though*. In the new sentence, the clause that begins with *because*, *although*, or *even though* is the **dependent clause**. The other clause is the main clause.

EXAMPLE: It was my mistake. I think the cashier was rude. →

DEPENDENT CLAUSE   MAIN CLAUSE
Even though it was my mistake, I think the cashier was rude.

The dependent clause can come first or second. When it comes first, a **comma** separates the two clauses.

1 | *Circle the correct words to complete the business letter. Underline the main clauses once and the dependent clauses twice.*

23 Creek Road
Provo, UT 84001
September 10, 2011

Customer Service Representative
Hardy's Restaurant
12345 Beafy Court
Provo, UT 64004

Dear Customer Service Representative:

I am writing this letter of complaint although / (because) one of your cashiers treated me rudely.

Because / Even though I was sure I paid her with a $20 bill, I only received change for $10. I told her

that there was a mistake. She said "You're wrong" and slammed the cash drawer shut. I reported the

incident. Later the manager called. He said the cashier was right although / because the money in the

cashier drawer was correct.

Because / Even though the mistake was mine, I believe the cashier behaved extremely rudely.

Although / Because I like Hardy's, I also value polite service. I hope I won't have to change

restaurants although / because I can't get it there.

Sincerely,

Ken Nelson

Ken Nelson

2 | *Look at the letter in Exercise 1. Circle the correct words in the sentences to complete the rules about dependent clauses and business letters.*

1. Use *because* to give a (reason) / contrasting idea.

2. Use *although* or *even though* to give a reason / contrasting idea.

3. When you begin a sentence with a dependent clause, use a colon / comma after it.

4. When a sentence has a dependent clause, it must also / doesn't have to have a main clause.

5. When a sentence has a main clause, it must also / doesn't have to have a dependent clause.

6. In a business letter, the sender's / receiver's address comes first.

7. The date comes before / after the receiver's address.

8. Use a colon / comma after the receiver's name.

3 | *Before you write . . .*

1. Work with a partner. Complete these complaints with dependent clauses and the correct punctuation. Use your own ideas.

   a. _____ I will not bring my car to your mechanic again.

   b. The server brought me a hamburger _____.

   c. My neighbor still won't turn down the TV _____.

2. Choose one of the above situations. Plan a role play about the conflict. Act out your role play for another pair of students.

3. Discuss what to write in a letter of complaint.

4 | *Write a letter of complaint. Use information from your role play in Exercise 3.*

5 | *Exchange letters with a different partner. Complete the chart.*

Did the writer . . . ?	Yes	No
1. use dependent clauses correctly	☐	☐
2. use modals correctly	☐	☐
3. give enough information about the complaint	☐	☐
4. use correct business-letter form	☐	☐

6 | *Work with your partner. Discuss each other's editing questions from Exercise 5. Then rewrite your own letter and make any necessary corrections.*

APPENDICES

1 Irregular Verbs

Base Form	Simple Past	Past Participle
arise	arose	arisen
awake	awoke	awoken
be	was/were	been
beat	beat	beaten/beat
become	became	become
begin	began	begun
bend	bent	bent
bet	bet	bet
bite	bit	bitten
bleed	bled	bled
blow	blew	blown
break	broke	broken
bring	brought	brought
build	built	built
burn	burned/burnt	burned/burnt
burst	burst	burst
buy	bought	bought
catch	caught	caught
choose	chose	chosen
cling	clung	clung
come	came	come
cost	cost	cost
creep	crept	crept
cut	cut	cut
deal	dealt	dealt
dig	dug	dug
dive	dived/dove	dived
do	did	done
draw	drew	drawn
dream	dreamed/dreamt	dreamed/dreamt
drink	drank	drunk
drive	drove	driven
eat	ate	eaten
fall	fell	fallen
feed	fed	fed
feel	felt	felt
fight	fought	fought
find	found	found
fit	fit/fitted	fit
flee	fled	fled
fling	flung	flung
fly	flew	flown
forbid	forbade/forbid	forbidden
forget	forgot	forgotten
forgive	forgave	forgiven
freeze	froze	frozen
get	got	gotten/got
give	gave	given
go	went	gone
grind	ground	ground
grow	grew	grown

Base Form	Simple Past	Past Participle
hang	hung	hung
have	had	had
hear	heard	heard
hide	hid	hidden
hit	hit	hit
hold	held	held
hurt	hurt	hurt
keep	kept	kept
kneel	knelt/kneeled	knelt/kneeled
knit	knit/knitted	knit/knitted
know	knew	known
lay	laid	laid
lead	led	led
leap	leaped/leapt	leaped/leapt
leave	left	left
lend	lent	lent
let	let	let
lie (lie down)	lay	lain
light	lit/lighted	lit/lighted
lose	lost	lost
make	made	made
mean	meant	meant
meet	met	met
pay	paid	paid
prove	proved	proved/proven
put	put	put
quit	quit	quit
read /rid/	read /rɛd/	read /rɛd/
ride	rode	ridden
ring	rang	rung
rise	rose	risen
run	ran	run
say	said	said
see	saw	seen
seek	sought	sought
sell	sold	sold
send	sent	sent
set	set	set
sew	sewed	sewn/sewed
shake	shook	shaken
shave	shaved	shaved/shaven
shine (intransitive)	shone/shined	shone/shined
shoot	shot	shot
show	showed	shown
shrink	shrank/shrunk	shrunk/shrunken
shut	shut	shut
sing	sang	sung
sink	sank/sunk	sunk
sit	sat	sat
sleep	slept	slept
slide	slid	slid

(continued on next page)

Base Form	Simple Past	Past Participle	Base Form	Simple Past	Past Participle
speak	spoke	spoken	swing	swung	swung
speed	sped/speeded	sped/speeded	take	took	taken
spend	spent	spent	teach	taught	taught
spill	spilled/spilt	spilled/spilt	tear	tore	torn
spin	spun	spun	tell	told	told
spit	spit/spat	spat	think	thought	thought
split	split	split	throw	threw	thrown
spread	spread	spread	understand	understood	understood
spring	sprang	sprung	upset	upset	upset
stand	stood	stood	wake	woke	woken
steal	stole	stolen	wear	wore	worn
stick	stuck	stuck	weave	wove/weaved	woven/weaved
sting	stung	stung	weep	wept	wept
stink	stank/stunk	stunk	win	won	won
strike	struck	struck/stricken	wind	wound	wound
swear	swore	sworn	withdraw	withdrew	withdrawn
sweep	swept	swept	wring	wrung	wrung
swim	swam	swum	write	wrote	written

2 Non-Action Verbs

Appearance	Emotions	Mental States		Possession and Relationship	Senses and Perceptions	Wants and Preferences
appear	admire	agree	know	belong	feel	desire
be	adore	assume	mean	come from (origin)	hear	hope
look (seem)	appreciate	believe	mind	contain	notice	need
represent	care	consider	presume	have	observe	prefer
resemble	detest	disagree	realize	own	perceive	want
seem	dislike	disbelieve	recognize	possess	see	wish
signify	doubt	estimate	remember		smell	
	envy	expect	see (understand)		sound	
Value	fear	feel (believe)	suppose		taste	
cost	hate	find (believe)	suspect			
equal	like	guess	think (believe)			
weigh	love	hesitate	understand			
	miss	hope	wonder			
	regret	imagine				
	respect					
	trust					

3 Verbs and Expressions Used Reflexively

allow yourself
amuse yourself
ask yourself
avail yourself of
be hard on yourself
be pleased with yourself
be proud of yourself
be yourself
behave yourself

believe in yourself
blame yourself
buy yourself
cut yourself
deprive yourself of
dry yourself
enjoy yourself
feel proud of yourself
feel sorry for yourself

forgive yourself
help yourself
hurt yourself
imagine yourself
introduce yourself
kill yourself
look at yourself
prepare yourself
pride yourself on

push yourself
remind yourself
see yourself
take care of yourself
talk to yourself
teach yourself
tell yourself
treat yourself
wash yourself

(s.o. = someone   s.t. = something)

PHRASAL VERB	MEANING
ask s.o. **over**	*invite to one's home*
blow s.t. **out**	*stop burning by blowing air on it*
blow s.t. **up**	*make explode*
bring s.o. or s.t. **back**	*return*
bring s.o. **up**	*raise (a child)*
bring s.t. **up**	*bring attention to*
burn s.t. **down**	*burn completely*
call s.o. **back**	*return a phone call*
call s.t. **off**	*cancel*
call s.o. **up**	*contact by phone*
calm s.o. **down**	*make less excited*
carry s.t. **out**	*complete (a plan)*
clean s.o. or s.t. **up**	*clean completely*
clear s.t. **up**	*explain*
close s.t. **down**	*close by force*
count on s.t. or s.o.	*depend on*
cover s.o. or s.t. **up**	*cover completely*
cross s.t. **out**	*draw a line through*
do s.t. **over**	*do again*
drink s.t. **up**	*drink completely*
drop in on s.o.	*visit by surprise*
drop s.o. or s.t. **off**	*take someplace in a car and leave there*
empty s.t. **out**	*empty completely*
figure s.o. **out**	*understand (the behavior)*
figure s.t. **out**	*solve, understand after thinking about it*
fill s.t. **in**	*complete with information*
fill s.t. **out**	*complete (a form)*
find s.t. **out**	*learn information*
get off s.t.	*leave (a bus, a couch)*
get over s.t.	*recover from*
give s.t. **back**	*return*
give s.t. **up**	*quit, abandon*
hand s.t. **in**	*give work (to a boss/teacher), submit*
hand s.t. **out**	*distribute*
hand s.t. **over**	*give*
help s.o. **out**	*assist*
keep s.o. or s.t. **away**	*cause to stay at a distance*
keep s.t. **on**	*not remove (a piece of clothing/ jewelry)*
keep s.o. or s.t. **out**	*not allow to enter*
lay s.o. **off**	*end employment*
leave s.t. **on**	*1. not turn off (a light/radio)*
	2. not remove (a piece of clothing/ jewelry)
leave s.t. **out**	*not include, omit*
let s.o. **down**	*disappoint*
let s.o. or s.t. **in**	*allow to enter*
let s.o. **off**	*allow to leave (from a bus/car)*
light s.t. **up**	*illuminate*
look s.o. or s.t. **over**	*examine*
look s.t. **up**	*try to find (in a book/on the Internet)*

PHRASAL VERB	MEANING
make s.t. **up**	*create*
pass s.t. **on**	*give to others*
pass s.t. **out**	*distribute*
pass s.o. or s.t. **over**	*decide not to use*
pass s.o. or s.t. **up**	*decide not to use, reject*
pay s.o. or s.t. **back**	*repay*
pick s.o. or s.t. **out**	*choose*
pick s.o. or s.t. **up**	*1. lift*
	2. go get someone or something
pick s.t. **up**	*1. get (an idea/a new book)*
	2. answer the phone
point s.o. or s.t. **out**	*indicate*
put s.t. **away**	*put in an appropriate place*
put s.t. **back**	*return to its original place*
put s.o. or s.t. **down**	*stop holding*
put s.t. **off**	*delay*
put s.t. **on**	*cover the body (with clothes/lotion)*
put s.t. **together**	*assemble*
put s.t. **up**	*erect*
set s.t. **up**	*1. prepare for use*
	2. establish (a business)
shut s.t. **off**	*stop (a machine/light)*
straighten s.o. **out**	*change bad behavior*
straighten s.t. **up**	*make neat*
switch s.t. **on**	*start (a machine/light)*
take s.o. or s.t. **back**	*return*
take s.t. **off/out**	*remove*
take over s.t.	*get control of*
talk s.o. **into**	*persuade*
talk s.t. **over**	*discuss*
tear s.t. **down**	*destroy*
tear s.t. **off**	*remove by tearing*
tear s.t. **up**	*tear into small pieces*
think s.t. **over**	*consider*
think s.t. **up**	*invent*
throw s.t. **away/out**	*put in the trash, discard*
try s.t. **on**	*put clothing on to see if it fits*
try s.t. **out**	*use to see if it works*
turn s.t. **around**	*make it work well*
turn s.o. or s.t. **down**	*reject*
turn s.t. **down**	*lower the volume (a TV/radio)*
turn s.t. **in**	*give work (to a boss/teacher), submit*
turn s.o. or s.t. **into**	*change from one form to another*
turn s.o. **off**	*[slang] destroy interest in*
turn s.t. **off**	*stop (a machine/light), extinguish*
turn s.t. **on**	*start (a machine/light)*
turn s.t. **up**	*make louder (a TV/radio)*
use s.t. **up**	*use completely, consume*
wake s.o. **up**	*awaken*
work s.t. **out**	*solve, find a solution to a problem*
write s.t. **down**	*write on a piece of paper*
write s.t. **up**	*write in a finished form*

5 Intransitive Phrasal Verbs

PHRASAL VERB	MEANING
blow up	explode
break down	stop working (a machine)
burn down	burn completely
call back	return a phone call
calm down	become less excited
catch on	1. begin to understand 2. become popular
clear up	become clear
close down	stop operating
come about	happen
come along	come with, accompany
come by	visit
come back	return
come in	enter
come off	become unattached
come on	do as I say
come out	appear
come up	arise
dress up	wear special clothes
drop in	visit by surprise
drop out	quit
eat out	eat in a restaurant
empty out	empty completely
find out	learn information
fit in	be accepted in a group

PHRASAL VERB	MEANING
follow through	complete
fool around	act playful
get ahead	make progress, succeed
get along	have a good relationship
get away	go on vacation
get back	return
get by	survive
get through	finish
get together	meet
get up	get out of bed
give up	quit
go ahead	begin or continue to do something
go away	leave
go on	continue
grow up	become an adult
hang up	end a phone call
keep away	stay at a distance
keep on	continue
keep out	not enter
keep up	go as fast
lie down	recline
light up	illuminate

PHRASAL VERB	MEANING
look out	be careful
make up	end a disagreement, reconcile
pass away	die
play around	have fun
run out	not have enough
set out	begin an activity or a project
show up	appear
sign up	register
sit down	take a seat
slip up	make a mistake
stand up	rise
start over	start again
stay up	remain awake
straighten up	make neat
take off	depart (a plane)
tune in	1. watch or listen to (a show) 2. pay attention
turn up	appear
wake up	stop sleeping
watch out	be careful
work out	1. be resolved 2. exercise

6 Irregular Plural Nouns

SINGULAR	PLURAL
half	halves
knife	knives
leaf	leaves
life	lives
loaf	loaves
shelf	shelves
wife	wives

SINGULAR	PLURAL
man	men
woman	women
child	children
foot	feet
tooth	teeth
goose	geese
mouse	mice

SINGULAR	PLURAL
deer	deer
fish	fish
sheep	sheep
person	people

7 Non-Count Nouns

REMEMBER: Non-count nouns are singular.

ACTIVITIES	COURSES OF STUDY	FOOD		IDEAS AND FEELINGS	LIQUIDS AND GASES	MATERIALS	VERY SMALL THINGS
baseball	archeology	bread	fruit	anger	air	ash	dust
biking	art	broccoli	ice cream	beauty	blood	clay	pepper
exploring	economics	butter	lettuce	fear	gasoline	cotton	rice
farming	English	cake	meat	freedom	ink	glass	salt
football	geography	cheese	pasta	friendship	milk	gold	sand
golf	history	chicken	pizza	happiness	oil	leather	sugar
hiking	mathematics	chocolate	salad	hate	oxygen	paper	
running	music	coffee	soup	hope	paint	silk	WEATHER
sailing	photography	corn	spaghetti	loneliness	smoke	silver	fog
soccer	psychology	fat	spinach	love	soda	stone	ice
swimming	science	fish	tea	truth	water	wood	rain
tennis		flour	yogurt			wool	snow
							wind

NAMES OF CATEGORIES		OTHER
clothing	(BUT: coats, hats, shoes ...)	(Some non-count nouns don't fit into any list. You must memorize these non-count nouns.)
equipment	(BUT: computers, phones, TVs ...)	
food	(BUT: bananas, eggs, vegetables ...)	
furniture	(BUT: beds, chairs, lamps, tables ...)	advice
homework	(BUT: assignments, pages, problems ...)	garbage/trash
jewelry	(BUT: bracelets, earrings, necklaces ...)	help
mail	(BUT: letters, packages, postcards ...)	information
money	(BUT: dinars, dollars, euros, pounds ...)	luggage
time	(BUT: minutes, months, years ...)	news
work	(BUT: jobs, projects, tasks ...)	traffic

8 Proper Nouns

REMEMBER: Write proper nouns with a capital letter. Notice that some proper nouns use the definite article *the*.

PEOPLE
- first names — Anne, Eduardo, Mehmet, Olga, Shao-fen
- family names — Chen, García, Haddad, Smith
- family groups — the Chens, the Garcias, the Haddads, the Smiths
- titles — Doctor, Grandma, President, Professor
- title + names — Mr. García, Professor Smith, Uncle Steve

PLACES
- continents — Africa, Asia, Australia, Europe, South America
- countries — Argentina, China, France, Nigeria, Turkey, the United States
- provinces/states — Brittany, Ontario, Szechwan, Texas
- cities — Beijing, Istanbul, Rio de Janeiro, Toronto
- streets — the Champs-Elysées, Fifth Avenue
- structures — Harrods, the Louvre, the Petronas Towers
- schools — Midwood High School, Oxford University
- parks — Central Park, the Tivoli Gardens
- mountains — the Andes, the Himalayas, the Pyrenees
- oceans — the Atlantic, the Indian Ocean, the Pacific
- rivers — the Amazon, the Ganges, the Seine
- lakes — Baikal, Erie, Tanganyika, Titicaca
- canals — the Suez Canal, the Panama Canal
- deserts — the Gobi, the Kalahari, the Sahara

DOCUMENTS
the Bible, the Koran, the Constitution

LANGUAGES
Arabic, Chinese, Portuguese, Russian, Spanish

NATIONALITIES
Brazilian, Japanese, Mexican, Saudi, Turkish

RELIGIONS
Buddhism, Christianity, Hinduism, Islam, Judaism

COURSES
Introduction to Computer Sciences, Math 201

PRODUCT BRANDS
Adidas, Dell, Kleenex, Mercedes, Samsung

TIME
- months — January, March, December
- days — Monday, Wednesday, Saturday
- holidays — Bastille Day, Buddha Day, Christmas, Hanukah, New Year's Day, Ramadan

9 Adjectives That Form the Comparative and Superlative in Two Ways

ADJECTIVE	COMPARATIVE	SUPERLATIVE
cruel	crueler/more cruel	cruelest/most cruel
deadly	deadlier/more deadly	deadliest/most deadly
friendly	friendlier/more friendly	friendliest/most friendly
handsome	handsomer/more handsome	handsomest/most handsome
happy	happier/more happy	happiest/most happy
likely	likelier/more likely	likeliest/most likely
lively	livelier/more lively	liveliest/most lively
lonely	lonelier/more lonely	loneliest/most lonely
lovely	lovelier/more lovely	loveliest/most lovely
narrow	narrower/more narrow	narrowest/most narrow
pleasant	pleasanter/more pleasant	pleasantest/most pleasant
polite	politer/more polite	politest/most polite
quiet	quieter/more quiet	quietest/most quiet
shallow	shallower/more shallow	shallowest/most shallow
sincere	sincerer/more sincere	sincerest/most sincere
stupid	stupider/more stupid	stupidest/most stupid
true	truer/more true	truest/most true

10   Irregular Comparisons of Adjectives, Adverbs, and Quantifiers

ADJECTIVE	ADVERB	COMPARATIVE	SUPERLATIVE
bad	badly	worse	the worst
far	far	farther/further	the farthest/furthest
good	well	better	the best
little	little	less	the least
many/a lot of	—	more	the most
much*/a lot of	much*/a lot	more	the most

*Much is usually only used in questions and negative statements.

11   Participial Adjectives

-ed	-ing	-ed	-ing	-ed	-ing
alarmed	alarming	disturbed	disturbing	moved	moving
amazed	amazing	embarrassed	embarrassing	paralyzed	paralyzing
amused	amusing	entertained	entertaining	pleased	pleasing
annoyed	annoying	excited	exciting	relaxed	relaxing
astonished	astonishing	exhausted	exhausting	satisfied	satisfying
bored	boring	fascinated	fascinating	shocked	shocking
charmed	charming	frightened	frightening	surprised	surprising
confused	confusing	horrified	horrifying	terrified	terrifying
depressed	depressing	inspired	inspiring	tired	tiring
disappointed	disappointing	interested	interesting	touched	touching
disgusted	disgusting	irritated	irritating	troubled	troubling

12   Order of Adjectives Before a Noun

REMEMBER: We do not usually use more than three adjectives before a noun.

1. Order of Adjectives from Different Categories

Adjectives from different categories usually go in the following order. Do not use a comma between these adjectives.

OPINION	SIZE*	AGE	SHAPE	COLOR	ORIGIN	MATERIAL	NOUNS USED AS ADJECTIVES	
beautiful	enormous	antique	flat	blue	Asian	cotton	college	
comfortable	huge	modern	oval	gray	European	gold	flower	
cozy	little	new	rectangular	green	Greek	plastic	kitchen	+ NOUN
easy	tall	old	round	purple	Pacific	stone	mountain	
expensive	tiny	young	square	red	Southern	wooden	vacation	

*EXCEPTION: Big and small usually go first in a series of adjectives: a **small** comfortable apartment

EXAMPLES: I bought an **antique Greek flower** vase.   NOT: a ~~Greek antique~~ flower vase
She took some **easy college** courses.   NOT: some ~~college easy~~ courses
We sat at an **enormous round wooden** table.   NOT: a ~~wooden enormous round~~ table

2. Order of Adjectives from the Same Category

Adjectives from the same category do not follow a specific order. Use a comma between these adjectives.

EXAMPLES: We rented a **beautiful, comfortable, cozy** apartment. OR
We rented a **cozy, comfortable, beautiful** apartment. OR
We rented a **comfortable, cozy, beautiful** apartment.

13 Verbs Followed by Gerunds (Base Form of Verb + -ing)

acknowledge	can't help	discuss	feel like	limit	prevent	resent
admit	celebrate	dislike	finish	mention	prohibit	resist
advise	consider	endure	forgive	mind (object to)	put off	risk
allow	delay	enjoy	go	miss	quit	suggest
appreciate	deny	escape	imagine	permit	recall	support
avoid	detest	excuse	justify	postpone	recommend	tolerate
ban	discontinue	explain	keep (continue)	practice	report	understand

14 Verbs Followed by Infinitives (To + Base Form of Verb)

agree	can('t) afford	deserve	hurry	neglect	promise	threaten
aim	can't wait	expect	intend	offer	refuse	volunteer
appear	claim	fail	learn	pay	request	wait
arrange	choose	help	manage	plan	rush	want
ask	consent	hesitate	mean (intend)	prepare	seem	wish
attempt	decide	hope	need	pretend	struggle	would like

15 Verbs Followed by Gerunds or Infinitives

begin	continue	like	remember*	stop*
can't stand	forget*	love	regret*	try
	hate	prefer	start	

*These verbs can be followed by either a gerund or an infinitive, but there is a big difference in meaning *(see Unit 32)*.

16 Verbs Followed by Object + Infinitive

advise	convince	get	need*	persuade	require	want*
allow	encourage	help*	order	prefer*	teach	warn
ask*	expect*	hire	pay*	promise*	tell	wish
cause	forbid	invite	permit	remind	urge	would like*
choose*	force			request		

*These verbs can also be followed by an infinitive without an object (example: *ask to leave* or *ask someone to leave*).

17 Adjective + Preposition Combinations

accustomed to	bad at	curious about	good at	responsible for	sorry for/about
afraid of	bored with/by	different from	happy about	sad about	surprised at/
amazed at/by	capable of	disappointed with	interested in	safe from	about/by
angry at	careful of	excited about	nervous about	satisfied with	terrible at
ashamed of	certain about	famous for	opposed to	shocked at/by	tired of
aware of	concerned about	fond of	pleased about	sick of	used to
awful at	content with	glad about	ready for	slow at/in	worried about

18 Verb + Preposition Combinations

admit to	believe in	deal with	look forward to	rely on	thank someone for
advise against	choose between	dream about/of	object to	resort to	think about
apologize for	complain about	feel like	pay for	succeed in	wonder about
approve of	count on	insist on	plan on	talk about	worry about

19 Modals and Their Functions

FUNCTION	MODAL OR EXPRESSION	TIME	EXAMPLES
Ability	can can't	Present	• Sam **can swim**. • He **can't skate**.
	could couldn't	Past	• We **could swim** last year. • We **couldn't skate**.
	be able to* not be able to*	All verb forms	• Lea **is able to run** fast. • She **wasn't able to run** fast last year.
Permission	can can't could may may not	Present or future	• **Can** I **sit** here? • **Can** I **call** tomorrow? • Yes, you **can**. • No, you **can't**. Sorry. • **Could** he **leave** now? • **May** I **borrow** your pen? • Yes, you **may**. • No, you **may not**. Sorry.
Requests	can can't could will would	Present or future	• **Can** you **close** the door, please? • Sure, I **can**. • Sorry, I **can't**. • **Could** you please **answer** the phone? • **Will** you **wash** the dishes, please? • **Would** you please **mail** this letter?
Advice	should shouldn't ought to had better** had better not**	Present or future	• You **should study** more. • You **shouldn't miss** class. • We **ought to leave**. • We'd **better go**. • We'd **better not stay**.
Necessity	have to* not have to*	All verb forms	• He **has to go** now. • I **had to go** yesterday. • I **will have to go** soon. • He **doesn't have to go** yet.
	have got to* must	Present or future	• He's **got to leave**! • You **must use** a pen for the test.
Prohibition	must not can't	Present or future	• You **must not drive** without a license. • You **can't drive** without a license.

*The meaning of this expression is similar to the meaning of a modal. Unlike a modal, it has -s for third-person singular.
**The meaning of this expression is similar to the meaning of a modal. Like a modal, it has no -s for third-person singular.

FUNCTION	MODAL OR EXPRESSION	TIME	EXAMPLES
Possibility	must must not have to*	Present	• This **must be** her house. Her name is on the door. • She **must not be** home. I don't see her car. • She **had to know** him. They went to school together.
	have got to* may may not might might not could	Present or future	• He**'s got to be** guilty. We saw him do it. • She **may be** home now. • It **may not rain** tomorrow. • Lee **might be sick** today. • He **might not come** to class. • They **could be** at the library. • It **could rain** tomorrow.
Impossibility	can't	Present or future	• That **can't be** Ana. She left for France yesterday. • It **can't snow** tomorrow. It's going to be too warm.
	couldn't	Present	• He **couldn't be** guilty. He was away . . .

*The meaning of this expression is similar to the meaning of a modal. Unlike a modal, it has *-s* for third-person singular.

20   Spelling Rules for the Simple Present: Third-Person Singular (*He, She, It*)

1. Add *-s* for most verbs.

work	work**s**
buy	buy**s**
ride	ride**s**
return	return**s**

2. Add *-es* for verbs that end in *-ch, -s, -sh, -x,* or *-z.*

watch	watch**es**
pass	pass**es**
rush	rush**es**
relax	relax**es**
buzz	buzz**es**

3. Change the *y* to *i* and add *-es* when the base form ends in **consonant** + *y.*

study	stud**ies**
hurry	hurr**ies**
dry	dr**ies**

Do not change the *y* when the base form ends in **vowel** + *y.* Add *-s.*

play	play**s**
enjoy	enjoy**s**

4. A few verbs have **irregular forms**.

be	**is**
do	**does**
go	**goes**
have	**has**

21 Spelling Rules for Base Form of Verb + *-ing* (Progressive and Gerund)

1. Add *-ing* to the base form of the verb.

read	read**ing**
stand	stand**ing**

2. If the verb ends in a **silent -e**, drop the final *-e* and add *-ing*.

leave	leav**ing**
take	tak**ing**

3. In **one-syllable** verbs, if the last three letters are a consonant-vowel-consonant combination (CVC), double the last consonant and add *-ing*.

C V C
↓ ↓ ↓
s i t   sit**ting**

C V C
↓ ↓ ↓
p l a n   plan**ning**

Do not double the last consonant in verbs that end in *-w, -x,* or *-y.*

sew	sew**ing**
fix	fix**ing**
play	play**ing**

4. In verbs of **two or more syllables** that end in a consonant-vowel-consonant combination, double the last consonant only if the last syllable is stressed.

admít	admit**ting**	*(The last syllable is stressed.)*
whísper	whisper**ing**	*(The last syllable is not stressed, so don't double the -r.)*

5. If the verb ends in *-ie*, change the *ie* to *y* before adding *-ing*.

die	d**ying**
lie	l**ying**

> **STRESS**
> ´ shows main stress.

22 Spelling Rules for Base Form of Verb + *-ed* (Simple Past and Past Participle of Regular Verbs)

1. If the verb ends in a **consonant**, add *-ed*.

return	return**ed**
help	help**ed**

2. If the verb ends in *-e*, add *-d*.

live	live**d**
create	create**d**
die	die**d**

3. In **one-syllable** verbs, if the last three letters are a consonant-vowel-consonant combination (CVC), double the last consonant and add *-ed*.

C V C
↓ ↓ ↓
h o p   hop**ped**

C V C
↓ ↓ ↓
g r a b   grab**bed**

Do not double the last consonant in verbs that end in *-w, -x,* or *-y.*

bow	bow**ed**
mix	mix**ed**
play	play**ed**

4. In verbs of **two or more syllables** that end in a consonant-vowel-consonant combination, double the last consonant only if the last syllable is stressed.

prefér	prefer**red**	*(The last syllable is stressed.)*
vísit	visit**ed**	*(The last syllable is not stressed, so don't double the -t.)*

5. If the verb ends in **consonant + y**, change the *y* to *i* and add *-ed*.

worry	worr**ied**
carry	carr**ied**

6. If the verb ends in **vowel + y**, add *-ed*. (Do not change the *y* to *i*.)

play	play**ed**
annoy	annoy**ed**

EXCEPTIONS:

lay	la**id**
pay	pa**id**
say	sa**id**

23 Spelling Rules for the Comparative *(-er)* and Superlative *(-est)* of Adjectives

1. With **one-syllable** adjectives, add *-er* to form the comparative. Add *-est* to form the superlative.

cheap	cheap**er**	cheap**est**
bright	bright**er**	bright**est**

2. If the adjective ends in *-e*, add *-r* or *-st*.

nice	nic**er**	nic**est**

3. If the adjective ends in **consonant** + *y*, change *y* to *i* before you add *-er* or *-est*.

pretty	pret**tier**	pret**tiest**

   Exception:

shy	shy**er**	shy**est**

4. If a one-syllable adjective ends in a consonant-vowel-consonant combination (CVC), double the last consonant before adding *-er* or *-est*.

   C V C
   ↓ ↓ ↓

b i g	big**ger**	big**gest**

   Do not double the consonant in adjectives ending in *-w* or *-y*.

slow	slow**er**	slow**est**
gray	gray**er**	gray**est**

24 Spelling Rules for Adverbs Ending in *-ly*

1. Add *-ly* to the corresponding adjective.

nice	nice**ly**
quiet	quiet**ly**
beautiful	beautiful**ly**

2. If the adjective ends in **consonant** + *y*, change the *y* to *i* before adding *-ly*.

easy	eas**ily**

3. If the adjective ends in *-le*, drop the *e* and add *-y*.

possible	possib**ly**

   Do not drop the *e* for other adjectives ending in *-e*.

extreme	extreme**ly**

   Exception:

true	tru**ly**

4. If the adjective ends in *-ic*, add *-ally*.

basic	basic**ally**
fantastic	fantastic**ally**

25 Spelling Rules for Regular Plural Nouns

1. Add *-s* to most nouns.

book	book**s**
table	table**s**
cup	cup**s**

2. Add *-es* to nouns that end in *-ch*, *-s*, *-sh*, or *-x*.

watch	watch**es**
bus	bus**es**
dish	dish**es**
box	box**es**

3. Add *-s* to nouns that end in **vowel** + *y*.

day	day**s**
key	key**s**

4. Change the *y* to *i* and add *-es* to nouns that end in **consonant** + *y*.

baby	bab**ies**
city	cit**ies**
strawberry	strawberr**ies**

5. Add *-s* to nouns that end in **vowel** + *o*.

radio	radio**s**
video	video**s**
zoo	zoo**s**

6. Add *-es* to nouns that end in **consonant** + *o*.

potato	potato**es**
tomato	tomato**es**

   Exceptions: kilo—kilos, photo—photos, piano—pianos

26 Contractions with Verb Forms

1. SIMPLE PRESENT, PRESENT PROGRESSIVE, AND IMPERATIVE

Contractions with *Be*

I am	=	I'm
you are	=	you're
he is	=	he's
she is	=	she's
it is	=	it's
we are	=	we're
you are	=	you're
they are	=	they're

SIMPLE PRESENT	PRESENT PROGRESSIVE
I'm a student.	I'm studying here.
He's my teacher.	He's teaching verbs.
We're from Canada.	We're living here.

I am not	=	I'm not		
you are not	=	you're not	OR	you aren't
he is not	=	he's not	OR	he isn't
she is not	=	she's not	OR	she isn't
it is not	=	it's not	OR	it isn't
we are not	=	we're not	OR	we aren't
you are not	=	you're not	OR	you aren't
they are not	=	they're not	OR	they aren't

SIMPLE PRESENT	PRESENT PROGRESSIVE
She's not sick.	She's not reading.
He isn't late.	He isn't coming.
We aren't twins.	We aren't leaving.
They're not here.	They're not playing.

Contractions with *Do*

do not	=	don't
does not	=	doesn't

SIMPLE PRESENT	IMPERATIVE
They don't live here.	Don't run!
It doesn't snow much.	

2. SIMPLE PAST AND PAST PROGRESSIVE

Contractions with *Be*

was not	=	wasn't
were not	=	weren't

Contractions with *Do*

did not	=	didn't

SIMPLE PAST	PAST PROGRESSIVE
He wasn't a poet.	He wasn't singing.
They weren't twins.	They weren't sleeping.
We didn't see her.	

3. FUTURE

Contractions with *Will*

I will	=	I'll
you will	=	you'll
he will	=	he'll
she will	=	she'll
it will	=	it'll
we will	=	we'll
you will	=	you'll
they will	=	they'll

will not	=	won't

FUTURE WITH *WILL*
I'll take the train.
It'll be faster that way.
We'll go together.
He won't come with us.
They won't miss the train.

Contractions with *Be going to*

I am going to	=	I'm going to
you are going to	=	you're going to
he is going to	=	he's going to
she is going to	=	she's going to
it is going to	=	it's going to
we are going to	=	we're going to
you are going to	=	you're going to
they are going to	=	they're going to

FUTURE WITH *BE GOING TO*
I'm going to buy tickets tomorrow.
She's going to call you.
It's going to rain soon.
We're going to drive to Boston.
They're going to crash!

4. Present Perfect and Present Perfect Progressive

Contractions with *Have*

I have	=	I**'ve**
you have	=	you**'ve**
he has	=	he**'s**
she has	=	she**'s**
it has	=	it**'s**
we have	=	we**'ve**
you have	=	you**'ve**
they have	=	they**'ve**
have not	=	**haven't**
has not	=	**hasn't**

You**'ve** already **read** that page.
We**'ve been writing** for an hour.
She**'s been** to Africa three times.
It**'s been raining** since yesterday.
We **haven't seen** any elephants yet.
They **haven't been living** here long.

5. Modals and Similar Expressions

cannot or can not	=	**can't**
could not	=	**couldn't**
should not	=	**shouldn't**
had better	=	**'d better**
would prefer	=	**'d prefer**
would rather	=	**'d rather**

She **can't dance**.
We **shouldn't go**.
They**'d better decide**.
I**'d prefer** coffee.
I**'d rather take** the bus.

27 Capitalization and Punctuation Rules

	USE FOR . . .	EXAMPLES
capital letter	• the pronoun *I* • proper nouns • the first word of a sentence	• Tomorrow **I** will be here at 2:00. • His name is **Karl**. He lives in **Germany**. • **When** does the train leave? **At** 2:00.
apostrophe (')	• possessive nouns • contractions	• Is that **Marta's** coat? • **That's** not hers. **It's** mine.
comma (,)	• after items in a list • before sentence connectors *and*, *but*, *or*, and *so* • after the first part of a sentence that begins with *because* • after the first part of a sentence that begins with a preposition • after the first part of a sentence that begins with a time clause or an *if* clause	• He bought **apples, pears, oranges,** and **bananas**. • They watched TV, **and** she played video games. • *Because* **it's raining,** we're not walking to the office. • *Across from* **the post office,** there's a good restaurant. • *After* **he arrived,** we ate dinner. • *If* **it rains,** we won't go.
exclamation mark (!)	• at the end of a sentence to show surprise or a strong feeling	• You're here! That's great! • Stop! A car is coming!
period (.)	• at the end of a statement	• Today is Wednesday.
question mark (?)	• at the end of a question	• What day is today**?**

28 Pronunciation Table

These are the pronunciation symbols used in this text. Listen to the pronunciation of the key words.

VOWELS

Symbol	Key Word	Symbol	Key Word
i	beat, feed	ə	banana, among
ɪ	bit, did	ɚ	shirt, murder
eɪ	date, paid	aɪ	bite, cry, buy, eye
ɛ	bet, bed	aʊ	about, how
æ	bat, bad	ɔɪ	voice, boy
ɑ	box, odd, father	ɪr	beer
ɔ	bought, dog	ɛr	bare
oʊ	boat, road	ɑr	bar
ʊ	book, good	ɔr	door
u	boot, food, student	ʊr	tour
ʌ	but, mud, mother		

CONSONANTS

Symbol	Key Word	Symbol	Key Word
p	pack, happy	ʃ	ship, machine, station, special, discussion
b	back, rubber		
t	tie	ʒ	measure, vision
d	die	h	hot, who
k	came, key, quick	m	men
g	game, guest	n	sun, know, pneumonia
tʃ	church, nature, watch	ŋ	sung, ringing
dʒ	judge, general, major	w	wet, white
f	fan, photograph	l	light, long
v	van	r	right, wrong
θ	thing, breath	y	yes, use, music
ð	then, breathe	t̬	butter, bottle
s	sip, city, psychology		
z	zip, please, goes		

29 Pronunciation Rules for the Simple Present: Third-Person Singular (He, She, It)

1. The third-person singular in the simple present always ends in the letter -s. There are, however, three different pronunciations for the final sound of the third-person singular.

/s/	/z/	/ɪz/
talks	loves	dances

2. The final sound is pronounced /s/ after the voiceless sounds /p/, /t/, /k/, and /f/.

top	tops
get	gets
take	takes
laugh	laughs

3. The final sound is pronounced /z/ after the voiced sounds /b/, /d/, /g/, /v/, /m/, /n/, /ŋ/, /l/, /r/, and /ð/.

describe	describes
spend	spends
hug	hugs
live	lives
seem	seems
remain	remains
sing	sings
tell	tells
lower	lowers
bathe	bathes

4. The final sound is pronounced /z/ after all **vowel sounds**.

agree	agrees
try	tries
stay	stays
know	knows

5. The final sound is pronounced /ɪz/ after the sounds /s/, /z/, /ʃ/, /ʒ/, /tʃ/, and /dʒ/. /ɪz/ adds a syllable to the verb.

miss	misses
freeze	freezes
rush	rushes
massage	massages
watch	watches
judge	judges

6. Do and say have a change in vowel sound.

do	/du/	does	/dʌz/
say	/seɪ/	says	/sɛz/

30 Pronunciation Rules for the Simple Past and Past Participle of Regular Verbs

1. The regular simple past and past participle always end in the letter -d. There are three different pronunciations for the final sound of the regular simple past and past participle.

/t/	/d/	/ɪd/
raced	lived	attended

2. The final sound is pronounced /t/ after the voiceless sounds /p/, /k/, /f/, /s/, /ʃ/, and /tʃ/.

hop	hopped
work	worked
laugh	laughed
address	addressed
publish	published
watch	watched

3. The final sound is pronounced /d/ after the voiced sounds /b/, /g/, /v/, /z/, /ʒ/, /dʒ/, /m/, /n/, /ŋ/, /l/, /r/, and /ð/.

rub	rubbed
hug	hugged
live	lived
surprise	surprised
massage	massaged
change	changed
rhyme	rhymed
return	returned
bang	banged
enroll	enrolled
appear	appeared
bathe	bathed

4. The final sound is pronounced /d/ after all **vowel sounds**.

agree	agreed
die	died
play	played
enjoy	enjoyed
snow	snowed

5. The final sound is pronounced /ɪd/ after /t/ and /d/. /ɪd/ adds a syllable to the verb.

start	started
decide	decided

GLOSSARY OF GRAMMAR TERMS

action verb   A verb that describes an action.
- *Alicia **ran** home.*

adjective   A word that describes a noun or pronoun.
- *That's a **great** idea.*
- *It's **wonderful**.*

adverb   A word that describes a verb, an adjective, or another adverb.
- *She drives **carefully**.*
- *She's a **very** good driver.*
- *She drives **really** well.*

adverb of frequency   An adverb that describes how often something happens.
- *We **always** watch that program.*

adverb of manner   An adverb that describes how someone does something or how something happens. It usually ends in *-ly*.
- *He sings **beautifully**.*

adverb of time   An adverb that describes when something happens.
- *We'll see you **soon**.*

affirmative   A statement or answer meaning *Yes*.
- *He **works**. (affirmative statement)*
- ***Yes**, he **does**. (affirmative short answer)*

article   A word that goes before a noun. The indefinite articles are *a* and *an*.
- *I ate **a** sandwich and **an** apple.*

The definite article is *the*.
- *I didn't like **the** sandwich. **The** apple was good.*

auxiliary verb   (also called **helping verb**) A verb used with a main verb. *Be*, *do*, and *have* are often auxiliary verbs. Modals (*can*, *should*, *may* . . .) are also auxiliary verbs.
- *I **am** exercising right now.*
- ***Does** he exercise every day?*
- *She **should** exercise every day.*
- *They**'ve** learned how to swim.*
- *They **can** swim very well.*
- *We **may** go to the pool tomorrow.*

base form   The simple form of a verb without any endings (*-s*, *-ed*, *-ing*) or other changes.
- ***be**, **have**, **go**, **drive***

capital letter   The large form of a letter. The capital letters are: *A, B, C, D, . . .*
- ***A**licia lives in the **U**nited **S**tates.*

clause   A group of words that has a subject and a verb. A sentence can have one or more clauses.
- ***We are leaving now.** (one clause)*
- ***When he calls, we'll leave.** (two clauses)*

common noun   A word for a person, place, or thing (but not the name of the person, place, or thing).
- *Teresa lives in a **house** near the **beach**.*

comparative   The form of an adjective or adverb that shows the difference between two people, places, or things.
- *Alain is **shorter** than Brendan. (adjective)*
- *Brendan runs **faster** than Alain. (adverb)*

comparison   A statement that shows the difference between two people, places, or things. A comparison can use comparative adjectives and comparative adverbs. It can also use *as . . . as*.
- *Alain is **shorter than** Brendan.*
- *Alain isn't **as tall as** Brendan.*
- *He runs **faster than** Brendan.*

consonant   A letter of the alphabet. The consonants are:
- ***b, c, d, f, g, h, j, k, l, m, n, p, q, r, s, t, v, w, x, y, z***

continuous   See **progressive**.

contraction   A short form of a word or words. An apostrophe (') replaces the missing letter or letters.
- ***she's** = she is*
- ***hasn't** = has not*
- ***can't** = cannot*
- ***won't** = will not*

count noun   A noun that you can count. It has a singular and a plural form.
- *one **book**, two **books***

definite article   *the*
This article goes before a noun that refers to a specific person, place, or thing.

* *Please bring me **the book** on the table. I'm almost finished reading it.*

dependent clause   (also called **subordinate clause**) A clause that needs a main clause for its meaning.

* ***When I get home**, I'll call you.*

direct object   A noun or pronoun that receives the action of a verb.

* *Marta kicked **the ball**. I saw **her**.*

formal   Language used in business situations or with adults you do not know.

* *Good afternoon, Mr. Rivera. Please have a seat.*

gerund   A noun formed with verb + -*ing*.
It can be the subject or object of a sentence.

* ***Swimming** is great exercise.*
* *I enjoy **swimming**.*

helping verb   See **auxiliary verb**.

imperative   A sentence that gives a command or instructions.

* ***Hurry!***
* ***Don't touch that!***

indefinite article   *a* or *an*
These articles go before a noun that does not refer to a specific person, place, or thing.

* *Can you bring me **a book**? I'm looking for something to read.*

indefinite past   Past time, but not a specific time. It is often used with the present perfect.

* *I've already **seen** that movie.*

indefinite pronoun   A pronoun such as *someone, something, anyone, anything, anywhere, no one, nothing, nowhere, everyone,* and *everything.* An indefinite pronoun does not refer to a specific person, place, or thing.

* ***Someone** called you last night.*
* *Did **anything** happen?*

indirect object   A noun or pronoun (often a person) that receives something as the result of the action of the verb.

* *I told **John** the story.*
* *He gave **me** some good advice.*

infinitive   *to* + base form of the verb

* *I want **to leave** now.*

infinitive of purpose   (*in order*) *to* + base form
This form gives the reason for an action.

* *I go to school **(in order) to learn** English.*

informal   Language used with family, friends, and children.

* *Hi, Pete. Sit down.*

information question   See **wh- question**.

inseparable phrasal verb   A phrasal verb whose parts must stay together.

* *We **ran into** Tomás at the supermarket.*

intransitive verb   A verb that does not have an object.

* *We **fell**.*

irregular   A word that does not change its form in the usual way.

* ***good → well***
* ***bad → worse***

irregular verb   A verb that does not form its past with -*ed*.

* ***leave → left***

main clause   A clause that can stand alone as a sentence.

* *When I get home, **I'll call you**.*

main verb   A verb that describes an action or state. It is often used with an auxiliary verb.

* *She **calls** every day.*
* *Jared is **calling**.*
* *He'll **call** again later.*
* *Does he **call** every day?*

modal   A type of auxiliary verb. It goes before a main verb or stands alone as a short answer. It expresses ideas such as ability, advice, obligation, permission, and possibility. *Can, could, will, would, may, might, should, ought to,* and *must* are modals.

* ***Can** you swim?*
* *Yes, I **can**.*
* *You really **should** learn to swim.*

negative   A statement or answer meaning *No*.

* *He **doesn't** work. (negative statement)*
* ***No**, he **doesn't**. (negative short answer)*

non-action verb (also called **stative verb**) A verb that does not describe an action. It describes such things as thoughts, feelings, and senses.
- I *remember* that word.
- Chris *loves* ice cream.
- It *tastes* great.

non-count noun A noun that you usually do not count (*air, water, rice, love, . . .*). It has only a singular form.
- The **rice** is delicious.

noun A word for a person, place, or thing.
- My **sister**, **Anne**, works in an **office**.
- She uses a **computer**.

object A noun or pronoun that receives the action of a verb. Sometimes a verb has two objects.
- She wrote **a letter to Tom**.
- She wrote **him a letter**.

object pronoun A pronoun (*me, you, him, her, it, us, them*) that receives the action of a verb.
- I gave **her** a book.
- I gave **it** to **her**.

paragraph A group of sentences, usually about one topic.

participial adjective An adjective that ends in *-ing* or *-ed*. It comes from a verb.
- That's an **interesting** book.
- She's **interested** in the book.

particle A word that looks like a preposition and combines with a main verb to form a phrasal verb. It often changes the meaning of the main verb.
- He looked the word **up**.
  (He looked for the meaning in the dictionary.)
- I ran **into** my teacher.
  (I met my teacher accidentally.)

past participle A verb form (verb + *-ed*). It can also be irregular. It is used to form the present perfect. It can also be an adjective.
- We've **lived** here since April.
- She's **interested** in math.

phrasal verb (also called **two-word verb**) A verb that has two parts (verb + particle). The meaning is often different from the meaning of its separate parts.
- He **grew up** in Texas. (became an adult)
- His parents **brought** him **up** to be honest. (raised)

phrase A group of words that forms a unit but does not have a main verb. Many phrases give information about time or place.
- **Last year**, we were living **in Canada**.

plural A form that means two or more.
- There **are** three **people** in the restaurant.
- **They are** eating dinner.
- **We** saw **them**.

possessive Nouns, pronouns, or adjectives that show a relationship or show that someone owns something.
- Zach is **Megan's** brother. (possessive noun)
- Is that car **his**? (possessive pronoun)
- That's **his** car. (possessive adjective)

predicate The part of a sentence that has the main verb. It tells what the subject is doing or describes the subject.
- My sister **works for a travel agency**.

preposition A word that goes before a noun or a pronoun to show time, place, or direction.
- I went **to** the bank **on** Monday. It's **next to** my office.
- I told him **about** it.

Prepositions also go before nouns, pronouns, and gerunds in expressions with verbs and adjectives.
- We rely **on** him.
- She's accustomed **to** getting up early.

progressive (also called **continuous**) The verb form *be* + verb + *-ing*. It focuses on the continuation (not the completion) of an action.
- She**'s reading** the paper.
- We **were watching** TV when you called.

pronoun A word used in place of a noun.
- That's my brother. You met **him** at my party.

proper noun A noun that is the name of a person, place, or thing. It begins with a capital letter.
- **Maria** goes to **Central High School**.
- It's on **High Street**.

punctuation Marks used in writing (period, comma, . . .). They make the meaning clear. For example, a period (**.**) shows the end of a sentence. It also shows that the sentence is a statement, not a question.

quantifier   A word or phrase that shows an amount (but not an exact amount). It often comes before a noun.

- Josh bought **a lot of** books last year, but he only read **a few**.
- He doesn't have **much** time.

question   See **yes/no question** and **wh- question**.

question word   See **wh- word**.

reciprocal pronoun   A pronoun (each other or one another) that shows that the subject and object of a sentence refer to the same people and that these people have a two-way relationship.

- Megan and Jason have known **each other** since high school.
- All the students worked with **one another** on the project.

reflexive pronoun   A pronoun (myself, yourself, himself, herself, itself, ourselves, yourselves, themselves) that shows that the subject and the object of the sentence refer to the same people or things.

- He looked at **himself** in the mirror.
- They enjoyed **themselves** at the party.

regular   A word that changes its form in the usual way.

- **play** —> play**ed**
- **fast** —> fast**er**
- **quick** —> quick**ly**

sentence   A group of words that has a subject and a main verb. It begins with a capital letter and ends with a period (**.**), question mark (**?**), or exclamation point (**!**).

- **Computers are** very useful.

EXCEPTION: In imperative sentences, the subject is you. We do not usually say or write the subject in imperative sentences.

- **Call** her now!

separable phrasal verb   A phrasal verb whose parts can separate.

- Tom **looked** the word **up** in a dictionary.
- He **looked** it **up**.

short answer   An answer to a yes/no question.

- **A:** Did you call me last night?
  B: No, I didn't. OR **No.**

singular   one

- They have **a sister**.
- **She** works in **a hospital**.

statement   A sentence that gives information. In writing, it ends in a period.

- Today is Monday.

stative verb   See **non-action verb**.

subject   The person, place, or thing that the sentence is about.

- **Ms. Chen** teaches English.
- **Her class** is interesting.

subject pronoun   A pronoun that shows the person or thing (I, you, he, she, it, we, they) that the sentence is about.

- **I** read a lot.
- **She** reads a lot too.

subordinate clause   See **dependent clause**.

superlative   The form of an adjective or adverb that is used to compare a person, place, or thing to a group of people, places, or things.

- Cindi is **the best** dancer in the group. (adjective)
- She dances **the most gracefully**. (adverb)

tense   The form of a verb that shows the time of the action.

- **simple present:** Fabio **talks** to his friend every day.
- **simple past:** Fabio **talked** to his teacher yesterday.

third-person singular   The pronouns he, she, and it or a singular noun. In the simple present, the third-person-singular verb ends in -s.

- **Tomás works** in an office. (Tomás = he)

time clause   A clause that begins with a time word such as when, before, after, while, or as soon as.

- I'll call you **when I get home**.

time expression   A phrase that describes when something happened or will happen.

- We saw Tomás **last week**.
- He'll graduate **next year**.

transitive verb   A verb that has an object.

- She **paints** beautiful pictures.

two-word verb   See **phrasal verb**.

verb A word that describes what the subject of the sentence does, thinks, feels, senses, or owns.

- They **run** two miles every day.
- I **agree** with you.
- She **loved** that movie.
- We **smell** smoke.
- He **has** a new camera.

vowel A letter of the alphabet. The vowels are:

- **a, e, i, o, u.**

wh- question (also called **information question**) A question that begins with a wh- word. You answer a wh- question with information.

- **A: Where** are you going?
  B: To the store.

wh- word (also called **question word**) A word such as *who, what, when, where, which, why, how,* and *how much.* It often begins a wh- question.

- **Who** is that?
- **What** did you see?
- **When** does the movie usually start?
- **How** long is it?

yes/no question A question that begins with a form of *be* or an auxiliary verb. You can answer a yes/no question with *yes* or *no.*

- **A: Are** you a student?
  B: Yes, I am. OR **No**, I'm not.
- **A: Do** you come here often?
  B: Yes, I do. OR **No**, I don't.

UNIT REVIEW ANSWER KEY

Note: In this answer key, where a short or contracted form is given, the full or long form is also correct (unless the purpose of the exercise is to practice the short or contracted forms).

UNIT 1

A
1. are you taking
2. don't
3. often speak
4. 's talking
5. Do

B
1. are . . . doing
2. 'm . . . playing
3. Do . . . want
4. don't eat
5. 'm feeling OR feel
6. looks
7. doesn't taste
8. are . . . shouting
9. Are
10. talk

C I live in Qatar, but right now I ~~stay~~ _'m staying_ in Wisconsin. I'm studying English here. I ~~have~~ _'m having_ a good time this summer, but in some ways it's a pretty strange experience. Summer in Wisconsin ~~feel~~ _feels_ like winter in Qatar! Every weekend, I go to the beach with some classmates, but I ~~go never~~ _never go_ into the water—it's too cold! I'm ~~enjoy~~ _enjoying_ my time here though, and my culture shock is going away fast.

UNIT 2

A
1. b
2. c
3. a
4. c
5. a
6. c

B
1. Did . . . go
2. called
3. didn't answer
4. Yes . . . did
5. went
6. did . . . see
7. saw
8. didn't like

C The poet Elizabeth Alexander was born in New York City, but she didn't ~~grew~~ _grow_ up there. Her father ~~taked~~ _took_ a job with the government, and her family moved to Washington, D.C. As a child, she ~~have~~ _had_ a loving family. Her parents were active in the civil rights movement, and Elizabeth ~~gots~~ _got_ interested in African-American history. In her first book, she wrote about important African leaders. She met Barack Obama at the University of Chicago. They both ~~teached~~ _taught_ there in the 1990s. On January 20, 2009, she ~~reads~~ _read_ a poem at President Obama's inauguration.

UNIT 3

A
1. Did . . . hear
2. saw
3. turned
4. Were . . . driving OR Did . . . drive
5. was working
6. was raining
7. was finishing
8. was leaving OR left
9. stopped
10. looked

B
1. . . . Danielle was watching TV, I was studying.
2. I closed my book . . . the show _Dr. Davis_ came on.
3. Dr. Davis was talking to his patient when the electricity went off.
4. . . . the electricity went off, we lit some candles.
5. We were talking (OR We talked) about a lot of things . . . we were waiting for the lights to come on.

C When I turned on the TV for the first episode of _Dr. Davis,_ I ~~unpacked~~ _was unpacking_ boxes in my freshman dorm room. I stopped and watched for an hour. After that, I ~~wasn't missing~~ _didn't miss_ a single show while I was attending school. While I was solving math problems, Dr. Davis was solving medical mysteries. And _just_ ~~while~~ _when_ my dumb boyfriend broke up with me, the beautiful Dr. Grace left Davis for the third time. I even watched the show from the hospital when I ~~was breaking~~ _broke_ my leg. The show just ended. I was sad when I ~~see~~ _saw_ the last episode, but I think it's time for some real life!

UNIT 4

A
1. did
2. used to
3. Did
4. play
5. used to
6. used to

B
1. used to look
2. used to have
3. used to let OR would let
4. wouldn't get
5. used to play
6. used to practice OR would practice
7. Did . . . use to go
8. used to love

C Celine Dion was born in Quebec, Canada. When she ~~used to be~~ _was_ five, her family opened a club, and Celine used to ~~sang~~ _sing_ there. People from the community ~~would to come~~ _would come_ to hear her perform.

At the age of 12, Celine wrote her first songs. Her
family used to record [~~used to record~~ *recorded*] one and sent it to a manager.
At first Celine used to singing [~~singing~~ *sing*] only in French. After
she learned English, she became known in more
countries. As a child, Celine Dion would be [~~would be~~ *was*] poor, but
she had a dream—to be a singer. Today she is one
of the most successful singers in the history of pop
music.

UNIT 5

A 1. h   3. f   5. g   7. c
   2. d   4. a   6. e   8. b

B 1. work   4. did she leave   6. is her boss
   2. did she   5. start   7. does
   3. told

C A: What did you did [~~did~~ *do*] with my math book? I can't
   find it.

   B: Nothing. Where you saw [~~you saw~~ *did you see*] it last?

   A: In the living room. I was watching *Lost* on TV.
   What [~~What~~ *What's*] Zack's phone number?

   B: I'm not sure. Why you [~~Why you~~ *Why do you*] want to know?

   A: He took the class last year. I'll call him. Maybe
   he still has his book.

   B: Good idea. What time does he gets [~~gets~~ *get*] out of
   work?

UNIT 6

A 1. 're going   3. is going to   5. is giving
   2. 'll   4. 's going to

B 1. are . . . going to do OR are . . . doing
   2. 're going to feel OR you'll feel
   3. is going to arrive OR will arrive
   4. is going to get
   5. 'll see
   6. 's going to cry
   7. does . . . start OR will . . . start OR is . . . starting
   8. Is . . . going to call OR Will . . . call OR Is . . .
      calling
   9. won't forget OR isn't going to forget
   10. 'll speak

C 1. When will Ed gets [~~gets~~ *get*] home tomorrow?
   2. The movie starts at 7:30, so I think I go [~~go~~ *'ll go* OR *'m going to go*].
   3. Do you want to go with me, or are you study [~~study~~ *studying* OR *going to study*]
      tonight?
   4. What you are [~~you are~~ *are you*] going to do next weekend?
   5. I'm going be [^ *to*] home all day.

UNIT 7

A 1. graduate   4. Will   6. until
   2. finish   5. learning   7. Are you
   3. When

B 1. works OR 's working
   2. won't register OR isn't going to register
   3. 'll spend OR 's going to spend
   4. studies OR is studying
   5. won't look OR isn't going to look
   6. graduates
   7. 'll take OR 's going to take

C A: Are you going to call Phil when we'll finish [~~we'll~~ *we*] finish
   dinner?

   B: No, I'm too tired. I'm just going to watch TV
   after [~~after~~ *before*] I go to sleep.

   A: Before I wash the dishes, I'm going answer [^ *to*]
   some emails.

   B: I'll help you, as soon as I'll drink [~~I'll drink~~ *I drink*] my coffee.

   A: No rush. I have a lot of emails. I won't be ready
   to clean up until you'll finish [~~you'll~~ *you*] finish.

UNIT 8

A 1. for   4. for   6. For
   2. since   5. Since   7. Since
   3. for

B 1. 've been   4. 've competed
   2. haven't had   5. 's won
   3. has loved   6. haven't seen

C 1. Marta and Tomás lived [~~lived~~ *have lived*] here since they got
      married in 1998.
   2. Tomás has been a professional tennis player
      since he has come [~~has come~~ *came*] to this country.
   3. He has won several competitions for [~~for~~ *since*] then.
   4. Since I have known Tomás, he had [~~had~~ *has had*] three
      different coaches.
   5. I haven't see [~~see~~ *seen*] Marta for several weeks.
   6. She have [~~have~~ *has*] been in Brazil since April 1.
   7. I've wanted to visit Brazil since [~~since~~ *for*] years, but I
      haven't had any vacation time since I got this
      new job.

A 1. already   3. yet   5. told
    2. still   4. Has   6. yet

B 1. has already graduated OR has graduated already

    2. still haven't had

    3. Have . . . delivered . . . yet

    4. still hasn't set

    5. 's already started OR 's started already

    6. still haven't arrived

    7. has arrived yet

    8. have . . . met . . . yet

C A: I can't believe it's the 10th already. And we still *haven't* ~~didn't~~ finished planning.

    B: We haven't checked the guest list for a while. Who hasn't ~~replies~~ *replied* yet?

    A: Sally hasn't called about the invitation ~~already~~ *yet*. I wonder if she's coming.

    B: Maybe she just forgot. Have you called ~~yet her~~ *her yet*?

    A: I've already ~~call~~ *called* her a couple of times. She ~~hasn't still~~ *still hasn't* called back.

A 1. ever   3. been   5. lately
    2. just   4. Has   6. has

B 1. Have . . . seen   5. 've . . . wanted
    2. 've . . . been   6. has taken
    3. has . . . read   7. 's . . . shown
    4. 's given

C 1. I've ~~lately~~ traveled a lot. *lately*

    2. We've ~~returned just~~ *just returned* ^ from an African safari.

    3. I've never ~~have~~ *had* so much fun before.

    4. Have you ~~been ever~~ *ever been* on a safari?

    5. No, but I've recently ~~went~~ *been* OR *gone* hot-air ballooning.

    6. My wife and I ~~has~~ *have* decided to go next summer.

    7. I've ~~saw~~ *seen* a lot of great photos on a hot-air ballooning website.

A 1. When did you move to Vancouver?

    2. How long have you been an engineer?

    3. Did you work in Vancouver for a long time?

    4. When did you get married?

    5. How many years have you lived in Singapore?

    6. Has your wife lived in Singapore long?

B 1. 've been   6. was
    2. saw   7. has learned
    3. 've crossed   8. ordered
    4. haven't seen   9. didn't learn
    5. took

C Tina and Ken lived apart for a while, but then Tina found a job in Singapore. She ~~has moved~~ *moved* there last month. Here are some of their thoughts:

KEN: I'm so glad Tina is finally here. Last year ~~has been~~ *was* the hardest time of my life.

TINA: Before I got here, I didn't ~~understood~~ *understand* Ken's experiences. But I ~~was~~ *'ve been* in culture shock since I ~~arrive~~ *arrived*, and I'm learning a new job too! Now I know what a rough time Ken had at first.

A 1. has written   4. has read
    2. has chosen   5. 've had
    3. 've been reading   6. 've taken

B 1. have . . . lived (OR been living)

    2. 've been

    3. 've been enjoying

    4. Have . . . read

    5. has . . . written

    6. 've been trying

    7. 've been studying

    8. has . . . been

    9. Has . . . chosen

C 1. Janet ~~hasn't been writing~~ *hasn't written* a word since she sat down at her computer.

    2. Since I've known Dan, he's ~~been having~~ *'s had* five different jobs.

    3. I've ~~drunk~~ *been drinking* coffee all morning. I think I've ~~been having~~ *had* at least 10 cups!

    4. We've been ~~lived~~ *living* here for several years, but we're moving next month.

UNIT 13

A **1.** a **2.** c **3.** b **4.** c **5.** b

B **1.** couldn't stay
2. could kick
3. couldn't keep
4. was able to win
5. can . . . dance
6. can jump
7. can stay
8. can't perform
9. can start
10. can raise

C **A:** I can't ~~to~~ see the stage. The man in front of me is very tall.

B: Let's change seats. You 'll be able to see from this seat.

A: Thanks. I don't want to miss anything. I *can't* ~~no can~~ believe what a great dancer Acosta is.

B: I know. He was so good as a kid that he *was able to* ~~could~~ win a breakdancing contest before he was nine.

A: I didn't know he was a street dancer! Well, I'm glad you were *able* ~~abled~~ to get tickets.

UNIT 14

A **1.** come **3.** borrow **5.** please shut
2. Do **4.** if

B **1.** I borrow a pen
2. my sister leave
3. if I open a window
4. my friend and I (OR me and a friend OR we) come early
5. I ask a question

C **1. A:** Do you mind if I *change* ~~changed~~ the date of our next meeting?
Not at all. OR *No, I don't.* OR *No problem.*
B: ~~Yes, I do.~~ When would you like to meet?

2. A: Could I *call* ~~calling~~ you tonight?
B: Sorry, but you *can't* ~~couldn't~~. I won't be home.

3. A: Mom, *may I* ~~I may~~ have some more ice cream?
B: No you *may not* ~~mayn't~~. You've already had a lot. You'll get sick.

4. A: Do you mind if my son *turns* ~~turn~~ on the TV?
Sorry, (but)
B: ~~Not at all.~~ I can't study with the TV on.

5. A: Can my sister *borrow* ~~borrows~~ your bike?
B: Could I *let* ~~letting~~ you know tomorrow?
A: Sure. No problem.

UNIT 15

A **1.** turning off
2. I'm sorry, I can't
3. please text
4. No problem
5. pick
6. I'd be glad to

B **1.** lending me five dollars
2. you drive me to school
3. you (please) explain this sentence to me (please)
4. you carry this suitcase for me
5. you (please) distribute the report (please)
6. walking the dog tonight

C

JASON: Hi Tessa. It's Jason. Could you *take* ~~taking~~ some photos of the game today?

TESSA: Sorry, Jason, but I *can't* ~~couldn't~~. My camera is broken. Maybe Jeri can help.

JASON: Hi Jeri. Would you *come* ~~came~~ to the game today? I need someone to take photos.

JERI: Jason, *would* ~~can~~ you mind calling me back in a few minutes? I'm busy right now.

JASON: Sorry, Jeri, I can't, but I'll email you. Would you *please give me* ~~give me please~~ your email address?
Sure OR *No problem* OR *Of course* OR *Certainly*
JERI: ~~Not at all.~~ It's Rainbows@local.net.

JERI: Hi Jason, it's Jeri. I'm sending you those photos. *Could you* ~~You could~~ call me when you get them?

JASON: Thanks, Jeri. The photos are great. Now will *you* teach me how to put them on Facebook?

UNIT 16

A **1.** a **2.** c **3.** a **4.** b **5.** a

B **1.** Should . . . call
2. 'd better do
3. should . . . contact
4. ought to call
5. Should . . . ask
6. Yes . . . should
7. Should . . . do
8. No . . . shouldn't
9. 'd better wait

C **1.** Vanessa should *get* ~~gets~~ a new computer. She should *not* ~~no~~ keep her old one.

2. She'd better not *buy* ~~buying~~ the first one she sees.

3. She ought *to* read reviews before she decides on one.

4. *Should* ~~Ought~~ she get one online or should she *go* ~~goes~~ to a store?

UNIT 17

A 1. a   2. b   3. c   4. c   5. a

B 1. Music is   4. Clothing shows
   2. photographs show   5. Food goes
   3. Money makes

C One night in ~~june~~ *June* 1,400 ~~Years~~ *years* ago, a volcano erupted in today's El Salvador and buried a village of the great Mayan civilization. Archeologists have already found many large ~~building~~ *buildings* from this time, but only a ~~little~~ *few* homes of farmers and workers. The village of El Ceren contains perfect examples of ~~a great deal of~~ *many* OR *a lot of* everyday objects. The archeologists have found some knives (with ~~foods~~ *food* still on them), ~~much~~ *many* OR *a lot of* pots made of ~~clays~~ *clay*, a lot *of* garden tools, a little fabric, and a book. On the wall of one room, they found a few ~~word~~ *words* in an unknown language. There is still a lot to learn from this time capsule, called "the Pompeii of Latin America."

UNIT 18

A 1. a   3. Ø   5. Some   7. the
   2. a   4. an   6. Ø   8. the

B 1. the   2. the   3. a   4. a   5. an

C Yesterday I downloaded ~~the~~ *some* movies. We watched *a* comedy and ~~a~~ *an* Argentinian thriller. ~~A~~ *The* comedy was very funny. I really enjoyed it. The thriller wasn't that good. There wasn't enough action in it. Tonight I think I'd rather read ~~the~~ *a* book than watch a movie. I recently bought ~~the~~ *a* book of fables and a mystery. I think I'll read ~~a~~ *the* mystery before I go to bed.

UNIT 19

A 1. annoying   4. hard
   2. late   5. surprisingly
   3. perfect

B 1. interesting old house
   2. big cheerful yellow kitchen OR cheerful big yellow kitchen
   3. peaceful residential street
   4. nice young international students
   5. didn't seem friendly at all (OR at all friendly)
   6. cute little Greek restaurant
   7. really beautiful garden
   8. wonderful old round wooden table
   9. decide pretty quickly
   10. rent awfully fast

C The conditions in Parker Dorm ar~~shocked~~ *shocking*. The rooms are ~~terrible~~ *terribly* sm furniture is incredibly ugly. The l don't work ~~good~~ *well*, so your stuff dorm counselors are great—th friendly people—but they can't m ~~badly~~ *bad* conditions.

UNIT 20

A 1. as   4. less
   2. better   5. longer
   3. more   6. the more impatient

B 1. more expensive than   4. more convenient
   2. bigger   5. farther
   3. larger than

C Last night, I had dinner at the new Pasta Place on the corner of Main Street and Grove. This new Pasta Place is just as good ~~than~~ *as* the others, and it has just as many sauces to choose from. No one makes a ~~more good~~ *better* traditional tomato sauce *than* them. But there are much ~~interestinger~~ *more interesting* choices. Their mushroom cream sauce, for example, is as ~~better~~ *good* as I've ever had. Try the mushroom and tomato sauce for a healthier ~~than~~ meal. It's just as delicious. The new branch is already popular. The later it is, *the* longer the lines. My recommendation: Go early for a ~~more short~~ *shorter* wait. And go soon. This place will only get more ~~popular~~ and more popular!

UNIT 21

A 1. shortest   4. rainiest
   2. biggest   5. most expensive
   3. driest   6. cheapest

B 1. the coldest   5. the least fun
   2. the most fantastic   6. the best
   3. the most popular   7. the funniest
   4. the most crowded

C Small towns aren't *the* most dynamic places to visit, and that's just why we love to vacation on Tangier Island. This tiny island is probably the ~~less~~ *least* popular vacation spot in the United States. Almost no one comes here. But it's also one of the ~~most~~ safest places to visit. And you'll find some of the ~~goodest~~ *best* seafood and the *most* beautiful beaches here. It's one of the easiest ~~place~~ *places* to get around (there are no cars on the island). If you get bored, just hop on the ferry. You're only a few hours from Washington, D.C., and a few more

...rom New York and the ~~excitingest~~ *most exciting* nightlife

UNIT 22

A
1. well
2. doesn't run
3. more accurately
4. of
5. as well as
6. the more tired he gets
7. harder
8. better

B
1. well
2. faster
3. the most accurately
4. the hardest
5. the worst

C Last night's game was a very exciting one. The Globes played the best they've played all season. But

they still didn't play as ~~good~~ *well* as the Stars. The Stars

hit the ball more ~~frequent~~ *frequently* and ran ~~more fast~~ *faster* than the Globes, and their pitcher, Kevin Rodriguez, threw the ball more accurately. Their catcher, Scott Harris,

handled ~~better the ball~~ *the ball better* than the Globes' catcher.

The Globes are good, but they are ~~less good than~~ *not as good as*

the Stars. All in all, the Stars just keep playing ~~good~~ *better*

and better. And the better they play, the ~~hardest~~ *harder* it is for their fans to get tickets! These games sell out quicker than hotcakes, so go early if you want to get a chance to see the Stars.

UNIT 23

A
1. not liking
2. smoking
3. feeling
4. joining
5. swimming
6. not eating
7. improving

B
1. Laughing is
2. suggests OR suggested watching
3. Telling . . . helps OR will help
4. advises OR advised against drinking
5. enjoy taking
6. think about smoking

C
1. You look great. Buying these bikes ~~were~~ *was* a good idea.
2. I know. I'm happy about ~~lose~~ *losing* weight too.
   ~~Didn't~~ *Not* exercising was a bad idea.
3. It always is. Hey, I'm thinking of ~~rent~~ *renting* a movie.
   What do you suggest ~~to see~~ *seeing*?
4. I've been looking forward to ~~see~~ *seeing* *Grown Ups*. Have you seen it yet?
5. Not yet. Do you recommend it? You're so good
   at ~~choose~~ *choosing* movies.

UNIT 24

A
1. to get
2. to meet
3. to finish
4. to go
5. to play
6. to call

B
1. invited Mary to visit us
2. agreed to come
3. wants to make new friends
4. told her to come early
5. decided not to invite Tom
6. needs to finish his project

C
1. **A:** I want ^*to* invite you to my party.
   B: Thanks. I'd love ~~coming~~ *to come*.
2. **A:** I plan ~~to not~~ *not to* get there before 8:00.
   B: Remember ~~getting~~ *to get* the soda. Don't forget!
3. **A:** Sara asked ~~I~~ *me* to help her.
   B: I agreed ~~helping~~ *to help* her too.
4. **A:** I promised ^*to* pick up some ice cream.
   B: OK. But let's do it early. I prefer ~~don't~~ *not to* arrive late.

UNIT 25

A
1. get
2. in order not
3. to take
4. too
5. clearly enough

B
1. easy enough to figure out
2. too hard for me to use
3. too fast for me to understand
4. too far for us to walk
5. in order not to be late
6. early enough for us to walk
7. too heavy for us to cross
8. my phone to get directions
9. clearly enough for it to work
10. a taxi to save time

C Is 16 too young ~~for~~ *to* drive? It's really hard to

~~saying~~ *say*. Some kids are mature enough to drive at 16, but some aren't. I think most 16 year-olds are still

too immature ^*to* drive with friends in the car, though.

It's ~~for them easy~~ *easy for them* to forget to pay attention with a

lot of kids in the car. In order ~~preventing~~ *to prevent* accidents, some families have a "no friends" rule for the first year. I think that's a reasonable idea.

UNIT 26

A
1. starting
2. to finish
3. trying
4. to join
5. seeing
6. to call
7. Studying

B
1. doing
2. to take
3. working OR to work
4. sitting
5. taking
6. to get
7. studying

C It's difficult to study in a foreign country, so

students need ~~preparing~~ *to prepare* for the experience. Most people look forward to living abroad, but they

worry about ~~don't feel~~ *not feeling* at home. They're afraid of not understanding the culture, and they don't want

~~making~~ *to make* mistakes. It's impossible to avoid ~~to have~~ *having* some problems at the beginning. No one escapes from feeling some culture shock, and it's important

~~realizing~~ *to realize* this fact. But soon most people stop ~~to feel~~ *feeling* uncomfortable and start to feel more at home in the new culture.

UNIT 27

A
1. each other
2. himself
3. one another
4. herself
5. myself
6. ourselves
7. yourselves
8. itself

B
1. talk to each other
2. greet each other
3. help yourself
4. enjoying themselves
5. drove herself

C When I first met Nicole, I told myself, "I'm not

going to like working with ~~herself~~ *her*." I was really

wrong. Nicole has helped ~~myself~~ *me* out with so many

things. When she ~~oneself~~ *herself* didn't know something, she

always found out for me. That way, both of ~~ourselves~~ *us* learned something. After I learned the job better, we

helped ~~each other's~~ *each other* OR *one another* out. Now the job ~~themselves~~ *itself* isn't that challenging, but I'm really enjoying myself.
Everyone here likes ~~each another~~ *one another* OR *each other*. That makes it a great place to work. I feel lucky to be here.

UNIT 28

A
1. out
2. up
3. on
4. out
5. up
6. over

B
1. Joe gets up early.
2. He turns on the TV OR He turns the TV on.
3. He sits down with Ana.
4. They get along well.
5. They look over his schedule OR They look his schedule over.
6. They talk it over.
7. They put it away.
8. They put on their coats OR They put their coats on.

C As soon as Ina wakes up, she finds Abby's leash

and puts it ~~away~~ *on* her. Then the two of them set *out* for

their morning walk ~~out~~. They keep ~~up~~ *on* walking until they get to the park, where there are a lot of other dogs and their owners. Abby is a very friendly animal,

and she gets ~~well along~~ *along well* with other dogs. Ina loves dogs and always had one when she was growing

~~over~~ *up*. There is a saying that "A dog is a man's best friend," but Ina knows it's a woman's best friend too. "I enjoy playing with Abby," she says, "and just being

with her cheers ~~up me~~ *me up*." Abby obviously enjoys being with Ina too. The two have become really good friends and have improved each other's lives a lot.

UNIT 29

A
1. don't have to
2. Does
3. can't
4. 've got to
5. had
6. have

B
1. don't have to do
2. have to pick up
3. 've . . . had to stand
4. don't have to wait OR won't have to wait
5. can't smoke
6. has to move OR will have to move
7. can't sit
8. have to have OR 'll have to have
9. had to eat OR 'll have to eat

C
1. He can't ~~boards~~ *board* the plane yet.
2. Passengers ~~must not~~ *don't have to* stay in their seats when the seat belt light is off.
3. Passengers: Please note that you ~~gotta~~ *have to* OR *must* pay extra for luggage over 50 pounds.
4. You don't ~~have got to~~ *have to* show your passport right now, but please have it ready.
5. Paul ~~will has~~ *will have* OR *has* to unpack some of his stuff. His suitcase is much too heavy.

A **1.** a   **2.** b   **3.** c   **4.** a   **5.** c

B **1.** 're supposed to be

2. isn't supposed to start

3. are . . . supposed to sit

4. 're supposed to go

5. Was (OR Am) . . . supposed to wear

6. 're (OR were) supposed to wear

7. isn't (OR wasn't) supposed to rain

8. was (OR is) supposed to be

C **1.** Dahlia was ~~suppose~~ *supposed* to drive. She was ~~supposed not~~ *not supposed* to fly.

2. She ~~is~~ *was* going to wear her blue dress, but she changed her mind.

3. What are we supposed to ~~doing~~ *do* after the ceremony?

4. My parents ~~will~~ *were* supposed to fly home tomorrow, but they're staying another day.

5. It was ~~no~~ *not* supposed to be this cold, and it ~~didn't suppose~~ *wasn't supposed* to rain.

A **1.** Will   **5.** get

2. might   **6.** could

3. going to   **7.** Maybe

4. may

B **1.** Are . . . going to go

2. may OR might OR could

3. Is . . . going to be

4. may not OR might not

5. are . . . going to

6. may OR might OR could stay

7. may not OR might not open

8. may OR might OR could open

C Suddenly, weather forecasts all over the world are predicting terrible storms. Climatologist Jack Hall understands weather trends, and he thinks that a new ice age could ~~to~~ begin very quickly. His son Sam is in New York with his high school class. One student is sick and ~~mayn't~~ *may not* live without medicine. ~~May~~ *Will* those kids survive by themselves? They ~~maybe~~ *may* OR *might* not. Jack bundles up and starts walking to New York to save them. There ~~might could~~ *may* OR *might* OR *could* be a happy ending. Or the world could end. You'll have to watch to find out!

A **1.** must   **4.** can't

2. has got to   **5.** Could

3. could   **6.** could

B **1.** couldn't be   **5.** can't be

2. could be   **6.** Could . . . lead

3. could . . . want   **7.** might know

4. Could . . . be

C **1.** Jason has been coughing all morning. He might ~~having~~ *have* a cold.

2. Diana must not ~~likes~~ *like* fish. She left most of it on her plate.

3. ~~May~~ *Could* OR *Can* the package be from your parents?

4. That's impossible! It ~~might not~~ *couldn't* OR *can't* be true.

5. Is the bank still open? That's a good question. I don't know. It might ˄ *be*.

6. She ~~could~~ *couldn't* OR *can't* be a thief! I trust her completely!

7. It's got ˄ *to* be a joke. I don't believe it's serious.

CREDITS

PHOTO CREDITS:

Page 1 (left) Asian Art & Archaeology, Inc./Corbis, (middle) Image Asset Management Ltd./SuperStock, (right) ©1985/1987 Entertainment Rights PLC; Characters ©1985/1987 Mattel Inc. All rights reserved. She-Ra, Princess of Power, and other character names are trademarks of Mattel Inc. Used with permission; **p. 13** (left to right) Getty Images, Shutterstock.com, Shutterstock.com, Shutterstock.com; **p. 16** Asian Art & Archaeology, Inc./Corbis; **p. 22** Bettmann/Corbis; **p. 24** Iwona Biedermann Photography; **p. 28** Pictorial Press Ltd/Alamy; **p. 30** Pictorial Press Ltd/Alamy; **p. 31** Image Asset Management Ltd./SuperStock; **p. 45** (top left) ©1985/1987 Entertainment Rights PLC; Characters ©1985/1987 Mattel Inc. All rights reserved. She-Ra, Princess of Power, and other character names are trademarks of Mattel Inc. Used with permission, (top right) Stefano Bianchetti/Corbis, (bottom left) Jon Riley/Index Stock Imagery, (bottom right) Paul Chesley/Getty Images, (bottom) Shutterstock.com; **p. 49** (top) Pac-Man © Namco/Image created for Photri 2005, (middle) Dorling Kindersley; (bottom) Shutterstock.com; **p. 51** Shutterstock.com; **p. 52** (top) Lisa O'Connor/ZUMA/Corbis, (bottom) iStockphoto.com; **p. 62** Fotolia.com; **p. 63** Shutterstock.com; **p. 73** (left) AFP/Getty Images, (middle) Sergei Remezov/Reuters/Corbis, (right) Birgid Allig/Getty Images; **p. 74** AFP/Getty Images; **p. 75** Shutterstock.com; **p. 79** Sergei Remezov/Reuters/Corbis; **p. 91** Birgid Allig/Getty Images; **p. 107** (left) Al Fuchs/NewSport/Corbis, (middle) Alison Wright/Corbis, (right) Shutterstock.com; **p. 108** Al Fuchs/NewSport/Corbis; **p. 114** Shutterstock.com; **p. 118** (left) Shutterstock.com, (right) Shutterstock.com; **p. 122** Shutterstock.com; **p. 125** Shutterstock.com; **p. 133** (left) Shutterstock.com, (middle) Alison Wright/Corbis, (right) Ken Redding/Corbis; **p. 139** Alison Wright/Corbis; **p. 154** Courtesy of Felicia Mabuza-Suttle; **p. 159** Shutterstock.com; **p. 165** © Jim Tetro Photography/Courtesy DOE; **p. 170** Shutterstock.com; **p. 175** (left) Shutterstock.com, (right) Mick Stevens from cartoonbank.com. All rights reserved; **p. 176** Walter Seng 1998; **p. 181** Dale Dong Photography; **p. 184** John Kane/Pilobolus Inc.; **p. 186** Shutterstock.com; **p. 188** Shutterstock.com; **p. 202** Mark Stevens/The New Yorker Collection/www.cartoonbank.com; **p. 215** Mick Stevens from cartoonbank.com. All rights reserved; **p. 219** Shutterstock.com; **p. 231** (left) Shutterstock.com, (middle) SuperStock/SuperStock, (right) Ralf-Finn Hestoft/Index Stock Imagery; **p. 237** Shutterstock.com; **p. 252** SuperStock/SuperStock; **p. 253** Alinari/Art Resource, NY; **p. 255** Ralf-Finn Hestoft/Index Stock Imagery; **p. 265** (left) Ariel Skelley/Corbis, (middle) Shutterstock.com, (right) Andrew Gunners/Getty Images; **p. 266** (top) Ariel Skelley/Corbis, (left) Shutterstock.com, (middle) Shutterstock.com, (right) Shutterstock.com; **p. 272** Ariel Skelley/Corbis; **p. 273** Shutterstock.com; **p. 276** Shutterstock.com; **p. 278** Shutterstock.com; **p. 282** Shutterstock.com; **p. 296** Andrew Gunners/Getty Images; **p. 307** AP Images/Andre Penner; **p. 313** Glyn Kirk/Getty Images; **p. 314** Fotosearch/Digital Vision; **p. 316** AP Images/Kyodo; **p. 321** (right) Shutterstock.com; **p. 322** www.CartoonStock.com; **p. 328** RubberBall Productions; **p. 334** RubberBall Productions; **p. 342** Nancy Ney/Getty Images; **p. 344** Shutterstock.com; **p. 348** Shutterstock.com; **p. 349** (1) Shutterstock.com, (2) Shutterstock.com, (3) David Allan Brandt/Getty Images, (4) Shutterstock.com, (5) Shutterstock.com, (6) Shutterstock.com, (7) Jon Arnold Images Ltd/Alamy, (8) Shutterstock.com; **p. 354** Marisa Acocella Marchetto/The New Yorker Collection/www.cartoonbank.com; **p. 368** Dreamstime.com; **p. 375** (middle) Shutterstock.com, (right) Rick Friedman/Corbis; **p. 376** (left) holbox/Shutterstock, (right) Lou Chardonnay/Corbis; **p. 380** Shutterstock.com; **p. 391** Douglas Kirkland/Corbis; **p. 397** Rick Friedman/Corbis; **p. 398** Photolibrary.com; **p. 407** (left) Fotosearch/Corbis; **p. 408** Fotosearch/Image Club; **p. 413** Shutterstock.com; **p. 422** Fotosearch/Corbis; **p. 429** Corbis; **p. 432** Shutterstock.com; **p. 443** (left) Shutterstock.com, (right) Shutterstock.com; **p. 457** (woman) Shutterstock.com, (plate) Joseph Sohm/Visions of America/Corbis, (paint) Shutterstock.com, (toys) Dreamstime.com, (shoes) Shutterstock.com.

ILLUSTRATION CREDITS:

Steve Attoe – pages 2, 66, 82, 83, 100, 175 (middle), 190, 225, 357; **Ron Chironna** – page 23; **Chi Chung** – pages 246, 247; **ElectraGraphics** – pages 152, 354; **Chris Gash** – pages 7, 8; **Paul Hampson** – page 232; **Jock MacRae** – pages 42, 387; **Tom Newsom** – pages 40, 54, 55, 140, 382, 383; **Dusan Petricic** – page 254; **Steve Schulman** – pages 164, 367, 370, 452 (left); **Gary Torrisi** – pages 58, 129, 131, 168, 207, 258, 260, 303, 452 (right)

INDEX

This index is for the full and split editions. All entries are in the full book. Entries for Volume A of the split edition are in black. Entries for Volume B are in red.